A POLITICAL CHRONOLOGY OF EUROPE

A POLITICAL CHRONOLOGY OF EUROPE

FIRST EDITION

First Edition 2001

© **Europa Publications Limited 2001**
11 New Fetter Lane, London EC4P 4EE, United Kingdom
(A member of the Taylor & Francis Group)

ISBN   1-85743-113-8

Printed and bound by
TJ International Ltd, Padstow, Cornwall

Foreword

This is the first title in a new six-volume series of Political Chronologies of the World. Forthcoming titles will deal with Central, South and East Asia, the Middle East, Africa, South-East Asia and Oceania, and the Americas. This volume covers the entirety of Western, Central and Eastern Europe, an area spanning from Greenland in the west to the Russian Federation in the east.

Although the book includes greater coverage of more-recent events – particularly in countries with a recent history of political upheaval – it also provides invaluable detail on the early history of each nation. Each chronology begins at least as early as the emergence of an entity resembling the modern nation, and in many cases considerably earlier.

In addition to coverage of purely political events, each title in the series also includes details of the principal economic, cultural and social landmarks in the history of each nation. Examples might include the adoption of new languages, alphabets, calendars or religions.

The principal events in the histories of dependencies and external territories lying within Europe may be found in the chapter dealing with the relevant sovereign state. Entries for territories and dependencies of European countries in other parts of the world will be found in the appropriate volume for that region.

This series aims to be the first point of reference for concise information on the history of each nation in the world. It is hoped that the volumes in the series will enable readers easily to locate self-contained entries on the period and area in which their interest lies.

February 2001

Contents

Abbreviations

AD	*anno Domini*
Adm.	Admiral
BC	before Christ
Brig.	Brigadier
c.	*circa*
Col	Colonel
Dr	Doctor
ECU	European Currency Unit
etc.	et cetera
Gen.	General
km	kilometre(s)
Lt	Lieutenant
m.	million
Maj.	Major
Mgr	Monsignor
MP	Member of Parliament
Prof.	Professor
SS	Saints
St	Saint
UN	United Nations
USA	United States of America
USSR	Union of Soviet Socialist Republics

Albania

168 BC: Illyria (which included modern-day Albania) was annexed by the Roman Empire.

AD 395: Following a division of the administration of the Roman Empire, Illyria was ruled by the Eastern Roman ('Byzantine') Emperor in Constantinople (now Istanbul in Turkey).

6th–7th centuries: Slavs invaded the Balkan Peninsula.

11th century: Vlachs (Wallachians) migrated into the territory still occupied by the remnants of the Thracian-Illyrian population.

1385: Ottoman (Turkish) forces reached the Albanian coast.

1443: Gjergj Kastrioti (Skënderbeu or Skenderbeg) led Albanians in a revolt against Ottoman dominance.

1468: Death of Skënderbeu.

1478: The Ottomans established full control over Albania and, under their rule, many Albanians converted to Islam.

1756: Mehemet of Bushan established an independent principality in northern Albania.

1787: Ali Pasha of Tepelenë (Janina) established an independent principality in southern Albania and neighbouring territories.

1822: Ottoman forces overthrew Ali Pasha.

1831: Mustafa Pasha, of the Bushan dynasty, was overthrown.

1878: The Congress of Berlin allotted parts of Albanian territory to Bulgaria, Greece, Montenegro and Serbia. The Albanian League for the Defence of the Rights of the Albanian Nation was established.

1881: The Albanian League was disbanded by the Ottomans.

1910: An uprising against Ottoman rule was suppressed by Turkish forces.

October 1912: The First Balkan War began; Albania was occupied by neighbouring powers.

28 November 1912: A national convention, convened in Vlorë, proclaimed the independence of Albania; Ismail Qemal was appointed President.

July 1913: The London Ambassadors' Conference recognized the principle of Albanian independence, but designated the country a protectorate, under the control of the Great Powers; Kosovo was granted to Serbia; other territories were gained by Greece.

March 1914: Prince William of Wied, who had been appointed ruler of the Albanian protectorate by the Great Powers, arrived in Albania.

August 1914: Italy and Greece occupied southern Albania at the outbreak of the First World War.

September 1914: Prince William of Wied left Albania, following local opposition to his rule.

April 1915: The secret Treaty of London was signed, which provided for much of Albania to be partitioned between Greece, Italy, Montenegro and Serbia.

January 1920: The Congress of Lushnjë reaffirmed Albania's independence and appointed a new Government; Tirana (Tiranë) was declared the capital of Albania.

August 1920: Italy agreed to withdraw its forces from Albania and recognize Albanian independence.

December 1920: Albania was admitted to the League of Nations.

10 June 1924: After an armed uprising, a Government headed by Fan Noli came to power.

24 December 1924: The Government of Fan Noli was overthrown by forces led by Ahmet Zogu.

January 1925: The Republic of Albania was proclaimed; Ahmet Zogu was appointed President.

September 1928: A monarchy was established, with Zogu proclaiming himself King Zog I.

April 1939: Italian troops invaded Albania; King Zog was forced into exile. The union of Albania and Italy under the Italian Crown was subsequently proclaimed.

November 1941: The Communist Party of Albania was founded; Enver Hoxha became its first leader.

September 1942: The National Liberation Front, a Communist-led resistance organization, was established.

September 1943: Italy surrendered to the Allies; Albania was invaded by Nazi German forces.

1943–44: Fierce fighting occurred between Nazi forces and resistance groups, and also between resistance groups of different political persuasions.

24–28 May 1944: The Congress of Përmet established, as a provisional government, the Anti-Fascist Committee for National Liberation, headed by Enver Hoxha.

29 November 1944: The National Liberation Front proclaimed the liberation of Albania.

2 December 1945: Elections with only Communist candidates took place; the Communists, as the Democratic Front, won some 90% of the votes cast.

11 January 1946: The People's Republic of Albania was proclaimed; King Zog was declared deposed.

1948: Close relations with Yugoslavia were ended after Yugoslavia was expelled from the Communist Information Bureau (Cominform). The Albanian Communist Party was renamed the Party of Labour of Albania (PLA).

1949: Albania joined the Council for Mutual Economic Assistance (CMEA). Koci Xoxe (former Minister of the Interior) and other officials were executed as alleged pro-Yugoslav traitors.

1954: Hoxha resigned as Chairman of the Council of Ministers (head of government), but retained effective power as First Secretary of the PLA. Mehmet Shehu was appointed head of government.

1955: Albania joined the Warsaw Treaty Organization (Warsaw Pact). The Soviet *rapprochement* with Yugoslavia strained Soviet–Albanian relations.

1961: The USSR denounced Albania and severed diplomatic relations after Hoxha announced his support for the Chinese Communist leader, Mao Zedong, in his ideological conflict with the USSR.

1962: Albania formally left the CMEA.

1967: Religious worship was outlawed and all mosques and churches were closed.

1968: Albania formally left the Warsaw Pact.

1972: Improved US–Chinese relations were denounced by Albania.

1975: Gen. Beqir Balluku, who had been dismissed as Minister of Defence in 1974, was executed as an alleged pro-Chinese traitor.

1976: A new Constitution was adopted; the country's name was changed to the People's Socialist Republic of Albania.

1978: Albania declared its support for Viet Nam, in its conflict with the People's Republic of China; China suspended all military and economic ties.

December 1981: Mehmet Shehu, head of government, died in a shooting incident. There were subsequent allegations that he had been murdered.

November 1982: Ramiz Alia replaced Haxhi Lleshi as Chairman of the Presidium of the People's Assembly (head of state).

April 1985: Death of Enver Hoxha. He was succeeded as First Secretary of the PLA by Ramiz Alia.

August 1987: In an attempt to improve relations, Greece ended the technical state of war which had existed between it and Albania since 1945.

December 1989: Despite some indication of reform, there were reports of anti-government demonstrations in the northern town of Shkodër (Scutari) and such activity increased throughout 1990.

May 1990: The People's Assembly adopted measures to liberalize the penal code, to end the ban on religious propaganda and to relax the constitutional prohibition on foreign investment, following some economic reforms announced by Alia the previous month.

July 1990: Some 5,000 Albanians were eventually allowed to leave the country after seeking asylum in the embassies of foreign countries. Diplomatic contact was resumed with the USSR.

December 1990: Opposition activists formed, and registered, the Democratic Party of Albania (DPA), while other proposed reforms included guaranteeing multi-party democracy and economic liberalization.

January 1991: Konstantinos Mitsotakis, the Prime Minister of Greece, visited Tirana, in an attempt to quell the exodus of ethnic Greeks from Albania. Later in the month a new Government included more reformists, such as Fatos Nano, an economist.

February 1991: Demonstrations in Tirana and student protests prompted Ramiz Alia to declare presidential rule and appoint a provisional government under Nano.

March 1991: The Italian navy was ordered to prevent any more vessels landing at the Italian port of Brindisi, after some 20,000 Albanians had arrived on ships seized in Albanian ports. Diplomatic relations with the USA were renewed.

31 March 1991: The PLA won over 60% of the votes cast in Albania's first multi-party election since the 1920s.

30 April 1991: Ramiz Alia was elected to the new post of President of the Republic, by the People's Assembly, which had renamed the country the

Republic of Albania and declared the 1976 Constitution invalid, replacing it, on an interim basis, with a Law on the Major Constitutional Provisions of the People's Assembly of the Republic of Albania.

June 1991: With continuing protests throughout the country and after a general strike, Ylli Bufi became head of government; he formed a Government which included the first non-Communist ministers since the Second World War. The PLA changed its name to the Socialist Party of Albania (SPA) and elected Nano its leader. Albania was finally admitted as a member of the Conference on Security and Co-operation in Europe (later Organization for Security and Co-operation in Europe—OSCE).

October 1991: The Assembly voted to recognize the 'Republic of Kosovo' (the predominantly ethnic Albanian area of neighbouring Yugoslavia), after protests at Serbian repression.

December 1991: The Bufi Government finally collapsed when the DPA withdrew from the coalition; Vilson Ahmeti was the new Chairman of the Council of Ministers. There were food riots in various parts of the country and increasing industrial unrest.

February 1992: A new electoral law prevented the Democratic Union of the Greek Minority (OMONIA), which held five seats in the Assembly, from putting forward candidates for the general election (the Greek community gained representation through the Union of Human Rights Party).

22–29 March 1992: Elections to the new Assembly were won by the DPA, which gained 62% of the votes cast in the first round (and 92 of the 140 seats), while the SPA only gained 26% (and 38 seats).

9 April 1992: Sali Berisha of the DPA was elected President of the Republic by the People's Assembly, following the resignation of Alia some days before. Berisha appointed Aleksander Meksi to lead a new coalition Government.

July 1992: The Albanian Communist Party was banned. At local elections the DPA gained the most votes (43% of the total), but the SPA improved its support, gaining 41%.

September 1992: There was a split in the DPA, following accusations that the Berisha regime was becoming more right-wing and authoritarian. Former President Alia was arrested and charged with corruption, joining several other prominent members of the old Communist regime in detention.

December 1992: Albania became a member of the Organization of the Islamic Conference (OIC).

February 1993: Former premier Ahmeti was placed under house arrest following allegations of corruption.

July 1993: Former premier Nano was charged with misappropriating state funds; he was found guilty in 1994.

6 November 1994: A draft constitution, in which enhanced powers for the executive were proposed, was rejected by 53.9% of participants in a referendum. The same month the Albanian Republican Party (ARP) and a faction of the Social Democratic Party withdrew from the governing coalition.

May 1995: In an effort to restrict the mass migration of Albanians to Italy, the two Governments increased coastal security.

June 1995: The sale of newspapers and magazines in Tirana was to be restricted to government-owned kiosks and state bookshops. Ilir Hoxha, the son of Enver Hoxha, was charged with inciting national hatred following the publication of a newspaper interview in which he denounced the DPA (he was later convicted). Such incidents were cited as evidence of growing government intolerance of criticism, even from within the DPA.

7 July 1995: The Government granted an amnesty to former President Alia and some 30 other political prisoners and, later, the case against Vilson Ahmeti was dismissed, owing to lack of evidence; Albania was accepted as a member of the Council of Europe.

September 1995: The 'Genocide Law', enacted by a small majority, prohibited the appointment of any person who held office during the Communist period to the executive, the legislature or the judiciary.

10 February 1996: Former President Alia was detained pending trial for several charges, among them allegations that he had ordered the killing of those attempting to flee across the border in 1991.

March 1996: Following several years of poor relations between the two countries, President Berisha and the Greek President, Konstantinos Stefanopoulos, signed a Treaty of Mutual Friendship and Co-operation.

26 May 1996: Elections to the People's Assembly, the conduct of which was widely condemned by international observers, were boycotted by the main opposition parties; the DPA, therefore, won 122 out of a total of 140 parliamentary seats.

12 July 1996: A new cabinet, again led by Meksi, was sworn in; it consisted mainly of DPA members, but the ARP, the Christian Democratic Party of Albania and the Union of Social Democrats were also represented.

October 1996: In local government elections, widely regarded to have been conducted fairly, the DPA secured the largest number of votes in 58 of the 64 municipalities and in 267 of the 309 communes.

January 1997: The collapse of several popular 'pyramid' investment schemes, resulting in huge losses of individual savings, prompted violent anti-government demonstrations.

1 March 1997: President Berisha declared a state of emergency, as anti-government protests escalated into insurgency and, often supported by rebel troops, opposition groups gained control of several towns.

3 March 1997: The People's Assembly re-elected Berisha, who was unopposed, for a second five-year term in the presidency.

11 March 1997: With the evacuation of foreign nationals and the flight of many Albanians, Berisha appointed Bashkim Fino, a former SPA mayor of Gjirokastër, to lead an interim Government of National Reconciliation, to include representatives of eight opposition parties, in advance of a general election.

11 April 1997: A UN-sanctioned Multinational Protection Force, established to facilitate the distribution of humanitarian assistance, was deployed, principally in government-controlled areas of northern and central Albania.

29 June 1997: The first round of voting in the general election took place. A simultaneous referendum on the restoration of the monarchy resulted in 66.7% of the participating electorate favouring the republic.

6 July 1997: With the second round of voting in the general election, the SPA secured 101 of the 155 seats in the enlarged People's Assembly, with the DPA winning 29 seats; the electoral process was declared satisfactory by the OSCE.

24 July 1997: Rexhep Mejdani, hitherto the Secretary-General of the SPA, was elected President by the People's Assembly. Subsequently, a new Council of Ministers was appointed, comprising representatives of the SPA and its allied parties, with former premier Nano as the head of government.

14 August 1997: The operation of the Multinational Protection Force formally ended, as the Government dispatched troops to the south of the country to restore order in areas which were still controlled by insurgents.

September 1997: A parliamentary commission was established to draft a new constitution in accordance with government proposals.

20–21 October 1997: Berisha was re-elected party chairman at the DPA's national conference. Former President Alia and three other senior officials of his administration were acquitted of charges of genocide.

November 1997: Negotiations between the Prime Minister, Nano, and the Yugoslav President, Slobodan Milošević, led to an announcement that relations between the two countries were to be normalized, although Milošević emphasized that the unrest in Kosovo remained an internal issue of the Federal Republic of Yugoslavia (FRY—Montenegro and Serbia).

6 March 1998: Following the use of the security forces by the Serbian authorities against ethnic Albanian villages, huge crowds gathered in protest in Tirana. President Mejdani condemned Serbian action against civilians and all leave for troops along Albania's northern border with Yugoslavia was cancelled.

June 1998: Reports indicated that about 20,000 ethnic Albanian refugees had crossed into Albania to escape fighting between Serb forces and Kosovar guerrillas.

21 June 1998: In partial local elections, the conduct of which was declared satisfactory by OSCE observers, an SPA-led electoral coalition, Alliance for the State, achieved a significant victory, winning control of five of the seven municipalities and six of the nine communes where voting took place.

6 July 1998: The People's Assembly approved the final report on the civil unrest of early 1997; it recommended the prosecution of several leading DPA officials, including former President Berisha, for the violation of constitutional provisions and the unlawful use of force against protestors. The following day the DPA announced a new, indefinite, boycott of parliament.

12 September 1998: Azem Hajdari, a leading DPA official, and his two bodyguards were shot and killed in Tirana; following two days of violent protest as Berisha alleged government responsibility for the murders, government troops regained control of the capital.

18 September 1998: A parliamentary commission lifted Berisha's immunity from prosecution and Nano stated that Berisha would be charged with an attempted *coup d'état*.

28 September 1998: The Prime Minister, Nano, resigned, claiming that a lack of support for him had contributed to the Government's weakness and the collapse of public order. The following day the SPA nominated its Secretary-General, Pandeli Majko, to succeed Nano, who remained Chairman of the SPA.

22 November 1998: In a referendum, 93.1% of the participating electorate voted in favour of the adoption of a new constitution. However, Berisha claimed the referendum was invalid, and urged DPA supporters to protest against the results; additional troops were deployed in Tirana to maintain public order.

28 November 1998: The new Constitution was officially adopted; the DPA announced that it would continue its refusal to recognize the Constitution.

20 January 1999: Nano resigned as Chairman of the SPA.

4 February 1999: The trial began of Ekrem Spahia, a prominent member of the Legality Movement Party, on charges of involvement with the alleged coup attempt in September 1998.

11–12 April 1999: Albanian border villages came under heavy bombardment by Serbian troops fighting the ethnic Albanian Kosovo Liberation Army (KLA), in Kosovo; Serbian forces later in the month advanced into Albanian territory, but were repelled by Albanian forces.

17 July 1999: The DPA voted to end its boycott of the legislature.

1 September 1999: The North Atlantic Treaty Organization (NATO) announced the end of its mission in Albania to help the country cope with the influx of Kosovar Albanians fleeing Serbian military action in the province. The troops were to be replaced by a 2,400-member contingent, to be known as Communications Zone West (COMMZ-W), which would assist international peace-keepers in Kosovo and help to maintain public order in Albania.

11 October 1999: Nano, who had resigned as SPA Chairman in January, was re-elected to the post, narrowly defeating the Prime Minister, Majko.

26 October 1999: Following his defeat in the party leadership contest, Majko resigned as premier; the Deputy Prime Minister, Ilir Meta, a close ally of Nano, was immediately nominated as Majko's successor. The DPA subsequently announced a boycott of a parliamentary motion to approve the new Council of Ministers formed by Meta, and the staging of protests following the return of Nano to the SPA leadership.

8 November 1999: Despite the DPA's, boycott the People's Assembly formally approved the new Government.

8 December 1999: Following the announcement of the formation of a moderate faction within the DPA, the party's deputy leader, Genc Pollo, was expelled from the party.

9 December 1999: The Constitutional Court formally abolished the death penalty.

11 January 2000: Meta dismissed the Minister of Public Economy and Privatization, Zef Preci, accusing him of having violated a law concerning the energy sector; at the same time, Prec Zogaj, a Minister of State, was also dismissed.

17 February 2000: Nano was elected speaker of an *Ad Hoc* Parliamentary Commission for the Stability Pact for South-Eastern Europe, adopted in Cologne (Germany) on 10 June 1999.

24 February 2000: Albania and Montenegro agreed to reopen the countries' border crossing, closed since 1997 after thousands of Kosovar Albanians had fled into Albania; however, by the end of February there were reports that the Yugoslav army had closed the crossing.

2 March 2000: Albania and Switzerland signed an accord on the voluntary repatriation of Kosovar Albanians who had fled to Switzerland during the war in Kosovo in 1999. The two countries also agreed to undertake joint operations to combat drugs-trafficking.

26 April 2000: The Governments of Albania and Montenegro signed a memorandum of understanding for economic, trade and cultural co-operation and a protocol of co-operation in foreign affairs.

19 May 2000: The Minister of Transport, Ingrid Shuli, resigned; she was replaced by Sokol Nako.

June 2000: A new political organization, the Albanian Workers' Movement, was founded in Vlore. Following the resignation of Namik Dokle, the Socialist Party of Albania elected Gramoz Ruci as Secretary-General.

7 July 2000: Four ministers, including the Ministers of Justice and of Defence, were replaced in an extensive government reorganization.

September 2000: An attempted attack on Berisha, who was visiting the southern town of Fier, was repulsed by his personal security guards. It was subsequently reported that the assailant was a local leader of the DPA.

1–15 October 2000: Local government elections were held, in which the SPA won 252 local council seats and the DPA 118 seats. However, many DPA supporters had boycotted the second round of voting following allegations of widespread electoral irregularities, and the DPA refused to accept the official results.

Late November 2000: Anti-Government demonstrators attempted to seize the police station in the northern town of Bajram Curri; two protesters were killed and some 20 injured in the suppression of the attack by security forces.

December 2000: Amid the continuing dispute over the local government elections, inter-party discussions over proposed amendments to the electoral regulations were initiated, prior to forthcoming elections to the People's Assembly in mid-2001.

29 December 2000: The new Prime Minister of the FRY, Zoran Zizić, declared that Yugoslavia would seek to establish diplomatic links with Albania as soon as was possible, a sentiment previously expressed by FRY President Vojislav Kostunica.

Andorra

768–814: Reign of Charles 'the Great' (Charlemagne), the ruler of the Franks and the first Holy Roman Emperor. He purportedly granted Andorra a charter guaranteeing its independence.

839: The Act of Consecration of the cathedral in the Spanish town of Urgel referred to the six parishes of Andorra—the Count of Urgel had assumed suzerainty over Andorra following the fracturing of the Frankish realm.

1133: The Count of Urgel ceded the six parishes of Andorra to the Bishop of Urgel.

1159: The Count of Foix, a French nobleman whose territory included much of the Pyrenean region near Andorra, laid claim to the parishes; he gained recognition of certain rights, but the dispute remained a source of conflict.

1278: A peace treaty, sponsored by the King of Aragon, provided for Andorran independence, under the joint sovereignty of the Count of Foix and the Bishop of Urgel, who were to be paid tribute in alternate years.

1289: A treaty confirming the agreement of 1278 first referred to the sovereign of Andorra as the 'co-princes' (coprínceps).

1419: The Co-Princes granted an Andorran request for the formation of a representative body for the debate of local issues; the Council of the Valleys, or General Council, comprised four members from each parish, elected by the heads of the leading families in that parish.

1589: Henry of Bourbon, who had inherited the title of Count of Foix, ascended the French throne as Henry IV; the French monarch, therefore, became one of Andorra's co-princes (Henry's son and successor, Louis XIII, reaffirmed Andorra's status).

1793: The proclamation of a republic in France left the title of French co-prince unclaimed, provoking Andorran fears of subordination to Spain.

1806: Napoleon I Bonaparte, who had proclaimed himself Emperor of France, issued a decree by which he assumed the title of Co-Prince of Andorra.

1870: With the final restoration of a republic, the President of France became the French co-prince of Andorra.

1912: Local defiance of the episcopal Co-Prince was provoked by his attempt to ban the vital tobacco trade.

1933: A Russian émigré, Boris Skosirev, attempted to proclaim himself King Boris I of Andorra, with some influential local support. The Bishop of Urgel sent troops to remove Skosirev from the Principality and the General Council was dissolved by the Andorran judicial authorities. The French Government subsequently sent forces to maintain order and the General Council was re-established.

1970: Women's suffrage was introduced and in the following year the voting age was lowered from 25 to 21 years.

1978: A seventh parish, Escaldes–Engordany, was created and the membership of the General Council was correspondingly expanded from 24 to 28.

January 1982: An executive body, known as the Government of Andorra (Govern d'Andorra) was formed from within the General Council (elected on 9 December 1981), with Oscar Ribas Reig as Head of Government (Cap de Govern).

April 1984: Ribas Reig, the Head of Government, was forced to resign upon the failure of his plan to introduce income tax. He was replaced in May by Josep Pintat Solans.

January 1986: Pintat Solans was re-elected to the post of Head of Government, following a general election the previous month.

January 1990: Following a general election in December 1989, the General Council elected Ribas Reig to his second term as Head of Government.

4 May 1993: Andorra's first Constitution was promulgated, having been approved by 74.2% of those participating in a referendum held in March and signed by the Co-Princes in April—the Co-Princes remained nominally sovereign, political parties and trade unions were legalized and proportional representation was introduced for electing 14 of the 28 General Council members. Ambassadors were exchanged with France and Spain.

July 1993: Andorra was admitted to the UN.

November 1994: Ribas Reig's taxation and budget proposals were defeated in the General Council and a motion of 'no confidence' in the Government was passed; Ribas Reig resigned the premiership and was succeeded by Marc Forné Molne, who formed a minority Government.

16 February 1997: In a general election, Forné Molne's Liberal Union (Unió Liberal) won 18 of the 28 seats in the General Council and returned to power;

Forné Molne formed a new Government, with an increased number of ministers and portfolios.

4 March 2001: The Partit Liberal d'Andorra (PLA), formerly the Liberal Union, won 15 of the 28 seats in the General Council in a general election. Forné Molné was re-elected Head of Government by the Council.

Austria

4th–5th centuries: Germanic tribes migrated westward into territory of the disintegrating Western Roman Empire; numerous Germanic kingdoms were established in much of western and central Europe and Christianity began to spread among the tribes.

6th–8th centuries: Slavic kingdoms were established in parts of modern Austria and Hungary.

768: Charles 'the Great' (Charlemagne) inherited the western half of the Frankish (German) kingdom upon his father's death, and gained the eastern half (which included parts of modern Austria) upon the death of his brother three years later. He undertook a campaign of further expansion, including movement eastward into central Europe.

843: The Treaty of Verdun formalized the divisions made since the death of Charlemagne, who had been crowned the first Holy Roman Emperor, and Austria was included in the eastern of the three kingdoms.

972: Emperor Otto I ('the Great') awarded the margravate of Austria to Leopold of Babenberg, following the expulsion of the invading Magyars (Hungarians).

1156: Henry II of Babenberg was awarded the title Duke of Austria.

1251: Przemsyl Ottokar II of Bohemia took control of the duchy of Austria, following the extinction of the Babenberg dynasty.

1278: Rudolf of Habsburg, the German Holy Roman Emperor, defeated Ottokar II, and gained possession of Austria, which he later awarded to his son, Albert.

1438: Albert II of Habsburg, King of Bohemia and Hungary, was elected Holy Roman Emperor. His successors acquired further territory (Burgundy, Naples, Spain) by marriage.

1515: The Vienna Treaties confirmed the inheritance of Bohemia and Hungary by the Habsburgs, who thereby established their dominance.

1519: Charles V, the Habsburg King of Spain, was elected Emperor, uniting the Habsburgs' central European and Mediterranean territories.

1526: The Habsburgs claimed Hungary as a hereditary possession upon the death of Louis II in battle against the conquering armies of the Ottoman Turks.

1555: The Peace of Augsburg concluded the conflicts occasioned by the religious Reformation (since 1517); Austria, under the Habsburgs, remained Roman Catholic.

1556: Charles V abdicated, leaving the Habsburg possessions of the Empire to his brother, Ferdinand I, and the Burgundian and Spanish possessions to his son, Phillip.

1648: The Peace of Westphalia concluded the Thirty Years' War: Austria remained Roman Catholic and the imperial power, but other German states increased in strength, while the Swiss and Dutch officially left the Empire.

1663: A permanent Assembly of the imperial territories (Reichstag) was convened at Regensburg.

1683: Ottoman Turkish armies laid siege to Vienna, the Austrian Habsburg capital, but were eventually defeated by the imperial army.

1699: The Ottomans formally ceded Hungary (including Transylvania and Slavonia) to the Habsburgs by the Peace of Karlowitz.

1718: The Peace of Passarowitz confirmed Habsburg hegemony in Hungary, including further gains at the expense of the Turks, and marked the apogee of the Habsburg Empire.

1740: Charles VI died without leaving a male heir; he had sought to ensure the succession of his daughter, Maria Theresa, who assumed control of Austria and the Habsburg territories (her husband was later elected Holy Roman Emperor). In what became known as the War of the Austrian Succession, Prussia invaded and took Silesia and retained it in all future conflicts with Austria.

1756–63: The Seven Years' War, provoked by Austria's response to the challenge from Prussia, embroiled many of the European Powers.

1772–95: The three Partitions of Poland gave Austria Galicia, although many of the other territories it claimed were awarded to Prussia.

1781: Serfdom was abolished.

1785: The League of German Princes (Fürstenbund) was established by Frederick II of Prussia, with the aim of undermining Habsburg control of Bavaria.

1792–1801: France declared war on both Austria and Prussia, which it accused of attempting to undermine the Revolution; Austria suffered losses to France in Germany, Italy and the Netherlands, and was forced to negotiate the Peace of Lunéville, which reorganized Germany, creating a pro-French buffer of states between France and Austria.

1804: Francis II assumed the imperial title for Austria, as well as being Holy Roman Emperor.

1805: The imperial forces were defeated by the French at Austerlitz and the Peace of Pressburg forced the Habsburgs to cede territory in Italy and Germany.

6 August 1806: Francis II, under pressure from the French leader, Napoleon Bonaparte (who proclaimed himself Emperor of the French, Napoleon I, in 1804), dissolved the Holy Roman Empire of the German Nation; he reigned henceforth as Francis I, Emperor of Austria.

1814–15: Under the terms negotiated at the Congress of Vienna, which ended the wars with revolutionary France, Austria lost its territory in the southern Netherlands (Belgium) and Hither Austria but gained the former Venetian territories of Dalmatia and Istria, in addition to Galicia and Upper Italy. Austria and Prussia agreed to form a new Germanic Confederation, comprising representatives from all German states, which was to meet in Frankfurt under Austrian presidency.

1848: Popular unrest throughout Europe included a number of uprisings on Habsburg territory, most notably with the formation of a nationalist government in Hungary, which refused to recognize Francis Joseph I in December, following the abdication of Ferdinand I.

1849: Imperial forces regained control of Hungary and a new, centralist Constitution was introduced (revoked in 1865).

1859: Austria was forced to cede Lombardy to Sardinia-Piedmont, an emerging Italian state, by the terms of the Peace of Zürich.

1866: Prussia invaded the Habsburg duchy of Holstein, so Austria mobilized the German Confederation against the Prussians, but the alliance was defeated at Sadowa (Königgratz), ending the Seven Weeks' War. The Treaty of Prague deprived the Habsburgs of Holstein and Venice and effectively excluded Austria from the emerging political entity of Germany; the German Confederation was dissolved (and subsequently replaced by the Prussian-dominated North German Confederation).

1867: The problem of the Imperial Constitution was resolved by the Compromise (*Ausgleich*), whereby the Habsburg territories were reorganized as the 'Dual Monarchy' of Austria (Cisleithania) and Hungary (Transleithania).

1873: Legislation providing for direct election to the Reichsrat (Imperial Council), rather than election through local diets, was enacted.

1879: Austria-Hungary formed the Dual Alliance with the new, Prussian-dominated, German state; their association was to last until 1918.

1897: Introduction of universal suffrage for all adult males.

5 October 1908: Austria-Hungary formally annexed Bosnia and Herzegovina, despite international objections, following the 'Young Turk' uprising in the Ottoman Empire.

1912–13: War among the Balkan states saw the removal of the Turks from the bulk of their European possessions and Habsburg opposition to Serbian expansion.

28 June 1914: The heir to the Austro-Hungarian throne, Archduke Francis Ferdinand, and his wife were assassinated in Sarajevo (Bosnia and Herzegovina) by a Bosnian Serb activist.

28 July 1914: Austria-Hungary declared war on Serbia, starting what would become known as the First World War (or 'Great War') between the Central Powers of Austria-Hungary, Germany and the Ottoman Empire (Turkey) and the Entente Powers of France, Russia, Serbia and the United Kingdom.

21 December 1916: Death of Francis Joseph I and the accession of his grand-nephew, Charles I.

4 October 1918: Austria-Hungary accepted the same armistice conditions as Germany, to come into effect on 3 November. Meanwhile, the Habsburg Monarchy proceeded to disintegrate and Charles I later abdicated.

1918–20: The treaties concluding the First World War saw the Dual Monarchy fragmented into the three new states of Austria, Czechoslovakia and Hungary, and other territories awarded to neighbouring countries; Austria gained the Burgenland from Hungary.

1920: The new Austrian Constitution was enacted, providing for a federal republic with a directly elected President and a bicameral legislature (amended in 1929).

1933: The Chancellor, Engelbert Dollfuss, dissolved Parliament and established an authoritarian state, linked to Catholicism. Public unrest resulted in the outbreak of civil conflict in early 1934, which was strongly suppressed.

1934: An attempted *coup d'état* by the Austrian branch of the National Socialist (Nazi) German Workers' Party, failed, despite the assassination of Dollfuss. He was succeeded by Kurt Schuschnigg, who attempted to unite neo-Nazi political forces against the movement for nationalist 'reunification' with Germany.

March 1938: Adolf Hitler, the German leader, ordered an invasion of Austria to protect his fellow Nazis, thereby bringing about the unification (*Anschluss*) of Austria with Germany.

1943: The Allied Powers fighting Germany in the Second World War (began in 1939) declared Hitler's annexation of Austria to be invalid.

April 1945: Austria, liberated from German control, established a provisional Government under the veteran Socialist, Dr Karl Renner.

1 May 1945: Restoration of the Constitution of 1920, as amended in 1929.

July 1945: Austria was partitioned into four zones, occupied by Allied troops from France, the USSR, the United Kingdom and the USA, as had been done in Germany.

November 1945: The first elections to the National Council (Nationalrat), the lower house of parliament, formalized the dominance of the Austrian People's Party (Österreichische Volkspartei—ÖVP) and the Socialist Party of Austria (Sozialistische Partei Österreichische), coalitions of which ruled Austria for much of the rest of the 20th century.

December 1945: Renner became the first Federal President of the Second Austrian Republic.

1955: The occupation of Austria ended and it resumed full sovereignty, joining the UN but declaring its neutrality.

April 1966: The ÖVP formed a single-party Government under Dr Josef Klaus.

March 1970: The SPÖ formed a single-party administration, with Dr Bruno Kreisky as Chancellor (which position he held until 1983).

June 1974: Dr Rudolf Kirchschläger won the presidential election held following the death of the incumbent President, Franz Jonas.

November 1978: A proposal to commission Austria's first nuclear power plant at Zwentendorf, near Vienna, was defeated in a national referendum, despite government support.

April 1983: The SPÖ lost its absolute majority, and a coalition Government of the SPÖ and the Freedom Party of Austria (Freiheitliche Partei Österreichs—FPÖ), with Dr Fred Sinowatz as Chancellor, subsequently came to power.

June 1986: Dr Kurt Waldheim was elected as President. The appointment aroused controversy, owing to his alleged involvement with atrocities committed by the army of Nazi Germany during the Second World War.

January 1987: Following a general election held in November 1986, the SPÖ and the ÖVP formed a coalition Government under the chancellorship of Dr Franz Vranitzky of the SPÖ.

July 1992: Dr Thomas Klestil assumed the Presidency.

June 1994: In a referendum on proposals for Austria's membership of the European Union (EU), 66.4% of the votes cast supported its membership (member from 1 January 1995).

January 1997: Vranitzky resigned as Chancellor; he was replaced by Dr Viktor Klima.

1 January 1999: Austria became one of 11 countries to participate in Stage III of the EU's Economic and Monetary Union (EMU), when a new single currency, the euro, was introduced.

3 October 1999: In a legislative election, the SPÖ obtained 33.2% of the votes cast and 65 of the 183 seats in the Nationalrat. The FPÖ (led by the Governor of Carinthia, Jörg Haider, who had been accused of maintaining neo-Nazi sympathies and of encouraging xenophobia) and the ÖVP both gained 29.6% of the ballot and 52 seats, and the Grüne Alternative Liste won 7.4% of the votes cast and 14 seats.

20 January 2000: Following protracted negotiations, the SPÖ and the ÖPV reached initial agreement on the renewal of their coalition. However, the arrangement could not be formalized and both parties withdrew the following day.

23 January 2000: The SPÖ announced that it would not seek to form a minority government; coalition negotiations began between the ÖPV and the FPÖ, in spite of domestic and international disquiet at the prospect of the FPÖ's participation in government.

1 February 2000: The Portuguese Government, which held the rotating presidency of the EU, announced that each member state would reduce its bilateral relations with Austria to the minimum level possible should an administration including members of the FPÖ take office.

5 February 2000: The new ÖVP-FPÖ coalition Government, led by Dr Wolfgang Schüssel of the ÖVP with a Vice-Chancellor and five ministers from the FPÖ, was sworn in by President Klestil. Israel and the USA subsequently recalled their ambassadors from Vienna in protest, while Austria's 14 fellow EU member states each suspended their participation in bilateral political co-operation.

28 February 2000: Haider announced his resignation from the leadership of the FPÖ; he was to be replaced by the Vice-Chancellor, Susanne Riess-Passer, in May.

29 June 2000: The Austrian Government agreed to a proposal from the European Commission involving the appointment of a panel of advisers to examine Austria's record on human rights, with particular regard to the status of its immigrant population.

8 September 2000: The European Commission's panel of advisers submitted a report containing no significant criticisms of Austria's observance of human rights and recommending that EU sanctions against Austria be removed.

12 September 2000: The EU announced that normal bilateral relations between Austria and its other member states would be restored.

January 2001: Austria signed an agreement with the USA to pay Jews US $500m. in compensation for property lost during the Nazi era, on the condition that a number of lawsuits were abandoned. The agreement was criticized by Haider.

Belarus

***c.* 878:** Kievan Rus, the first unified state of the Eastern Slavs, was founded, with Kiev (now in Ukraine) as its capital.

***c.* 988:** Vladimir, ruler of Kievan Rus, converted to Orthodox Christianity.

10th century: The principality of Polotsk (Polatsak or Połacak) became the main centre of power on Belarusian territory, rivalling Kiev and Novgorod for predominance within Rus.

1054: The death of Yaroslav I ('the Wise') signalled the dissolution of the Kievan state into rival principalities, the main ones in Belarus being those of Polotsk and Turov (Turau).

1240–63: Rule of Mindaugas (Mindouh), in Novogrudok (Navahradak), who formed the Grand Duchy of Lithuania (Litva) and Rus. His state covered the western territories of Rus, including Minsk (Miensk), Vitebsk (Vitsebsk or Viciebsk) and Polotsk, and eastern Lithuania. Orthodox Slavs predominated in the state and a precursor of Belarusian was the official language. The capital was later moved to Vilnius.

1386: Marriage of Jagiełło (Jahaila; baptized Władysław in 1386) of Lithuania and Jadwiga (Hedwig) of Poland established the union of the two states; subsequent treaties ensured Litva and Rus remained an autonomous Grand Duchy under Poland.

1569: The Grand Duchy of Litva, Rus and Samogitia (the latter—the 'lowlands', in western Lithuania—having been added in the 15th century) surrendered its separate status by the Union of Lublin, as part of an attempt to strengthen the Jagiellonian Polish-Lithuanian state, which was threatened by Sweden, the Ottoman Turks and the Russians.

1596: The Union of Brest ('Lithuanian' Brest or Brest-Litovsk) secured the allegiance of part of the Eastern Orthodox Church for the Pope, the head of the Roman Catholic Church; the creation of this 'Greek Catholic' or Uniate Church was part of a process of attempting to catholicize the confessionally mixed Polish state.

1696: Old Belarusian was replaced by Polish as the language of official documentation in the Grand Duchy.

1772: Parts of Belarus were incorporated into the Russian Empire (the ruler of which had been proclaimed 'Tsar of all the Russias' in 1721) at the First Partition of Poland.

1793: Second Partition of Poland; acquisition by Russia of the rest of Belarus.

1839–40: The tsarist authorities intensified russification in the North-Western Territories, as Belarusian lands were known: the Uniate Church was disbanded and the terms Belarus and Belarusian were banned.

1861: Emancipation of the serfs throughout the Russian Empire.

1902: The Belarusian Revolutionary (later Socialist) Hramada was founded; it became the leading Belarusian nationalist organization.

1 August 1914: Russia entered the First World War against Germany, Turkey and Austria-Hungary (the Central Powers); the tsarist military headquarters (Stavka) was based in Mogilev (Mahilou or Mahiloŭ); from 1915 western Belarus was occupied by the Germans.

2 March (New Style: 15 March) 1917: Abdication of Tsar Nicholas II after demonstrations and strikes in Petrograd (St Petersburg), the imperial capital.

5 August (18 August) 1917: A Rada (Council) was proclaimed in Belarus, following the assembly of a 'national council' in the previous month; the Rada was predominantly Socialist Revolutionary in nature, aiming for an autonomous republic under the Petrograd Provisional Government.

15 November (28 November) 1917: Bolshevik troops arrived in Minsk from Petrograd, where Lenin (Vladimir Ilych Ulyanov) and his Bolshevik allies had assumed power; the Bolsheviks took control of the city against little resistance.

28 December 1917 (10 January 1918): An All-Belarusian Congress proclaimed Belarus a democratic republic and refused to recognize Bolshevik power on Belarusian territory; the Bolsheviks disbanded the Congress, but it elected a Rada, which continued to work in secret.

14 February (Old Style: 1 February) 1918: First day upon which the Gregorian Calender took effect in the Bolshevik territories.

21 February 1918: Bolshevik troops were forced to withdraw, as German forces occupied Minsk.

3 March 1918: By the Treaty of Brest-Litovsk, Soviet Russia ceded much territory to Germany, including Belarus, and recognized Ukrainian independence.

25 March 1918: The Belarusian Rada declared the independence of the state, as the Belarusian National Republic, but it only achieved limited autonomy under German military rule.

23 December 1918: Following the collapse of German power, the Russian Communist leadership decided a Soviet Socialist Republic (SSR) should be established in the largely reoccupied Belarus.

1 January 1919: Proclamation of an independent Belarusian SSR, despite sentiments in Russia for the absorption of the territory.

February 1919: The Bolsheviks replaced the Belarusian SSR with a short-lived Lithuanian–Belarusian SSR ('Litbel'—in recognition of their common history).

March 1919: Polish armies invaded Belarus (declared part of Poland), Lithuania and Ukraine.

11 July 1920: Soviet troops recaptured Minsk, after more than one year of civil war and war with Poland; the following day, by the Treaty of Moscow, the Soviet regime recognized Lithuanian independence and subsequently ceded some Belarusian territory; the Belarusian SSR was re-established in the following month.

16 January 1921: Soviet Russia recognized the Belarusian SSR and signed an alliance with the nominally independent state.

18 March 1921: Poland retained about one-third of Belarus, in the west, by the Treaty of Rīga, which formally concluded the Soviet–Polish War.

30 December 1922: Four Soviet 'Union Republics' proclaimed the Union of Soviet Socialist Republics (USSR), of which the Belarusian SSR was a constituent and nominally independent member, despite a union with Russia being urged by Stalin (Iosif V. Dzhugashvili).

1924: The Belarusian SSR was virtually doubled in size when the territories of Vitebsk (Vitsebsk or Viciebsk) and Mogilev (Mahilou or Mahiloŭ) were formally transferred from Russian jurisdiction.

October 1926: Gomel (Homel or Homiel) was transferred from the Russian Federation to the Belarusian SSR.

1933: The Soviet Government claimed to discover a 'Belarusian National Centre', sponsored by Poland, which was the excuse for mass arrests of Belarusian officials and Party members; furthermore, the peasantry were enduring much hardship during the forcible collectivization of agriculture.

September 1939: The Soviet army occupied western Belarus (Polish since 1921), in accordance with the Treaty of Non-Aggression with Germany (the Nazi–Soviet Pact), signed in August.

3 November 1939: The Communists ensured that the new territories (which increased the Belarusian SSR by one-half in area) voted for incorporation into the USSR.

22 June 1941: The Germans violated the Nazi–Soviet Pact by invading the USSR in 'Operation Barbarossa'; according to the plans of the German leader, Adolf Hitler, Belarus was marked for ethnic German settlement (*Ostland*) and the expulsion of natives.

28 June 1941: Minsk was occupied by German forces; a 'puppet' regime under Ivan Yermachenko was subsequently established, although the Germans also encountered partisan resistance.

December 1943: At an Allied conference in Tehran, Iran, the USSR insisted that it should not only have all of Belarus and Ukraine, but its western border should be along the Oder (Odra) river.

4 July 1944: Soviet troops recaptured Minsk; during the war about one-quarter of the population of Belarus died (pre-1941 population levels were not regained until 1970) and massive damage was done throughout the republic.

26 June 1945: The USSR, the USA, the United Kingdom, China and 46 other countries, including the Belarusian and Ukrainian SSRs, in their own right, signed the Charter of the United Nations.

1946–48: A mass purge of the Communist Party of Belarus (CPB) resulted in the replacement of many ethnic Belarusian officials by Russians.

October 1980: Piotr Masherau, First Secretary of the CPB since 1965, was killed in suspicious circumstances, apparently after an argument with Leonid Brezhnev, General Secretary of the all-Union Communist Party.

April 1986: An explosion occurred at a nuclear reactor in Chernobyl (Chornobyl), Ukraine, 10 km south of the Belarusian border, which resulted in discharges of radioactive material; much of the 30-km exclusion zone around the disaster site was in Belarusian territory and over 20% of the republic was severely affected.

30 October 1988: A demonstration in Minsk to commemorate the victims of Stalinism (partly prompted by the discovery of mass graves at Kurapaty, near Minsk) was violently dispersed by security forces.

June 1989: The Belarusian Popular Front (BPF) held its inaugural congress in Vilnius, Lithuania.

28 January 1990: The Supreme Soviet (Supreme Council) enacted a law replacing Russian as the official language with Belarusian.

25 February 1990: A BPF rally in Minsk was attended by some 150,000 protesters, demanding extra funds to deal with the consequences of the Chernobyl disaster, a major focus of opposition activity in Belarus.

4 March 1990: For the elections to the republican Supreme Council, the BPF was obliged to join the Belarusian Democratic Bloc; although the Bloc won about one-quarter of the seats decided by popular ballot, the Communists still controlled some 84% of the total number of seats in the legislature.

27 July 1990: The Supreme Council, after increasing popular pressure, declared the state sovereignty of Belarus (claiming the right to form its own armed forces, issue its own currency and conduct its own foreign policy), but rejected the possibility of secession.

17 March 1991: In the all-Union referendum on the future of the USSR, 83% voted for a reformed Soviet federation, the highest proportion in any republic outside Central Asia.

25 August 1991: Following the collapse of the attempted coup in Moscow, Russia (the Soviet capital), the Supreme Council of Belarus adopted a declaration of independence; the Communist leadership resigned and the CPB was suspended.

19 September 1991: Formal election of Stanislau Shushkevich, a physicist with a reputation as a reformist, as Chairman of the Supreme Council (Head of State), replacing Nikolai Dementei (Mikalai Dzemyantsei); the name of the state was changed to the Republic of Belarus.

18 October 1991: Representatives of Belarus joined seven other Union Republics in signing a treaty that established an Economic Community between the signatories.

8 December 1991: The leaders of Belarus, the Russian Federation and Ukraine met near Brest and agreed to form a Commonwealth of Independent States (CIS) to replace the USSR; the headquarters of the organization was to be in Minsk. On 21 December the leaders of 11 Soviet republics, including Belarus, signed a protocol, the Almaty (Alma-Ata) Declaration, on the formation of the CIS.

20–22 July 1992: A series of agreements between Belarus and the Russian Federation advocated increased co-operation and seemed to envisage some sort of confederation. The USA agreed to provide Belarus with US $59m., in order to assist with the removal of its nuclear weapons to Russia. The last remaining nuclear warhead was removed from Belarus on 26 November 1996.

29 October 1992: The Supreme Council rejected a petition, signed by 383,000 people, in support of the BPF's demand for new parliamentary elections.

3 February 1993: The Supreme Council approved adherence to the Treaty on the Non-Proliferation of Nuclear Weapons and ratified the first Strategic Arms Reduction Treaty (START 1). The following day the Supreme Council voted to end the suspension of the CPB, which had been in force since August 1991.

26 January 1994: Shushkevich, who had been in conflict with the conservative parliament for some time, also lost reformist support and was dismissed from office. Vyacheslau Kuznetsou, the First Deputy Chairman of the Supreme Council, became acting Head of State.

28 January 1994: Mechislau Gryb (Myacheslau Hryb), a pro-Russian conservative, was elected the new Chairman of the Supreme Council.

15 March 1994: The Supreme Council approved a new Constitution; it was formally adopted on 28 March and came into effect on 30 March.

10 July 1994: In the second round of voting in the presidential election (the first round was on 23 June) Alyaksandr Lukashenka, the head of the Supreme Council's anti-corruption committee and a conservative supporter of closer integration with Russia, received 85% of the votes cast. He was inaugurated as the first President of Belarus on 20 July.

January 1995: Belarus joined the Partnership for Peace programme of military co-operation of the North Atlantic Treaty Organization (NATO).

14 May 1995: The results of a referendum enhanced presidential authority, restored Russian as an official language and approved a change to the state symbols and closer integration with the Russian Federation. The first round of parliamentary elections was held.

28 May 1995: After a second round of elections, only 119 deputies had been elected to the 260-member Supreme Council. Another two rounds of voting, on 29 November and 10 December, brought the total number of new deputies to a quorate 198; the CPB gained the largest number of seats, followed by the Agrarian Party (AP), the United Civic Party of Belarus (UCP) and the Party of People's Accord.

2 April 1996: Despite nationalist protests President Lukashenka and the Russian President, Boris Yeltsin, signed a Treaty on the Formation of a Community of Sovereign Republics, which expressed the intention of closer integration and eventual confederation; opposition rallies were dispersed by police, provoking accusations of brutality.

9 August 1996: President Lukashenka formally proposed a referendum on constitutional amendments to enhance his powers and increase his term of office (to 2001), after an increasing number of confrontations with parliament (the Constitutional Court ruled that the results of such a referendum were not legally binding, but the President revoked this decision by decree).

18 November 1996: Mikhail Chigir, who had been Lukashenka's first premier, was replaced by Syargey Ling, owing to his criticism of the President with regard to the referendum.

24 November 1996: Voting in the referendum on changes to the Constitution, despite drafts of the amendments being unavailable to the public and reports of widespread irregularities, indicated substantial support for the President; the impeachment proceedings against Lukashenka initiated by 75 parliamentary deputies were, therefore, halted.

27 November 1996: The amended Constitution was published and came into immediate effect; it provided for a bicameral National Assembly, the lower house of which, a 110-member House of Representatives, was established the previous day by the majority in the old Supreme Council. Fifty deputies denounced the referendum results and declared themselves the legitimate legislature.

4 December 1996: The Chairman of the Constitutional Court, Valery Tsikhinya, and several other judges resigned in protest at the imposition of the constitutional changes.

13 December 1996: The President approved legislation inaugurating the new upper house of parliament, the 64-member Council of the Republic, consisting of regional representatives and presidential appointees.

8 January 1997: The deputies of a continuing 'Supreme Council' formed a 'shadow' cabinet, the Public Coalition Government—National Economic Council, chaired by Genadz Karpenka.

19 February 1997: Ling was confirmed as premier by the National Assembly.

2 April 1997: Presidents Lukashenka and Yeltsin signed the Treaty of Union between Belarus and Russia and initialled the Charter of the Union; anti-Union demonstrations were suppressed by the security forces.

29 July 1997: Negotiations between representatives of the new and old legislatures, continued from June, collapsed, following disagreement over which Constitution (the 1994 version or the 1996 version) was to form the basis of the discussions.

10 November 1997: The BPF initiated a petition campaign, known as Charter-97 (Khartyya-97), with the aim of forcing new elections.

2 April 1998: On the anniversary of the Treaty of Union with Russia, anti-Government protestors disrupted celebrations with an unauthorized demonstration; the police arrested about 40 people, including several BPF officials and the leader of the Malady Front (the youth wing of the BPF), Pavel Sevyarynets.

22–29 June 1998: Bulgaria, France, Germany, Greece, Italy, Japan, Poland, the United Kingdom and the USA withdrew their ambassadors from Belarus, in protest at the breach of international law involved in the effective eviction of the staff of 22 embassies housed in a residential compound outside Minsk. Subsequently, the European Union (EU) and the USA banned President Lukashenka and his ministers from entering their territory. In December Lukashenka gave assurances that, henceforth, he would comply with international agreements. (All ambassadors had returned to Minsk by September 1999.)

11 September 1998: About 30 left-wing and centrist parties, among them the CPB and Liberal Democratic Party of Belarus, formed a new alliance to promote further integration with Russia and to support Lukashenka's candidacy in the presidential election scheduled for 2001. The alliance, the Belarusian People's Patriotic Union, declared its intention to contest future legislative elections as a single bloc. In the same month Belarus became a permanent member of the Non-aligned Movement.

2 November 1998: The Parliamentary Assembly of the Russia–Belarus Union voted for the creation of a unified parliament, to consist of two chambers.

15 December 1998: A new law was approved by the House of Representatives, effectively banning candidates with a police record or fine from standing in local elections to be held in April 1999. Numerous opposition candidates who had incurred fines for participating in anti-Government demonstrations were, thus, excluded.

25 December 1998: Presidents Lukashenka and Yeltsin signed a document providing for the creation of a union state within one year and equal rights for their citizens in Belarus and Russia.

10 January 1999: The Central Electoral Commission of the former Supreme Council called a presidential election to be held in May, in accordance with the 1994 Constitution. Despite the arrest of its Chairman, Viktar Ganchar, the Commission registered two candidates, the exiled leader of the BPF, Zyanon Paznyak, and the former premier, Mikhail Chigir.

27 January 1999: President Lukashenka decreed that political parties, trade unions and other organizations must re-register by July; those failing to do so were to be disbanded. By September only 17 of the 28 existing official parties had been re-registered; owing to the imposition of stringent minimum levels of membership.

6 April 1999: The Chairman of the Public Coalition Government–National Economic Council, Genadz Karpenka, died. He was replaced on 21 April by Mechislau Gryb, who was officially elected to the post in November.

8 April 1999: Mikhail Chigir was charged with embezzlement and abuse of office, one month before the presidential election in which he had planned to stand as a candidate (the embezzlement charge was subsequently dropped).

6–16 May 1999: The Central Electoral Commission of the former Supreme Council was unable to organize fixed polling stations for the presidential election; Zyanon Paznyak withdrew his candidacy on 13 May, owing to alleged illegalities in the voting procedure. Neither the Government nor the international community recognized the election as valid.

30 May 1999: Over 50 people were killed following a stampede in a Minsk underground railway station. Stricter security measures were subsequently introduced.

20 July 1999: President Lukashenka did not stand down at the end of his five-year term, in contravention of the nullified 1994 Constitution.

21 July 1999: Over 2,000 people gathered in Minsk to protest at President Lukashenka's 'illegitimate rule', leading to clashes with police and numerous arrests.

22 July 1999: Syamyon Sharetski, the leader of the AP and the former Chairman of the Supreme Council, fled to Lithuania to seek support, following his election as acting Head of State by the former Supreme Council.

September 1999: Nine independent newspapers were closed down by the Government, amid a climate of increased government control and the disappearances of several opposition figures, including Viktar Ganchar, from May.

26 September 1999: Following an inconclusive leadership vote in July, members of the BPF formed a breakaway faction, known as the Conservative Christian Party of the BPF, with Paznyak as Chairman. Vintsuk Vyachorka was elected Chairman of the BPF in late October.

17 October 1999: Up to 20,000 demonstrators participated in an anti-Government Freedom March. Leading opposition officials were among the 90 protesters arrested.

8 December 1999: A Union Treaty was signed between Russia and Belarus which, ultimately, intended to merge the two countries into a confederal state; a number of the Treaty's proposed political and economic aims, such as the introduction of a common monetary unit, were not to be introduced before 2005.

18 February 2000: Syargey Ling resigned as Prime Minister. Parliament subsequently approved Uladzimir Yermoshin, hitherto the Governor of Minsk City, as his replacement.

22 February 2000: The Consultative Council of Opposition Parties and Movements adopted a decision not to participate in the parliamentary elections due to take place in October, in protest at not having been consulted about the preparation of a new draft electoral code.

15 March 2000: Up to 25,000 people took part in a second Freedom March in Minsk.

25 March 2000: A demonstration to mark the 82nd anniversary of the proclamation of the Belarusian National Republic was prevented from taking place in the centre of Minsk, and up to 300 people were detained by police, including members of the press and international observers, attracting international criticism of what was deemed to be excessive police force. Despite the cancellation of the demonstration, up to 10,000 people gathered on the outskirts of the city.

25 April 2000: The joint Council of Ministers of Belarus and the Russian Federation met for the first time.

April–May 2000: A number of prominent opposition politicians were arrested and charged with organizing unrest, relating to the Freedom Marches; all were subsequently acquitted.

19 May 2000: Mikhail Chigir was convicted of abuse of office and received a three-year suspended prison sentence. The verdict was condemned as politically motivated by the international community.

2 July 2000: The opposition parties published a list of conditions for their participation in future elections, including reform of electoral legislation, confirmation of the National Assembly as the legislative body, free access to the media, and freedom of assembly and expression. A decision to boycott the parliamentary elections scheduled for 15 October was confirmed on 24 July.

14 August 2000: President Lukashenka wrote to the European Union and the Organization for Security and Co-operation in Europe (OSCE) detailing his proposals for the free and fair conduct of the parliamentary elections scheduled for 15 October. Both organizations had previously expressed concern in that regard.

6 September 2000: Further charges were brought against Chigir, relating to alleged non-payment of taxes. Chigir claimed the charges against him and other prominent opposition politicians were politically motivated and were intended to prevent them participating in the legislative election.

27 September 2000: Uladzimir Navumau, hitherto head of the presidential security service, was appointed Minister of Internal Affairs, replacing Yuriy Sivakow, who had been transferred to a post within the presidential administration.

9 October 2000: Opposition figures established a committee, known as 'Choice-2001', to promote the interests of politicians considered capable of defeating Lukashenka in the presidential election scheduled to take place in 2001.

10 October 2000: President Lukashenka and his counterparts in the Russian Federation, Kazakhstan, Kyrgyzstan and Tajikistan signed a treaty creating a new customs union, to be known as the Eurasian Economic Community.

15 October 2000: Despite a large anti-election rally and boycotts by a number of opposition parties, elections to the National Assembly were held and 41 members were elected. The OSCE declared the elections to be neither free, fair, nor open and the international community refused to recognize the results. Amid numerous allegations of electoral irregularities, voting was declared invalid in 13 of 110 constituencies.

29 October 2000: A second round of voting was held, following which 56 seats in the National Assembly remained to be allocated. The Central Election Commission announced in December that further elections to fill these vacancies would be held on 18 March 2001.

November 2000: An independent electoral monitoring group petitioned the Supreme Court to invalidate the results of the election. President Lukashenka made a number of changes to the Government and security services: most notably, Prof. Ural Latypaw, hitherto Deputy Prime Minister and Minister of Foreign Affairs, was appointed State Secretary of the Security Council and replaced in his previous position by Mikhail Khvastow. The President was widely considered to be dissatisfied with the progress made in investigating the disappearances of numerous public figures.

December 2000: The Supreme Court overturned the sentence received by Mikhail Chigir in May and ordered a reinvestigation of the evidence on the grounds of legal irregularities during the trial.

27 December 2000: The Government and central bank announced that the value of the Belarusian rouble would be linked to that of the Russian rouble through a maximum permitted monthly devaluation of 3% from January 2001, in order to facilitate the proposed currency union between the two countries from 2008.

1 January 2001: A new, purportedly more-liberal, criminal code was introduced.

Belgium

3rd–5th centuries: Germanic tribes migrated from the east into western Europe; the Franks settled in an area between the Scheldt and Meuse rivers, including much of modern Belgium, and began to expand into the surrounding territory.

567: The Frankish empire was divided into three: the eastern kingdom included modern Belgium, Lorraine and the right bank of the Rhine (precursor of the Holy Roman Empire); the western kingdom became France; and Burgundy.

900–11: The eastern Frankish kingdom was divided by internal feuds and tribal duchies were established. The County of Flanders, the west of modern Belgium, was later declared to be part of the Kingdom of France.

944: Lorraine, which included eastern Belgium, was created a duchy within the Holy Roman Empire.

1305: Flanders fell to France, despite the wealth of its trading cities, owing to the loss of English support.

1382: At the Battle of Roosbeeke the cities of Flanders, still discontent with French rule, were defeated by Phillip II of Burgundy and, together with the rest of the Low Countries (which lay within the Holy Roman Empire), were subjected to the Duchy of Burgundy.

1477: Maximilian of Habsburg, the son of the Emperor, married Maria, heiress of Burgundy; he subsequently defeated King Louis XI of France to confirm his succession to the Burgundian throne.

1489: Flanders recognized the claims of Maximilian to Burgundy and the provinces of the Low Countries came under Habsburg rule.

1519: Maximilian's grandson, Charles, the King of Spain as well as the Duke of Burgundy, was crowned Emperor (as Charles V).

1551: Charles V formally vested the possessions of the Imperial Circle of Burgundy in the Spanish Crown.

1556: Charles V abdicated, leaving the Spanish and Burgundian possessions to his son, Phillip II.

1568: After years of unrest, spurred by the rise of Calvinism in the north, the Low Countries (Netherlands) rose in revolt against Spain; the rebels were led by William of Orange and relied on naval superiority.

1576: The Pacification of Ghent was formed by all the provinces of the Netherlands, opposing Spanish rule.

1579: The Union of Arras re-established Spanish control over the southern provinces of Artois and Hainault; it was immediately opposed by the northern provinces, which formed the Union of Utrecht.

1581: The Union of Utrecht proclaimed its independence from Spain.

1584: The Spanish recaptured the provinces of Flanders and Brabant. The United Provinces of the Netherlands enacted its Constitution and, thus, the Low Countries were divided.

1648: Spain recognized the independence of the United Provinces, long assisted by the European powers, and formalized the borders of the rump 'Spanish Netherlands' (roughly, modern Belgium).

1701–13: The War of the Spanish Succession, which ended in the Peace of Utrecht, retained the Spanish Netherlands, if not Spain itself, for the Habsburgs; the southern provinces of the Low Countries, therefore, became known as the Austrian Netherlands.

1787: There was a popular uprising in the Austrian Netherlands, long uneasy with the reforms of Emperor Joseph II and his predecessor, and unrest spread to other Habsburg lands.

1789: The Austrian Netherlands seceded from Habsburg control, proclaiming itself the 'Republic of the United Belgian Provinces', but the revolt was defeated in the following year.

1795: Revolutionary France formally annexed the Austrian Netherlands (which it had first invaded in 1792), occupying the territory until the end of the Napoleonic Wars.

1815: The Congress of Vienna, which ended the European wars with revolutionary France, reunited the northern and southern Low Countries in the new Kingdom of the United Netherlands. The new state experienced strong religious and cultural antipathy between the Catholic, Latin south and the Protestant, Germanic north.

1828: A Liberal-Catholic union was formed in the southern provinces (by this point, increasingly known as Belgium) to oppose Dutch rule.

14 October 1830: National Congress declared Belgian independence after a short period of violent unrest, notably in Brussels and Antwerp. Supported by France and the United Kingdom, Belgium was able to resist Dutch attempts to maintain the United Netherlands.

1831: A Belgian Constitution, providing for a monarch and a bicameral parliament, and declaring Belgium permanently neutral, was enacted; French was declared the only official language, causing anger among the country's Dutch speakers, and Prince Leopold of Saxe-Coburg was awarded the throne.

1839: The Treaty of London guaranteed the neutrality and inviolability of Belgium and the Netherlands recognized Belgian independence.

1865: France aimed to annexe Belgium, as compensation for an increase in Prussian power in central Europe; the outbreak of the Franco–Prussian War later removed the issue from the agenda.

1879: The ruling Liberal party caused political confrontation with its proposals to secularize the education system and relations between Belgium and the Vatican (the seat of the Pope, the head of the Roman Catholic Church) were temporarily broken.

1885: The Berlin Conference awarded a vast territory along the Congo river in Africa to King Leopold II of Belgium, as a personal possession; (he later granted it to the Belgian state). The Catholic Party made religious education compulsory in schools.

1893: Universal suffrage was introduced (the electoral system was changed to allow proportional representation in 1899). Complaints of brutality by the Belgian administration in the Congo Free State began to arise, both from its residents and from neighbouring colonial powers.

1906: Exposure of the Schlieffen Plan (a recommendation of strategy to be used by Germany in the event of a war in Europe, inspired by a former Chief of the General Staff, Count Alfred von Schjylieffen, which included the invasion of Belgium in moves against France) caused great alarm in Belgium.

1908: Congo Free State officially became a Belgian colony, the Belgian Congo (now the Democratic Republic of the Congo—formerly Zaire 1971–97).

1914–18: At the outbreak of the First World War, German forces invaded Belgian territory, in accordance with the Schlieffen Plan but in violation of the Treaty of London, prompting the guarantors of Belgian neutrality, the Entente Powers of France and the United Kingdom, to declare war. Belgium and the bordering area of France were the principal theatre of war in Europe and some 6m. people are estimated to have died here.

1919: The Treaty of Versailles removed the requirement of Belgian neutrality, restored the Constitution and awarded Belgium a small amount of territory previously belonging to Germany (Eupen and Malmédy).

1920: A military alliance was concluded with France.

1921: The Belgium–Luxembourg Economic Union was founded.

1925: Belgium was a signatory to the Locarno Agreement, which established Germany's western border and guaranteed a demilitarized zone in the Rhineland.

1932: The Dutch language was given equal status in national public affairs.

1936: The alliance with France was terminated, and the British, French and German Governments instead agreed to guarantee the frontiers and the neutrality of Belgium. The German Government, however, under Adolf Hitler's National Socialist (Nazi) German Workers' Party, abrogated the Locarno Agreement.

1940: Following the outbreak of the Second World War in Europe in the previous year, Germany invaded Belgium. King Leopold III was taken prisoner and held in Belgium until liberation; a Government-in-Exile sat in Paris (France) and then in London (the United Kingdom).

September 1944: Allied forces liberated Belgium.

1945: Belgium became a founding member of the UN.

1945–74: Flanders traditionally supported the Christian Social Party (Christelijke Volkspartij—CVP) and later the People's Union (Volksunie—VU), whereas Wallonia typically expressed support for the Socialist Party (Parti Socialiste—PS).

1948: The Benelux Economic Union was formed by Belgium, Luxembourg and the Netherlands (the Union became effective in 1960 and a single customs area was established in 1970).

18 April 1951: Belgium and five other countries formed the European Coal and Steel Community (ECSC), the first institution of the three European Communities. Leopold III abdicated and was succeeded by his son, Baudouin.

25 March 1957: Belgium signed the Treaty of Rome, which established the European Economic Community (EEC). The European Atomic Energy Community (Euratom) was established on the same day. Brussels was to be one of the three main bases for the Communities (collectively, the Communities came to be known as the European Community and then, from November 1993, as the European Union—EU).

1960: After an uprising in the Belgian Congo, Belgium agreed to grant independence to the colony; the hurried departure of the colonial authorities engendered some disorder in the newly independent state, even requiring a UN troop presence.

1963: The Constitution was amended to make Belgium officially bilingual, giving Dutch (Flemish) equal status with French.

24 December 1970: Legislation was enacted expressing a commitment to a system of regional government in Belgium and providing for the creation of two largely autonomous regions, Dutch-speaking Flanders and French-speaking Wallonia, within a federal Belgium. Each linguistic community was given a Cultural Council with the power to pass decrees in particular areas.

1974: A Christian Social–Liberal coalition came to power, led by Léo Tindemans.

August 1980: The Flemish and Walloon regions became operational. The Cultural Council were made more independent of central government and the number of areas in which they could pass decrees was increased.

December 1981: Owing to a lack of Socialist support, a new Government was formed, comprising a coalition of the Dutch- and French-speaking wings of the Christian Social and Liberal parties and led by Dr Wilfried Martens of the CVP.

May 1988: The Socialists returned to government, in a coalition of the Dutch- and French-speaking wings of the Christian Social and Socialist parties, and the VU, also led by Martens.

July 1989: Under modifications to the Constitution, Brussels became the third federal region, with its own Executive, and further autonomy was conferred on the country's communities.

April 1990: King Baudouin objected in principle to legislative proposals permitting abortion, so abdicated to permit promulgation of the law; after 36 hours Parliament restored him to the throne.

March 1992: A new Government, comprising the Dutch- and French-speaking Christian Social and Socialist parties, but without the VU, came to power. Jean-Luc Dehaene of the CVP became Prime Minister.

Mid-July 1993: The Constitution was amended to create a federal state of Belgium, comprising the largely autonomous regions of bi-lingual Brussels, Dutch-speaking Flanders and French-speaking Wallonia. Assemblies were also created for the 'Language Communities', including one for the small German-speaking minority.

9 August 1993: Prince Albert of Liège acceded to the throne as King Albert II.

1994–95: A highly public investigation into a number of prominent Socialist ministers took place, following allegations of their involvement in a bribery scandal.

August 1996: A paedophile network was uncovered, which led to accusations of police incompetence and official corruption.

April 1998: Marc Dutroux, a convicted paedophile and murderer, whose arrest in August 1996 was the central incident of the controversy, briefly escaped from police custody. The incident occasioned renewed mistrust of the police and other national institutions and precipitated the resignations of the commander of the national gendarmerie and the Ministers of the Interior and of Justice.

1 January 1999: A common currency to Belgium and 10 other EU countries, the euro, was introduced as part of Stage III in the process of Economic and Monetary Union (EMU).

May 1999: Revelations that livestock had been provided with animal feed containing the carcinogen dioxin led to export bans being imposed by both the European Commission and the USA.

13 June 1999: The Flemish Liberals and Democrats—Citizen's Party (Vlaamse Liberalen en Demokraten—Partij van de Burger, VLD) emerged from the legislative election as the largest single party in the Chamber of Representatives, with 23 of the 150 seats, having received 14.3% of the total votes cast; the CVP won 22 seats (with 14.1% of the ballot), the Socialist parties secured a combined 33 seats (19.8%), the ecologist parties 20 seats (14.4%) and the Vlaams Blok 15 seats (9.9%).

12 July 1999: A new coalition Government took office, led by Guy Verhofstadt of the VLD and comprising members of that party, its Francophone homologue, the Parti Réformateur Libéral, and the Flemish- and French-speaking wings of the Socialist and ecologist parties. The new administration ended a 40-year period of CVP participation in government.

8 July 2000: The Democratic Republic of Congo (DRC) recalled its ambassador from Belgium in protest at the issue by a Belgian court of a warrant for the arrest of the DRC's Minister of State for Foreign Affairs and International Co-operation, Yerodia Abdoulaye Ndombasi. The minister was alleged to have incited violence against members of minority ethnic groups in the DRC in 1998.

8 October 2000: In local elections, the Government faced competition from the right-wing Vlaams Blok, which advocated Flemish independence and anti-immigration policies. The party made its most significant gains in Flanders, receiving 33% of votes cast in Antwerp, and doubled its share of the vote, compared with the previous election, in several districts of Brussels.

Bosnia and Herzegovina

168 BC: Illyria (which included Bosnia and Herzegovina and other former Yugoslav territories) was annexed by the Roman Empire.

AD 395: Following a division of the administration of the Roman Empire, Illyria was ruled by the Eastern Roman ('Byzantine') Emperor in Constantinople (Istanbul, now in Turkey); this marked the beginning of the history of Bosnia and Herzegovina as a region on the borders of Western and Eastern Europe.

5th century: Southern Slav peoples began to move from the north into Illyria and the Balkans.

7th–8th centuries: Western Christian missionaries, from Aquileia (Trieste, now in Italy) and Salzburg (now in Austria), were active among the Croats and the Slovenes, respectively, introducing the Latin script and a Western cultural orientation.

863: The missionary activity of the Byzantine brothers, SS Constantine (Cyril) and Methodius, led to the conversion of the Serbs (including the ancestors of the Bosnians) and the Bulgars to Eastern Orthodox Christianity; a Slavonic liturgy was introduced with a written language, in the Cyrillic script.

11th century: Emergence of the Serb principality of Rama, the original Bosnian state, although it soon fell under the influence of the Catholic Croat kingdom.

1102: Croatia's personal union with Hungary effectively, if not finally, linked it to the Hungarian Crown.

1180–1204: The local ruler (ban) under the Hungarian Crown, Kulin, despite the disapproval of the Catholic authorities, was tolerant of the emergence of a local Christian heresy, sometimes equated with the dualism of the Bogomils; this was widely adopted by the local élite of a territory strongly disputed for by not only the Hungarians, but also the Serbs, Byzantines and Venetians.

1187: The Emperor in Constantinople acknowledged Serbian independence and Hungarian conquests in Croatia and Bosnia, but authority in the area remained uncertain. By the middle of the next century the local élite enjoyed sufficient independence from the Catholic and Orthodox powers that the heretical Bosnian Church (*ecclesia Sclavoniae*) was virtually a state religion.

1322–53: Reign of Stjepan II Kotromanić, who established a powerful Bosnian state, nominally subject to Hungary.

1346: Coronation of Uroš IV (Stefan Dušan of Raška, who reigned 1331–55) as Tsar (King) of the Serbs and Greeks, at Skopje; his short-lived empire incorporated the territory subsequently known as Herzegovina.

1377: Stjepan Trvtko I (1353–91) proclaimed himself Tsar of the Bosnians and Serbs, renouncing Hungarian overlordship; his kingdom secured control of much of the Adriatic coast.

1389: The Turkish Ottoman Empire destroyed the Serbian nobility at a battle on the plain of Kosovo Polje.

1448: Herzegovina became a border duchy of Austria (herceg means duke), as the Habsburgs attempted to improve the security of the Serbian princes and the Bosnian kingdom against the encroaching Ottomans.

1463: The Ottomans finally ended Bosnian independence.

1483: The province of Herzegovina was annexed to the Ottoman Empire.

1624: After some 150 years of Ottoman rule and the often political conversion of the Slav élite, two-thirds of the population of the provinces of Bosnia and Herzegovina were officially reckoned to be Muslim.

July 1878: At the Congress of Berlin, the Habsburg Empire of Austria-Hungary (already having regained Croatia) secured administration rights in Bosnia and Herzegovina; the Bosnian élite's National Muslim Organization (later the Yugoslav Muslim Organization), which sought to protect the Muslim community against competing Croat and Serb claims, was tolerated, but had less influence under the Habsburgs.

5 October 1908: Austria-Hungary formally annexed Bosnia and Herzegovina, despite international objections, following the 'Young Turk' uprising in the Ottoman Empire, which led to disturbances in the Balkans; the Habsburg ally, Germany, prevented war against Serbia.

1910: The secret 'Greater Serb' society, Union or Death (the 'Black Hand'), was founded by Col Dimitrijević-Apis.

28 June 1914: The heir to the Habsburg throne, Archduke Francis Ferdinand, and his wife were assassinated in Sarajevo, by a Bosnian student acting for the Serb Black Hand group.

28 July 1914: Austria-Hungary declared war on Serbia, which started the First World War between the Central Powers, of Austria-Hungary and Germany, and the Entente Powers, of France, Russia, Serbia and the United Kingdom.

July 1917: Serbia and the other Southern Slavs (excluding the Bulgarians) declared their intention to form a unitary state, under the Serbian monarchy.

29 October 1918: Following the defeat and dissolution of the Danubian Monarchy, the Southern Slav (Yugoslav) peoples separated from the Austro-Hungarian system of states (a Southern Slav republic was established on 15 October); Dalmatia, Croatia and Slavonia, Bosnia and Herzegovina, parts of Carinthia, Carniola and the Banat were, subsequently, ceded formally to the new state.

4 December 1918: Proclamation of the Kingdom of Serbs, Croats and Slovenes (Kingdom of Yugoslavia from 1929), which united Serbia and Montenegro with the former Habsburg lands.

1937: Tito (Josip Broz) became General Secretary of the Communist Party of Yugoslavia (later the League of Communists of Yugoslavia—LCY), which was to become the main partner in the Partisan (National Liberation Army) resistance to invasion during the Second World War.

10 April 1941: Following the German-Italian invasion and partition of Yugoslavia, an Independent State of Croatia (including Bosnia and Herzegovina) was proclaimed, with the Italian, Duke Aimone of Spoleto (Split), as King, and a Government under Ante Pavelić, leader of the fascist Ustaša (Rebel) movement; Bosnia and Herzegovina experienced some of the worst fighting in the internecine struggles of the war period.

29 November 1943: In the Bosnian town of Jajce, following fierce resistance and civil conflict with the Serb royalist Četniks (Yugoslav Army of the Fatherland) and with the Ustaša regime, Gen. (later Marshal) Tito's Partisans proclaimed their own government for liberated areas (including much of eastern Bosnia).

29 November 1945: Following elections for a Provisional Assembly, the Federative People's Republic of Yugoslavia was proclaimed, with Tito as prime minister.

January 1946: A Soviet-style Constitution, establishing a federation of six republics, of which one was Bosnia and Herzegovina, and two autonomous regions, was adopted. The Communist regime subsequently banned the 'Young Muslims' organization, which sought to champion the rights of Muslims, but was condemned as a terrorist group.

April 1963: A new Constitution changed the country's name to the Socialist Federal Republic of Yugoslavia (SFRY).

1971: The Slav Muslims (mainly the Bosnian Muslims or Bosniaks) achieved recognition as a distinct ethnic group and the status of one of the six 'nations of Yugoslavia'. Greater autonomy was granted to the federal units and the system of collective leadership and the regular rotation of posts was adopted in the federation and in the administration of Bosnia and Herzegovina.

February 1974: A new federal Constitution was adopted.

4 May 1980: Tito died; his responsibilities were transferred to the collective federal State Presidency and to the Presidium of the LCY.

18 November 1990: Elections to the collective State Presidency of Bosnia and Herzegovina were held (the three nationalist parties—representing the main Bosnian Muslim, Serb and Croat ethnic groups—secured all seven seats); the first round of voting for the new, bicameral Assembly also took place (the second round was on 2 December).

9 December 1990: The final round of voting for the Assembly took place; of the 240 seats, the predominantly Muslim Party of Democratic Action (PDA) won 86, the Serb Democratic Party (SDP) 72 and the Croatian Democratic Union of Bosnia and Herzegovina (CDU—BH) 44.

20 December 1990: The three main parties, all nationalist groups, announced their coalition agreement: Dr Alija Izetbegović, the leader of the PDA, was to be President of the republican State Presidency; Jure Pelivan of the CDU—BH, the Premier; and Momčilo Krajišnik of the SDP, President of the Assembly.

26 April 1991: In the first indication that the political crises in Yugoslavia could be reflected in Bosnia and Herzegovina, Serb-dominated districts in the north-west unilaterally announced the formation of the 'Municipal Community of Bosanska (Bosnian) Krajina'; the move was repudiated by the republican authorities, who feared a link with the Serb 'Krajina' territory in Croatia.

15 May 1991: The 'Serbian bloc' (the representatives of Serbia, Kosovo and Metohija, Vojvodina and Montenegro) on the federal State Presidency prevented the accession, as its first non-Communist President, of Stipe Mesić of Croatia, effectively depriving Yugoslavia of a head of state.

30 June 1991: A European Community (EC, known as the European Union— EU—from November 1993) mediating team secured agreement to a cease-fire in Slovenia and Croatia (both of which had declared their independence six days previously), with the threat of EC sanctions, and the immediate proclamation of Stipe Mesić as President of the federal State Presidency; there was to be a three-month moratorium on further implementation of the Croatian and Slovenian declarations of dissociation.

September 1991: Despite EC efforts to negotiate peace, fighting continued in Croatia. Meanwhile, in Bosnia and Herzegovina various groups of Serb-dominated municipalities formed four 'Serb Autonomous Regions' (SARs) and ethnic tensions resulted in shooting incidents along the borders with Croatia and Montenegro—prompting a declaration of neutrality by the State Presidency in the following month.

15 October 1991: The Assembly declared the sovereignty of Bosnia and Herzegovina, emphasizing the inviolability of its borders and its willingness to consider a form of Yugoslav association; this resolution was rejected by the SARs, which declared themselves subject only to the federation.

24 October 1991: The Serb deputies of the republican Assembly announced the formation of an 'Assembly of the Serb Nation of Bosnia and Herzegovina' (Serb Assembly).

9–10 November 1991: A referendum organized by the Serb Assembly was reported to have indicated overwhelming support for remaining in a common Serb state.

February 1992: Following an agreement in the previous month, a UN Protection Force (UNPROFOR) was established by the Security Council; it was based in Sarajevo and its peace-keeping role in Croatia was extended to Bosnia and Herzegovina later in the year.

29 February–1 March 1992: In a referendum, boycotted by the Serb community, 99.4% of those voting (comprising 63% of the electorate) supported full independence. The country was declared independent and renamed the Republic of Bosnia and Herzegovina.

27 March 1992: The formation of the 'Serb Republic of Bosnia and Herzegovina' was announced, to be headed by the leader of the SDP, Dr Radovan Karadžić.

7 April 1992: Two days after the beginning of the siege of Sarajevo by Serb forces, Bosnia and Herzegovina's independence was formally recognized by the EC countries and the USA.

19 May 1992: The Yugoslav People's Army (YPA) announced the withdrawal of its troops from Bosnia and Herzegovina.

22 May 1992: Bosnia and Herzegovina was accepted as a member of the UN.

30 May 1992: The UN introduced sanctions against the Federal Republic of Yugoslavia (FRY—Serbia and Montenegro) as a result of its continuing intervention in the civil war in Bosnia and Herzegovina.

7 July 1992: The formation of the 'Croat Union of Herzeg-Bosna' was announced; led by Mate Boban, it claimed about 30% of the territory of Bosnia and Herzegovina.

26–27 August 1992: The London Conference was held in the United Kingdom, co-chaired by mediators from the UN (Cyrus Vance, former US Secretary of State) and the EC (Lord Owen, former British Secretary of State for Foreign and Commonwealth Affairs); a peace plan was announced in October, in Geneva (Switzerland).

December 1992: Following allegations of 'ethnic cleansing' and organized rape, the UN Human Rights Commission condemned the Serbs as largely responsible for violations of human rights in the country. Later in the month the UN Security Council demanded access to all Serb detention centres.

22 February 1993: The UN Security Council decided to prosecute war criminals by establishing an International Criminal Tribunal for the Former Yugoslavia (ICTY), based in The Hague (Netherlands).

May 1993: The Serb Assembly at Pale decisively rejected the Vance–Owen Plan. France, the Russian Federation, Spain, the United Kingdom and the USA proposed the formation of six 'safe areas' for the Bosniaks—effective from 22 July.

July 1993: Representatives of the three sides in the conflict reached a constitutional agreement in Geneva, whereby the country would become the 'Union of Republics of Bosnia and Herzegovina'—a loose confederation of three ethnically based states.

27 August 1993: During a session of the State Presidency, the Croat Prime Minister, Mile Akmadžić, was dismissed, in a sign of growing tensions between the Muslims and the Croats. He was to be succeeded by a Muslim, Haris Silajdžić.

28 August 1993: An assembly met in Grude and officially proclaimed the 'Croat Republic of Herzeg-Bosna'; the deputies accepted the Geneva Plan on condition that the other two sides in the conflict also accepted it. On the same day the Serb Assembly voted in favour of the Plan.

31 August 1993: At a session of the Bosnia and Herzegovina Assembly the Geneva Plan was rejected in its existing form, but deputies agreed that it should be a basis for further peace negotiations.

27 September 1993: In Velika Kladusa, one of the chief towns of the district of Bihać, the 'Autonomous Province of Western Bosnia' was established; a Muslim member of the State Presidency, Fikret Abdić, was elected President by its 'Constituent Assembly'; a state of martial law was imposed by Izetbegović on the whole of 'Western Bosnia'.

28 September 1993: The majority of delegates at a 'Bosnian Convention' voted in favour of accepting the Geneva Plan, but only if the territories captured from the Bosnian Muslims (or, as the Convention favoured, Bosniaks) were returned.

October 1993: The Muslim Democratic Party was established in Velika Kladusa; Abdić was named Chairman. There was fighting between forces loyal to Izetbegović and those supporting Abdić.

5 February 1994: The shelling of a Sarajevo market-place by Serb forces, causing many casualties, provoked the UN to threaten military intervention; this led to a cease-fire around Sarajevo, particularly following a Russian diplomatic initiative.

8 February 1994: Boban resigned as President of Herzeg-Bosna, to be replaced by a Presidential Council.

25 March 1994: The premier of the Serb Republic, Vladimir Lukić, resigned.

31 March 1994: A Constituent Assembly of mainly Bosniak and Croat deputies declared the formation of the Federation of Bosnia and Herzegovina, in accordance with a US-brokered plan to end almost one year of fighting between Croat and government forces.

10 April 1994: The UN ordered the first North Atlantic Treaty Organization (NATO) air strike against Serb ground forces, which were attacking Goražde; earlier in the year similar threats had improved the situation in Sarajevo (both towns were 'safe areas').

May 1994: Zubak was elected President of the new Federation, Ejup Ganić (a Bosniak and deputy leader of the State Presidency) Vice-President and Silajdžić Prime Minister; the following month a joint Government was elected.

July 1994: A plan presented by the 'Contact Group' (consisting of France, Germany, Russia, the United Kingdom and the USA), which granted 51% of Bosnian territory to the Federation, and 49% to the Bosnian Serbs, was accepted by Izetbegović and President Tudjman of Croatia.

August 1994: NATO air strikes against the Bosnian Serbs resumed, following Serb attacks against UN forces and the renewed bombardment of Sarajevo. The Serbian President, Slobodan Milošević, the most powerful figure in the FRY leadership, formally severed relations with the Bosnian Serbs. Government troops defeated Abdić's forces in Bihać; thousands of rebel troops and civilians, including Abdić, escaped to Serb-held territory in Croatia.

1 September 1994: The Bosnian Serb Assembly unanimously approved the result of a referendum in which 96% of participants voted against the Contact Group Plan.

3 October 1994: In order to secure the relaxation of all remaining sanctions (some had been lifted the previous month) and to force the Bosnian Serbs to accept the peace plan, the FRY closed its border with Serb-occupied Bosnia and Herzegovina to all but humanitarian supplies.

31 December 1994: The mediation of a former US President, Jimmy Carter, resulted in the acceptance by both sides of a revised version of the Contact Group Plan (providing for possible confederal links between the Bosnian Serbs and the FRY) and a four-month cease-fire agreement was signed, with effect from the next day.

February 1995: Against a background of increasing violation of the cease-fire, the Bosnian Serbs and the Croatian Serbs established a joint Supreme Defence Council and guaranteed mutual military assistance.

March 1995: A formal military alliance was announced between the Croatian, Bosnian Croat and Bosnian government forces, and military action against the Serbs intensified.

April 1995: At a meeting in Bonn (Germany), the Bosnian Croats and the Muslim-dominated Bosnian Government agreed to unite their police forces, local governments and, eventually, their armed forces. A Russian plan for FRY recognition of Bosnia and Herzegovina failed.

May 1995: Heavy shelling of Sarajevo by the Serbs provoked the UN to request air strikes by NATO forces, carried out on Serb ammunitions depots. Relations between the Serb forces and UNPROFOR continued to deteriorate and a large number of peace-keepers were taken hostage, prompting the UN to create, in the following month, a 10,000-strong 'rapid reaction force', to provide the peace-keepers with added protection.

July 1995: The Serbs captured the 'safe area' of Srebrenica and then, despite punitive NATO air strikes, the 'safe area' of Žepa.

4 August 1995: The Croatian army began a major offensive that routed the Krajina Serbs, thereby causing a massive influx of refugees into Bosnian Serb territory and depriving the Serb Republic of vital military and strategic support.

6–7 August 1995: The siege of Bihać, which was begun on 20 July by the Bosnian Serbs, the Krajina Serbs and Bosniak supporters of Abdić, was effectively ended by Bosnian government and Croatian troops.

9 August 1995: The US Assistant Secretary of State, Richard Holbrooke, proposed a peace plan based on earlier proposals by the Contact Group, but acknowledging the Serb possession of Srebrenica and Žepa.

30 August 1995: Two days after a mortar attack in central Sarajevo (presumed to be the work of the Serbs), which left 41 civilians dead and over 80 wounded, a series of devastating NATO air and artillery strikes (known as 'Operation Deliberate Force') began against Serb positions across the country; this continued despite Russian objections.

8 September 1995: At a meeting in Geneva, which was chaired by the Contact Group, the foreign ministers of Bosnia and Herzegovina, Croatia and the FRY (acting for the Bosnian Serbs) agreed the basic principles for a peace accord (including recognition that Bosnia and Herzegovina should comprise two existing 'entities'—the Federation and the Serb Republic—and that the country should be divided between them, with 51% for the Federation).

11 September 1995: Joint Bosnian government and Croatian forces began an assault on Serb-held territory in western and central Bosnia.

20 September 1995: The Bosnian Serbs completed the withdrawal of heavy weapons from around Sarajevo.

26 September 1995: In New York (USA) the foreign ministers of Bosnia and Herzegovina, Croatia and the FRY agreed the basic principles of an elected national parliament and presidency, with the Bosnian Serbs guaranteed representation by one-third of both bodies.

12 October 1995: A 60-day cease-fire, agreed under US pressure, came into force. In spite of the truce, forces on both sides continued attempts to gain more territory before a final peace settlement.

1 November 1995: The 'Peace Proximity Talks' began at the Wright-Patterson Air Force Base near Dayton, Ohio (USA), under the aegis of the Contact Group.

21 November 1995: At Dayton leaders of the Federation of Bosnia and Herzegovina, Croatia and the FRY initialled a General Framework Agreement for Peace in Bosnia and Herzegovina; this, with its attached accords, provided for the division of the country between the Federation (51%) and the Serb Republic (49%); the city of Sarajevo was to have special status.

22 November 1995: The UN suspended the remaining sanctions against the FRY and agreed to end the arms embargo, imposed on the former Yugoslavia in September 1991.

14 December 1995: The Dayton accords were signed into treaty at the Elysées Palace in Paris (France).

18 December 1995: The Serb Republic's parliament elected Rajko Kasagić premier in a new Government.

20 December 1995: According to the terms of the Dayton accords, the mandate of the 60,000-strong NATO-controlled Implementation Force (IFOR) began, and the formal transfer of power from UNPROFOR took place.

21 December 1995: Bosnia and Herzegovina became a member of the International Monetary Fund (IMF).

12 January 1996: Silajdžić resigned as premier and formed a new Party for Bosnia and Herzegovina.

30 January 1996: The republican Assembly elected a new Government for the Republic of Bosnia and Herzegovina, to be chaired by Hasan Muratović. The following day Izudin Kapetanović was confirmed as head of a new federal Government by the Constituent Assembly of the Federation.

19 March 1996: With the final suburb of Sarajevo, Grbavica, coming under the control of the federal police, the Bosnian capital was reunified; much of its Bosnian Serb population, however, had fled the city for Serb-held areas.

15 May 1996: Karadžić dismissed Kasagič, the moderate premier of the Bosnian Serbs and their main contact with the international community,and replaced him with the more extreme Gojko Klicković .

18 May 1996: Karadžić deputized one of the Vice-Presidents, Biljana Plavšić, to execute most of his presidential functions, including dealings with the international community.

30 June 1996: Controversial local elections were finally held in Mostar; List for a United Mostar, a Bosniak electoral alliance which included the PDA, won some 47.4% of the votes and the CDU—BH 44.6%. The Croat representatives refused to accept the results or to attend the new city assembly until August, when a compromise was agreed.

19 July 1996: Under considerable pressure from the international community, Karadžić agreed formally to resign his posts of President of the Serb Republic and leader of the SDP. Plavšić became Acting President.

14 September 1996: The Organization for Security and Co-operation in Europe (OSCE) organized elections to the state Presidency and the federal legislature, to the presidency and legislature of the Serb Republic, and to the legislature and cantonal authorities of the Bosnian Federation. Izetbegović was elected Chairman of the Presidency, while the PDA won the majority of seats in the Federation's section of the national House of Representatives and in the Federation's own legislature. Similarly, the SDP obtained a majority in the Serb section of the House of Representatives and in the Serb National Assembly; Plavšić was elected President of the Serb Republic, with some 59% of the votes cast.

30 September 1996: One day after being sworn in the three members of the Presidency of Bosnia and Herzegovina, Izetbegović, Zubak and Krajišnik, convened for the first time, in a meeting organized by the overseer of the Dayton accords, the High Representative of the International Community, Carl Bildt, a former premier of Sweden.

1 October 1996: The UN Security Council resolved finally to end sanctions (suspended at the end of 1995) against the Serb Republic and the FRY.

3 October 1996: Full diplomatic relations between Bosnia and Herzegovina and the FRY were agreed, following mediation by the French President, Jacques Chirac: the FRY agreed to respect the territorial integrity of Bosnia and Herzegovina; and Bosnia and Herzegovina recognized the FRY as the successor state of the former Yugoslavia.

5 October 1996: The inaugural session of the state Presidency was held in Sarajevo; Krajišnik refused to attend, however, claiming his life would be at risk in the city. The inaugural session of the republican Assembly was postponed, owing to a boycott by Serb deputies.

8 November 1996: President Plavšić dismissed Gen. Ratko Mladić as commander of the Serb armed forces, replacing him with Maj.-Gen. Pero Colić; it was not until 28 November, however, that Mladić, who was wanted for the investigation of war crimes, agreed to relinquish his post.

27 November 1996: A new Serb Government was appointed, again headed by Klicković.

17 December 1996: The Government of the Republic of Bosnia and Herzegovina formally transferred its remaining functions to the Federation and, therefore, officially ceased to exist; it was also announced that the Croat polity of Herzeg-Bosna no longer existed.

18 December 1996: Edhem Bičakčić replaced Kapetanović as Prime Minister of the Federation.

20 December 1996: The successor to IFOR, known as the Stabilization Force (SFOR), formally began operations in the country. SFOR was about one-half the size of IFOR and had a mandate of 18 months, subsequently extended.

3 January 1997: The inaugural session of the Bosnia and Herzegovina Assembly was finally held; it approved the Council of Ministers nominated by the Co-Prime Ministers, Silajdžić of the Party for Bosnia and Herzegovina and Boro Bosić of the SDP, who had been appointed by the state Presidency in the previous month—each of the Bosnian ethnic groups held an equal number of offices in the new cabinet.

28 February 1997: The Governments of the Serb Republic and the FRY signed an agreement to foster mutual economic co-operation and to collaborate on regional security; the Serb Republic's legislature ratified the agreement in March, despite opposition from President Plavšić and from some Bosniak and Bosnian Croat leaders.

30–31 May 1997: A conference of the Peace Implementation Council met in Sintra (Portugal): Carlos Westendorp, a former Spanish foreign minister, was appointed the new High Representative; NATO officials stipulated deadlines for the approval by the entities of a number of laws on property, passports and citizenship; a new list of ambassadors was demanded, to better reflect the ethnic diversity of the country.

28 June 1997: President Plavšić suspended the Serb Republic's Minister of Internal Affairs, Dragan Kilac, over his alleged failure to consult her on important issues; the suspension was opposed by the National Assembly.

3 July 1997: Supported by the UN and the OSCE, President Plavšić dissolved parliament and announced that elections were to be held in early September; the decision was opposed by the legislature and, following the Constitutional Court's ruling in August that Plavšić's decision was illegal, it voted to disregard future decrees by the Bosnian Serb President.

9 July 1997: The EU announced the suspension of aid to the Serb Republic owing to its failure to extradite suspected war criminals to the ICTY.

22 August 1997: Mark Pavić replaced Kilac as Serb Minister of Internal Affairs; his appointment was rejected by the Bosnian Serb legislature, which subsequently appointed an alternative interior minister and promoted Kilac to Deputy Prime Minister.

13–14 September 1997: Local elections in both entities, originally scheduled for September 1996, finally took place, observed by the OSCE; of the 91 parties that contested the elections, the three main nationalist groups, the PDA, the CDU and the SDP, received the vast majority of the votes cast.

24 September 1997: Plavšić and Krajišnik attended a meeting in Belgrade at which details for elections to both the Bosnian Serb legislature and Presidency and to the Bosnian collective state Presidency were agreed.

1 October 1997: SFOR troops seized television transmitters allegedly being used for propaganda purposes by Karadžić's supporters; the action was condemned by Krajišnik, who was a member of the station's management, and other Bosnian Serb politicians.

22–23 November 1997: In elections to the Serb Republic's National Assembly, the SDP won the largest number of seats (24 of a total of 70), but had a reduced representation in parliament, and the Coalition for a Single and Democratic Bosnia, an alliance including the PDA and the Party for Bosnia and Herzegovina, gained 16 seats, while President Plavšić's recently formed Serb National Alliance and the Serb Radical Party each secured 15 seats.

17 December 1997: The Parliamentary Assembly approved the law on passports within the deadline set by the international community, but failed to ratify the citizenship law; the following day Westendorp, the High Representative, announced that the citizenship law would be imposed on Bosnian territory from 1 January 1998.

27 December 1997: At the inaugural session of the National Assembly, the Serb President, Plavšić, nominated an independent, Mladen Ivanić, as premier; following objections by the SDP, Ivanić proposed an inter-party agreement on an interim 'government of national unity', until new elections.

18 January 1998: Following the failure of Ivanić's all-party negotiations, a moderate, Milorad Dodik, won sufficient parliamentary support to form a new

Bosnian Serb Government; he announced his intention to govern in adherence to the terms of the Dayton accords.

26 January 1998: The EU approved 26m. ECU-worth of aid to the Serb Republic.

31 January 1998: Following the swearing in of the new cabinet, the Bosnian Serb Assembly voted to relocate the Republic's capital from Pale, where the extremist Karadžić and his supporters were based, to Banja Luka.

15 February 1998: Two Bosnian Serbs, Miroslav Tadić and Milan Simić, became the first indicted war crimes suspects to voluntarily surrender to the ICTY.

1 April 1998: Following a devaluation of the Yugoslav dinar, the Serb Republic declared Germany's Deutsche Mark to be its official currency.

9 June 1998: At the third conference of the Peace Implementation Council, in Luxembourg, foreign ministers resolved to accelerate the implementation of the Dayton peace agreement; both Krajišnik and Prime Minister Dodik condemned the declaration as another attempt to transfer authority from the Serb Republic to the central government.

20 June 1998: As agreed in February, SFOR's new mandate, which stated that a multinational specialized unit would remain in the region indefinitely and that six-monthly reviews would take place, was enforced.

22 June 1998: A new national currency, the convertible mark, was introduced; it was to be 'pegged' to the Deutsche Mark and was valid for 18 months.

12–13 September 1998: Elections to the Bosnian collective Presidency and national legislature, the Federation's House of Representatives, and the Serb Republic's Presidency and National Assembly took place. Izetbegović was re-elected to the state Presidency, and Zivko Radišić, a moderate representative of the Serbs, and Ante Jelavić, a nationalist Croat, were elected for the first time; Radišić was inaugurated as Chairman of the state Presidency for an eight-month term. The national legislature and Federation's House of Representatives continued to be dominated by nationalist parties: a PDA-led alliance gained 14 of the 42 seats in the Bosnian House of Representatives and 68 of the 140 seats in the Federation House of Representatives. In the election to the Bosnian Serb Presidency, the Chairman of the Serb Radical Party (SRP), Nikola Poplasen, defeated the Western-backed Plavšić. The SDP retained the largest number of seats (19 out of 83) in the National Assembly of the Serb Republic, although the moderate parties kept significant representation.

12 December 1998: Ganić was re-elected President of the Federation of Bosnia and Herzegovina and a new Federation Council of Ministers was established.

9 January 1999: SFOR troops shot and killed a Bosnian Serb suspected of war crimes, after he resisted arrest near the town of Foca; Bosnian Serbs subsequently staged violent protests at the local UN headquarters.

5 March 1999: Following his attempt to dismiss Dodik from the post of Prime Minister of the Serb Republic, President Poplasen was removed from office on the grounds that he had exceeded his authority; Mirko Sarović hitherto Vice-President, provisionally assumed the presidential role.

7 March 1999: International arbitrators in Vienna (Austria) ruled that Serb control of Brčko would end, and that the town would henceforth be governed jointly by the Serb Republic and the Federation, under international supervision. The decision was rejected by the Bosnian Serb National Assembly and by Prime Minister Dodik, who resigned in protest (he later rescinded his resignation); nevertheless, in mid-April a new municipal government, comprising Serbs, Muslims and Croats was elected in the town.

15 June 1999: Jelavić replaced Radišić as Chairman of the state Presidency.

18 June 1999: The UN Security Council voted to extend the mandate of SFOR and the principally civilian security force, the UN Mission in Bosnia and Herzegovina (UNMIBH) for a further 12 months; at the same time, NATO announced a reduction in the SFOR contingent, to approximately 16,500 troops.

August 1999: Wolfgang Petritsch, hitherto Austrian ambassador to the FRY, succeeded Westendorp as High Representative of the international community in Bosnia and Herzegovina.

1 October 1999: Petritsch prohibited Poplasen and a further two SRP officials from contesting forthcoming local elections, on the grounds that they had consistently obstructed the implementation of the Dayton peace agreement.

29 November 1999: Petritsch dismissed nine Bosnian Serbs, seven Bosniaks and six Bosnian Croats from their posts in local government in the Federation and the Serb Republic, mainly for obstructing the return of minority group refugees.

December 1999: Ivo Andrić-Luzanski, hitherto the Federation Vice-President, assumed the Federation Presidency, in accordance with the one-year rotational mandate stipulated in the Constitution.

29 January 2000: The Deputy Prime Minister of the Serb Republic, Tihomir Gligorić, was dismissed by Prime Minister Dodik, who accused him of causing disunity within the entity's Government.

9 February 2000: Legislation allowing for the restructuring of the state Presidency was agreed upon, following the Constitutional Court's decision, in the previous month, that certain tenets of the Presidency were unconstitutional; henceforth, the collective Presidency would consist of two Ministers of

State and a Chairman, which would rotate between Muslim, Serb and Croat representatives every eight months.

11 February 2000: Haris Siladžić, the Bosniak co-premier of the national Council of Ministers, resigned his post in protest at the Government's perceived failure to ensure the safe return of refugees.

14 February 2000: Alija Izetbegović took over from Ante Jelavić as Chairman of the state Presidency.

19 February 2000: The Socialist Party of the Bosnian Serb Republic (SPRS) withdrew from the ruling Accord Coalition following disagreement with Prime Minister Dodik and the other coalition partners; the Bosnian Serb premier's refusal to reinstate the dismissed SPRS Deputy Prime Minister, Tihomir Gligorić, resulted in the resignation, two days later, of the four other SPRS ministers.

3 March 2000: The Bosnian Croat general, Tihomir Blaskič, the most senior officer to be brought to trial by the ICTY, was convicted of war crimes and sentenced to 45 years' imprisonment, the most severe sentence issued by the Tribunal thus far.

8 March 2000: Following the completion of demilitarization in the disputed northern town of Brčko, an Interim District Government was officially inaugurated; the new structure, which was announced by the international supervisor for Brčko, Robert Farrand, was to consist of four Serbs, four Bosniaks and one Croat member, and was to be headed by Sinisa Kisić, hitherto mayor of Brčko.

9 March 2000: The Serb Republic premier, Dodik, and the Croatian foreign minister, Tonino Picula, signed a statement on the return of refugees and displaced persons; both ministers agreed to submit legislation on the issue to their respective parliaments, to improve border relations and to allow 2,000 persons from each territory to return home within three months.

21 March 2000: Robert Farrand appointed the 29 deputies that would comprise the transitional assembly of Brčko; the legislature, the mandate of which would last until district elections were held, consisted of 13 Serb, nine Bosniak and seven Croat representatives. Mirsad Djapo of the Socialdemocratic Party was appointed Speaker.

3 April 2000: The former joint President of the Presidency and a close ally of Karadžić, Momćilo Krajišnik, was arrested in Pale by SFOR troops and extradited to the ICTY in the Netherlands to answer charges of war crimes.

8 April 2000: Local elections were held; according to results released by the OSCE, the SDP gained a majority in 49 of the country's 145 municipalities, mainly in the Bosnian Serb Republic. The CDU—BH won control of 25 councils and the PDA gained control of 23 municipalities, mainly in the Federation. The moderate, multi-ethnic Socialdemocratic Party made significant electoral gains, however, winning control of 15 municipalities in the Federation (compared to one in the previous ballot) and achieving representation in 98 municipalities, including 26 in the Serb Republic. The elections, which were deemed free and fair by the OSCE, attracted a voter turn-out of 66%.

12 April 2000: The state House of Representatives adopted legislation on changes to the composition of the Council of Ministers; henceforth, the state Government would consist of a Council Chairman and five ministries. The Chairman would be appointed by the state Presidency for an eight-month term, and subject to approval by the legislature.

16 April 2000: Following the poor performance of their party in the local elections, the PDA governors of Sarajevo and Tuzla resigned their posts.

28 April 2000: After losing a vote of confidence within his party, Ejup Ganić, the PDA Deputy Chairman, resigned his party posts. His party colleague, Edhem Bičakčić, the Federation Prime Minister, survived a vote of confidence.

3 May 2000: The Stara Gradiska–Bosanska Gradiska international border crossing between Bosnia and Herzegovina and Croatia was re-opened, facilitating the return of displaced persons and contributing to better transport connections and stronger trade relations between the two countries.

24 May 2000: The PDA-led Federation Government survived a vote of 'no confidence' in the House of Representatives, proposed by the Socialdemocratic Party. On the same day, Ganić was expelled from the PDA, owing to his failure to comply with the party board's decision that he resign as Federation Vice-President.

6 June 2000: Izetbegović announced his intention to resign from the collective state Presidency in October, when his eight-month term as Chairman was due to end, on grounds of ill health and advancing age; however, he intended to continue in his post as PDA leader.

22 June 2000: The new republican Government of Spasoje Tusevljak (who had been elected Chair of the Council of Ministers earlier in the month) was approved in the House of Representatives.

27 July 2000: Petritsch dismissed the Minister of Agriculture, Water Management and Forestry in the Federation Government, Ahmed Smajić, and the head of the tax service, for impeding economic reform.

7 September 2000: The Bosnian Serb National Assembly endorsed a motion of 'no confidence' in the Government of Milorad Dodik, proposed by the SDP.

11 September 2000: The Bosnian Serb Government challenged the constitutionality of the vote of 'no confidence' and referred the matter to the Constitutional Court, stating that it would remain in office until the legislative elections scheduled for November.

11 November 2000: Elections were held at cantonal, entity and republican level. Mirko Sarović and Dragan Cavić were elected as President and Vice-President respectively of the Serb Republic and, in elections to the Bosnian Serb National Assembly, the SDP won 38% of votes (31 seats). The PDA won 27% of votes (38 seats) in elections to the Federation House of Representatives, the Socialdemocratic Party won 26% (37 seats), the CDU–BH 18% (25 seats) and the SBiH 15% (21 seats). In elections to the republican House of Representatives, the Socialdemocratic Party won 22% of votes (nine seats), the PDA 20% (eight seats), the SDP 15% (six seats), and the SBiH and CDU–BH 12% (five seats) each.

December 2000: Mladen Ivanić was designated by Sarović as Prime Minister of the Serb Republic.

January 2001: Ivanić formed the Serb Republic's first multi-ethnic Council of Ministers. Amid international concerns over the inclusion of several SDP members, Ivanić replaced the new Minister of Trade and Tourism, a prominent SDP member.

10 January 2001: Former Bosnian Serb President Biljana Plavšić, who had been indicted in April 2000, surrendered to the ICTY but denied accusations of having played a major part in the organization of a campaign of genocide and deportation against Muslims and Croats between July 1991 and December 1992.

7 February 2001: The national Parliamentary Assembly rejected the designated Prime Minister, CDU–BH member Martin Raguz. A newly formed coalition, the Alliance for Change, comprising the SDP BiH and nine other non-nationalist parties, held 17 of the 42 seats in the House of Representatives, in addition to 69 seats in the federal legislature.

22 February 2001: SDP BiH member Bozidar Matić nominated a new national Council of Ministers, which was approved by the House of Representatives.

23 February 2001: Three Bosnian Serbs were convicted by the ICTY of the systematic rape and sexual enslavement of Muslim women in the town of Foca in 1992; they received a combined sentence of 60 years. Three days later Bosnian Croat official Dario Kordic was convicted of authorizing murders and war crimes against Bosnian Muslims in 1993–94; he was sentenced to 25 years' imprisonment.

4 March 2001: A rebel assembly of Bosnian Croats voted to secede from the Federation; the decision was condemned by western powers overseeing the implementation of the 1995 Dayton agreement as a serious threat to the peace process in the region.

7 March 2001: Jelavić was dismissed from the collective state Presidency by Petritsch following the declaration by the CDU–BH of its intention to create a separate Croat state.

Bulgaria

865: The Khan of the Bulgars, Boris (852–89), converted to Eastern Orthodox Christianity, following the missionary activity of the Eastern Roman ('Byzantine') brothers, SS Constantine (Cyril) and Methodius, 'the Apostles of the Slavs'.

893–927: Reign of Simeon, first Tsar (Caesar) of the Bulgars, who failed in his ambition to take Constantinople (Istanbul, now in Turkey) and the Byzantine throne, but established a powerful empire and instituted the Bulgarian Church as the first new autocephalous Orthodox church.

971: Annexation of eastern Bulgaria as a Byzantine province.

1014: The Bulgar ruler, Samuel, was defeated at the battle of Balathista by the Emperor Basil II ('the Slayer of the Bulgars'), who subsequently designated western Bulgaria a Byzantine province.

1187: Following a decline in Byzantine power the Emperor in Constantinople recognized the establishment of the second Bulgarian Empire, under the Asen dynasty.

1330: The Bulgars were defeated by Serbian forces at the battle of Küstendil (Velbuzhde).

1396: Bulgaria became a province of the Turkish Ottoman Empire.

1870: Establishment of an autocephalous Exarchate of the Bulgarian Orthodox Church (not recognized by Constantinople until 1945).

1876: Violent suppression of Bulgarian uprisings by the Ottomans.

1877: Russia declared war on the Turks in support of the Orthodox, Slav subjects of the Ottoman Empire.

1878: The Ottomans recognized an autonomous principality of Bulgaria, at the Congress of Berlin; Eastern Rumelia and Macedonia remained under Turkish rule.

1879: The First Grand National Assembly of Bulgaria, meeting in the town of Turnovo (now Veliko, 'Grand', Turnovo), adopted a liberal constitution (the 'Turnovo Constitution') and invited the nephew of the Russian tsarina, Alexander (Aleksandur) von Battenburg, of the House of Hesse-Darmstadt, to become the ruling prince.

1885: Eastern Rumelia was annexed by Bulgaria. Serbian forces were defeated at the battle of Slivnitsa.

1887: Election of Ferdinand of Saxe-Coburg as Prince of Bulgaria, following the abdication of Aleksandur.

2 August 1903: Bulgarians in Pirin Macedonia took part in the Ilinden uprising—a revolt against the Ottoman authorities organized by the Internal Macedonian Revolutionary Organization (IMRO). The revolt was suppressed.

October 1908: Upheavals in the Ottoman Empire included the proclamation of Tsar (King) Ferdinand I of an independent Bulgarian kingdom.

August 1913: The Peace of Bucharest concluded the Second Balkan War: Bulgaria lost Macedonia and the Dobrudzha.

12 October 1915: Bulgaria declared war on Serbia, thus entering the First World War on the side of the Central Powers of Germany, Austria-Hungary and the Ottoman Empire (Turkey).

29 September 1918: Bulgaria surrendered unconditionally to the Entente Powers, with the consequent abdication of Ferdinand I and the accession of Boris III.

29 November 1919: The Treaty of Neuilly was signed: Bulgaria was forced to cede its Thracian territories and Mediterranean coast to Greece; it also ceded territory on its western frontier to Yugoslavia (then known as the Kingdom of Serbs, Croats and Slovenes); and returned the Dobrudzha (which it had regained by the Peace of Bucharest of May 1918) to Romania.

1923: A *putsch* by army officers resulted in the suppression of the Peasants Party and the Communist Party.

19 May 1934: A coup by two nationalist organizations, Zveno and the Association of the Officers of the Reserve, led to the establishment of the authoritarian regime of Col Kimon Georghief.

January 1935: Col Georghief resigned; authoritarian rule was continued by Boris III.

30 August 1940: The second Arbitration Award of Vienna restored Southern Dobrudzha to Bulgaria (confirmed in 1947).

1 March 1941: Bulgaria signed a pact with the Axis Powers of Germany and Italy and, following the commencement of war in the Balkans, gained western Macedonia from Yugoslavia.

August 1943: Death of Boris III; a regency was established for the young Tsar, Simeon II.

5 September 1944: The USSR declared war on Bulgaria.

8 September 1944: Bulgaria declared war on Germany.

9 September 1944: Following a coup by the Fatherland Front, a left-wing alliance dominated by the Bulgarian Communist Party (BCP), the Soviet army occupied Bulgaria.

28 October 1944: An armistice was signed with the Allies.

August 1945: The Agrarian and Social Democratic Parties left the Front and the Government.

15 September 1946: Tsar Simeon II was formally deposed and a Republic was declared, following a referendum.

November 1946: Georgi Dimitrov, First Secretary of the BCP, became Chairman of the Council of Ministers (Prime Minister).

22 February 1947: A peace treaty was signed with the Allies.

December 1947: A new Constitution abolished all opposition parties and established a system based on the Soviet model. Bulgaria became a People's Republic.

March 1949: Dimitrov was replaced as Chairman of the Council of Ministers by Vasil Kolarov.

July 1949: Vulko Chervenkov became leader of the BCP, following Dimitrov's death.

February 1950: Chervenkov became Chairman of the Council of Ministers.

March 1954: Todor Zhivkov became leader of the BCP.

April 1956: Anton Yugov replaced Chervenkov as Chairman of the Council of Ministers.

November 1962: Zhivkov replaced Yugov as Chairman of the Council of Ministers.

1965: An army coup attempt was discovered and suppressed, enabling Zhivkov to consolidate his position.

16 May 1971: A new Constitution was adopted, following a referendum; the Constitution established the Council of State as the supreme executive and legislative body. Zhivkov relinquished his former government posts to become

President of the Council of State (head of state) and was succeeded as Prime Minister by Stanko Todorov.

June 1981: Following elections to the National Assembly, Grisha Filipov became Chairman of the Council of Ministers.

December 1985: On the occasion of a national census the Government was accused of trying forcibly to assimilate the ethnic Turkish population ('Bulgarian Muslims'), through a 'regenerative programme'.

20 March 1986: Filipov was replaced as Prime Minister by Georgi Atanasov.

July 1987: Zhivkov promised liberalization and pluralism in government in his so-called 'July Concept'.

February 1988: The dissident Independent Association for Human Rights was founded; environmental protests in northern areas led to the foundation of Ecoglasnost.

March 1988: Candidates other than those nominated by the BCP were permitted to stand in local elections, although in July a number of prominent proponents of reform were dismissed from office.

November 1988: Eighty leading intellectuals founded the Club for the Support of Glasnost and Perestroika.

22 August 1989: The Turkish Government closed the border with Bulgaria, some 310,000 refugees having fled the programme of assimilation and the violent suppression of protests.

10 November 1989: Zhivkov was forced to resign his post as General Secretary of the BCP, following demonstrations against him and was replaced by the Minister of Foreign Affairs, Petur Mladenov. One week later Mladenov was elected by the National Assembly to succeed Zhivkov as President of the Council of State. The Government announced the dissolution of the secret police.

December 1989: Following a strike by Podkrepa (Support), the independent trade-union movement, the Government agreed to begin negotiations about 'round-table' meetings between the BCP, the Bulgarian Agrarian People's Union (BAPU) and the Union of Democratic Forces (UDF—a recently established alliance of opposition groups). The Government approved measures to end discrimination against the Muslim minority.

January 1990: The National Assembly revoked the leading role of the BCP.

February 1990: Aleksandur Lilov replaced Petur Mladenov as head of the Supreme Council of the BCP. Atanasov resigned as Prime Minister and was replaced by Andrei Lukanov, who headed a Government comprising only members of the BCP. Later, the official trade-union congress completed its renunciation of any party or state affiliations and changed its name to the Confederation of Independent Trade Unions in Bulgaria (CITUB).

3 April 1990: Petur Mladenov was elected to the new post of President of the country by the National Assembly. The BCP changed its name to the Bulgarian Socialist Party (BSP).

17 June 1990: The second round of voting in elections to a constituent Grand National Assembly (GNA) took place, amid widespread allegations of electoral irregularities. However, the BSP received 211 seats out of 400, the UDF 144 and the Muslim Movement for Rights and Freedoms (MRF) won 23.

July 1990: Mladenov announced his resignation as President, following a series of protests and strikes. The GNA convened in Veliko Turnovo, but the BSP soon lost its majority as the reformist Alternative Socialist Party faction left the party (joining the UDF in October).

1 August 1990: Zheliu Zhelev, hitherto leader of the UDF, was eventually elected President of the country by the GNA. President Zhelev proposed that Lukanov form a new Government, although the UDF refused to join a coalition with the BSP.

September 1990: Bulgaria was elected to membership of the International Monetary Fund (IMF).

November 1990: Despite some reforms, including renaming the country the Republic of Bulgaria, there were increasing protests at the lack of progress in the GNA on a new constitution. A general strike prompted the resignation of Lukanov once there was agreement on a multi-party administration under a non-party premier (later decided to be Dimitur Popov).

December 1990: The major political groups signed the Agreement Guaranteeing the Peaceful Transition to a Democratic Society, which committed support to the Popov Government, the drafting of a new constitution, the introduction of a market economy and general elections to be held in 1991.

May 1991: A group of 39 UDF deputies withdrew from the GNA session, protesting at its delays (lack of progress on constitutional issues had provoked violent demonstrations in March); this boycott was resolved, but marked the beginning of a split in the UDF and its constituent parties.

12 July 1991: The GNA finally ratified the Constitution, which was signed by 309 of the 400 deputies and came into effect on 13 July.

13 October 1991: Despite internal divisions, in the elections to the National Assembly the UDF emerged as the largest party, gaining 110 seats. The UDF nominated the leader of the Green Party, Filip Dimitrov, as Prime Minister.

19 January 1992: Zheliu Zhelev won the presidential election with 53% of the votes cast, having been forced into a second round of voting by the BSP-backed candidate, Vulko Vulkanov.

30 August 1992: President Zhelev, speaking on television, strongly criticized Dimitrov and his cabinet.

September 1992: The MRF and the BSP voted to remove Stefan Savov, the UDF-nominated Chairman of the National Assembly, from office.

December 1992: Lyuben Berov was eventually nominated for the post of Prime Minister (Dimitrov had lost a vote of censure in October) by the MRF; he was subsequently elected by the National Assembly to head a cabinet largely without party affiliation (with the parliamentary support of the MRF, the BSP and a faction of the UDF).

29 June 1993: Blaga Dimitrova, the Vice-President, resigned, alleging that she had been insufficiently consulted while in office; this followed increasing criticism of the President by the UDF, which had organized demonstrations against him and was also in disagreement with the Government.

August 1993: Bulgaria's former leader Todor Zhivkov was charged with the diversion of state funds abroad and placed under house arrest (he was acquitted of all charges in 1996 and died two years later).

September 1994: Berov resigned, after failing to negotiate a reduction in Bulgaria's foreign debt.

October 1994: The BSP and the UDF refused to form a government to replace the Berov administration, so President Zhelev dissolved parliament and appointed Reneta Indzhova to head an interim Government.

18 December 1994: In the general election the BSP, led by Zhan Videnov, gained an outright majority in the National Assembly, receiving 52.1% of the votes cast. Videnov was appointed Prime Minister of a new Government at the end of January 1995.

1 February 1995: A 'Europe Agreement' between Bulgaria and the European Union (EU) came into force; the following year Bulgaria officially applied for membership.

June 1995: The heads of the state television and radio services, and the Director-General of the national news agency, were dismissed by the BSP-led Government, which claimed their reporting lacked objectivity.

May 1996: Escalating problems in the banking sector and a steadily deteriorating currency culminated in a financial crisis, with a massive withdrawal of funds and a series of measures which failed to improve government finances or to halt the devaluation of the lev.

2 June 1996: In US-style primary elections for a presidential candidate for a united opposition, President Zhelev was defeated by Petar Stoyanov of the UDF, who gained 66% of the vote.

2 October 1996: The former Prime Minister, Andrei Lukanov (who had remained an influential member of the BSP and critic of the Videnov regime), was assassinated.

3 November 1996: In the second round of voting in the presidential election, Stoyanov was elected to the presidency, with 59.7% of the votes cast.

December 1996: Following increasing dissatisfaction within his own party and demonstrations by the UDF, Videnov offered his resignation as Prime Minister and party leader.

January 1997: The BSP designated the Minister of the Interior, Nikolai Dobrev, as Prime Minister, but, following an increase in demonstrations by the UDF, President Zhelev revoked Dobrev's mandate. On 19 January Stoyanov was inaugurated as President, and he again invited the BSP to form an administration.

February 1997: The UDF again rejected the proposed Government under Dobrev; amid fears of civil conflict, Dobrev resigned and President Stoyanov nominated the Mayor of Sofia, Stefan Sofianski, as Prime Minister; he formed an interim Council of Ministers and the National Assembly was dissolved on 19 February.

March 1997: The interim Government announced that the former Prime Minister, Videnov, and other members of his regime were to be charged with criminal negligence, over the severe economic hardship which resulted from his policies.

19 April 1997: In elections to the National Assembly the UDF secured 52.6% of the votes cast and 137 seats, while the BSP, which contested the elections in the Democratic Left alliance, obtained 22.1% of the votes and 58 seats; the Alliance for National Salvation, a coalition dominated by the MRF, won 19 seats; the newly established Euro-Left gained 14 seats; and the Bulgarian Business Bloc (BBB) secured 12 seats.

8 May 1997: A formal political consensus was adopted by the National Assembly, on economic reform, on the restoration of agricultural land to its rightful, pre-Communist ownership and on entry to the EU and to the North Atlantic Treaty Organization (NATO).

21 May 1997: The National Assembly elected Ivan Kostov of the UDF as Prime Minister.

1 July 1997: As stipulated by the IMF, a currency board was introduced to halt the continuing economic decline.

5 September 1997: The BBB was forced to dissolve its parliamentary group, after the expulsion of its two representatives left the group with less than the required minimum of representatives.

24 June 1998: The agreement demarcating the border between Turkey and Bulgaria was ratified by the National Assembly.

8 September 1998: With 11 other countries of Central Asia, the Caucasus and the Black Sea region, Bulgaria signed an agreement in Baku (Azerbaijan) to recreate the 'Silk Road' trade route between China and the West.

December 1998: Following the Constitutional Court's ruling that the Communist confiscation of property was illegal, King Simeon returned to Bulgaria, after 52 years in exile.

5 May 1999: Despite public opposition, which increased after a misdirected missile damaged a suburb of Sofia in the previous month, the legislature approved the Government's decision to grant NATO use of its airspace in its bombardment against the Federal Republic of Yugoslavia, in return for security guarantees.

5 July 1999: The lev was redenominated, in order to ease the worsening financial situation, one new lev being equal to 1,000 old leva.

16 and 23 October 1999: In municipal elections the UDF won the largest number of votes cast (31.3%), narrowly defeating the BSP, which obtained 29.4% of the ballot.

10 December 1999: Bulgaria was invited to begin negotiations on entry into the EU.

21 December 1999: Prime Minister Kostov effected a widescale reorganization of the Council of Ministers; among the changes were the reduction in the number of deputy premiers, from three to one, and the appointment as defence minister of Boiko Noev, replacing Georgi Ananiev.

9 February 2000: Euro-Left deputy, Tsvetelin Kunchev, was sentenced to six years' hard labour after being convicted of charges of robbery, extortion and kidnapping.

14 March 2000: Representatives of the Bulgarian and Romanian Governments signed an agreement on the position of a second bridge to be built on the River Danube, linking the two countries.

15 March 2000: Bulgaria and Turkey ratified an agreement to remove, destroy and discontinue the use of anti-personnel mines in areas adjoining their common borders.

28 March 2000: Negotiations for Bulgaria's entry into the EU opened in Brussels (Belgium).

19 May 2000: Kostov survived a vote of 'no confidence' in the National Assembly.

June 2000: Relations between Bulgaria and Libya deteriorated as a result of matters related to the impending trial of six Bulgarian medics, a doctor and several nurses accused of deliberately infecting 393 Libyan children with the human immunodeficiency virus (HIV).

1 June 2000: Former President Mladenov died, aged 63.

9 June 2000: The Bulgarian and Macedonian ministers responsible for the environment signed a bilateral treaty on co-operation in environmental protection.

10 June 2000: Bulgaria's principal EU negotiator, Alexander Bozhkov, resigned amid allegations of corruption.

17 August 2000: President Stoyanov dismissed the Chief Secretary of the Ministry of the Interior, Bozhidar Popov, following a report by a special ministerial commission into the discovery in late July of illegal surveillance equipment in the homes of the Prosecutor-General, other senior officials and members of parliament.

23 October 2000: President Stoyanov urged the country's political parties to form a broad coalition after the legislative elections scheduled for 2001, in order to optimize Bulgaria's possibilities of EU membership.

26 October 2000: Two senior officials of the UDF, who had advocated that Kostov be replaced as Prime Minister, resigned following the party's expression of support for the premier.

1 December 2000: The EU announced the removal, from May 2001, of the requirement for Bulgarian nationals seeking to enter an EU member state to be in possession of a visa. As a consequence, Bulgaria terminated its free-travel agreement with the Russian Federation.

9 December 2000: Bogomil Bonev, who had been removed from his post as Minister of the Interior in December 1999, was elected Chairman of the Civic Party, formed in October.

7 March 2001: The Government announced that it would send military aid to Macedonia to combat attacks by Albanian rebels on its border with Kosovo.

Croatia

168 BC: Illyria (which included modern-day Croatia) was annexed by the Roman Empire.

AD 395: Following a division of the administration of the Roman Empire, Illyria was ruled by the Eastern Roman ('Byzantine') Emperor in Constantinople (Istanbul, now in Turkey).

5th century: Southern Slav peoples began to move from Pannonia into Illyria and the Balkans.

7th–8th centuries: Western Christian missionaries, from Aquileia (Trieste) were active among the Croats, introducing the Latin script and a Western cultural orientation.

812: By the Treaty of Aix-la-Chapelle (Aachen), the Byzantine Emperor, Michael I, acknowledged the Frankish (German) ruler, Charles ('the Great'— Charlemagne), as Emperor in the West; Byzantine suzerainty over Istria and Dalmatia was confirmed and German influence to the north of the Croats was established.

1076: Coronation, by the Pope (the leader of the Roman Church), of Dimitar Zvonimir, who had rejected Eastern, Byzantine overlordship of the Croatian kingdom established in the 10th century.

1082: Venice was granted trading privileges in the Eastern Empire, securing its independence and growing influence along the formerly Byzantine Dalmatian coast.

1102: Croatia's personal union with Hungary (under the *Pacta Conventa*) linked it to the Hungarian Crown, together with parts of Dalmatia.

1187: The Emperor in Constantinople acknowledged Hungarian conquests in Croatia and Bosnia.

1490: Death of the Hungarian King, Matthias I Corvinus, who had secured modern Croatia and the Vojvodina (Slavonia and the Banat) for Hungary and, temporarily, conquered the Habsburg lands.

1526: Louis II and the Hungarian forces were destroyed by the Ottomans at the Battle of Mohács; the Hungarian Crown was claimed as a hereditary possession of the House of Habsburg, but the kingdom itself was subsequently partitioned between the Habsburgs (northern Croatia) and the Ottomans (southern Croatia and Slavonia).

1718: The Peace of Passarowitz confirmed the Habsburg liberation of Hungary, including Croatia and Slavonia; the Ottomans ceded the Banat and northern Serbia (but the latter was held only until 1739).

1815: The Congress of Vienna confirmed Austrian rule over Istria and Dalmatia, which were formerly Venetian.

1848: At a time of revolution in Habsburg and other territories, the Croatian assembly, in Agram (Zagreb), was forced to end consideration of a Southern Slav (Yugoslav) state.

1868: Croatia, united with Slavonia, was granted autonomy by Hungary, which, since the *Ausgleich* or Compromise of the previous year, was now a partner in the Habsburg 'Dual Monarchy'.

1881: Final abolition of the 'Military Frontier' or Vojna Krajina, in which, since the 17th century, the Habsburgs had allowed some autonomy to Serb settlers defending the borders against the Ottomans in Bosnia. (Austria-Hungary had secured administration rights in Bosnia and Herzegovina in 1878.)

1903: Accession of Petar I Karadjordjević, leader of the Radical party, to the throne of Serbia; he was anti-Habsburg and encouraged the Southern Slav movement ('Yugoslavism'), the champion of which in Croatia-Slavonia was Bishop Josip Strossmayer.

28 June 1914: The heir to the Habsburg throne, Archduke Francis Ferdinand, and his wife were assassinated in Sarajevo (Bosnia and Herzegovina).

28 July 1914: Austria-Hungary declared war on Serbia, which started the First World War between the Central Powers, of Austria-Hungary and Germany, and the Entente Powers, of France, Russia, Serbia and the United Kingdom.

July 1917: Representatives of the Croats, Serbia and the other Southern Slavs (excluding the Bulgarians) declared their intention to form a unitary state, under the Serbian monarchy.

29 October 1918: Following the defeat and dissolution of the Danubian Monarchy, the Southern Slav peoples separated from the Austro-Hungarian system of states (a Southern Slav republic was established on 15 October); Dalmatia, Croatia-Slavonia, Bosnia and Herzegovina, parts of Carinthia, Carniola and the Banat were, subsequently, ceded formally to the new state.

4 December 1918: Proclamation of the Kingdom of Serbs, Croats and Slovenes, which united the former Habsburg lands with Serbia and Montenegro.

August 1921: Prince Aleksandar, Regent of Serbia since 1914 and of the new Kingdom since its formation, became King, upon the ratification of the 'Vidovdan' (St Vitus Day) Constitution.

August 1928: A separatist Croatian assembly convened in Zagreb.

3 October 1929: Following the imposition by King Aleksandar of a royal dictatorship, the country was formally named Yugoslavia.

1931: The dictatorship was suspended by the introduction of a new Constitution, although this did not prevent Croat unrest and the rise of the fascist Ustaša (Rebel) movement.

October 1934: King Aleksandar I of Yugoslavia was assassinated in France by Croatian extremists; his brother, Prince Paul, became Regent, on behalf of the young King Petar II.

1937: Tito (Josip Broz) became General Secretary of the Communist Party of Yugoslavia (CPY), which was to become the main partner in the Partisan (National Liberation Army) resistance to the German invasion.

March 1941: A *coup d'état* installed King Petar II, who reversed previous policies and aligned himself with the Allied Powers of the Second World War.

9 April 1941: An Independent State of Croatia (Nczavisna Država Hrvatska) was established, following the invasion of Yugoslavia by German and Italian forces; the State included much of Bosnia and Herzegovina, while the rest of Yugoslavia was dismembered by Albania, Bulgaria, Germany, Hungary and Italy (the last annexing some of the Dalmatian coast); the Italian, Duke Aimone of Spoleto, was King of Croatia, with an Ustaša Government under Ante Pavelić.

29 November 1943: Proclamation of a government for 'liberated' areas by the Partisans, following a savage resistance struggle and civil war with the Ustaša regime and the royalist Četniks (Yugoslav Army of the Fatherland) of western Serbia; Tito's leadership was subsequently acknowledged by the Allies and the royal Government-in-Exile.

1944: King Petar II was declared deposed.

29 November 1945: Following elections for a Provisional Assembly, the Federative People's Republic of Yugoslavia was proclaimed, with Tito as prime minister.

January 1946: A Soviet-style Constitution was adopted, establishing a federation of six republics, one of which was Croatia (including Dalmatia and Slavonia).

1954: Istria was partitioned between Italy, which gained the city of Trieste, and Yugoslavia (mostly becoming part of Croatia, but the north going to Slovenia—denying Croatia a border with Italy). The so-called Novi Sad Agreement proclaimed Serbo-Croat to be one language with two scripts.

1966: Reformists, who had already achieved some economic liberalization, secured the fall of Vice-President Aleksandar Ranković, the head of the secret police and an advocate of strong central government.

July 1971: Following the granting of the rights of autonomy to the federal units, Tito introduced a system of collective leadership and the regular rotation of posts.

December 1971: The reformist Croatian leadership was forced to resign following criticism from Tito; the suppression of the Croatian 'mass movement', or *Maspok*, and a purge of liberals throughout Yugoslavia followed.

1974: A new Constitution came into force, aimed at containing nationalist tendencies, particularly within Croatia.

4 May 1980: Tito died; his responsibilities were transferred to the collective State Presidency of the federation and to the Presidium of the League of Communists of Yugoslavia (LCY).

March 1989: Against a background of increasing tension in the Serbian province of Kosovo and declining economic conditions, a new Federal Government, under Ante Marković, was appointed.

22 April 1990: The first-round elections to the three chambers of the Croatian Assembly (for a maximum of 356 seats) were held.

6–7 May 1990: A second round of voting took place; in the final results, the nationalist opposition party, the Croatian Democratic Union (CDU), gained 205 of the eventual 351 seats in the Assembly.

30 May 1990: The Assembly elected Franjo Tudjman, leader of the CDU, as President of the State Presidency of Croatia; Stjepan ('Stipe') Mesić was elected President of the Executive Council (Premier).

25 July 1990: The Croatian Assembly approved constitutional changes, including: the removal of the word 'Socialist' from the Republic's title; the redesignation of the republican Executive Council as a 'Government'; the replacement of the republican State Presidency with a President and six Vice-Presidents; and the downgrading of the use of the Cyrillic alphabet. The leaders of the Serb minority in Croatia, who had formed a 'Serb National Council', denounced the amendments and demanded a referendum on immediate cultural autonomy.

August 1990: The Assembly dismissed Croatia's member of the federal State Presidency, a Communist, and nominated their Premier, Mesić, instead (endorsed by the Federal Assembly on 19 October); Josip Manolić was elected Premier.

1 October 1990: The Serb National Council, after announcing their referendum results, proclaimed autonomy for the Serb-dominated Krajina areas of Croatia (the 'Serb Autonomous Region—SAR of Krajina', which was based in Knin).

November 1990: The Assembly placed the Territorial Defence Force under republican control.

21 December 1990: The Croatian Assembly (Sabor) promulgated a new Constitution, which proclaimed the Republic's full sovereignty and its right to secede from Yugoslavia.

20 January 1991: Croatia and Slovenia concluded a mutual defence pact, amid rising tension between the republican authorities and the Yugoslav People's Army (YPA).

25 January 1991: The YPA agreed to end its state of alert and the Croatians agreed to demobilize, if not disband, all paramilitary groups. However, 10 days later, the YPA ordered the arrest of Croatia's Minister of Defence on sedition charges.

21 February 1991: Croatia asserted the primacy of its Constitution and laws over those of the federation and declared its conditions for participation in a confederation of sovereign states.

28 February 1991: The self-proclaimed SAR of Krajina declared its separation from Croatia and its desire to unite with Serbia (on 16 March it formally resolved on its adherence to the Yugoslav federation).

11 April 1991: Croatia established an army, the Croatian National Guard Corps (to replace the Territorial Defence Force), after increasing anxieties about the intentions of the YPA following clashes between it and Croatian forces.

30 April 1991: The SAR of Krajina's self-proclaimed government or executive council announced the formation of a Krajina Assembly.

19 May 1991: In a referendum in Croatia, some 94% of participants voted in favour of an independent republic (possibly as part of a confederation of sovereign states).

29 May 1991: The SAR of Krajina announced that its basic statute was a constitutional law; its Assembly appointed a government led by Milan Babić.

25 June 1991: The Sabor declared the independence and sovereignty of the republic, beginning the process of 'dissociation' from the federation at the same time as Slovenia. Two days later the union of the two Krajinas was announced: the SAR in Croatia; and Bosanska (Bosnian) Krajina in Bosnia and Herzegovina.

30 June 1991: Following fighting, mainly in Slovenia, a cease-fire was secured; one condition was implemented forthwith—the proclamation of Stipe Mesić as President of the federal State Presidency; it was subsequently agreed that Croatia and Slovenia should have a three-month moratorium on further implementation of their declarations of dissociation.

18 July 1991: In Croatia, as fighting continued to escalate, Josip Manolić was appointed the head of a new war cabinet or state council, being replaced as Premier (Prime Minister) by his deputy, Franjo Gregurić.

1 August 1991: Tudjman reorganized the Croatian Government, forming an administration of 'democratic unity', with 16 of the 27 posts being filled by opposition parties.

13 August 1991: An SAR of Western Slavonia was declared; later that month the SAR of Slavonia, Baranja and Western Srem (Eastern Slavonia) also proclaimed its autonomy.

25 September 1991: The UN Security Council unanimously ordered an arms embargo on Yugoslavia. In the SAR of Slavonia, Baranja and Western Srem, its 'Grand National Assembly' enacted a constitutional law.

8 October 1991: The Sabor declared all federal laws null and void, the European Community (EC—known as the European Union, EU, from November 1993) moratorium on the Croatian and Slovenian processes of dissociation having expired the previous day. Later in the month the SARs of Krajina and Bosanska Krajina announced their unification, subsequently being joined by the SAR of Slavonia, Baranja and Western Srem; Babić, leader of the Knin regime, was authorized to represent the areas at a peace conference for Yugoslavia in the Hague (Netherlands).

October 1991: The siege of Dubrovnik by the YPA began (it did not end until 28 May 1992).

18 November 1991: The town of Vukovar, on the Danube (Dunav) river, was captured by Serb forces.

19 November 1991: Croatians were ordered to leave all federal offices and subsequently to serve only the Croatian state.

5 December 1991: Stipe Mesić resigned as President of the Yugoslav federation; two weeks later the federal prime minister, Ante Marković, also left office. In the same month, the 'Republic of Serb Krajina' (RSK) was proclaimed, formed by the union of the three SARs.

23 December 1991: A Croatian dinar was introduced.

2 January 1992: The UN negotiated a cease-fire between the Croatian National Guard and the YPA.

15 January 1992: An independent Republic of Croatia was recognized by the EC.

February 1992: The UN Protection Force in Yugoslavia (UNPROFOR) was deployed in Croatia to supervise the withdrawal of the YPA and the demilitarization of Serb-held enclaves.

May 1992: Croatia was formally admitted to the UN. The Croatian People's Party left the coalition Government, over a law that gave special rights to Serbs residing in areas with a Serb majority. The YPA began to withdraw from Croatia.

June 1992: Following attacks by Croatian forces on several Serb areas, a UN Security Council resolution demanded the immediate withdrawal by Croats to the positions they had held before 21 June.

2 August 1992: Parliamentary and presidential elections were held; Tudjman, one of eight candidates, was re-elected President (winning 56% of the votes cast), and the ruling CDU obtained 85 of the 138 seats in the new Chamber of Representatives, the lower house of the Sabor. The new Government, headed by Hrvoje Šarinić, took office on 8 September.

26 August 1992: Following the failure of the peace negotiations in The Hague in 1991, the London Conference opened in the United Kingdom; it was decided that a permanent conference would be established in Geneva, Switzerland.

22 January 1993: In an effort to win control of the Maslenica bridge Croatian troops breached UNPROFOR peace-keeping lines and began an offensive in Serb-held Krajina.

7 February 1993: In elections to the Chamber of Municipalities, the upper house of the Sabor, the CDU won a majority (37 seats out of 67).

29 March 1993: The Šarinić Government resigned under pressure; President Tudjman appointed Nikica Valentić as Prime Minister.

14 July 1993: Serb paramilitary forces began to reoccupy the regions of Karlovac and Zemunik, in response to the continued presence of Croatian troops in the Maslenica area.

15–16 July 1993: The so-called Erdut Agreement, negotiated by the UN, was signed by the Serbian and Croatian Presidents. On 13 August, however, the Agreement was declared null and void by the Croatian Minister of Foreign Affairs, Mate Granić.

4 October 1993: UN Security Council Resolution 871 required the extension of UNPROFOR's mandate; it also demanded the disarming of Serb paramilitary groups and the transferral of all 'pink zones' (areas with majority Serb populations lying outside the official UN Protected Areas—UNPAs) to Croatian control; eight days later the Krajina Serb Assembly voted to reject the resolution and ordered the mobilization of all conscripts.

23 January 1994: Milan Martić was elected President of the RSK, beating his rival, Milan Babić, in a second round of voting.

30 March 1994: Following the expiry of a three-month cease-fire the rebel Serbs and the Croatian Government signed a new agreement which provided for the creation of a 'buffer zone' between the two front lines, to be monitored by UNPROFOR.

5 April 1994: Josip Manolić, the President of the Chamber of Municipalities, and Stipe Mesić, the President of the Chamber of Representatives, left the CDU in protest at President Tudjman's anti-Muslim stance. They founded a new party, the Croatian Independent Democrats, later in the month, with Mesić as Chairman.

30 May 1994: A new currency, the kuna, was introduced.

October 1994: A negotiating forum, the Zagreb Group or 'Z4', was created with the aim of finding a solution to the conflict in the RSK; the Group comprised two EU representatives, and the US and Russian ambassadors to Croatia.

December 1994: The Zagreb Group secured the agreement of the Croatian Government and the RSK to the re-establishment of basic infrastructural links between the Krajina and the rest of Croatia.

12 January 1995: President Tudjman announced that UNPROFOR's mandate would not be renewed at the end of March. Later that month, the Croatian Serbs rejected proposals of the Zagreb Group involving the surrender of territory and guarantees of autonomy.

8 February 1995: In an attempt to force President Tudjman to reverse his decision to expel UN troops, the RSK parliament voted to suspend implementation of the enclave's economic agreement with Croatia. Also in this month the RSK agreed a military alliance with the Bosnian Serbs.

12 March 1995: President Tudjman agreed to a continued UN presence in Croatia, but only of a smaller force (known as the UN Confidence Restoration Operation—UNCRO). In the same month a formal military alliance between Croatia, the Bosnian Croats and the Bosnian Government was announced.

13 April 1995: Bosnian Serb artillery began an assault on Dubrovnik and its airport, in which one person was killed.

1–2 May 1995: Croatian government troops reoccupied the territory of Western Slavonia (despite its status as a UNPA), forcing many Serbs to flee the area. The Serbs retaliated with attacks on Karlovac and Sisak. A UN-brokered cease-fire was agreed the following day.

4–8 August 1995: In a major offensive, Croatian government forces seized Knin and gained control of most of the Krajina; some 150,000 Croatian Serb refugees fled to Serb-held areas in Bosnia and Herzegovina and Yugoslavia. Of the former RSK territories, only Eastern Slavonia remained under Serb control, effectively reinforced by the presence of Yugoslav troops on its border.

September 1995: A new electoral law reduced from 13 to three the number of parliamentary seats allocated to the Serb minority, while a further 12 seats were granted to Croatian *émigrés*; amendments to the law on minorities further reduced the rights of the Krajina Serbs.

3 October 1995: After heavy fighting in Eastern Slavonia an 11-point agreement was signed by Croatian government officials and Serb leaders; this agreement provided for a 'transitional period' during which the enclave would be demilitarized.

29 October 1995: At a general election the CDU won 45 out of 80 elected seats in the Chamber of Representatives and 37 out of 63 seats in the Chamber of Municipalities. A new Government was subsequently appointed, headed by the former Minister of the Economy, Zlatko Mateša.

12 November 1995: The Basic Agreement on the Region of Eastern Slavonia, Baranja and Western Sirmium was signed at Erdut. The accord provided for the reintegration of Eastern Slavonia into Croatia, under UN supervision.

15 January 1996: On the same day that UNCRO's mandate expired, the UN Security Council established the UN Transitional Administration for Eastern Slavonia, Baranja and Western Sirmium (UNTAES), to supervise the region's demilitarization and reintegration over a period of two years.

1 May 1996: The Croatian Government dissolved the opposition-led Zagreb City Assembly and appointed a Government Commissioner in its place.

14 May 1996: The foreign ministers of the member states of the Council of Europe refused to endorse Croatia's admission to the organization, citing the country's failure to comply with a 21-point programme on democracy and human rights.

21 May 1996: Following the full deployment of UNTAES a 30-day period of demilitarization began in Eastern Slavonia.

1 July 1996: Transitional police forces, under the command of Petar Djukić, assumed control of Eastern Slavonia.

23 August 1996: An agreement on mutual recognition, signed by the foreign ministers of Croatia and the Former Republic of Yugoslavia (FRY), formally ended five years of hostility between the two countries.

16 October 1996: The Council of Europe agreed to accept Croatia's application for membership, following its Government's pledge to ratify the European Convention on Human Rights within one year of admission.

January 1997: The Croatian Government announced a Memorandum on the Completion of the Peaceful Reintegration of Eastern Slavonia, which attempted to appease the largely Serb population there by offering new voting rights and senior posts in the enclave's government, as well as making military service optional.

1 April 1997: In a referendum in Eastern Slavonia 99.5% of the participating electorate voted in favour of the enclave remaining a single administration under Serb control after its return to Croatia.

13 April 1997: In elections to the upper house the CDU secured 42 of the 63 elective seats, while the Croatian Peasants' Party gained nine, the Croatian Social-Liberal Party (CSLP) six and the Social Democratic Party (SDP) four; the remaining two seats were won by the IDA. In simultaneously held local elections in Eastern Slavonia, in which some 85% of the voting population participated, the Independent Democratic Serb Party, led by Vojislav Stanimirović, gained control of 11 of the 28 contested municipalities.

15 June 1997: In spite of reports that he was seriously ill, Franjo Tudjman was re-elected to the presidency, with 61.4% of the votes cast although the Organization for Security and Co-operation in Europe (OSCE) alleged that the elections had not been carried out fairly, the Constitutional Court endorsed the results later in the month.

1 July 1997: International institutions suspended financial aid to Croatia in protest at the lack of progress in the resettlement of refugees in Eastern Slavonia, as well as the Government's failure to comply with extradition orders by the International Criminal Tribunal for the Former Yugoslavia (ICTY) in The Hague (Netherlands) on those suspected of war crimes.

10 October 1997: The International Monetary Fund approved the resumption of aid to Croatia following the surrender of 10 Bosnian Croat war-crimes suspects to the ICTY.

21 November 1997: The Chamber of Representatives approved constitutional changes, proposed by President Tudjman and already endorsed by the upper house earlier in the month, which, notably, prohibited the re-establishment of a union of Yugoslav states.

13 January 1998: The UN Security Council voted to extend the mandate of the UN Mission of Observers in Prevlaka (UNMOP), deployed in the peninsula since February 1996, until 15 July (the mandate was subsequently extended further).

15 January 1998: The Croatian Government formally resumed control of Eastern Slavonia following the expiry of the mandate of UNTAES in the Serb-dominated enclave.

12 February 1998: Following international criticism, the Government annulled a decree, issued the previous month, which had effectively allowed the eviction of Serbs from their homes in Eastern Slavonia by permitting the mainly Croat former occupants to reclaim state-owned apartments left during the Serb–Croat conflict.

20 February 1998: More than 15,000 people participated in a demonstration in Zagreb to protest at deteriorating social and economic conditions in the country.

31 March 1998: The Government proposed the legal provisions under which Serb refugees could return to Croatia; the plan was immediately criticized by the OSCE, which maintained that the right to return to one's country was inalienable and could not be dependent on the fulfilment of other conditions.

14 April 1998: In a meeting with representatives of the international community President Tudjman warned that a mass return of Serb refugees to Croatia would destabilize the country.

8 May 1998: The 'Article 11' Commission, which was established by the international community to oversee the reintegration of Eastern Slavonia into Croatia, declared that sanctions would be imposed on Croatia if the Government failed to allow the free return of displaced persons.

14 May 1998: The Government announced a relaxation of the conditions of the Serb refugees' return, which it claimed was a compromise between the demands of the international community and the national interests of Croatia.

23 June 1998: A draft agreement on the status of the disputed area of Prevlaka was presented to the UN Security Council; the plan proposed the establishment of a joint Croatian–Yugoslav Commission to demarcate borders, around which there would be a five-year demilitarization zone.

26 June 1998: The Chamber of Representatives voted to adopt the Government's Programme for the Return and Accommodation of Displaced Persons, Refugees and Exiled Persons, which contained the Programme for the Return, a document that met with the approval of the international community.

21 July 1998: After a break of more than three years Croatia and Slovenia resumed negotiations on maritime border issues.

19 September 1998: In a meeting in Zagreb the Minister of Foreign Affairs, Mate Granić, and the US Ambassador to Croatia, William Montgomery, agreed to establish Croatian–US working groups to implement the Dayton peace accords and to accelerate Croatia's inclusion in NATO's Partnership for Peace programme.

12 October 1998: The Minister of Defence and Vice-Chairman of the CDU, Dr Andrija Hebrang, resigned from his posts following disagreement with President Tudjman over allegations that the military intelligence service had been used to undermine moderates within the CDU. He was replaced in his government post by Gen. Pavao Miljavac, hitherto Chief of Staff of the Army.

24 November 1998: Croatia and Bosnia and Herzegovina signed an accord which gave Bosnia and Herzegovina the right to use the Croatian port of Plŏce; in return, Croatia was granted free transit through Neum, a small section of Bosnian territory on the Adriatic coast.

21 January 1999: Croatia and Montenegro (FRY) reached an agreement on the reopening of two border crossings.

5 February 1999: Branko Salaj resigned as director of the state news agency, HINA, in protest at alleged state interference in the media. His stance was supported by the publication, in early March, of a US government report which criticized the Croatian Government's control of the press. The report also accused Croatia of failing to co-operate with the ICTY, and of failing to reintegrate displaced ethnic Serbs.

8 April 1999: Milan Ramljak, the Deputy Prime Minister and Minister of Justice, resigned from his cabinet posts in protest at the Government's increasingly authoritarian stance; the Cabinet was subsequently reorganized.

18 May 1999: An OSCE report severely criticized Croatia's progress in implementing its international commitments.

7 July 1999: Croatia and Bosnia and Herzegovina agreed on a common border.

9 August 1999: Following his indictment by the ICTY, Vinko Martinović was extradited to the Hague to answer charges of crimes committed during the Croatian-Muslim conflict in 1993-94. However, Croatia's reluctance to extradite Mladen Naletilić, indicted on similar charges, invoked severe international criticism.

1 November 1999: President Tudjman underwent emergency medical treatment after becoming seriously ill.

26 November 1999: The Sabor declared President Tudjman to be 'temporarily incapacitated' and provisionally transferred the powers of Head of State to the parliamentary Speaker, Vlatko Pavletić, who postponed the forthcoming parliamentary elections, due to be held on 22 December, to 3 January 2000. Six principal opposition parties, the 'Opposition Six', signed an agreement on the establishment of a coalition Government in the event of winning the elections.

10 December 1999: President Tudjman died. His funeral, three days later, was attended by large crowds. However, President Suleyman Demirel of Turkey was the only international head of state to attend the occasion.

3 January 2000: Elections to the Chamber of Representatives were held. A coalition comprising the SDP, CSLP and two regional groups won the largest share (47.0%) of the votes cast and 71 of the 152 legislative seats; the ruling CDU gained 30.5% of the votes cast and 40 seats, and the alliance of the other four main opposition parties, together with the Croatian Social Democrats' Action, won 15.9% of the ballot and 25 seats.

14 January 2000: In what was considered to be the first significant international judgement on 'ethnic cleansing' in Croatia, the ICTY found five Bosnian Croats guilty of crimes against more than 100 Muslims in 1993; Vladimir Santić received the most severe sentence of 25 years' imprisonment.

24 January 2000: Voting in the first round of the presidential elections took place; opposition candidate Stipe Mesić gained 41.1% of the votes cast, compared to Dražen Budiša, the CSLP leader, who attracted 27.7%, and the CDU's Mate Granić, who won 22.5% of the ballot. As no candidate received more than 50% of the votes cast, a second ballot between the two leading candidates was to take place.

27 January 2000: SDP leader Ivica Račan was formally appointed Prime Minister; he immediately announced the establishment of a new coalition Government, comprising members of the Opposition Six.

2 February 2000: Zlatko Tomcić, leader of the Croatian Peasants' Party, was elected President of the Sabor and acting head of state.

7 February 2000: In the second round of the presidential election, Mesić defeated Budiša, winning 56.1% of the votes cast, compared to the latter's 43.9%. Mesić was sworn in as President on 18 February.

14 February 2000: Negotiations on Croatia's possible EU membership began in Brussels (Belgium) between Prime Minister Račan and EU officials.

2 March 2000: Mate Granić announced his decision to leave the CDU and establish the Democratic Centre, a pro-European party of the moderate centre, with Vesna Skare-Ozbolt.

3 March 2000: After being found guilty of war crimes, Tihomir Blaskić was sentenced to 45 years' imprisonment by the ICTY, the harshest sentence meted out by the Tribunal thus far.

9 March 2000: The Minister of Foreign Affairs of Croatia, Tonino Picula, and the Prime Minister of the Bosnian Serb Republic, Milorad Dodik, signed a joint statement on the return of refugees and displaced persons. The two ministers agreed to submit legislation to their respective parliaments regarding the return of refugees to areas controlled by other ethnic groups, and in the meantime allowed 2,000 refugees to return to their homes within three months.

21 March 2000: The indicted war criminal, Mladen Naletilić ('Tuta'), was extradited to the ICTY to face charges.

31 March 2000: The Croatian Government established a council for co-operation with the ICTY, which was to be attended by a deputy premier and the foreign minister; on 14 April the Sabor approved a Declaration of Co-operation between Croatia and the ICTY.

3 May 2000: The Stara Gradiska–Bosanska Gradiska international border crossing between Croatia and Bosnia and Herzegovina was re-opened, facilitating the return of displaced persons and contributing to improved transport connections and stronger trade relations between the two countries.

7 May 2000: Municipal elections were held in Zagreb. The SDP—Croatian Pensioners' Party coalition gained the largest share of the votes cast (20.99%) and 15 of the 50 councillor seats, the CPP won 19% of the votes cast, and the CSLP and the CDU gained 14.8% and 11.6%, respectively, of the ballot. The newly formed Democratic Centre won 6.77% of the votes cast and the Croatian Peasants' Party received 2% of the vote. The low voter turnout (33.7%) was attributed to the frequency of elections.

19 May 2000: Eleven of the 22 people indicted for genocide and war crimes against civilians during the siege and fall of Vukovar in 1991 were found guilty by the ICTY. The longest sentence meted out was 20 years' imprisonment.

25 May 2000: Croatia officially joined NATO's Partnership for Peace programme. Five days later Croatia was granted associate membership of NATO's Parliamentary Assembly.

28 August 2000: Milan Levar, an important witness in the ICTY's investigation into atrocities allegedly committed by Croatian forces in 1991, was killed in an explosion at his home; in subsequent months the frequency of arrests of those suspected of involvement in war crimes increased.

29 September 2000: A number of senior military figures, including seven generals, were ordered to retire after they published a letter critical of the Government's policy of co-operation with the ICTY.

October 2000: Transcripts of recordings of conversations held by Tudjman during his time in office began to be released; the recordings were held to support allegations of corruption on the part of Tudjman, his family and his associates. In December Tudjman's family began legal proceedings to prevent the release of any further transcripts or recordings.

9 November 2000: The Sabor adopted amendments to the Constitution, transferring the power to appoint the government from the President of the Republic to the Sabor and restricting the powers of the Chamber of Counties in the legislative process. The restrictions on the role of the presidency displeased Mesić and the amendments were only approved following protracted discussions between the President and the Government.

9 December 2000: Miroslav Tudjman, the son of the late President and the former head of Croatia's security services, announced the formation of a new, right-wing political organization, the Association for Croatia's Identity and Prosperity.

12 December 2000: It was announced that the former head of Croatia's secret police, Ivan Brzović, was to be prosecuted on charges of intercepting telephone calls made by President Mesić between 1998 and his election to the presidency.

21 December 2000: It was confirmed that the army Chief of the General Staff, Col-Gen. Petar Stipetić, had been summoned to appear before the ICTY as a possible suspect. Stipetić had previously been summoned to the Tribunal as a witness.

January 2001: The UN Security Council extended the mandate of UNMOP to mid-July.

February 2001: The Government announced that it planned to abolish the opposition-controlled Chamber of Counties, following the expiry of its mandate in April; the proposal was to be referred to the Chamber of Representatives.

15 February 2001: In a rally organized by Tudjman's followers, 100,000 nationalists protested in Split against government attempts to arrest Gen. Mirko Norac, who was suspected of involvement in the murder of more than 40 Serb civilians in 1991.

23 February 2001: Gen. Norac surrendered himself to a district court and was remanded in custody.

26 February 2001: Croatian military commander Mario Cerkez was convicted by the ICTY of numerous counts of murder and other war crimes committed against Bosnian Muslims between 1993 and 1994; he received a 15-year sentence.

The Czech Republic

5th–7th centuries: Slavic tribes migrated to central Europe from the eastern plains.

830: The establishment of the Great Moravian Empire, which comprised Bohemia, Moravia and Slovakia.

907: Following the Battle of Bratislava (Pressburg), the Great Moravian Empire was overthrown and the Kingdom of Bohemia was established.

1041: Bohemia became a fief of the Holy Roman Empire, after the subjugation of Prince Bretislav of Bohemia, by the forces of Henry III, the German Emperor.

1310: After a four-year struggle over the succession, the Bohemian nobles granted the throne to John of Luxembourg, thus ending the Přemyslid dynasty in Bohemia.

1346–78: The reign of Charles I of Bohemia (Charles IV as Holy Roman Emperor), who encouraged the cultural and commercial development of the Czech Lands.

1419: Following the martyrdom of Jan Hus (1415), the leader of a reformist religious movement centred in Prague, his followers, the Hussites, rebelled against German rule after the first 'Defenestration of Prague'.

1420–33: The Hussite Wars were fought, in which forces loyal to the Holy Roman Empire attempted to suppress the Hussite rebellion.

1526: Czech nobles elected the Habsburg Archduke Ferdinand I to the throne.

1620: After a two-year rebellion, which began with the Second Defenestration of Prague, Czech troops were defeated at the Battle of the White Mountain.

1781–85: Serfdom was abolished in the Czech Lands.

1848: An unsuccessful uprising against the Habsburgs took place in Prague.

30 May 1918: The Pittsburgh Agreement, which provided for the creation of a common Czech–Slovak state, was signed between Slovak and Czech exiles in the USA.

28 October 1918: The Republic of Czechoslovakia was proclaimed; Tomáš Garrigue Masaryk was elected President.

28 June 1919: The Treaty of Versailles provided international recognition to the Czechoslovak state and confirmed its frontiers.

November 1935: Masaryk resigned as President; he was succeeded by Edvard Beneš.

29 September 1938: The Munich Conference took place in Germany between the leaders of France, Germany, Italy and the United Kingdom; an agreement was signed, which permitted the cession of the Czechoslovak territories known as Sudetenland to Germany.

5 October 1938: Beneš resigned as President.

15–16 March 1939: Adolf Hitler, the German leader, invaded the Czech Lands: Bohemia and Moravia became a German Protectorate; Slovakia was proclaimed an independent state, under the pro-fascist leadership of Mgr Jozef Tiso.

3 April 1945: Beneš and his Government-in-exile returned to Czechoslovakia.

9 May 1945: Soviet troops entered Prague.

16 May 1946: National elections took place; the Czechoslovak Communist Party (CPCz) won 38% of the votes cast; Klement Gottwald, leader of the CPCz, was appointed Prime Minister.

25 February 1948: The Communists seized power, following the resignation of 12 non-Communist ministers.

9 May 1948: A new Constitution was approved, which declared Czechoslovakia a 'people's democracy'.

30 May 1948: Elections took place, with only Communist-approved candidates nominated.

June 1948: Beneš resigned, after refusing to sign the new Constitution.

December 1952: Rudolf Slánský, former Secretary-General of the CPCz, and other prominent Communists were executed after 'show trials'.

March 1953: Klement Gottwald died. Antonín Novotný was appointed First Secretary of the CPCz; Antonín Zápotocký became President; Viliám Široký was appointed Prime Minister.

1957: First Secretary of the CPCz, Antonín Novotný, replaced Zápotocký as President.

July 1960: A new Constitution was enacted; Czechoslovakia was renamed the Czechoslovak Socialist Republic.

1963: Prime Minister Široký was replaced by Jozef Lenárt, who launched the mildly reformist New Economic Model. Rudolf Slánský and other Communists who had been purged in the 1950s were rehabilitated.

October 1967: A student rally was violently dispersed by police.

5 January 1968: Antonín Novotný resigned as First Secretary of the CPCz; he was replaced by Alexander Dubček, leader of the Communist Party of Slovakia (CPS).

March 1968: Censorship of the press was ended.

April 1968: The Central Committee of the CPCz adopted an Action Programme, which proposed constitutional and economic reforms. Gen. Ludvík Svoboda was appointed President. Oldřich Černík was appointed Prime Minister.

3 August 1968: Representatives of the Communist Parties of member countries of the Warsaw Pact (except Romania) met in Bratislava (Slovakia) to discuss Czechoslovakia's 'Prague Spring' reforms.

20–21 August 1968: Warsaw Pact troops invaded Czechoslovakia; Dubček and other government and Party leaders were abducted to Moscow.

1 January 1969: A federal system of government was introduced.

16 January 1969: A student, Jan Palach, immolated himself and died, in protest at the ending of reforms.

17 April 1969: Gustáv Husák replaced Dubček as First Secretary of the CPCz.

January 1970: Černík was dismissed as Prime Minister.

11 December 1973: A treaty, signed between the Federal Republic of Germany (West Germany) and Czechoslovakia, normalized relations between the two countries and formally annulled the 1938 Munich Agreement.

May 1975: Svoboda resigned as President and was replaced by Husák.

1 January 1977: A group of dissidents, including Václav Havel, the playwright, published the 'Charter 77' manifesto, which demanded an end to the abuse of civil and political rights.

December 1987: Miloš Jakeš replaced Gustáv Husák as General Secretary of the CPCz.

21 August 1988: Large anti-government demonstrations took place in Prague, on the 20th anniversary of the 1968 Soviet invasion; further demonstrations took place on the same day in the following year.

10 October 1988: Lubomír Štrougal resigned as federal Prime Minister; he was replaced by Ladislav Adamec.

16 January 1989: A large demonstration took place to mark the 20th anniversary of the suicide of Jan Palach; Václav Havel and 13 other dissidents were arrested (international protests later secured Havel's release).

1 May 1989: The traditional May Day rally was disrupted when police dispersed demonstrators protesting against human-rights violations.

28 October 1989: Anti-government demonstrations took place, on the 71st anniversary of the establishment of a Czechoslovak state.

17 November 1989: Students participating in an officially sanctioned demonstration were attacked by riot police; 140 people were injured. Later some 300 opposition activists from various non-Communist organizations united to form Civic Forum, a broad anti-government coalition (in Slovakia, its counterpart was known as Public Against Violence—PAV).

21 November 1989: Adamec began discussions with Civic Forum.

24 November 1989: With protests and strikes continuing to take place, Miloš Jakeš, General Secretary of the CPCz, and all other members of the Presidium of the Central Committee and the Secretariat of the CPCz, resigned; Karel Urbanek was elected leader of the CPCz. Alexander Dubček returned to Prague and spoke to a large crowd in Wenceslas Square.

28 November 1989: Civic Forum was officially registered as a legal organization.

29 November 1989: The Federal Assembly abolished the CPCz's constitutional monopoly of power.

7 December 1989: Adamec resigned as Prime Minister; he was replaced by Marián Čalfa.

10 December 1989: Čalfa announced a new federal Government, with a majority of non-Communist members. Husák resigned as President.

28 December 1989: Dubček was elected Chairman of the Federal Assembly. The following day it elected Václav Havel President of Czechoslovakia.

1 February 1990: The abolition of the StB (Státni bezpečnost—the secret police) was announced.

6 February 1990: Petr Pithart was appointed Prime Minister of the Czech Republic.

7 February 1990: The National Front, the Communists' political organization, was disbanded.

27–28 March 1990: The Federal Assembly approved new laws guaranteeing freedom of association and freedom of the press, and allowing exiles to reclaim their citizenship.

29 March 1990: The name of the country was changed to the Czech and Slovak Federative Republic.

27 May 1990: Václav Klaus, federal Minister of Finance, announced a reform-orientated budget.

June 1990: Elections to the Federal Assembly took place; Civic Forum (in Bohemia and Moravia) and PAV (in Slovakia) won an overall majority. A coalition Government was formed, with participation from all major parties, except the CPCz.

5 July 1990: Havel was re-elected as President for a transitional two-year period.

12 December 1990: The Federal Assembly approved constitutional legislation delimiting the powers of the federal, Czech and Slovak governments.

23 February 1991: Civic Forum was formally disbanded; its members formed two new political parties, the conservative Civic Democratic Party (CDP) and the liberal Civic Movement.

26 February 1991: Legislation allowing privatization of state-owned enterprises was approved.

2 March 1991: Thousands of people took part in demonstrations in Moravia, demanding autonomous status for their region.

10–14 March 1991: There were large demonstrations in Slovakia, in favour of independence for the Republic; President Havel was attacked by crowds when he visited Bratislava.

27 April 1991: The Civic Movement officially constituted itself as an independent political party.

13 June 1991: The first phase of the 'large privatization' programme began, with the sale of 50 state-owned enterprises to Western companies.

21 June 1991: The withdrawal of Soviet forces, which had been stationed in Czechoslovakia since 1968, was completed.

1 July 1991: Leaders of the member countries of the Warsaw Pact met in Prague to complete the dissolution of the organization, by formally ending the work of its Political Consultative Committee.

5–6 June 1992: At federal and republican legislative elections there were strong performances by the Movement for a Democratic Slovakia (MDS) and other parties favouring separation between the Czech Lands and Slovakia. However, the pro-federal CDP became the single largest party; the successors to the Communists (Left Bloc in the Czech Lands, Party of the Democratic Left in Slovakia) came third and fourth. Negotiations commenced between the CDP and MDS to form a federal government. Meanwhile Mečiar was appointed Slovak Prime Minister.

July 1992: A transitional federal Government was appointed, dominated by members of the CDP and MDS, with Jan Stráský of the CDP as Prime Minister. Czech politicians accepted that total separation of Czech Lands and Slovakia was preferable to the compromise measures proposed. Václav Klaus was appointed Prime Minister of the new Czech Government. Three rounds of voting in the Federal Assembly failed to elect a new President, with the MDS and Slovak National Party blocking re-election of Havel, who duly resigned.

26 October 1992: A Customs Union treaty and other accords were agreed between the Czech and Slovak Governments.

25 November 1992: The Federal Assembly adopted legislation enabling the constitutional disbanding of the federation, with the assets divided 2:1 in the Czech Republic's favour, in accordance with the balance of population.

December 1992: A treaty of good neighbourliness, friendly relations and co-operation was signed between the two Republics, followed by the exchange of diplomatic relations. A new Constitution of the Czech Republic was adopted; the Czech National Council became the Chamber of Deputies (lower house), retaining the existing 200 members. Czechoslovakia, Hungary and Poland signed an agreement with the European Community (EC, known as the European Union—EU from November 1993) granting them associate member status.

1 January 1993: Separation of the Czech Republic and Slovakia took effect.

26 January 1993: Havel was elected President of the Czech Republic.

February 1993: Separate Czech and Slovak currencies (both called koruna) were introduced. Final rejection of amendment to establish a Senate (upper house) with membership transferred from the former Federal Assembly; elections for the Senate were repeatedly postponed and eventually scheduled for November 1996.

June 1993: Parliament voted to establish a Constitutional Court and a Supreme Control Office (an independent body to audit government finances). At the congress of the Communist Party of Bohemia and Moravia (CPBM), neo-Stalinists were expelled and reformists left to form a new party, the Party of the Democratic Left.

July 1993: The former Czechoslovak Communist regime was declared illegitimate and criminal. Border controls were introduced on the Czech–Slovak frontier to stem flow of 'third-party' refugees, mainly heading for Germany; Slovak citizens, however, were to be unaffected.

March 1994: The Czech Republic joined the North Atlantic Treaty Organization's (NATO) Partnership for Peace programme of military co-operation.

September 1994: A law introduced new qualifications, of two years' established residence and five years without any criminal record, for nationality and associated rights and benefits.

August 1995: Former Czechoslovak Communists, including Miloš Jakeš and Jozef Lenárt, who had co-operated with the USSR in suppressing the 1968 'Prague Spring' uprising, were charged with treason.

1 October 1995: An act to make the koruna widely convertible came into effect.

28 November 1995: The Czech Republic became the first former Communist country to join the Organisation for Economic Co-operation and Development (OECD).

January 1996: The Ministers of the Interior of the Czech Republic and Slovakia approved a treaty to finalize the Czech–Slovak border (following opposition among citizens to be transferred to Slovak jurisdiction, the Chamber of Deputies rejected the treaty in April). The Prime Minister, Klaus, submitted the Czech Republic's application to join the EU.

31 May–1 June 1996: In the Czech Republic's first general election as an independent state the CDP-led government alliance won 99 seats—CDP 68, Christian Democratic Union—Czechoslovak People's Party (CDU—CPP) 18, Civic Democratic Alliance (CDA) 13—two seats short of an overall majority; the opposition Czech Social Democratic Party (CSDP) won 61 seats, the CPBM 22 and the Association for the Republic—Republican Party of Czechoslovakia (AFR—RPC) 18. Negotiations on the formation of a new Government involved the CDP, CDU—CPP, CDA and CSDP, but not the CPBM and AFR—RPC.

27 June 1996: Klaus was reappointed Prime Minister of a minority coalition Government, which included the CDP, CDU—CPP and CDA; Miloš Zeman, the leader of the CSDP, was appointed Chairman (speaker) of the Chamber of Deputies.

November 1996: The head of the counter-intelligence service resigned amid allegations that official surveillance had been improperly used to benefit the interests of the ruling CDP.

15–16 November 1996: Only 30% of the electorate voted in the delayed Senate elections; after a second round on 22–23 November the CDP had 32 of the 81 seats and the CSDP 25.

July 1997: Severe flooding in Moravia and eastern Bohemia caused 50 deaths and damage to property and infrastructure estimated at 60,000m. koruny.

August 1997: Hundreds of Gypsies (Roma) sought asylum in Canada and the United Kingdom, claiming persecution, and drawing international attention to allegations of institutional racism in the Czech Republic; the status of the Roma minority remained a significant political issue in the Czech Republic throughout the late 1990s and early 2000s.

23 October 1997: Jozef Zieleniec resigned his position as Minister of Foreign Relations and as Deputy Chairman of the CDP, indicating continued factionalism in the coalition, under pressure from severe economic problems.

30 November 1997: The Prime Minister, Klaus, and the Government resigned, after the withdrawal of the CDU—CPP and CDA from the coalition, following allegations of corruption against the CDP.

17 December 1997: Jozef Tošovský, hitherto central bank governor, was appointed Prime Minister, to head a 'caretaker', largely non-political administration, supported by the old coalition, in advance of an early general election.

8 January 1998: Ivan Pilip, the finance minister, resigned from the CDP after Klaus declared that CDP members serving in the interim Government did not have party authorization; subsequently, the other three CDP ministers also resigned from the party.

18 January 1998: A new party, the Freedom Union (FU), was established by 30 of the 69 CDP deputies; Ruml was elected leader.

20 January 1998: Havel was re-elected President for a second five-year term.

15 April 1998: The Chamber of Deputies approved Czech membership of the North Atlantic Treaty Organization (NATO).

19–20 June 1998: In the general election the CSDP gained 32.3% of the votes cast and 74 seats in the 200-seat Chamber of Deputies; the CDP gained 27.7% of the poll and 63 seats; the other parties to gain representation in parliament were the CPBM (24 seats), the CDU—CPP (20) and the FU (19).

17 July 1998: Zeman was appointed Prime Minister of a minority CSDP Government supported by the CDP, which had failed to negotiate a coalition with the CDU—CPP and the FU.

January 1999: The head of the Czech counter-intelligence service, Karel Vulterin, was dismissed following allegations that he had not informed the Government of planned terrorist attacks in Prague.

16 March 1999: The Czech Republic was granted full membership of NATO, along with Hungary and Poland.

29 July 1999: Ivo Svoboda was dismissed from his position as Minister of Finance after it was announced that he was to be prosecuted over his involvement in a failed company.

13 October 1999: The municipality of Ústí nad Labem constructed a wall, 60 m (210 ft) long and 2 m high, in front of houses occupied by members of the Roma minority; the wall, ostensibly built to protect other local residents from noise and disorder, was demolished on 24 November following national and international condemnation.

17 November 1999: At demonstrations to mark the 10th anniversary of the fall of Communism protesters urged several senior political figures to allow younger politicians to succeed them; a further demonstration held in Prague in early December attracted some 50,000 people.

January 2000: The CDP reaffirmed its agreement to maintain the minority CSDP Government, on the condition that the premier reorganize the Council of Ministers and propose measures of electoral reform.

April 2000: A book was published containing allegations that the Deputy Prime Minister and Minister of Foreign Affairs, Jan Kavan, had worked as a secret agent in the United Kingdom during the era of Communist rule in Czechoslovakia and had been involved with the StB; two weeks previously, Kavan had been appointed the minister in charge of the Czech security services.

26 April 2000: As stipulated by the extension to the co-operation agreement with the CDP, signed in January there was a reorganization of the Council of Ministers; four ministers were replaced, portfolios were unaffected.

24 May 2000: Miloš Zeman, the Prime Minister, and his Slovak counterpart, Mikuláš Dzurinda, signed a declaration resolving property disputes arising from the distribution of the assets of the Czechoslovak state upon its dissolution at the end of 1992.

25 May 2000: The Chamber of Deputies endorsed a series of amendments to electoral legislation, increasing the number of electoral districts in the Czech Republic from eight to 35, establishing a single round of voting in elections to the Chamber of Deputies and increasing the minimum percentage of votes cast required for coalitions to gain parliamentary representation.

5 June 2000: President Havel underwent surgery for an abdominal complaint, the third time he had required surgery during his terms of office.

8 June 2000: Libor Novák, the former Deputy Chairman of the CDP, was acquitted of tax offences with regard to party funds, an issue which forced the resignation of the CDP Government in November 1997.

9 June 2000: The premiers of the four countries of the Visegrad Group (the Czech Republic, Hungary, Poland and Slovakia) signed accords providing for the creation of a fund to promote co-operation in culture, education and science and research.

October 2000: The first reactor became operational at the Temelín nuclear power station in southern Bohemia. The construction of the facility had strained relations with Austria, which had concerns as to the plant's safety and objected to the presence of such a facility some 60 km (35 miles) from its frontier. The Austrian President warned that his country may obstruct Czech accession to the EU over the issue.

November 2000: Austrian environmentalists blocked the Czech frontier in protest at the commencement of power generation at Temelín. A meeting regarding the problem between government officials from the two countries was cancelled as a result.

30 November 2000: Tošovský, who had returned to his position as Governor of the central bank after the end of his period of office as Prime Minister, resigned from the post. President Havel appointed Zdenek Tuma, hitherto a Vice-Governor of the bank, to replace Tošovský. The appointment was widely criticized as new legislation was to come into effect in December transferring the right to nominate the Governor to the Prime Minister. The Government referred the matter to the Constitutional Court, but withdrew its complaint in December because of fears that the controversy was adversely affecting the value of the koruna.

13 December 2000: Czech and Austrian officials agreed on a programme of international monitoring of the Temelín power station.

15 December 2000: The Minister of Defence, Vladimir Vetchý, was dismissed amid allegations of incompetent management of the ministry.

20 December 2000: Jiří Hodac, thought to have sympathies with the CDP, was appointed Director-General of the state television company. Staff members claimed that Hodac's appointment was politically motivated and campaigned for his removal, citing fears of political bias in news coverage preceding the legislative elections scheduled for 2001. The dispute led to an occupation of the station buildings by staff and the interruption of news programming.

11 January 2001: Hodac resigned as Director-General of the state television company.

Denmark

795: Localized and democratic Scandinavian communities, specialising in hunting and fishing, had gradually become more aggressive and sought to expand their territories. Viking (as the communities are now designated) raids of Danish, Swedish and Norwegian warriors began, primarily on coastal settlements and along navigable rivers. The attacks continued for 200 years and spanned from Pisa (Italy) to the Shetland Islands (now part of the United Kingdom).

965: Harold Bluetooth, King of Denmark (958–87), was obliged to accept Christianity, following defeat by Germanic forces.

1016: After repeated incursions into England from 980, the Viking king, Knud (Canute) II 'the Great', was elected King of England. He ruled a short-lived Anglo-Scandinavian Empire, consisting of Denmark, Norway and England.

1035: After the death of Knud 'the Great', the Danes were expelled from Norway.

1204–20: Waldemar II conquered Holstein (Holsten), Norway, Pomerellen, Estonia and Courland.

1282: King Erik Klipping, grandson of Waldemar II, was obliged to sign a charter, providing for the annual reunion of a parliament (Danehof), and for provincial assemblies (Ding), and which reduced the powers of the monarchy.

1346: Following peasant uprisings in Estonia against oppressive Danish and German nobles, King Waldemar IV of Denmark considered the region too difficult to control and sold Estonia to the Livonian Order of Teutonic Knights (an alliance of the Sword Bretheren and the German Order of Teutonic Knights).

1348: Waldemar IV gained Funen (Fyn) island from Holstein by force and the Jutland peninsula in an attempt to unite the Danish kingdom.

1370: Denmark was forced to agree to the Peace of Straslund, surrendering commercial pre-eminence in the Baltic region to the Hanseatic League (a mercantile federation of North German towns).

1380: Olaf, the grandson of Waldemar IV of Denmark and son of Haakon of Norway, ascended the thrones of both countries, with his mother, Margrethe, as regent; the Faroe Islands, Iceland and Greenland, previously under Norwegian rule, thus came under Danish sovereignty.

1397: Sweden agreed to join in a political union (the Union of Kalmar) with Denmark and Norway, but rejected assimilation into the Danish monarchy.

1509–12: A series of conflicts from 1501 between the Swedes and the Danes, led to open war between Denmark and the Hanseatic League (who had been supporting Sweden).

1520–23: The Danish King, Christian II, invaded Sweden and ordered the 'Stockholm massacre' of Swedish opponents in order to retain his dominant position over Sweden. In response a Swedish noble led a successful attack and expelled Christian II, thus, effectively, ending the Union of Kalmar.

1527: The Diet (Assembly) of Odense gave official toleration to Lutheranism in the Danish kingdom, encouraging the Reformation.

1533: The Norwegians regained self-government.

1531–36: The port city of Lübeck (leader of the Hanseatic League), in an effort to gain trading supremacy in the Baltic region, declared war on Denmark and Sweden, capturing Copenhagen and Malmö. An expedient alliance between the two countries drove out the invaders and ended Lübeck's monopolization of trade in the Baltic region.

1536: At the end of the Civil War, Christian III was restored to the throne. The Diet of Copenhagen established Lutheranism as the state religion in Denmark.

1544: Slesvig-Holsten (Schleswig-Holstein, in German) was divided between Christian III and his two brothers.

1643–45: Sweden occupied much of the Danish mainland and Christian IV accepted the unfavourable Peace of Brömseboro.

1657–58: The First Northern War was ended by the Peace of Roskilde, by which Denmark ceded its remaining territory in southern Sweden and the Trondheim region of Norway to the Swedish and the Union of Kalmar was conclusively dissolved.

1702: Serfdom was abolished in Denmark.

1802: The formal abolition of the slave trade in 1792 came into effect.

1814: Norway was given over to Sweden from Denmark by the Treaty of Kiel.

1848: The duchies of Slesvig and Holsten, with predominantly German populations, revolted against Danish control and were occupied by Prussian troops.

1849: Under the 'June Constitution', absolute monarchy was ended and Denmark became a constitutional monarchy with universal male suffrage.

1850: With the diplomatic support of Russia, Sweden and the United Kingdom, the Peace of Berlin awarded the duchies of Schleswig and Holstein to Denmark.

1863: The 'November Constitution' ended the unity of Denmark's territorial claim with regard to Schleswig and Holstein, by annexing the former region.

1864: A series of disputes over the sovereignty of Schleswig led to war with the Austro-Prussian Alliance. The resulting Treaty of Vienna settled the dispute in favour of the Alliance, and the duchy was placed under Prussian administration. The subsequent dissatisfaction with Parliament, in Denmark, led to restoration of monarchial supremacy.

1901: The principle of ministerial accountability to the Parliament (Folketing) was accepted, restoring its authority.

1903: Iceland was granted autonomy.

1915: A new Constitutional Charter vested legislative authority in the Monarch and the Parliament (Rigsdag), and executive authority in the Monarch and the Council of Ministers.

1918: Iceland was recognized as a separate possession of the Danish Crown.

1920: Although Denmark had remained neutral during the First World War, a plebiscite in North Schleswig, held as a result of German defeat, occasioned that territory's reabsorption into Denmark.

1939: A non-aggression pact was signed with Germany, immediately preceding the outbreak of the Second World War in Europe.

1940: Denmark surrendered to German invasion (although the Faroe Islands were occupied by British forces during the Second World War). A German plenipotentiary in Copenhagen was appointed, and the Danish Government was allowed to continue in office until 1943.

29 August 1943: German forces seized control of the Danish administration.

1944: Iceland was proclaimed a sovereign republic, and was recognized as such by Denmark upon liberation the following year.

1945: Denmark was liberated after the surrender of German armed forces. Denmark became a founder member of the UN.

23 March 1948: The Faroe Islands were granted autonomy in internal affairs.

1949: Denmark became a founder member of the North Atlantic Treaty Organization (NATO).

1952: The Nordic Council was established, a body comprising parliamentary delegations from Denmark, Norway, Sweden, Finland and Iceland, which sought to introduce extensive co-operation between the member states in several policy areas, but not that of security.

5 June 1953: A New Constitutional Charter was adopted, consolidating developments over the previous half-century. The bicameral legislature was replaced by the unicameral Folketing, provisions for a legislative referendum and female accession to the throne were introduced, and Greenland became part of the Kingdom.

1973: In a general election 10 parties gained representation in Parliament, bringing to an end the stable political system of four or five parties, which had lasted since the 1920s. A minority Liberal Government led by Poul Hartling was formed.

January 1973: Following a referendum held in the previous year Denmark officially joined the European Economic Community (EEC), along with the Republic of Ireland and the United Kingdom. The Faroe Islands declined to join. Although the population of Greenland had voted overwhelmingly against joining in October 1972, they were bound by the Danish decision.

1975: Anker Jørgensen became Prime Minister of a minority Social Democrat Government and led various coalitions and minority governments until 1982.

May 1979: Home Rule was granted to Greenland, Denmark retaining control of foreign, security and currency policies.

1982: Increasing economic problems and internal disagreements led to the resignation of the Jørgensen Government—a minority coalition of Conservatives and Liberals formed a Government led by Poul Schlüter; he and his Conservative Party led a series of minority coalitions until 1993.

Febuary 1982: A referendum began the process of Greenland's withdrawal from participation in the EEC.

January 1984: A general election brought Schlüter's coalition back into power, now relying on the support of the Social Liberal members of the Folketing, rather than on the right-wing Progress Party.

1 February 1985: Greenland officially withdrew from the EEC, being accorded the status of an overseas territory in association with the Community.

January 1986: The left-wing parties united to reject the Single European Act (proposals for extensive co-operation and integration within the European Community), arguing that it would lead to the diminution of Denmark's power to maintain strict environmental controls.

February 1986: A referendum approved the Government's support for the Single European Act; the Act was officially ratified in May.

91

May 1987: The Schlüter Government enlisted the support of the Social Liberals, thereby breaking an anti-government majority on 'green' and foreign-policy issues.

1988: The government coalition was reconstituted, with the Conservative People's Party, the Liberal Party and the Social Liberals represented in the Cabinet.

May 1988: An election took place, ostensibly on the issue of Demark's membership of NATO and defence policy, after the Folketing demanded that the Government inform visiting warships, including those of Denmark's allies, of the country's ban on nuclear weapons.

June 1988: After inconclusive election results and three weeks of negotiations, a Cabinet was formed under Poul Schlüter, comprising members of the Conservative People's Party, Liberals and the Social Liberals. Good relations with NATO allies were resumed with a compromise, whereby visiting warships would only be asked to respect Danish law in its territorial waters, without mention of nuclear weapons.

December 1990: Against a background of increasing popular support for the Progress Party (which favoured a reduction in taxes), the Schlüter Government proposed large decreases in social-welfare expenditure. An early general election was called.

January 1991: Schlüter's fourth coalition Government was formed from the Conservative People's Party and the Liberal Party only.

27 August 1991: Denmark and Sweden agreed to construct a 17 km road/rail link over the Øresund strait linking Copenhagen and Malmö (Sweden).

May 1992: The Folketing voted, by 130 votes to 25, to approve the EC's Treaty on European Union (known, after the town in the Netherlands where it was signed, as the 'Maastricht Treaty'—a further series of proposals for greater political and economic integration, including a common defence policy and common currency).

2 June 1992: A referendum narrowly rejected Danish ratification of the Maastricht Treaty, requiring Denmark to be conceded an 'opt-out' clause which exempted it from participating in aspects that were a perceived threat to national sovereignty (such as a common currency or common defence policy).

15 June 1992: Europe's longest suspension bridge, spanning the Store Bælt (Great Belt), and completing a link from the island of Zealand to the Jutland peninsula, was officially opened by Queen Margrethe II.

14 January 1993: Schlüter was forced to resign as Premier, after a judicial enquiry disclosed that he had misled the Folketing in a long-running case concerning Tamil immigrants from Sri Lanka. Poul Nyrup Rasmussen, a

Social Democrat, commanded enough support to form the first majority Government for 11 years.

May 1993: In the second referendum on the Maastricht Treaty, 56.7% of the votes cast were in favour of ratification (it duly took effect in November).

September 1994: Parliamentary elections were held, leading to a new coalition of the Social Democrat, Social Liberal and Centre Democrat parties.

11 March 1998: A general election returned Rasmussen's Government to office with a narrow majority in the Folketing.

6 April 1998: The Supreme Court ruled that Danish membership of the European Union (EU) was permissible under the Constitution, in response to a petition brought by a citizens' group challenging the validity of the Maastricht Treaty.

27 April–7 May 1998: An industrial dispute paralysed Denmark's transport and distribution network, only ending after legislative intervention.

28 May 1998: Government support for ratification of the EU Treaty of Amsterdam (expanding on the provisions of the Maastricht Treaty) secured a narrow majority in a national referendum.

May 1999: Denmark, the Faroe Islands and the United Kingdom signed an agreement ending a 30-year dispute concerning boundaries of territorial waters in an area of the North Sea potentially rich in petroleum reserves.

1 July 2000: A bridge connecting Denmark to Sweden across the Øresund strait was opened to traffic.

28 September 2000: In a referendum on Denmark's proposed membership of Stage III of the EU's programme of Economic and Monetary Union, including its adoption of the new currency unit, the euro, 53.1% of the votes cast opposed Danish membership.

December 2000: In a reorganization of the Cabinet, the most notable among the appointments were those of the politically inexperienced Anita Bay Bundegaard and Arne Rolighed as Minister for Development and Co-operation and Minister of Health respectively.

February 2001: The Government of the Faroe Islands called a referendum for 26 May on the question of sovereignty for the islands. Under the proposal, Queen Margrethe II would remain head of state and there would continue to be a common monetary system with Denmark, but Danish subsidies would be phased out.

Estonia

3,000 BC: Finno-Ugric peoples, the ancestors of the Estonians, first began to migrate from eastern Europe to the north-east coast of the Baltic Sea.

AD 1219: Valdemar II of Denmark and the German Sword Brethren, a crusading order, conquered Estonia.

1346: The Danes sold their share of Estonian territory to the Livonian Order of Teutonic Knights (an alliance of the Sword Brethren and the German Order of Teutonic Knights).

1524–39: The State of Teutonic Knights renounced religious allegiance to Rome and converted to Lutheranism.

1561: In the secularization and partition of the State of Teutonic Knights, Estonia (now northern Estonia) became part of Sweden. Livonia (now Latvia and southern Estonia) was placed under Polish rule, as part of the Lithuanian–Polish Duchy of Courland (Kurland).

1595: Sweden's right to Narva and Estonia was recognized by the Peace of Teusin, signed by Sweden and the Russian Empire, although Sweden did not assume full control of Estonia until 1607.

1629: Sweden gained the territory of Livonia by the Armistice of Altmark, after the Swedish–Polish Wars.

1721: The Treaty of Nystad, between Russia and Sweden, ended the Great Northern War and brought Estonia and Livonia under Russian rule.

1817: Serfdom was abolished in Estonia.

November 1905: Following a revolution in Russia the previous month, an increase in Estonian nationalist feeling resulted in a demand for autonomy by the all-Estonian Assembly; the uprising was eventually suppressed.

1 August 1914: Russia entered the First World War against the Empires of Austria-Hungary, Germany and the Ottomans (the Central Powers).

2 March (New Style: 15 March) 1917: Abdication of the last Tsar, Nicholas II, after demonstrations and strikes in Petrograd (St Petersburg); a Provisional Government, led by Prince Lvov, took power.

30 March (12 April) 1917: The Provisional Government granted Estonia its autonomy.

24 February (Old Style: 11 February) 1918: The independent Republic of Estonia was declared; Konstantin Päts led a Provisional Government, although this was not recognized by the German occupiers.

3 March 1918: The Bolsheviks, in control of the Government of Russia, signed the Treaty of Brest-Litovsk with Germany, thereby ceding large areas of western territory, including Estonia, to Germany.

November 1918: Following Germany's surrender, the Provisional Government assumed control in Estonia.

2 February 1920: The Treaty of Tartu (Dorpat) ended hostilities between Estonia and Soviet Russia; the Soviet Government recognized Estonian independence and renounced any claims on its territory. In August a parliamentary Constitution was introduced.

January 1921: Estonia was recognized as an independent state and admitted to the League of Nations.

1924: An attempt by Communists to seize power in Estonia failed.

1933: The increasing influence of the right-wing War of Independence Veterans' League, or movement of freedom fighters, forced the introduction of a constitutional system with an executive presidency.

12 March 1934: The parliamentary system in Estonia was replaced by a period of dictatorship, after premier Päts seized control in a bloodless coup and curbed the influence of the right.

April 1938: Following the adoption of a new Constitution, which provided for a presidential system of government and a bicameral parliament, Päts was elected President.

23 August 1939: The Treaty of Non-Aggression (the Nazi–Soviet Pact) was concluded by Joachim von Ribbentrop and Vyacheslav Molotov, the foreign ministers of Germany and the USSR, respectively; the 'Secret Protocols' to this Pact provided for the annexation of Estonia and Latvia by the USSR.

June 1940: The Baltic states (Estonia, Latvia and Lithuania) and Bessarabia were occupied by the USSR; the Estonian Government resigned and was replaced by a Soviet-appointed administration, led by Johannes Vares-Barbarus.

21 July 1940: The new Estonian parliament (consisting entirely of members sympathetic to the Soviet regime) proclaimed the Estonian Soviet Socialist Republic.

6 August 1940: Estonia was admitted to the USSR as a constituent Union Republic of the federation.

June 1941: More than 10,000 Estonians were deported to Siberia by the Soviet authorities; deportations continued until the death of Stalin (Iosif V. Dzhugashvili) in 1953.

July 1941: German forces entered Estonia, having invaded the USSR the previous month.

September 1944: Despite expelling all German troops from Estonia, the Soviet regime endured a series of armed attacks by the so-called 'forest brethren' (*metsavennad*), a pro-independence guerrilla movement, which continued its campaign until 1955.

1947–March 1949: Collectivization, and continuing mass deportations, occurred in Estonia.

October 1980: The brutal suppression of a protest by schoolchildren at the 'russification' of Estonia prompted a critical 'Letter of the Forty' from prominent intellectuals to the authorities.

23 August 1987: A crowd of 2,000 demonstrators commemorated the anniversary of the Molotov-Ribbentrop Pact; soon afterwards, an Estonian Group for the Publication of the Molotov-Ribbentrop Pact was established, becoming the Estonian National Independence Party (ENIP) in 1988.

13 April 1988: The Estonian Popular Front (EPF) was formed; mass demonstrations against the Soviet regime were organized by the EPF throughout July and August.

16 June 1988: Vaino Väljas replaced Karl Vaino (leader of Estonia since 1978) as First Secretary of the Communist Party of Estonia (CPE). In the following month Intermovement, a political group intended to counteract the influence of the increasingly popular opposition, was formed.

16 November 1988: The Estonian Supreme Soviet declared the sovereignty of the Republic. The declaration, which included the right to annul all-Union legislation, was declared unconstitutional by the USSR's Supreme Soviet, but was affirmed by the Estonian Supreme Soviet the following month.

18 January 1989: Estonian was adopted as the state language and the tricolour of independent Estonia was reinstated as the official flag.

March 1989: In elections to the all-Union Congress of People's Deputies, the EPF won 27 of the 36 Estonian seats, while Intermovement won five. The ENIP refused to participate in the elections and proposed a rival parliament, the 'Congress of Estonia', to be elected only by citizens of pre-1940 Estonia and their descendants.

May 1989: Estonia declared its economic independence from the all-Union authorities; this decision was ratified by the Supreme Soviet of the USSR in November.

August 1989: A new electoral law, increasing the residency requirements for voters and candidates, was strenuously opposed (mainly by ethnic Russians); the legislation was eventually suspended.

November 1989: The Estonian Supreme Soviet voted to annul the 1940 decision to join the USSR.

22 February 1990: The Estonian legislature approved a declaration demanding immediate negotiations with the all-Union Supreme Soviet on the restoration of independence. The following day the legal pre-eminence of the Communists was abolished.

11–12 March 1990: The Congress of Estonia, to which elections had been held in late February and early March, convened and declared itself the constitutional representative of the Estonian people.

18 March 1990: In elections to the Estonian Supreme Soviet the EPF won 43 of the 105 contested seats; other pro-independence groups gained 35 seats, with the remainder secured by the Intermovement group. At the first session of the new legislature, Arnold Rüütel, previously Chairman of the Presidium of the Supreme Soviet, was elected Chairman.

30 March 1990: The Supreme Soviet declared a transitional period towards independence; at the same time, the validity of Soviet power in Estonia was denied.

3 April 1990: Edgar Savisaar, leader of the EPF, was elected Prime Minister by the Supreme Soviet (Supreme Council).

8 May 1990: The first five articles of the 1938 Constitution were reinstated; the formal name of independent Estonia, the Republic of Estonia, was restored, as well as the state emblems, the flag and the anthem. The following week the Soviet President annulled Estonia's declaration of independence and some 2,000 protesters against the declaration attempted to occupy the parliament building.

3 March 1991: In a referendum, 77.8% of the participants (comprising 82.9% of the registered electorate) voted in favour of independence.

17 March 1991: Of the 225,000 Slavs in north-eastern Estonia who participated in the all-Union referendum, approximately 95% voted in favour of keeping the USSR as a 'renewed federation'.

19 August 1991: At the same time as an attempted coup in Moscow (Russia—the Soviet capital), Gen. Fedor Kuzmin, Commander of the Soviet Baltic Military District, declared that he was assuming control of Estonia.

20 August 1991: Military vehicles entered Tallinn; at a session of the Estonian Supreme Council full and immediate independence was declared.

21 August 1991: Soviet troops occupied the television station in Tallinn, but, in Moscow, the *coup d'état* collapsed.

22 August 1991: Among measures against those who had allegedly supported the coup, the Estonian Government banned the all-Union Communist Party, Intermovement and the United Council of Work Collectives.

6 September 1991: The newly formed State Council of the USSR recognized Estonia's independence.

17 September 1991: Estonia was admitted to the UN.

9 October 1991: The USSR (which was finally to be dissolved in December) established diplomatic relations with Estonia.

6 November 1991: A new citizenship law stated that only persons who had been citizens of Estonia prior to 1940, and their descendants, were eligible to vote.

30 January 1992: Edgar Savisaar resigned as Prime Minister and was replaced by Tiit Vähi.

20 June 1992: The Estonian crown or kroon replaced the rouble as sole legal tender.

3 July 1992: Following approval by 91% of the electorate in a referendum in late June, a new Constitution came into force, providing for a 101-member parliament, the Riigikogu (State Assembly), and a presidency with limited powers.

20 September 1992: In legislative elections the largest number of seats (29) was won by the Pro Patria (Fatherland) Union (in Estonian, Isamaaliit). No presidential candidate secured an absolute majority.

5 October 1992: The Riigikogu, choosing between the two leading candidates for the presidency, elected Lennart Meri, a former Minister of Foreign Affairs, rather than Rüütel, previously Chairman of the old Supreme Council. President Meri appointed a coalition Government under Mart Laar of the Pro Patria (Fatherland) Union.

14 May 1993: Notwithstanding opposition from the Russian Government, Estonia was admitted to the Council of Europe.

June 1993: Despite significant protests by ethnic Russians against the citizenship laws, all non-Estonians were required to apply for citizenship or for a residence permit by 1 January 1996 (provoking further tensions with Russia). In January 1995 the residency requirement was extended to five years.

13 November 1993: Members of the EPF agreed to disband the organization.

February 1994: Estonia was admitted to the North Atlantic Treaty Organization's (NATO) Partnership for Peace programme of military co-operation.

29 August 1994: The last former Soviet troops were finally withdrawn from Estonia.

26 September 1994: With the coalition weakening, following a revelation that he had contravened an agreement with the International Monetary Fund (IMF), Laar was forced to resign as Prime Minister.

27 October 1994: Andres Tarand of the Moderates' Party was appointed Prime Minister for the coalition.

5 March 1995: In legislative elections an alliance of the Estonian Coalition Party (ECP) and the Rural Union won the largest number of seats (41) in the Riigikogu; a coalition of the Estonian Reform Party (ERP) and liberal groups gained 19 seats, followed by the Estonian Centre Party with 16 seats. Six seats were secured by the Our Home is Estonia pact, an alliance representing the Russian-speaking minority.

23 March 1995: Tiit Vähi, leader of the ECP, was asked to form a Government by President Meri and, on 31 March, the newly appointed Prime Minister agreed a coalition with the Rural Union and the Estonian Centre Party.

17 April 1995: A new Council of Ministers was appointed; the former premier and the leader of the Centre Party, Edgar Savisaar, was appointed Deputy Prime Minister and Minister of the Interior.

10 October 1995: Following Savisaar's dismissal from the cabinet, following revelations that he had secretly recorded political negotiations in March, and the effective collapse of the coalition, Vähi and the rest of the Council of Ministers resigned.

3 November 1995: Vähi, who had been reappointed premier, succeeded in forming a new coalition of his ECP and the Rural Union with the ERP.

15 November 1995: The European Parliament ratified Estonia's associate membership of the European Union (EU).

February 1996: The Estonian Apostolic Orthodox Church was declared to be under the jurisdiction of the Constantinople Patriarchate (based in Istanbul, Turkey); in response, the Moscow Patriarchate, which had exercised jurisdiction since 1940 and represented the interests of the russophone congregations, suspended relations with Constantinople; these were restored in May.

12 July 1996: Estonia and Latvia signed an agreement on the demarcation of maritime boundaries, following a dispute over fishing rights in the Gulf of Rīga.

26–27 August 1996: After three rounds of voting in the Riigikogu, neither Meri nor Rüütel gained sufficient votes to be elected to the presidency. A larger electoral college continued the presidential election; none of the five candidates in the first round achieved an overall majority; the second-round candidates were once again Meri and Rüütel, with Meri finally being re-elected in September.

November 1996: Estonia agreed to omit consideration of the 1920 Treaty of Tartu from an agreement demarcating the Russian–Estonian border; the Government had previously insisted that Russia recognize the Treaty as the basis of relations between the two countries.

22 November 1996: The six ERP ministers resigned, after a co-operation agreement was signed by the ECP and the Estonian Centre Party, without informing the ERP; this initiated the collapse of the ruling coalition.

1 December 1996: A minority Government, still headed by Vähi and supported by the ECP, the Rural Union and independent members, was finally appointed.

25 February 1997: Vähi resigned, following a series of allegations, which he continued to deny, concerning the abuse of office. Mart Siimann, the leader of the ECP, was appointed Prime Minister two days later.

14 March 1997: The ECP, the Rural Union and some independents again formed a minority Government.

13 December 1997: Estonia was invited to be one of the six countries to be considered for the next phase of EU enlargement; negotiations began on 31 March 1998.

16 January 1998: The Presidents of Estonia, Latvia, Lithuania and the USA signed a US–Baltic Charter of Partnership.

13 March 1998: The Riigikogu voted to abolish the death penalty.

14 October 1998: Raul Malk, hitherto ambassador to the United Kingdom, was appointed Minister of Foreign Affairs following the resignation, in the previous month, of Toomas Hendrik Ilves.

8 December 1998: The Riigikogu approved amendments to the citizenship law providing for the naturalization of the children of ethnic Russians and other minorities resident in Estonia for at least five years. The amendments came into effect on 12 July 1999.

15 December 1998: In spite of opposition from the Organization for Security and Co-operation in Europe (OSCE), the Riigikogu approved legislation requiring elected officials to demonstrate sufficient command of Estonian to be able to participate in basic burearcratic procedures of office. The legislation, which came into force in May 1999, was also condemned by the Russian Government.

7 March 1999: In legislative elections the Estonian Centre Party won the largest number of seats (28) in the Riigikogu; the ERP and Pro Patria (Fatherland) Union won 18 seats each, the Moderates' Party (in alliance with the People's Party) gained 17 seats, followed by the Estonian Country People's Party (seven) and the United People's Party of Estonia (six).

25 March 1999: A centre-right coalition Government was formed by the ERP, Pro Patria (Fatherland) Union and the Moderates' Party, each taking five ministerial posts; the leader of Pro Patria (Fatherland) Union, Mart Laar, was appointed Prime Minister.

21 May 1999: Estonia's admittance to the World Trade Organization was approved.

1 July 1999: A further amendment to the language law came into force, which stipulated that service-sector workers be proficient in Estonian.

July 1999: At a meeting in Palanga (Lithuania), the Prime Ministers of Estonia, Latvia and Lithuania agreed to develop the Baltic Common Economic Area and to promote further implementation of regional free-trade agreements.

August 1999: The leader of the Tallinn Union of Russian Citizens in Estonia, Oleg Morozov, was charged with violating Estonian residency laws because of his refusal to obtain a residency permit, owing to the fact he had been born in Estonia and had been resident there all his life. On being sentenced to 20 days' imprisonment, Mozorov went on hunger strike and demanded recognition as a political prisoner. He was subseqently ordered to leave Estonia by 30 January 2000.

17 October 1999: In local elections, a coalition of the Pro Patria (Fatherland) Union and the Moderates' Party gained control of 13 of the 15 counties in Estonia.

7 November 1999: Tarmo Loodus was appointed interior minister following the resignation of Juri Mois, who was appointed Mayor of Tallinn.

13 April 2000: Vello Vensel, a professor of statistics at Tallinn Technical University, was appointed the new President of the central bank; however, 12 days later he announced he was unable to take up the post, owing to ill health. Vahur Kraft, the previous incumbent, was reappointed bank President in June.

14 June 2000: Following four years of deliberation, legislation on workers' rights was finally approved by the Riigikogu. The new law protected the right to collective bargaining.

30 June 2000: The Commander of the Defence Forces, Lt-Gen. Johannes Kert, was dismissed by President Meri on the grounds of his supposed opposition to structural reform in the armed forces. Kert was temporarily replaced by Lt-Col Aare Ermus.

28 August 2000: A motion of 'no confidence' in the Minister of Economic Affairs, Mikhel Pärnoja, was defeated in the Riigikogu.

31 August 2000: Estonia expelled two Russian diplomats from the country, accusing them of 'activities incompatible with their status'. The Russian Federation responded by terming the expulsions a 'deliberate provocation' and ordering two Estonian diplomats to leave its territory.

8 September 2000: Rear-Adm. Tarmo Kouts, hitherto head of the border guards, was nominated by President Meri to the position of Commander of the Defence Forces; Kouts' appointment was subsequently confirmed by the Riigikogu.

14 October 2000: Two political parties, the Estonian Blue Party and the Development Party, officially merged to form the Estonian Democratic Party.

21 November 2000: Following numerous incidents of persons unwittingly crossing the unmarked Estonian–Russian frontier, the two countries agreed to improve delineation and signposting. In December an agreement on the establishment of a number of border crossings was reached.

4 December 2000: The United Nations Development Programme (UNDP) announced that it no longer considered its work necessary in Estonia and that its office in the country would close during 2001.

5 December 2000: The Russian-Baltic Party, established in early 2000, was formally registered.

Early 2001: A new right-wing Republican Party was registered; the party was opposed to membership of the EU.

February 2001: Laar was the subject of an inquiry into an incident in 1999 in which he and other officials were alleged to have taken aim at a picture of the Estonian Centre Party leader, Edgar Savisaar, during an informal shooting practice. A vote of 'no confidence' in the Prime Minister was suspended, pending the completion of the inquiry.

Finland

862: Swedish Vikings conquered territory in southern Finland, inhabited by descendants of Finno-Ugric tribes which had migrated from eastern Europe.

950: Finnic settlements in the eastern Baltic accepted Swedish Viking settlements among them, eventually forming part of the Viking (Rus) kingdom based at Novgorod.

1157: Eric of Sweden made further conquests in Finland.

1284: The Swedish Duchy of Finland was established.

1617: Sweden took Karelia, inhabited by Finnic peoples, from Russia by the Treaty of Stolbevo.

1714: During the Great Northern War between Sweden and the Baltic Alliance of Denmark, Poland and Russia, Russia invaded and took Finland; it was returned to Sweden by the Treaty of Nystad in 1721.

1772: The Duchy of Finland gained a degree of autonomy within Sweden, including its own assembly.

1809: The Treaty of Fredrickshamn awarded Finland to Russia; Finland became a Grand Duchy and retained the autonomy it had established in earlier years, but under Tsar Nicholas I (1825–55), the assembly was never convened.

1878: A Finnish Army was established, amid growing pro-independence sentiment.

1899: The autonomy of Finland within the Russian Empire was officially discontinued; the Army was dissolved and Russian was introduced as the official language.

1905: During political protests throughout the Russian Empire an uprising took place in Finland, and the assembly reasserted its authority.

1917: With the Russian Revolution, Finland was granted autonomy within a Russian confederation; but following the Bolshevik seizure of power and supported by several European countries seeking the establishment of 'buffer' states on Russia's borders, it declared itself independent on 6 December.

1918: Finland was a 'White' (anti-communist) stronghold during the Russian civil war and was attacked by the Bolshevik Red Army; the leading Finnish-based White general, Carl Gustav Baron von Mannerheim, became interim head of state.

1919: A Constitution was enacted, providing for an indirectly elected President and a unicameral Parliament (Eduskunta), directly elected by universal suffrage.

1920: The Treaty of Dorpat (Tartu) with Soviet Russia fixed the borders in the north-eastern Baltic at their 1914 positions, excepting the Petsamo region in the Arctic, which was granted to Finland, and Eastern Karelia, which was awarded to Russia.

1921: The League of Nations recognized Finnish sovereignty over the Åland Islands and established the Islands' neutral status.

1922: Land reform was enacted, redistributing the property of the largely Swedish-speaking land-owning class. Finland, Estonia, Latvia and Poland signed a treaty of non-aggression and co-operation, in the face of Soviet expansionism; the Finnish legislature did not ratify the treaty, however, fearing forced involvement in any future conflict between Poland and the Soviet state (known as the USSR from December).

1932: Finland signed a non-aggression pact with the USSR.

1939: With the outbreak of the Second World War in Europe, the USSR demanded that Finland allow it to construct military and naval bases on its territory; when Finland refused, the Soviets invaded. The conflict, known as the Winter War, was resolved in the following year, when Finland ceded the Karelian isthmus to the USSR and leased other strategically important sites in the Baltic and Arctic Seas.

1941: Finland allied with Germany to attack the USSR and was, consequently, invaded again by the Soviets, in the so-called Continuation War; Finland regained territory in Karelia and Petsamo.

1944: Finland dissolved its alliance with Germany and signed a separate armistice with the USSR.

1946: Juo Kusti Paasikivi was elected President, in succession to Mannerheim.

November 1947: A final peace treaty was concluded between the USSR and Finland: Finland was required to cede territory to the USSR, including the Karelian isthmus, and to pay reparations.

April 1948: Finland and the USSR signed a Treaty of Friendship, Co-operation and Mutual Assistance (known as the YYA Treaty): Finland was obliged to repel any attack on the USSR through Finnish territory; and was prevented from joining any international organization which could pose a threat to the USSR.

1955: Finland joined the United Nations (UN), and the Nordic Council, an organization established by Denmark, Iceland, Norway and Sweden in 1952 with the aim of promoting policy co-operation between the Nordic states. The YYA Treaty was extended for a period of 20 years.

1956: Dr Urho Kekkonen was elected to the presidency; he remained in office until 1981.

1961: Finno-Soviet relations were threatened when the Finnish Government rejected a Soviet plan for a common defence policy. Finland became an associate member of the European Free Trade Association (EFTA), acceding to full membership in 1986.

1969: By virtue of Finland's neutrality, negotiations for the first Strategic Arms Limitation Treaty (SALT), on the nuclear capability of the USSR, the USA and their respective allies, began in Helsinki.

1970: The YYA Treaty was extended for a further 20 years (a third extension was agreed in 1983).

1973: Finland signed a free-trade agreement with the European Economic Community (EEC).

1979: Despite economic problems bringing conservative gains in the general election, a new centre-left coalition Government was formed by Dr Mauno Koivisto, comprising his Social Democratic Party (Suomen Maaseudun Puolue—SDP) and three others.

1982: President Kekkonen having resigned in the previous year, Koivisto was elected to replace him, with Kalevi Sorsa, a Social Democrat, in turn replacing him as head of government.

1983: The SDP won 57 of the 200 seats in the Eduskunta and Sorsa formed a new centre-left governing coalition.

1987: Following a general election, Harri Holkeri, former Chairman of the conservative National Coalition Party (Kansallinen Kokoomus—Kok), formed a coalition comprising, among others, his own party and the Social Democrats. Government and President embarked on a programme of constitutional reforms: notably, limiting the powers of the presidency and simplifying the majority requirements in the conduct of parliamentary business.

1988: In the first presidential election to incorporate a popular vote, Koivisto was re-elected as President.

1989: Mikhail Gorbachev became the first Soviet head of state to visit Finland since 1975.

1991: At the general election, the Finnish Centre Party (Suomen Keskusta—Kesk) obtained 55 of the 200 seats in the Eduskunta and its leader, Esko Aho, became Prime Minister of a Government including the SDP, Kok and a small party.

1992: The 1948 YYA Treaty with the USSR was replaced by a new agreement with its main successor state, the Russian Federation; the new treaty placed no military obligations on Finland and did not preclude Finland's membership of any international organization not overtly hostile to Russia.

1994: After two rounds of voting, Martti Ahtisaari, the SDP candidate and a senior UN official, became President. Much of the year was dominated by debate and controversy over Finland's planned entry to the European Union (EU—as the EEC had become), a move approved by 56.9% of those voting in a referendum.

1 January 1995: Finland formally acceded to the EU.

1995: At the general election, the SDP obtained 63 seats of the 200 in the Eduskunta, Kesk 44 seats, Kok 39 seats and the Left Alliance (Vasemmistoliitto-Vänsterförbundet) 22; Paavo Lipponen of the SDP became premier and Sauli Niinistö of Kok his deputy in a coalition also joined by the Left Alliance, the Swedish People's Party (Svenska folkpartiet) and the Green League (Vihreä Liitto).

1996: Finland joined the Exchange Rate Mechanism of the EU's European Monetary System and the Government expressed interest in participating in Economic and Monetary Union (EMU).

1997: Closer relations with Poland led to a customs agreement being signed and, in the following year, a state visit by the Polish President, Aleksander Kwaśniewski.

1 January 1999: Finland and 10 other EU countries introduced the euro as a common currency eventually intended to replace national currencies in the process of EMU.

4 January 1999: The Minister for Transport and Communications, Matti Aura, resigned from his post following revelation of a scandal surrounding the flotation of 20% of the state-owned telecommunications operator, Sonera.

21 March 1999: At the general election, the SDP was returned with 51 seats, while Kesk and Kok improved their representation (obtaining 48 and 46 seats, respectively) and the Left Alliance retained 20 seats; these four parties and an independent formed a new Government.

16 January 2000: In the first ballot of the presidential election, Tarja Halonen, the SDP candidate and Minister of Foreign Affairs, received 40.0% of the votes cast, while Esko Aho (Kesk) obtained 34.4%.

6 February 2000: Halonen obtained 51.6% of the votes cast in the second ballot and was duly elected President.

1 March 2000: A new Constitution entered into force, providing for a reduction in the executive powers of the President, including an obligation on the President to co-operate more closely with the Council of State on matters of foreign policy and the transferral to the Eduskunta of responsibility for nominating the Prime Minister.

France

51 BC: Gaul (roughly, modern day France) was finally fully incorporated into the Roman Empire.

***c.* AD 400:** Gaul was invaded by Germanic tribes, the Franks becoming the dominant ruling class in the north.

481: Clovis became King of the Franks, establishing his court in Paris.

500: Clovis converted to Christianity; this confirmed the naturalization of the Germanic tribes in the Frankish (French) realm and helped spread Christianity east as the kingdom later expanded into modern Germany.

732: Frankish forces defeated Arab invasions at Tours and Poitiers.

751: Pepin, the first ruler of what became known as the Carolingian dynasty, was recognized as King of the Franks, in succession to the defunct Merovingians.

768: Pepin died and divided his kingdom between his two sons; Charles 'the Great' (Charlemagne) inherited the west, but reunited the Frankish realm upon his brother's death in 771.

800: Charlemagne was crowned Holy Roman Emperor by the Pope.

843: The Treaty of Verdun formally divided the Frankish empire into three: in the west lay most of modern France; Burgundy was to be the nucleus of the middle kingdom; and the east remained the territory of the Germanic Holy Roman Empire.

887: Odo, the Count of Paris, was installed as King, establishing a rivalry between his Robertian dynasty and the Carolingians—effectively, power moved to the individual states within the kingdom.

987: Louis V, the last Carolingian, died without leaving an heir; the monarchy officially became elective, although in reality it was transferred permanently to the Robertians, initially under Hugh Capet.

1066: William, Duke of Normandy, became King of England, bringing English influence into France.

1154: Upon accession to the English throne, Henry II, who was married to Eleanor of Aquitaine, also possessed the French territories of Anjou, Brittany, Gascony, Guyenne, Maine, Normandy, Poitou and Touraine.

1202: King Phillip II of France declared King John of England 'without land' in France, preparatory to beginning a campaign of reconquest.

1209–29: As well as consolidating possession of former English territory north of the Loire, the French Crown conquered lands in the south of the country, extending the kingdom's authority to the Mediterranean coast.

1297: Flanders was occupied by French forces, despite help for the cities of the Low Countries from England, which had continued to lose land to the French monarchy.

1309: King Phillip IV, whose marriage had extended royal territory to the east, forced the Pope to transfer his seat to Avignon.

1329: The Capetian branch of the ruling dynasty became extinct and the throne passed to the House of Valois, although this claim was contested by Edward III of England.

1337: The Hundred Years' War between France and England began.

1377: The Pope returned his official residence to Rome.

1420: Henry V of England, who, with the help of Burgundy, had occupied Normandy and Paris, was declared regent of France, marking the apogee of English power in the kingdom.

1429: The intervention of Joan of Arc prevented the fall of Orleans to the English.

1430: The infant English monarch, Henry VI, was crowned King of France.

1436: Paris was liberated by the French Crown, following the restoration of its alliance with Burgundy, and the decline of English power continued.

1453: The final peace with England left it only Calais and the Channel Islands and marked the reassertion of the French Crown's power vis-à-vis that of its feudal, princely subjects; moreover, the conflict had given rise to a concept of French nationhood.

1482: A treaty between France and the Holy Roman Empire partitioned Burgundy, giving the western part to France, and the east, the Franche Comté, as well as the Low Countries, to the Empire.

1494: Charles VIII claimed the throne of Naples, which he argued was a possession of the House of Anjou, and French troops advanced into Italy.

1525: King Francis I, continuing French ambitions in Italy (which had suffered varying fortunes), had come into conflict with the Habsburg ruler of both

Spain and the Holy Roman Empire, Charles V, but was defeated at Pavia. The resultant peace treaty forced Francis to cede Burgundy to the Empire and to abandon his territorial claims in Milan and Naples.

1534: Francis' policy towards the Reformation became hardened, and persecutions of minority groups began.

1536: Francis resumed war against Charles V, gaining Piedmont but, more importantly, by utilizing the support of the Protestant German princes against the Empire (while maintaining France as Roman Catholic).

1552: France's enlargement in the east was assisted by the conclusion of an agreement with a league of anti-imperial German princes, which promised France control over the cities of Metz, Toul and Verdun.

1558: Calais was regained from England.

1559: By the Peace of Cateau-Cambrésis, France definitively surrendered its ambitions in Italy, allowing Spain to become the dominant power there.

1562: Catherine de Medici, regent for her son, Charles IX, issued an edict granting limited religious freedom to Protestant groups, but thereby provoked the Wars of Religion. This series of civil wars was not only a contest between Protestants (the French Calvinists were known as Huguenots) and Roman Catholics (led by the Holy League) and between the Crown and nobility, but also involved Spain.

1588: Although Henry III deprived all Protestants of the right to inherit the throne (a Huguenot prince, Henry of Navarre, had become heir in 1584), the Holy League formed a government in Paris; the King was forced to ally with Henry of Navarre to restore royal legitimacy.

1589: Henry of Navarre succeeded to the throne as Henry IV, the first monarch of the House of Bourbon, and secured his acceptance on the throne by renouncing Protestantism and defeating Spain.

1598: The Edict of Nantes guaranteed freedom of worship to the Huguenots and gave them certain other liberties within France but, with a still Roman Catholic strengthened Crown, the Wars of Religion ended.

1603: The first French colonies in North America were established.

1624: Louis XIII admitted Cardinal Armand de Richelieu to his Council, the Cardinal swiftly rising to the leadership of that body; Richelieu's policies centred on the enforcement of absolute obedience to the monarch and his opposition to Protestantism *within* France.

1648: The Treaty of Westphalia ended the Thirty Years' War, with France (which had supported the Protestant princes) receiving significant territorial gains, notably the establishment of the Rhine as the border of its and the

Empire's zones of influence. The conflict between France and Spain continued, however.

1652: The defeat of an uprising known as the Fronde, supported by Spain, confirmed the absolute power of the monarchy, to the benefit of the still-infant Louis XIV ('the Sun King').

1659: The Peace of the Pyrenees ended the conflict with Spain, with France making significant territorial gains, particularly on its borders with the Spanish Netherlands.

1678: The Peace of Nijmegen ended a six-year war with the Habsburg Empire, the Netherlands and Spain, gaining Louis XIV the Franche Comté and several towns in the Low Countries.

1681: Louis XIV's policy of 'reunion' (absorbing territory so as to establish the Rhine as France's eastern frontier) led to the annexation of several imperial towns in Alsace, including Strasbourg.

1685: The Edict of Nantes was revoked and an estimated 500,000 Huguenots fled the country.

1701: Louis XIV's grandson, Phillip of Anjou, was nominated as the successor to the Spanish throne upon the death of Charles II, the last Spanish Habsburg; the rival claimant, Charles, an Austrian Habsburg, was supported in the ensuing conflict by most of the powers of Europe, again united in opposing French expansionism.

1713: The Treaty of Utrecht ended the War of the Spanish Succession, with the Bourbons receiving Spain and its overseas territories (although a union of the French and Spanish Crowns was forbidden), its European possessions reverting to the Habsburgs.

1756: Conflicting colonial ambitions, together with continuing disputes in Europe, led to the Seven Years' War, with France fighting the United Kingdom overseas and (in alliance with Habsburg Austria, Russia and Sweden) against Hanover, Prussia and the United Kingdom in Europe.

1763: By the Treaty of Paris France lost its North American and most of its Indian possessions, as well as Senegal, to the United Kingdom, but the Treaty of Hubertusburg ended the European war without significant territorial implications for France.

1774: Louis XVI succeeded to the throne; his attempts to institute administrative reforms, reducing the feudal rights of the nobility, and to liberalize the economy were defeated by the nobles.

1778: France agreed to support the rebel British colonies in their struggle to secure the independence of the United States of America (USA), but the cost of further war added to domestic discontent.

1783: The Peace of Paris ended the American War of Independence, with France regaining Senegal and its future influence in West Africa.

1788: Jacques Necker, a former minister who had complained about the magnitude of France's debt, was appointed Prime Minister, with the condition that the Estates General (a hitherto largely powerless Parliament) was convened.

1789: The meeting of the Estates General unleashed popular discontent, with the Third Estate (bourgeoisie) representing the people against the monarch and the other two Estates (representing clergy and the nobility). The Third Estate eventually sat separately and declared a National Assembly, and royal power was undermined by rioters occupying the Bastille prison and by the dissolution of the army. The Assembly abolished feudalism, freed the peasantry, confiscated ecclesiastical property and issued the Declaration of the Rights of Man.

1791: A new Constitution provided for a unicameral legislative assembly, and for executive power to be nominally vested in the monarch, exercised through a council of ministers; the King (who had earlier failed in an attempt to flee Paris) retained a temporary right of veto over legislation.

1792: France declared war on Austria, while unrest in Paris continued. The revolutionary leaders arranged for the Assembly to be dissolved; it was succeeded by a National Convention, which declared France a Republic.

1793: The Convention voted narrowly in favour of the imposition of the death penalty on Louis XVI ('Citizen Capet'), although the execution provoked a Coalition of other countries (including Prussia, Spain and the United Kingdom) to support Austria in its war with France. The Constitution promulgated by the Convention vested legislative power in the people, by means of plebiscites on every law; executive power was vested in a number of committees, drawn from the members of the Convention; this unwieldy system led, effectively, to government by decree.

1794: The head of the powerful Committee for Public Safety, Maximilien de Robespierre, united the factional opposition in the Convention against him by his absolutist tendencies; he was ousted from power and executed. Christian worship, meanwhile, was prohibited and replaced by the so-called Cult of Reason.

1795: The Convention ratified a new Constitution; legislative power was vested in two new bodies (the Council of the Elders and the Council of the 500) and executive power rested with the five-member Directory, appointed by the Councils. Prussia and Spain left the Coalition against France.

1797: The French invasion of Italy in the previous year, under Napoleon Bonaparte, forced Austria and Piedmont to conclude peace with France: Austria ceded the Austrian Netherlands (Belgium) and the left bank of the Rhine; France also established a number of satellite republics in the Alps and Italy.

1799: The United Kingdom succeeded in forming a second Coalition against France. Bonaparte returned from a campaign in Egypt and took power from the Directory. A plebiscite approved a system of government dominated by a First Consul (which post Bonaparte duly received) and two assistant consuls.

1800: Christian worship was permitted and the majority of the *émigré* nobles and others expelled from France in previous years were allowed to return. Victories over Austria at Marengo and Hohenlinden began the dissolution of the Second Coalition. France acquired Louisiana from Spain.

1801: Russia signed a peace treaty with France, leaving the British isolated within Europe.

1802: France signed the Treaty of Amiens with the United Kingdom, ending the Second War of the Coalition.

1804: France and its colonies were declared a hereditary Empire, with Bonaparte becoming Napoleon I. The Napoleonic Code established equality for all citizens in matters of civil law, its introduction having lasting influence throughout Europe.

1805: The Third Coalition was formed: the British navy defeated the French and Spanish fleets at the Battle of Trafalgar, but in central Europe French troops entered the Austrian imperial capital, Vienna, and defeated the Austro-Prussian forces in the Battle of Austerlitz.

1806: After victory over Prussia, Napoleon I declared the 'Continental System', which aimed to block British trade in Europe. A Fourth Coalition was defeated and the Confederation of the Rhine was imposed by France on the western German states.

1808: Napoleon I, having already invaded Portugal, installed his brother, Joseph, as King of Spain, but this provoked a direct British intervention on mainland Europe (the Peninsula War lasted until 1813, when the French withdrew).

1812: With the French Empire at its greatest extent, armies advanced eastward into Russia; although Napoleon I reached Moscow, a combination of Russian resistance and severe winter weather forced a costly retreat.

1814: A Prussian-led force invaded France and reached Paris, deposing Napoleon I and exiling him to the Italian island of Elba. The brother of the executed Louis XVI assumed the throne as Louis XVIII, restoring absolutist rule. By the Peace of Paris France lost its Napoleonic conquests, excepting Savoy.

1815: Napoleon I secretly returned to France and marched on Paris; Louis XVIII fled, but the European powers refused to accept the restoration of Bonaparte. British and Prussian forces defeated the French armies decisively near the Belgian village of Waterloo; Napoleon I was forced to abdicate and his final exile, this time under British supervision, was to the remote Atlantic island of St Helena. Louis XVIII was restored to the throne. The Congress of Vienna restored France to its 1792 borders.

1818: A more moderate French Government secured the removal of foreign troops from French territory, although reactionary government returned in 1820, following the assassination of the Duke of Berry, a nephew of the King, by a Bonapartist.

1830: A confrontation between the Chamber of Deputies and Charles X led to popular insurrection and the fall of the King. Despite demands for a republic, the bourgeois-led legislature installed the Duke of Orleans, from a cadet branch of the House of Bourbon, as King Louis Philippe, in a limited monarchy. France captured Algiers and Oran, and became the leading power in North Africa.

1848: Amid growing dissatisfaction with the 'July Monarchy' of Louis Philippe, a Second Republic was proclaimed and a Constituent Assembly elected. An insurrection against the bourgeois domination of the Assembly was suppressed, causing several thousand deaths. The new Constitution provided for a unicameral legislative Assembly and a directly elected President. In the presidential election, Louis Napoleon Bonaparte, the nephew of Napoleon I, gained a significant majority.

1852: A new Constitution was enacted, strengthening the position of the President. A plebiscite re-established France as an Empire, with Bonaparte assuming the style Napoleon III.

1854–56: France joined Piedmont, Turkey and the United Kingdom in an alliance against the Russians in the Crimean War.

1860: The imperial Government permitted opposition parties to hold seats in the Chamber of Deputies and a greater extent of press freedom.

1862: France began to establish colonies in Indo-China.

1869: The opposition won a clear victory in the elections to the Chamber of Deputies and proposed a plebiscite on the liberalization of the Empire.

1870: The plebiscite revealed a majority of voters in favour of liberalizing the Empire. Meanwhile, Napoleon III provoked war with Prussia over the vacancy of the Spanish throne, but the French were defeated at Sedan and Napoleon III was taken prisoner; a provisional Government was established, deposing Napoleon III *in absentia*, and proclaiming a Third Republic. In September Prussian forces besieged Paris.

1871: Paris capitulated and France was defeated. By the Peace of Versailles, France lost Alsace-Lorraine to the new, Prussian-led German Empire.

1875: A new Constitution was enacted, providing for a President indirectly elected by the Chamber of Deputies and the Senate for a seven-year term.

1894: France and Russia concluded the 'Dual Alliance', a mutual co-operation treaty, which included defence against the perceived threat from Germany.

1904: France extended its alliance system by the so-called Entente Cordiale with the United Kingdom.

1905: The state was officially secularized.

1914: France and its Entente allies declared war on Germany, over its support for Austria-Hungary in the 'Balkan Crisis'. Germany invaded northern France through Belgium.

1919: Under the terms of the Treaty of Versailles, which formally concluded the First World War (fighting had ceased towards the end of the previous year), France regained Alsace-Lorraine and insisted on punitive war compensation from Germany (now a republic).

1935: France and Russia signed a mutual assistance treaty.

1939: France guaranteed the integrity of Poland and, upon the German invasion of the country, declared war on Germany, as did the United Kingdom.

1940: German troops invaded France, capturing much of the country, including Paris. An armistice was signed, confirming German occupation of much of the north, and a Government of unoccupied France was established in Vichy, led by Marshal Henri Pétain. Gen. Charles de Gaulle, exiled in London (United Kingdom), established the Provisional National Committee of the Free French, which formed a Government-in-Exile, and supported resistance groups within occupied France. Fearing its use by Germany, the United Kingdom destroyed the French fleet.

1943: Pétain refused to lead the 'rump' French state back into the war, on the side of Germany and its Axis allies, and German forces occupied the south of the country.

1944: France was invaded in the west and south by Allied troops and, eventually, liberated. De Gaulle led a Government of National Unity.

1945: The Fourth Republic was established. The Second World War concluded with France restored to its pre-1940 borders (including Alsace-Lorraine) and empire. France was a founding member of the United Nations (UN) and was accorded a permanent seat on the UN Security Council.

1946: The Constitution of the Fourth Republic was enacted, providing for a parliamentary system of government with a bicameral legislature.

1949: Viet Nam was awarded independence within the French Union of overseas possessions.

1954: After two years of war in Viet Nam, and the defeat of French forces at Dien Bien Phoo, complete independence was granted to Cambodia, Laos and Viet Nam (the last was partitioned).

1956: Tunisia and Morocco were granted independence. France and the United Kingdom took military action to prevent the nationalization by Egypt of the Suez Canal. The action was condemned by the UN and the USA, and the British and French forces were compelled to withdraw, damaging the two countries' standings in international affairs.

1957: France was an original signatory to the Treaty of Rome, which founded the European Economic Community (EEC—which evolved into the European Union—EU).

1958: A referendum approved the transformation to a presidential system of government, creating the Fifth Republic. The new Constitution provided for a President, indirectly elected to a seven-year term, and a bicameral Parliament, comprising a directly elected National Assembly (Assemblée Nationale—lower house) and an indirectly elected Senate (Sénat—upper house). De Gaulle was elected President.

1960: Unrest in Algeria escalated into more serious violence, and additional French troops were stationed there.

1962: After a bitter civil war, Algeria was granted independence from France. The French Constitution was amended to provide for the direct election of the President. De Gaulle was duly re-elected.

1968: Demonstrations by students and workers' groups opposed to the prevailing political system frequently escalated into violent unrest; order was restored after a series of concessions was made by the Government of Georges Pompidou.

1969: De Gaulle resigned from the presidency after the defeat of his reform proposals in a referendum. He was temporarily replaced by Alain Poher, the President of the Senate. At the presidential election in June, Pompidou defeated Poher and was duly elected President.

1974: Pompidou died while in office. The subsequent presidential election was won by Valéry Giscard d'Estaing.

1981: François Mitterrand became France's first Socialist President, after defeating Giscard d'Estaing in the presidential election.

1986: The centre-right coalition won the general election, and formed a Government, led by Jacques Chirac. This state of 'cohabitation' (the President being from the opposite political bloc to the Government) was unprecedented in France.

1988: Mitterrand was re-elected to the presidency. A minority Socialist Government was appointed, thus ending the period of cohabitation. The Socialists emerged from a subsequent general election in a stronger position.

1992: In a referendum, 51% of voters supported French ratification of the EC's Treaty on European Union ('Maastricht Treaty').

1995: Chirac defeated the Socialist candidate, Lionel Jospin, in the presidential election.

1997: Following elections to the National Assembly, the Socialist Party was able to form a coalition Government, led by Jospin, thus beginning a second period of cohabitation.

1 January 1999: France joined 10 other EU countries in the introduction of a common currency, the euro, designed, eventually, to replace the French franc as the national currency.

January 2000: The European Commission began legal proceedings against France, which had continued its prohibition of imports of British beef on the grounds of its possible infection with bovine spongiform encephalopathy (BSE) antigens. The EU's own ban on British beef exports had ended in July 1999.

21 July 2000: Proposals for the granting of a degree of legislative autonomy to the island of Corsica were presented by Jospin. The plans attracted some opposition from within the governing coalition, culminating in the resignation of the Minister of the Interior, Jean-Pierre Chevènement, on 30 August.

24 September 2000: In a referendum, a proposal to amend the Constitution, reducing the President's term of office from seven to five years, received 72.9% of valid votes cast. The amendment was to take effect following the presidential elections scheduled for 2002.

January 2001: Dissenting members of the Front Libération National de la Corse (FLNC), who had formed Armata Corse in opposition to the peace process in Corsica, claimed responsibility for two executions and eight bombings on the island.

Germany

4th–5th centuries: Germanic tribes migrated westwards into territory of the disintegrating Western Roman Empire; numerous Germanic kingdoms were established in much of western and central Europe, with the Franks becoming the dominant power in northern France.

481: Clovis, King of the Franks, converted to Christianity, indicating the neutralization of the 'barbarian' tribes on the territory of the former Roman Empire—the Frankish expansion eastwards was to take those values into the original Germanic heartland beyond the Rhine.

771: Charles 'the Great' (Charlemagne), already king in the western part of the Frankish realm (much of modern France), inherited the eastern kingdom (western Germany and the Low Countries) upon the death of his brother. He expanded his territory into central Europe.

800: Charlemagne was crowned the first Holy Roman Emperor by the Pope.

843: The Treaty of Verdun formally divided the Frankish empire into three: the western kingdom acquired the Franks' name; Burgundy was to be the nucleus of the middle kingdom; while the eastern kingdom retained the German heartland. The imperial title passed between different princes of the Carolingian dynasties.

962: Otto I 'the Great', ruler of the dominant eastern state of Saxony and leader of the German resistance to the Magyars (Hungarians), was crowned Emperor at Rome. Henceforth, the Holy Roman Empire of the German Nation was to have a continuous existence until its dissolution in 1806.

1122: After a period of struggle between Emperor, Pope and the German princes, the Concordat of Worms was concluded between the Emperor, Henry V, and Pope Calixtus II—imperial control over the Church was weakened and the position of the princes in relation to the Emperor was strengthened.

1125: The accession of Lothair II, last of the Franconian dynasty (which had succeeded the House of Saxony in 1024), marked the beginning of the principle of elected emperors.

118

1138: The first of the Hohenstaufen Emperors came to the throne and a further period of conflict with the papacy and dynastic rivalry in Germany ensued.

1220: The ecclesiastical princes gained further autonomy from the Holy Roman Emperor. The secular princes gained the same rights in 1232.

1273: The elective imperial monarchy was formally established, the right to vote being limited to seven princes (electors), three of them ecclesiastical, demonstrating the weakening of the imperial institution after 23 years of disputed succession.

1356: The Golden Bull was issued by Emperor Charles IV (of the main ruling dynasty, of Luxembourg), removing the majority of imperial rights in seven principalities, but prohibiting the formation of leagues of cities, which had begun during the previous century.

1376: The Swabian League of Cities was formed, to protect city rights against the Empire and the princes, in direct contravention of the Golden Bull, but the leagues were finally crushed by the army of the princes in 1388.

1438: With the extinction of the Luxemburg dynasty, Albert II of Bohemia and Hungary was elected Emperor and, henceforth, the imperial title remained an inheritance of the Austrian House of Habsburg, consolidated by the acquisition of territories throughout Europe (Burgundy, Naples, Spain).

1517: The religious Reformation began under Martin Luther, eventually dividing Germany into those who adhered to the Roman Church (Roman Catholics) and those who protested the authority of the Pope (Protestants). The Habsburg King of Spain was elected Emperor as Charles V—his power was contested by many of the German princes in a conflict complicated by religious discord.

1555: The Peace of Augsburg concluded the conflicts immediately occasioned by the Reformation and resolved that subjects of a prince should be obliged to adhere to the denomination of that prince—the Emperor could only secure Roman Catholicism in his hereditary, Habsburg possessions. The next year Charles V abdicated, leaving Austria and the imperial title to his brother and Spain to his son.

1648: The Peace of Westphalia concluded the Thirty Years' War, occasioned by a Habsburg attempt to reimpose Roman Catholicism and imperial power, but instead involving other states (France, Sweden) in German territory and increasing the powers of the stronger princes; the Swiss and the Dutch left imperial jurisdiction completely.

1663: The first permanent assembly of the imperial territories (Reichstag) was convened at Regensburg, comprising eight electors, 165 princes, and 61 city representatives.

1713: Frederick William I succeeded to the throne of Prussia, consolidating its position as the most powerful of the German principalities with social, administrative and military reforms.

1740: The death of Emperor Charles VI without a male heir provoked the War of the Austrian Succession, in which Prussia took Silesia from the Habsburgs.

1756–63: In the Seven Years' War, Prussia was saved from defeat at the hands of Austria's anti-Prussian coalition initially by its alliance with the United Kingdom and then by the disunity of the coalition.

1772–95: The three Partitions of Poland were favourable to Prussia, expanding its territory greatly.

1785: Frederick II of Prussia established the League of German Princes (Fürstenbund), initially to oppose Habsburg control of Bavaria.

1792: France declared war on Austria and Prussia, which it accused of trying to undermine the French Revolution; in the following year, the other German imperial states joined the anti-French coalition.

1801: The Peace of Lunéville was the first attempt of the French leader, Napoleon Bonaparte, to reorganize Germany, compensating the German princes for territory on the left bank of the Rhine lost to France with territory elsewhere in Germany.

1803: The deputies of the imperial states decided to reorganize Germany, concentrating power on the largest states.

1804: The last Holy Roman Emperor assumed the imperial title for Austria, as Francis II.

1805: After Austria's defeat at Austerlitz, the Peace of Pressburg forced it to cede territory to Baden, Bavaria and Württemburg (the latter two became kingdoms, the first a Grand Duchy).

1806: France insisted on 16 southern and western German states forming the Confederation of the Rhine (eventually including all the German principalities except Brunswick, Hesse and Prussia). Meanwhile, Francis I of Austria renounced his original title and the Holy Roman Empire of the German Nation was dissolved. Prussia was seriously defeated by France and saved from total dissolution only by Russian intervention.

1813: Prussia declared war on France and, eventually, decisively defeated the French armies at the Battle of Leipzig—the Confederation of the Rhine was dissolved with the liberation from French influence.

1815: Under the terms negotiated at the Congress of Vienna, Prussia gained territory in the Rhineland, Saxony and Westphalia. Austria, which also gained from the Congress, acted with Prussia to establish a new Germanic Confederation, comprising 39 states, each of which sent an ambassador to the

Federal Assembly (Bundestag), which met in Frankfurt under Austrian presidency. The new order provoked a flourishing of nationalist sentiments, which many of the princes perceived as a threat.

1829: The Prussian customs union (introduced for all Prussian territories in 1819) began to include other German states.

1830: Political unrest in France led to repercussions in Germany, with Brunswick, Hanover, Hesse and Saxony abandoning absolute rule and introducing constitutions.

1834: The German Customs Union (Zollverein), introducing unified tariffs for most of Germany (the principal exceptions being some northern states), was established.

1847: King Frederick William IV of Prussia was obliged to convene a united provincial assembly, as a consultative body, representing all the estates.

1848: Political unrest throughout Europe encouraged the Baden Assembly to vote in favour of the convocation of a national German Parliament and began a movement which resulted in the Vorparlament, which met at Frankfurt and resolved to hold elections for a national assembly.

1849: The National Assembly, meeting in Frankfurt, divided over the definition of Germany: whether Austria should be included in a German federation ('Great Germans'); or whether it should be excluded from a constitutional monarchy under Prussia ('Small Germans'). Frederick William IV of Prussia refused the throne of a new Small German federation and the Assembly dissolved.

1850: Prussia abandoned its own attempt to create a united Small Germany, owing to Austrian objections, and the plan was withdrawn. The 1815 Confederation was re-established.

1862: Otto von Bismarck became the Prussian premier.

1865: Denmark having been forced to cede the duchies of Schleswig (Slesvig) and Holstein (Holsten), the Convention of Gastein awarded administrative rights over Holstein to Austria and over Schleswig to Prussia.

1866: The Prussians invaded Holstein and Austria mobilized the Confederation to declare war on Prussia. Prussia gained a decisive victory at Sadowa (Königgratz), thereby ending the Seven Weeks' War, and Austria was excluded from Germany's political future.

1867: Prussia established a North German Confederation, with William I of Prussia as President, Bismarck as Chancellor and a Parliament consisting of an appointed upper house or Federal Council (Bundesrat) and an elected lower house (Reichstag). The southern states joined a renewed Customs Union and took seats in the Zollparlament, the first genuinely all-German body.

1870: France, indignant at a possible Hohenzollern candidacy for the Spanish crown, declared war on Prussia, but lost Alsace and Lorraine to a German invasion.

1871: With the defeat of France, the allied German states agreed to the proclamation of a German Empire, with William I of Prussia as Emperor (Kaiser). The Empire had a federal structure, with similar institutions to those of the old North German Confederation.

1882: Germany's conclusion of the Triple Alliance with Austria-Hungary and Italy, as well as its pacts with Russia, sealed Bismarck's policy to forestall French revenge.

1884–85: The German desire to add prestige to the new state prompted Bismarck to claim a colonial empire, initially in Africa, although care was taken to avoid a conflict with the other colonial Powers.

1890: Bismarck was dismissed as Chancellor, following a series of disagreements with the new Emperor, William II.

1898: The German Government resolved to invest in its navy, which was perceived as a direct challenge to British maritime supremacy and fuelled an 'arms race' in Europe.

1907: The Triple Entente of France, Russia and the United Kingdom was concluded, increasingly at odds with Germany and its increasingly dependent Central Power allies, Austria-Hungary and Ottoman Turkey.

1914: Conflict between Austria-Hungary and Serbia brought the power blocs into the First World War, with Germany invading France (through Belgium) in the west and Russian Poland in the east.

1918: Revolution in Russia permitted German success on the eastern front, but its troops in northern France were withdrawn as victory was deemed impossible. With civil unrest at home and the loss of its possessions abroad, in right-wing mythology the German defeat became associated with the democracy of the socialist-led republic proclaimed after the abdication of the Emperor.

1919: The Treaty of Versailles imposed massive reparations on Germany, which debilitated its economy for many years, deprived it of its colonial empire and gave Alsace-Lorraine to France and West Prussia to Poland. The new republic enacted the so-called Weimar Constitution.

1921: Adolf Hitler, a former army colonel, became leader of the extreme right-wing National Socialist (Nazi) German Workers' Party (NSGWP).

1923: Germany's failure to comply with its reparation duties led to a French-led invasion of the Ruhr. 'Hyperinflation' caused economic distress, creating an environment in which Hitler attempted a coup in Munich, but was imprisoned.

1925: The Locarno Agreement established Germany's western border and guaranteed a demilitarized zone in the Rhineland.

1926: Germany became a member of the League of Nations.

1933: Hitler was appointed Chancellor, in a coalition with the traditional right-wing parties which had, hitherto, excluded him from government, although the NSGWP had been the largest single party in the Reichstag since the previous year. Nazi power was soon established and political, racial and social repression begun.

1934: A non-aggression pact was signed with Poland. The Saarland territory was reabsorbed, following a plebiscite.

1936: German troops occupied the Rhineland, in contravention of the Treaty of Versailles. Germany also cancelled the Locarno Agreement and signed an anti-Soviet pact with Japan (later joined by Italy).

1938: Union (Anschluss) with Austria was secured by invasion and plebiscite, and France and the United Kingdom conceded the secession of the Czechoslovakian territory of the Sudetenland in order to preserve peace in Europe.

1939: Germany concluded a non-aggression pact with the USSR. It then invaded Poland, provoking France and the United Kingdom to declare war, the Second World War.

1940: Germany invaded Belgium, Denmark, France, the Netherlands, Norway and Romania.

1941: Germany, still fighting elsewhere in Europe, invaded the USSR. The USA joined the war after an attack by Germany's ally, Japan.

1945: Germany was invaded and occupied by the Allies, ending the war in Europe. An Allied Control Council was formed and Germany was partitioned into British, French, Soviet and US zones of administration. Berlin, which lay within the Soviet sector, was similarly divided. The Saarland was made an autonomous French protectorate; West and East Prussia and Silesia were placed under Polish administration. Political parties were re-established.

1948: The three 'Western' zones were integrated economically following the London Conference; a new, reformed German currency, the Deutsche Mark, was introduced. The USSR barred all access to the Western sectors of Berlin through the Soviet zone of Germany, but Allied airlifts resolved the problem.

1949: A new German state, the Federal Republic of Germany (FRG or 'West' Germany) was established in the British, French and US zones, with Konrad Adenauer of the Christian Democratic Union (Christlich-Demokratische Union—CDU) as the first Chancellor. In the Soviet zone a German Democratic Republic (GDR or 'East' Germany) was declared, with the Soviet zone of Berlin as its capital; executive power was held by the Socialist Unity Party of Germany (Sozialistische Einheitspartei Deutschlands—SED).

18 April 1951: The FRG signed a treaty (along with five other countries) founding the European Coal and Steel Community (ECSC), the first of the European Communities.

1955: The occupation of Germany by the Western powers was ended and the FRG was admitted to the North Atlantic Treaty Organization (NATO), the Warsaw Pact and the Western European Union (WEU).

1957: Saarland acceded to the FRG. The FRG signed the Treaty of Rome and became a founder member of the European Economic Community.

1960: Walter Ulbricht became Chairman of the Council of State (head of state) of the GDR.

1961: The Berlin Wall was erected by the Government of the GDR, ostensibly to defend the Eastern sector against a Western attack.

1969: In West Germany the CDU and its sister party, the Christian Social Union (Christlich-Soziale Union—CSU), lost support at the general election, allowing the Social Democratic Party of Germany (Sozialdemokratische Partei Deutschlands—SPD) to form a coalition Government with the Free Democratic Party (Freie Demokratische Partei—FDP), under Willy Brandt of the SPD.

1973: With improved East–West relations , both the FRG and the GDR became members of the United Nations (UN). Willi Stoph became the GDR head of state.

1974: Brandt resigned as Chancellor, after discovering that his assistant was a clandestine agent of the GDR; he was succeeded by Helmut Schmidt, also of the SPD.

1976: Erich Honecker replaced Stoph as Chairman of the Council of State of the GDR.

1982: The CDU and CSU formed a Government with the FDP, under the chancellorship of Helmut Kohl of the CDU.

1989: The collapse of the Communist regimes in Eastern Europe culminated in the breaching of the Berlin Wall and the disintegration of state authority in the GDR.

1990: With a general election in the West confirming Kohl as Chancellor, unification was able to proceed: German Economic, Monetary and Social Union took place on 1 July; treaties on unity and the final sanction of the four former occupying Powers in August and September; and, on 3 October, the dissolution of the GDR and the accession of the East German Länder as five federal provinces of the FRG.

January 1991: Following a general election held in December 1990, the first Government of the unified Germany took office, still under Chancellor Kohl.

June 1991: The Bundestag voted in favour of Berlin as the future seat of the legislature and of government by 2000.

December 1992: The Bundestag ratified the Treaty on European Union (the 'Maastricht Treaty'), which provided, among other things, for closer economic and political integration within what became known as the European Union (EU), a move which Germany (and, in particular, its Chancellor) strongly supported.

September 1996: The Bundesrat voted to move from Bonn to the capital, Berlin.

27 September 1998: The ruling parties lost heavily at a general election and a leftist coalition of the SPD and Alliance 90/Greens (Bündnis 90/Die Grünen), led by Gerhard Schröder of the SPD, came to power.

1 January 1999: Germany was a member of the first group of countries to participate in Stage III of the EU's Economic and Monetary Union (EMU), whereby the Deutsche Mark was to be fully replaced by the euro from 2002.

March 1999: German aircraft participated in active service in Europe for the first time since 1945, when NATO airstrikes were carried out against Yugoslavia.

April 1999: The Reichstag was inaugurated in Berlin.

June 1999: The first German ministry relocated to Berlin, and was followed by most other government institutions during the course of the year.

1 July 1999: Prof Dr Johannes Rau of the SPD, formerly the Minister-President of North Rhine-Westphalia, was inaugurated as Federal President.

November 1999: A system of secret bank accounts held by the CDU and used to manage undisclosed donations to party funds was discovered. Former Chancellor Kohl later admitted knowledge of some secret funding, and he and the party became the subjects of a criminal investigation.

December 1999: The German Government agreed to pay a substantial sum in compensation to people who had worked as forced labourers or been deprived of their assets under the Nazi regime.

February 2000: An initial fine of DM43.1m. was imposed on the CDU following the investigation into its accounts. The party Chairman, Dr Wolfgang Schäuble, who had succeeded Kohl in that position and had been a close ally during his period in office, resigned.

9 January 2001: The Minister of Health, Andrea Fischer, and the Minister of Food, Agriculture and Forestry, Karl-Heinz Funke, were forced to resign over the mishandling of the bovine spongiform encephalopathy (BSE) crisis in Germany.

8 February 2001: Kohl agreed to pay a DM300,000 fine rather than stand trial on the charge of accepting illegal donations to the CDU.

2 March 2001: It was announced that the criminal investigation into CDU funding would close. However, the parliamentary inquiry into the affair was to continue.

Greece

c. **1500 BC:** The early Greeks migrated to the Balkan Peninsula from north of the River Danube, displacing the Minoan civilization which had spread from Crete to the southern coast of modern Greece; they established independent states and colonized the coastal regions of the Mediterranean.

1000 BC: Foundation of the Greek state of Sparta, a military society which eventually dominated the southern Peloponnese.

776 BC: The first pan-Hellenic games were held; athletes from all over the Aegean competed; the event is often cited as the first indication of a Greek national consciousness.

7th–6th centuries BC: The city state of Athens (Athínai) developed the traditions of democracy.

490 BC: Persian forces (under the rule of Emperor Darius I) landed at Marathon in Greece and were eventually defeated by the Athenians.

480–479 BC: The Persians again invaded Greece, this time under the command of Darius's son, Xerxes; they advanced on Athens and burned down the city but were eventually defeated at the Battle of Plataea.

431–421 BC: The first Peloponnesian War was fought between Athens and Sparta.

413–404 BC: Second Peloponnesian War.

359 BC: Philip II acceded to the throne in Macedon; Philip's military campaigns in Greece ended the independence of the city states.

333 BC: Philip II's son, Alexander 'the Great', defeated the Persians in Asia Minor at the Battle of Issus and began his advance through the territories of the Persian Empire; Alexander died in 323 BC, having extended his territories into Mesopotamia.

168 BC: Macedon was conquered by the Romans.

133 BC: The last king of Pergamon bequeathed his land to the Roman Empire.

AD 394: The Roman Emperor Theodosius I made Christianity the official religion in Greece and prohibited the worship of Greek and Roman gods.

395: Following a division of the administration of the Roman Empire, Greece was ruled by the Eastern Roman ('Byzantine') Emperor in Constantinople (now Istanbul, Turkey).

6th–7th centuries: Slavs invaded the Balkan Peninsula.

1196: The Normans invaded Greece; the Venetians agreed to help the Greeks defend themselves in return for the use of Byzantine trade routes.

1204: The Fourth Crusade arrived in Constantinople and created the so-called 'Latin Empire of Constantinople', dividing the Byzantine Empire into feudal states, ruled mostly by Frankish dynasties.

1259: The Byzantine Emperor Michael VIII captured the Peloponnese from its Frankish rulers; his forces liberated Constantinople in 1261.

1453: Ottoman troops captured Constantinople, thus ending the Byzantine Empire and beginning the period of Ottoman dominance in Greece.

1571: At the Battle of Lepanto, off the northern coast of the Peloponnese, the Venetians and Spanish defeated the Ottoman navy, ending Ottoman naval dominance of the area's seas.

1687: Corinth and Athens were captured by Venetian forces.

1770: A nationalist rebellion in the Peloponnese, supported by Russia, was defeated; in the same year unrest on the island of Crete was suppressed.

1786: Ottoman forces defeated a Russian-inspired rebellion in Epirus.

1814: Three Greeks resident in Odessa (then Russia, now Ukraine) founded a movement in support of Greek independence, the Philiki Etairia (Friendly Society); branches of the organization were established throughout Greece, meeting in secret.

1820: Ali Pasha, the Ottoman governor of Ioannina, began a rebellion against central Ottoman rule.

25 March 1821: The Greek flag was raised at a monastery in the Peloponnese, beginning the War of Independence.

1821–22: Ottoman forces suppressed a rebellion on the island of Crete (Kríti), which supported union with an independent Greek state.

13 January 1822: The independence movement having captured much territory, including Athens, Greek independence was proclaimed at Epidaurus.

1824–27: Internal differences within the independence movement enabled the Imperial forces were able to regain large portions of the territory they had lost, including Athens.

April 1827: Ioannis Kapodistrias was elected President of Greece.

20 October 1827: France, Russia and the United Kingdom ('the Powers'), eager to reduce Ottoman strength in Europe, joined the conflict in support of Greek independence; the Powers combined to defeat the Ottoman fleet at Navarino.

1828: French forces having expelled Egyptian forces from Greece, Russia declared war on the Ottoman Empire; the Russians gained an advantage on several fronts and the following year the Ottomans were forced to negotiate a peace.

16 September 1829: By the Treaty of Adrianople, which concluded the war between Russia and the Ottomans, the latter recognized Greek autonomy; Greece henceforth considered itself independent, although its independence was not officially recognized until the signing of the Protocol of London, in the following year.

1831: Kapodistrias was assassinated; the Powers created a hereditary monarchy; in 1833 the Bavarian Prince Otto accepted the throne and moved the capital (hitherto at Nafplion) to Athens.

1832: The Ottoman Empire formally recognized the independence of Greece.

1843: Otto convened a National Assembly, which drafted a Constitution providing for a bicameral parliament.

1862: King Otto was deposed by the military and replaced by the Danish Prince, William, who assumed the style of King George I.

1864: The United Kingdom officially ceded the Ionian Islands (a British protectorate since 1815) to Greece; a new Constitution, reducing the powers of the monarchy, was enacted.

1866: A further uprising in Crete saw many Ottoman casualties, but was eventually suppressed.

1897: Greece's plans to annex Crete resulted in the 'Thirty Day War' with the Ottomans; Greece was defeated and withdrew from the island; according to the terms of a peace settlement the Ottomans also withdrew and Crete became an international protectorate under King George I.

1905: The president of Crete's autonomous assembly, Eleftherios Venizelos, declared the island to be in union with Greece.

1910: Following a *coup d'état* by the military, Venizelos was elected Prime Minister of Greece.

30 May 1913: The Treaty of London (United Kingdom) concluded the First Balkan War, in which a league of Bulgaria, Greece, Montenegro and Serbia succeeded in removing the Turks from the bulk of their European possessions; Crete was united with Greece.

August 1913: The Treaty of Bucharest (Romania) concluded the Second Balkan War; Bulgaria lost Macedonia, which was divided between Serbia and Greece.

October 1916: Owing to a difference in opinion about Greece's alignment in the First World War (Venizelos supported the Entente Powers, of France, Russia, Serbia and the United Kingdom, whereas King Konstantinos (Constantine) I imposed a policy of neutrality), Venizelos established a rival Government in Thessaloníki (Salonika).

June 1917: France and the United Kingdom ousted the King and imposed Venizelos as Prime Minister of the whole of Greece.

29 November 1919: The Treaty of Neuilly ceded Bulgarian territory to Greece; the Allied Powers had also granted Greece permission to occupy the predominantly Greek region of Smyrna (now Izmir, Turkey) on the coast of Asia Minor.

1920: Venizelos was defeated in legislative elections; a new, royalist administration restored the monarchy's power.

1922: The Turks drove back Greek forces which had advanced far into Anatolia, forcing them to evacuate from Smyrna; the Turks then set the city alight; thousands of refugees fled to Greece.

1923: The Treaty of Lausanne ordered the exchange of religious minorities in Greece and Turkey; Muslims resident in Greece resettled in Turkey and Christians from Turkey moved to Greece.

1924: The monarchy was abolished when King Konstantinos I was asked to abdicate by the military.

1928: Venizelos was reappointed Prime Minister.

1935: Following an attempted *coup d'état*, a plebiscite (now considered to have been manipulated) resulted in the restoration of the monarchy and the accession of King George II. Venizelos fled to France (where he died in 1936).

April 1936: King George II appointed Gen. Ioannis Metaxas as Prime Minister, resulting in the organization of industrial action by the Kommunistiko Komma Ellados (KKE—Communist Party of Greece).

4 August 1936: Metaxas persuaded the King to impose what became known as the 'Regime of the Fourth of August 1936', in which significant constitutional clauses were suspended; Parliament was dissolved.

28 October 1940: Italy's leader, Benito Mussolini, demanded that Italian forces occupying Albania be permitted to pass through Greece; Metaxas refused this demand, resulting in an invasion of Italian forces from Albania.

April 1941: Germany invaded Greece, which became subject to Bulgarian, German and Italian occupation; the King and his self-appointed ministers fled into exile in London (United Kingdom) and then Cairo (Egypt).

October 1944: Greek and British forces succeeded in liberating Greece from occupation.

December 1944: Communist groups that had formed part of the resistance movement launched an armed insurgency against the Government of Georgios Papandreou, recently returned from exile; fighting continued until early 1945, when a peace agreement was reached, the terms of which included the holding of elections.

1946: A general election in March resulted in an overwhelming victory for royalist parties. A referendum confirmed support for the restoration of the monarchy. Communist groups formed a Democratic Army, whose confrontations with the official Greek army escalated into civil war.

1949: The Communist forces were defeated and the civil war ended.

1952: A new Constitution was enacted, providing for a parliamentary democracy, with a monarch as head of state. The Greek Rally, led by Field Marshal Alexandros Papagos, won a decisive victory in the general election.

1953: Greece, Turkey and Yugoslavia signed a treaty of friendship.

1955: Papagos died in office and was succeeded by Konstantinos Karamanlis. The new premier dissolved the Greek Rally and founded the Ethniki Rizospastiki Enosis (ERE—National Radical Union).

1956: The ERE won an absolute majority of parliamentary seats in the general election; Karamanlis was reappointed Prime Minister.

May 1958: Following legislative elections the ERE increased its representation in the Vouli (Parliament).

1961: The ERE won absolute majorities of votes and parliamentary seats in the general election; the Enosis Kentrou (Centre Union) was founded by Georgios Papandreou.

1963: Karamanlis resigned; in the resultant general election the Centre Union won the greatest number of seats, though it failed to gain an absolute majority.

1964: King Konstantinos II acceded to the throne on the death of his father, King Paul. In further legislative elections, the Centre Union won an absolute majority of parliamentary seats.

21 April 1967: A group of army officers seized power and imposed military rule; political leaders were arrested and the general election, scheduled for May, was indefinitely postponed.

13 December 1967: Col Georgios Papadopoulos, who had emerged as the most powerful figure in the 'regime of the Colonels', became Prime Minister; he assumed the foreign affairs portfolio in January 1970 and became regent in March 1972.

1 June 1973: Following a failed naval mutiny, allegedly inspired by King Konstantinos, the monarchy was abolished and Greece declared a republic, with Papadopoulos assuming the presidency in the following month.

November 1973: Amid increasing public disenchantment with the military regime, unrest among students at the National Polytechnic was violently suppressed by the army; Papadopoulos was ousted in an internal military coup led by the head of the military police, Brig.-Gen. Demetrios Ioannidis; Lt-Gen. Phaedon Ghizikis was appointed President and a largely civilian cabinet, led by Adamantios Androutsopoulos, was installed; however, effective power remained with Ioannidis.

July 1974: Following an unsuccessful attempt to depose the President of Cyprus, Archbishop Makarios, and the subsequent failure to prevent the Turkish invasion and occupation of northern Cyprus, the Androutsopoulos Government collapsed; the military regime was unable to retain power and Karamanlis was asked to return from exile to form a Government of National Salvation.

November 1974: Karamanlis' new party, Nea Demokratia (New Democracy— ND) won an absolute majority of parliamentary seats at the general election.

December 1974: A proposal to restore the monarchy was defeated in a plebiscite. Michael Stassinopoulos, head of the Council of State, was appointed President.

11 June 1975: A new Constitution was enacted, providing for a parliamentary republic with certain executive powers vested in the presidency; Konstantinos Tsatsos replaced Stassinopoulos as President. In the same month Greece submitted a formal application for membership of the European Communities (EC—known as the European Union, EU, from November 1993).

November 1977: ND was returned to power, albeit with a reduced majority, following legislative elections; the Panellinion Socialistikon Kinema (Panhellenic Socialist Movement—PASOK), led by Andreas Papandreou, became the second-largest party in Parliament.

May 1980: Karamanlis was elected President; Georgios Rallis succeeded him as premier and ND leader.

1 January 1981: Greece formally acceded to membership of the EC.

October 1981: In a general election, PASOK obtained an absolute majority in Parliament; Papandreou subsequently formed Greece's first socialist Government.

March 1985: Karamanlis resigned in protest at government plans to amend the Constitution, reducing presidential powers; Christos Sartzetakis was appointed head of state.

June 1985: PASOK retained the largest number of seats (161) in elections to the 300-member Parliament.

August 1985: Greece and Albania reopened their common frontier, closed since 1940; Greece renounced its claim to the Albanian region of North Epirus, which contained a significant minority of ethnic Greeks.

March 1986: In spite of opposition, the Parliament approved constitutional amendments which transferred many of the President's executive powers to the legislature.

March 1987: Greece narrowly avoided military confrontation with Turkey in a dispute over petroleum-exploration rights in the Aegean Sea; in the following January the premiers of both countries signed an agreement not to engage in military conflict.

August 1987: The Greek Government proclaimed that it no longer considered the country to be at war with Albania, a state which had persisted since the Second World War.

November 1988: Several prominent members of the PASOK Government resigned after being implicated in a major financial scandal involving alleged embezzlement from the Bank of Crete.

June 1989: ND won the greatest number of seats in parliamentary elections, but failed to gain an overall majority, leading to the formation of a non-political, interim Government, headed by Tzannis Tzannetakis, which announced its intention to implement a *katharsis*, or a campaign of purification, of Greek politics.

November 1989: No party gained a majority at further legislative elections; another coalition administration was formed, led this time by Xenofon Zolotas; however, this Government collapsed in February 1990 and a non-political cabinet was reinstated until a further ballot could be held.

April 1990: ND secured a one-seat majority in another round of elections, and was thus able to form a single-party Government, led by Konstantinos Mitsotakis. In the following month, Karamanlis was appointed President for a second five-year term.

April 1992: Mitsotakis assumed responsibility for the foreign-affairs portfolio in order to co-ordinate his Government's opposition to attempts by the former Yugoslav republic of Macedonia (FYRM) to gain international recognition; Greece feared that the inclusion of the word 'Macedonia' in that country's title might result in territorial claims on the Greek province of the same name; the Government withdrew its objection in early 1993.

October 1993: The loss of the Government's narrow majority following the defection of several deputies led to its resignation and the holding of legislative elections; PASOK won the largest number of seats and formed a Government, led once again by Papandreou, who had been acquitted of all charges relating to the Bank of Crete financial scandal in January 1992.

February 1994: The PASOK Government implemented what was effectively a trade embargo, preventing the transport of any goods, other than humanitarian aid, into the FYRM via the Greek port of Thessaloníki; the initiative was condemned by the international community.

10 March 1995: Konstantinos Stefanopoulos, leader of the Komma Dimokratikis Ananeosis (Party of Democratic Renewal—DIANA), was elected President by the legislature.

October 1995: Relations between Greece and the FYRM were normalized, following the implementation of agreements on access to Thessaloníki and alterations to the FYRM's flag.

15 January 1996: Andreas Papandreou resigned as Prime Minister, owing to ill health (he died in June); he was succeeded by Konstantinos (Costas) Simitis.

31 January 1996: In spite of considerable domestic opposition, Prime Minister Simitis complied with a US petition to withdraw Greek military vessels from the area surrounding Imia (Kardak), a small group of uninhabited islands in the Aegean Sea, following Turkish attempts to claim sovereignty of them.

22 September 1996: PASOK, led by Simitis, won 162 seats in the legislative election, having obtained 41.5% of the votes cast; ND won 38.2% of the votes and 108 seats. A Government, similar in composition to the previous one, was subsequently formed.

July 1997: Direct talks held in Madrid (Spain) between Simitis and the Turkish President, Süleyman Demirel, led to the so-called 'Madrid Declaration', in which the two countries pledged not to use violence or the threat of violence to resolve bilateral disputes; nevertheless, relations between the two countries remained strained.

27 May 1998: A widely-observed general strike was held throughout the country, in protest at the Government's privatization plans and the continuing implementation of austerity measures; industrial action continued throughout 1998 and 1999.

18 February 1999: Several members of the cabinet, including the Ministers of Foreign Affairs and of the Interior, Public Affairs and Decentralization resigned, after it emerged that Abdullah Ocalan, leader of the Kurdistan Workers' Party (PKK—the proscribed Kurdish movement which sought secession from Turkey), who was wanted in Turkey on terrorist charges, had been given refuge at the Greek embassy in Kenya.

17 August 1999: Following a severe earthquake in north-western Turkey, Greece provided financial and material assistance and renounced its veto on EU financial aid to that country; Turkey reciprocated in the following month when an earthquake in Athens left more than 60,000 people homeless.

20 November 1999: A visit by US President Bill Clinton prompted a series of public protests against the USA's involvement in the North Atlantic Treaty Organization's (NATO) bombing of the Federal Republic of Yugoslavia earlier in the year.

10–11 December 1999: At the EU summit meeting in Helsinki (Finland), Greece supported Turkey's candidacy for EU membership.

20 January 2000: Georgios Papandreou became the first Greek Minister of Foreign Affairs to visit Turkey since 1962; the two countries agreed to hold direct talks on their military presence in the Aegean Sea area and signed a number of economic co-operation agreements.

9 February 2000: President Stefanopoulos became the first incumbent Greek head of state to be re-elected to the post, by 269 of the 300 parliamentary deputies.

9 April 2000: In the legislative elections, PASOK, again led by Simitis, won 43.8% of the votes cast and 158 parliamentary seats, narrowly defeating ND, which obtained 42.7% of the votes and 125 seats; the KKE won 5.2% of the ballot and 11 seats, and the Coalition of the Left and Progress secured 3.2% and six seats; three days later Simitis formed a new Government, the principal portfolios remaining with their previous incumbents.

3 May 2000: The European Commission announced that Greece would be permitted to join EMU on 1 January 2001.

8 June 2000: The assassination, in Athens, of a British diplomat by what were believed to be members of the 17 November Revolutionary Organization led to international concern that Greece was failing to co-operate fully with international anti-terrorist efforts.

19 June 2000: Greece received a formal invitation to join Stage III of the EU's programme of Economic and Monetary Union (EMU), from 1 January 2001; the Government had submitted its application in March.

1 January 2001: Greece formally became the 12th member of Stage III of EMU.

Hungary

906: The Magyars, under the leadership of Árpád (896–907), migrated to the Hungarian plains.

1000: The coronation of St Stephen I (997–1038), with a crown sent by the Pope, established Hungary as a western Christian kingdom.

1458–90: Reign of Matthias I Corvinus, who prevailed against the rival claims to the throne by the House of Habsburg, extended Hungarian hegemony and moved his capital to Vienna (now in Austria).

1526: The Hungarian army was destroyed by the forces of the Ottoman Empire at the battle of Mohács; with the death of Louis II, the Habsburgs inherited Hungary's Crown of St Stephen.

1541: Hungary was partitioned between the Habsburgs and the Ottomans.

1687: The Imperial Diet of Pressburg (Bratislava) declared the Hungarian Crown to be a hereditary possession of the Austrian House of Habsburg.

1699: The Ottomans ceded Hungary (including Transylvania and Slavonia) to its conqueror, the Habsburg Holy Roman Emperor.

1711: The Peace of Sathmar granted self-administration to Hungary, subject to the laws of the Imperial Diet.

6 August 1806: Francis II, under pressure from Napoleon I of France, dissolved the Holy Roman Empire of the German Nation and reigned henceforth as Francis I, having assumed the imperial title for Austria in 1804.

1848: An uprising in Hungary under Louis Kossuth established a national government, but, in December, refused to recognize the new Emperor, Francis Joseph I.

1849: Imperial armies regained control of Hungary.

1867: The Compromise (*Ausgleich*) of 1867 reorganized the Habsburg Empire as the Dual Monarchy of Austria (Cisleithania) and Hungary (Transleithania); Emperor Francis Joseph I was crowned as King of Hungary.

28 June 1914: The assassination of the heir to the Dual Monarchy, Archduke Francis Ferdinand, in Sarajevo (Bosnia and Herzegovina) led to the start of the First World War.

21 November 1916: Death of Francis Joseph I and the accession of his grand-nephew, Charles I.

4 October 1918: Austria-Hungary accepted the same armistice conditions as Germany (to take effect on 3 November).

25 October 1918: Count Mihály Károlyi established a national council following the decision of the Hungarian Diet to recall its troops and the effective dissolution of the Danubian Monarchy.

31 October 1918: Károlyi became premier with the backing of Charles I, who then renounced participation in government.

16 November 1918: Hungary was declared a republic, Károlyi becoming President.

20 December 1918: The Hungarian Communist Party was established by Béla Kun.

21 March 1919: Károlyi resigned in protest at the Allies' territorial demands; Kun formed a coalition Government of Communists and Social Democrats.

August 1919: A Romanian counter-offensive, following Hungarian incursions into Slovakia and Transylvania, resulted in the flight of Kun and a brief occupation of Budapest.

March 1920: Adm. Miklós Horthy de Nagybánya restored Hungary as a monarchy, but with a vacant throne and himself as Regent.

4 June 1920: Signature of the Treaty of Trianon concluding peace at the end of the First World War: Hungary ceded Slovakia and Carpatho-Ukraine (Sub-Carpathian Ruthenia) to Czechoslovakia, Transylvania to Romania, the Banat to Romania and Yugoslavia, Croatia-Slavonia to Yugoslavia and the Burgenland to Austria; the consequent desire of the Hungarians to revise the borders resulted in close relations with Germany.

February 1939: Hungary joined Germany and Italy in the Anti-Comintern Pact.

11 April 1941: Hungary entered the Second World War on the side of Germany.

March 1944: German troops occupied Hungary.

October 1944: Regent Horthy secretly concluded an armistice with the USSR, but was forced to rescind it and was then arrested and replaced by the Fascist, Ferenc Szálasi.

20 January 1945: A provisional government signed an armistice with the USSR and agreed to the Hungarian borders of 1937 (as established at Trianon).

November 1945: Following a general election, the Smallholders Party, the largest party, formed a coalition Government with the Communists.

August 1947: The Communists became the largest single party in the general election, after the discrediting of the KGP.

June 1948: The Communist Party merged with the Social Democratic Party to form the Hungarian Workers' Party (HWP).

May 1949: The Hungarian People's Front for Independence (dominated by the HWP) presented a single list of candidates.

August 1949: A People's Republic was established.

1953: Imre Nagy became Prime Minister.

April 1955: Nagy was forced to resign by Mátyás Rákosi, the First Secretary of the HWP, and was expelled from the Party.

July 1956: Rákosi was forced to resign and was replaced by Ernő Gerő.

23 October 1956: Demonstrations and rioting broke out in Budapest against the Communist Government.

24 October 1956: Soviet tanks were sent in to quell the rioting.

25 October 1956: The Communist Government was replaced by a reformist regime headed by Imre Nagy; Soviet forces withdrew.

3 November 1956: Nagy established an all-party coalition Government, having already renounced membership of the Warsaw Pact.

4 November 1956: Some 200,000 Soviet troops invaded the country; Nagy was overthrown and János Kádár was installed by the USSR as the new premier in an all-Communist Government.

June 1958: Nagy and four associates were executed for their part in the 1956 uprising. Kádár became leader of the newly formed Hungarian Socialist Workers' Party (HSWP).

1 January 1968: The New Economic Mechanism, which combined central-planning and market instruments, was introduced.

June 1985: The legislative elections permitted voters a wider choice of candidates under the terms of a new electoral law.

October 1986: A group of academics, supported by Imre Pószgay and other reformers in the HSWP, drew up a paper, 'Change and Reform', which heralded the breakdown in consensus both inside and outside the Party.

June 1987: Károly Grósz was appointed Chairman of the Council of Ministers; he introduced some reforms aimed at alleviating the economic problems of the country.

15 March 1988: Some 10,000 people marched through Budapest, on the 140th anniversary of the 1848 uprising against Austrian rule, demanding the introduction of genuine reforms.

April 1988: Four reformers within the HSWP were expelled from the Party for demanding radical political and economic reform. A radical youth group formed an opposition party, the Federation of Young Democrats (FYD).

May 1988: At a special ideological conference of the HSWP János Kádár was replaced as General Secretary of the Central Committee by Károly Grósz; Kádár also lost his membership of the Politburo. Various opposition groups formed the Network of Free Initiatives—subsequently renamed the Alliance of Free Democrats (AFD).

June 1988: Some 50,000 people demonstrated in Budapest against the Romanian Government's proposed destruction of 7,000 villages, including 1,500 ethnic Hungarian villages.

July 1988: The Central Committee of the HSWP approved an austere economic reform programme which would lead to a reduction in subsidies, a devaluation of the forint and a rapid rise in unemployment.

21 November 1988: Miklós Németh replaced Grósz as Chairman of the Council of Ministers.

20 December 1988: The National Assembly voted to allow the right to demonstrate and the establishment of independent political organizations.

February 1989: The HSWP agreed to the establishment of a multi-party system; its Central Committee agreed to abandon the clause in the Constitution guaranteeing the HSWP's leading role in society.

15 March 1989: Some 100,000 people took part in an anti-government demonstration in Budapest.

May 1989: The Chairman of the Council of Ministers, Németh, reorganized his cabinet and declared that it would henceforth be answerable to the National Assembly before the HSWP; Kádár was relieved of his post as Chairman of the HSWP. 'Round-table' negotiations between the HSWP and various opposition groups began.

16 June 1989: Following the rehabilitation of Imre Nagy he was reburied with four associates at a state funeral in Budapest which was attended by 300,000 people.

23 July 1989: An opposition deputy was elected to the National Assembly, in a by-election, for the first time since 1947 (by September there were seven opposition deputies, who then formed a parliamentary group).

10 September 1989: The border with Austria was opened allowing the exodus of thousands of East Germans seeking to emigrate to the West.

18 September 1989: Against a background of continuing demonstrations and industrial unrest, during round-table negotiations it was decided that the Constitution and electoral law be modified and that the Presidential Council be dissolved.

7–8 October 1989: The HSWP voted to dissolve itself and reconstitute as the Hungarian Socialist Party (HSP); Rezső Nyers was elected Chairman of the new party.

18 October 1989: Mátyás Szűrös was elected to the newly created post of President of the Republic, in an acting capacity.

23 October 1989: The country was renamed the Republic of Hungary.

12 March 1990: Following an agreement with the USSR, the withdrawal of Soviet troops began (completed by June 1991).

March–April 1990: After two rounds of voting in the general election, the Hungarian Democratic Forum (HDF) won 165 of the 386 seats in the National Assembly, while the AFD gained 92, the Independent Smallholders' Party (ISP) 43 and the HSP only 33. The HDF agreed a coalition Government with the ISP, the Christian Democratic People's Party (CDPP) and independents.

2 May 1990: Árpád Göncz (AFD) was elected interim President and Speaker of the National Assembly (and was supported by the HDF in the presidential election); the following day József Antall (HDF) was appointed Chairman of the Council of Ministers.

June 1990: The Ibusz travel agency became the first Hungarian company to be privatized and trading resumed on the Budapest Stock Exchange after a 42-year break. Hungary began a process of disengagement from the activities of the Warsaw Pact.

3 August 1990: Göncz was elected President of the Republic by the National Assembly.

October 1990: The Government offered all state industries for sale; later in the month price rises had to be limited in order to end the disruptions and protests throughout the country.

February 1991: Hungary, Czechoslovakia and Poland agreed a common approach to a number of foreign-policy and defence issues at a meeting in the town of Visegrad, thereby earning the epithet of the 'Visegrad Group'.

28 June 1991: A protocol providing for the dissolution, within 90 days, of the Council for Mutual Economic Assistance (CMEA or Comecon) was signed in Budapest.

February 1992: József Torgyán, the leader of the ISP, announced his party's departure from the government coalition; however, only 13 ISP deputies followed his lead.

April 1993: Hungary and Slovakia agreed to submit the dispute over Slovakia's re-routeing of the Danube, to feed the hydroelectric plant at Gabčikovo, to the International Court of Justice (based in The Hague, Netherlands), after European Community (EC) mediation had failed.

June 1993: After having been expelled from the HDF at the beginning of the month, the right-wing István Csurka formed his own party, the Hungarian Justice and Life Party (HJLP).

12 December 1993: The Prime Minister, Antall, died; Péter Boross, hitherto the interior minister, succeeded himas premier.

1 February 1994: Hungary's associate membership of the European Union (EU, as the EC was known from November 1993) came into effect.

May 1994: The general election was decided in two rounds of voting; the HSP obtained a clear parliamentary majority, winning a total of 209 out of 386 seats; the AFD won 70 seats; the HDF 37; and the ISP (renamed the Independent Smallholders' and Peasants' Party—ISPP) 26. The CDPP and the FYD won 22 and 20 seats, respectively. The HSP and the AFD subsequently signed a coalition agreement, which installed Gyula Horn of the HSP as Prime Minister.

January 1995: László Bekesi resigned as Minister of Finance, following a disagreement with the Prime Minister over the economic reform programme. He was succeeded by Dr Lajos Bokros the following month.

March 1995: An austerity programme was announced by the Government, which included drastic reductions in government spending and a 9% devaluation of the forint. Later, despite nationalist opposition in Hungary, a Treaty of Friendship and Co-operation was signed between Hungary and Slovakia, which guaranteed the rights of ethnic minorities in the two countries and recognized the inviolability of their joint border (it came into effect in May 1996).

April 1995: The FYD renamed itself the Federation of Young Democrats— Hungarian Civic Party (FYD—HCP).

19 June 1995: President Göncz was re-elected by an overwhelming majority in the National Assembly.

March 1996: Iván Szabó and other members of the HDF broke away from the party to form the Hungarian Democratic People's Party (HDPP), a moderate, conservative body.

16 September 1996: Hungary and Romania signed a Treaty of Understanding, Co-operation and Good-Neighbourliness, according to which Hungary renounced any claim on Transylvania and Romania agreed to guarantee rights to its ethnic Hungarian minority.

October 1996: The directors of the Hungarian Privatization and State Holding Company (ÁPV Rt) were dismissed, following the revelation of improper financial dealings (in February 1997 a parliamentary investigative committee attributed responsibility for the scandal to the Government).

25 September 1997: The International Court of Justice concluded that both Hungary and Slovakia had contravened international law by their actions in the Gabčikovo-Nagymarós hydroelectric scheme.

16 November 1997: In a referendum, 85.3% of the participants (comprising 49% of the registered electorate) voted in favour of Hungary's accession to the North Atlantic Treaty Organization (NATO), which the country had been formally invited to join, from 1999, in July.

27 February 1998: Hungary and Slovakia finally negotiated the basis of an agreement on the Gabčikovo-Nagymarós project (the next month Hungary confirmed that it would not build a dam at Nagymarós, but would conduct environmental impact studies).

30 March 1998: Hungary began negotiations on accession to the EU, in the first phase of the EU's eastward enlargement, expected early in the next decade.

10 and 24 May 1998: The general election was decided in two rounds of voting. The second round of voting in the general election, in which 57% of the electorate took part, resulted in: the FYD—HCP obtaining a parliamentary majority, with a total of 147 out of 386 seats; the HSP winning 134 seats; the ISPP 48 seats; and the AFD 24 seats. The HDF and the HJLP won 18 and 14 seats, respectively.

June 1998: The FYD—HCP, the ISPP and the HDF signed a coalition agreement; the leader of the FYD—HCP, Viktor Orbán, was appointed Prime Minister.

3 September 1998: Slovakia announced its decision to refer once again the issue of the Gabčikovo-Nagymarós hydroelectric scheme to the International Court of Justice.

5 September 1998: Following the resignation of Horn from the leadership of the HSP in response to the party's electoral defeat, a former foreign minister, László Kovács, was elected Chairman.

18 October 1998: In municipal elections, the government coalition received 39.6% of votes cast, while the HSP and AFD won 35.1% of the votes.

12 March 1999: Following approval by an overwhelming majority in the National Assembly in the previous month, Hungary officially became a full member of NATO.

May 1999: Hungary allowed NATO use of its air space and military bases to facilitate NATO's aerial bombardment of the neighbouring Federal Republic of Yugoslavia (FRY); however, there were widespread fears that the Government's co-operation with NATO would lead to reprisals against the ethnic Hungarian population in the Serbian province of Vojvodina.

7 December 1999: György Matolcsy was appointed Minister of Economic Affairs following the resignation of Attila Chikán and Zoltán Rockenbauer acceded to the post of Minister of National Cultural Heritage following József Hámori's appointment as scientific policy adviser to the premier.

29 January 2000: Following the FYD—HCP's decision to separate the posts of party Chairman and Prime Minister, László Kövér, Minister without Portfolio responsible for National Security, replaced Orbán as party leader.

2 February 2000: Ibolya Dávid, the justice minister and leader of the HDF, announced the formation of an alliance which included the HDPP and the Entrepreneur's Party; the initiative, to be known as Olive Branch 2000 (Bekejobb 2000), would allow the parties to better promote centre-right Christian values in Hungarian politics.

February 2000: A leak of mineral waste from the Baia Mare gold mine in Romania led to the accidental poisoning of the Danube and Tisza rivers and consequent widespread environmental damage in the region.

13 April 2000: Two right-wing independent deputies, former members of the FYD—HCP and the HJLP, formed their own parliamentary grouping, to be known as the Alliance for Eastern Hungary.

16 May 2000: Following disagreement with the Prime Minister over changes to the responsibilities of several ministries, the Minister for Transport, Communications and Water Management, Kalman Katona, was dismissed; he was replaced by László Nogradi.

31 May 2000: The Ministry of Finance established a fuel price-monitoring system, following a sharp increase in petroleum prices; the Hungarian Oil and Gas Company (MOL—Magyar Olajés Gáziparirt Rt) began to reduce prices in June.

5–6 June 2000: In the presidential election the sole candidate, Ferenc Madl, gained 251 out of a possible 386 votes in the National Assembly; as he failed to win the requisite 258 votes, a second round of voting was required, held the next day; however, after this ballot too proved inconclusive, a third round of voting took place, in which Madl secured the presidency.

15 June 2000: The Minister of the Environment, Pál Pepó, resigned; he was succeeded by Ferenc Ligetvari of the ISCP.

21 June 2000: The Chairman of MOL, Janos Csak, resigned in protest at the Government's decision to allow an increase of 12% in the price of natural gas.

4 August 2000: Ferenc Madl took office as President of the Republic.

6 November 2000: László Nogradi resigned as Minister of Transport, Communications and Water Management following an incident in which his official car, travelling in excess of the local speed limit on his orders, was involved in an accident resulting in the deaths of two people.

23 November 2000: The Minister of Finance, Zsigmond Járai, announced that the Government intended to abandon the so-called 'crawling peg' policy of progressive devaluation of the forint relative to the euro in 2001.

29 November 2000: The Governments of Hungary and Poland began negotiations on the formation of an alliance between MOL and the partially state-owned Polish petroleum company, PKN Orlen.

13 December 2000: The Prime Minister, Viktor Orbán, announced that he would request President Madl to appoint Járai as Governor of the Hungarian National Bank, upon the departure in March 2001 of György Surányi. Járai would be succeeded as Minister of Finance by Mihaly Varga, hitherto deputy minister. Orbán also announced the retirement of the Minister of Health, Árpád Gógl, who was replaced in January 2001 by István Mikola.

Iceland

860: Norwegian (Viking) explorers reached Iceland, hitherto inhabited only by hermitical Celtic monks.

874: The Norwegian settlement and colonization of Iceland began.

930: The codification of laws in Norway provided for a separate Icelandic state. The Althing (Alþing), the world's oldest surviving assembly and claimed to be the first Parliament in Europe, was founded.

1262: Iceland passed under Norwegian rule.

1380: The union of the Norwegian and Danish thrones saw Iceland become a possession of the Danish Crown.

1536: Lutheranism, which had began to spread in Iceland, was declared the established religion by the Danish Crown.

1602: A trade monopoly for Denmark was established in Iceland.

1915: Female suffrage was granted.

1918: Amid growing nationalist sentiment in Iceland, the Danish Government granted the country the status of a separate possession of the Danish crown.

17 June 1944: Iceland severed its link with Denmark (occupied by German forces since 1940) and became a sovereign republic. The Constitution provided for a directly elected President and for the Althing to be directly elected on the basis of proportional representation.

1949: Iceland became a member of the North Atlantic Treaty Organization (NATO).

1951: By agreement with Iceland, the USA began using Keflavík as a base for an airborne early warning system and also for observation in the North Atlantic Ocean.

1952: Iceland joined Denmark, Norway and Sweden in establishing the Nordic Council.

1959: A coalition between the Independence Party (IP—Sjálfstædisflokkurinn) and the Social Democratic Party (SDP—Althýduflokkurinn) was formed, lasting in government until 1971.

1964: Iceland declared its territorial waters to extend for 12 nautical miles (22 km) from its coast; opposition to this extension was led by the United Kingdom, which was concerned about the impact on fishing rights, and resulted in the first of the disputes known as the 'cod wars'.

1970: Iceland's membership of the European Free Trade Association (EFTA) was formalized.

1971: A general election led to a coalition of the Progressive Party (PP—Framsóknarflokkurinn), the People's Alliance (PA—Althýdubandalag) and the Union of Liberals and Leftists; the premier was Ólafur Jóhannesson (PP).

1972: The territorial waters around Iceland were again extended, to 50 nautical miles and the resulting second 'cod war' was not resolved until the signing of a fishing-rights agreement the following year.

1974: In the general election, right-wing parties increased their share of the vote; the IP and the PP formed a coalition, led by Geir Hallgrímsson (IP).

1975: Iceland unilaterally imposed a limit for foreign fishing vessels of 200 nautical miles from its coast provoking the third and most serious 'cod war'; the United Kingdom deployed several naval ships to protect fishing vessels and there were a number of casualties.

1976: Iceland temporarily severed diplomatic relations with the United Kingdom, the first ever such disruption between two NATO member countries; an agreement was reached later in the year, and the British fishing fleet withdrew from the area.

1978: Owing to disagreements over economic policy and the PA's advocacy of Iceland's withdrawal from NATO, coalition negotiations continued for two months after the general election before Ólafur Jóhannesson formed a Government of the PP with the PA and the SDP.

1979: Iceland declared its exclusive fishing rights in waters within a boundary 200 nautical miles from its coastline; fishing rights were to remain the main area of contention between Iceland and its closest neighbours.

1979: The SDP withdrew from the ruling coalition and its leader, Benedikt Gröndal, then led an interim administration which continued in office after an inconclusive general election.

February 1980: The IP, the PA and the PP formed a coalition led by Gunnar Thoroddsen (IP).

1 August 1980: Vigdís Finnbogadóttir, the world's first popularly elected female head of state, took office as President of Iceland.

April 1983: In the general election, two newly formed parties, the Social Democratic Alliance (SDA) and the Women's List (WL—Samtök um kvennalista), obtained almost 13% of the votes cast; the IP won 38.7% of the vote and formed a Government with the PP, although Steingrímur Hermannsson of the PP became premier.

May 1985: The Althing unanimously declared Iceland a 'nuclear-free zone', banning the entry of nuclear weapons.

April 1987: A general election for an enlarged, 63-seat Althing was held; both ruling parties suffered losses, but mainly the IP, to the right-wing Citizen's Party (CP—Borgaraflokkurinn), which had been formed one month earlier by Albert Guðmundsson, a former minister and IP member.

July 1987: A coalition of the IP, the PP and the SDP was formally constituted, with Thorsteinn Pálsson, leader of the IP since November 1983, as Prime Minster.

September 1988: The SDP and the PP withdrew from the coalition following disagreements concerning economic policy; the PP's Steingrímur Hermannsson formed a centre-left coalition with the SDP and the PA, although the Government committed itself to a number of economic austerity measures.

September 1989: The CP (now without Guðmundsson as leader) and the Association for Equality and Social Justice entered the coalition Government.

1991: The Constitution was amended, ending the system of dividing the Althing into an Upper House (one-third of the elected deputies) and a Lower House.

April 1991: In a general election, the IP (Davíd Oddsson replaced Pálsson as leader in the previous month) was returned as the largest single party, but the incumbent coalition only collapsed when the SDP withdrew over failure to agree policy towards the creation of a European Economic Area (EEA). A new coalition comprising the IP and the SDP, led by Oddsson, was formed.

June 1992: Iceland withdrew from the International Whaling Commission (IWC) over its hunting restrictions.

August 1993: Iceland and Norway began a dispute over fishing rights in an area of the Barents Sea fished by Iceland, but over which Norway claimed jurisdiction. The dispute continued through 1994 during which the Norwegian coastguards cut the nets of Icelandic trawlers fishing for cod in the disputed region. Canada officially recognized Norway's sovereign rights over the disputed area in January 1995.

January 1994: An agreement between the European Union (EU) and Iceland came into force, whereby Iceland's fisheries products were made tariff-free to the EU and Iceland permitted EU vessels to catch 3,000 metric tons of fish per year in its waters.

April 1995: In a general election, the IP secured 25 seats (37% of the votes cast) and Oddsson remained premier, but formed a new coalition with the PP—both parties opposed the Common Fisheries Policy of the EU, hindering Iceland's application to join.

29 June 1996: An election to succeed Vigdís Finnbogadóttir after four terms as President was won by Ólafur Ragnar Grímsson, a former leader of the PA, with 41% of the votes cast.

August 1996: Denmark and Iceland entered into a fishing dispute over the area in the Atlantic Ocean between Iceland and Greenland, a dependency of Denmark.

8 May 1999: In a general election, the incumbent coalition retained a majority in the Althing: the IP gained 40.7% of the votes cast (26 seats) and the PP gained 18.4% (12 seats); the opposition Alliance (Samfylkinginn), formed in January by the SDP, the WL and the PA, obtained 26.8% of the votes cast (17 seats).

2 August 2000: Grímsson was reappointed President; no alternative candidate stood for election.

Ireland

444: The establishment of the island's first episcopal see at Armagh marked a successful evangelization of Ireland by a Roman Briton, St Patrick, even though the island had never been occupied by the secular Roman Empire.

839: Dublin was founded by Viking (Norse) invaders, who were beginning to settle the coast rather than merely raiding.

979: The Norsemen were defeated at Tara, in a rebellion led by Malachi, an indigenous Celt of the interior.

1014: Brian Boru (Bhriain Boroimhe), king of much of southern Ireland, defeated the Norsemen at Clontarf, although he himself was killed.

1102: The Norwegian Viking king, Magnus Barefoot, was killed on an expedition to Ireland as Norse influence began to decline and the Celtic clans and the five kingdoms enjoyed some unity under a High King.

1155: King Henry II of England received a papal bull authorizing the invasion of Ireland.

1171: The English conquest of Ireland began, meeting strong resistance; Henry declared himself Lord of Ireland in 1175, although English influence was limited to the major towns on the coastal fringe.

1494: The reassertion of the English Crown's authority in a fractious Ireland began after the turbulence of dynastic civil war in England: the Irish Parliament was made subordinate to the English Parliament.

1541: King Henry VIII of England was proclaimed King of Ireland and Head of the Irish Church; attempts to introduce the Reformation into Ireland were largely unsuccessful, the majority of the population retaining the Roman Catholic faith.

1558: Under Elizabeth I, the policy of 'plantation' was introduced, entailing the confiscation of lands owned by Roman Catholics and their being awarded to Protestants; the policy led to a further increase in the number and intensity of insurrections against English rule.

1595–1603: An uprising, led by Hugh O'Neil, Earl of Tyrone, attracted financial and military support from Roman Catholic Spain, but was defeated.

1607–08: Further land confiscations caused a flight of former landowners from the northern province of Ulster, where several Protestant groups from England and Scotland had chosen to settle.

1641: A rebellion broke out in Ulster, over the policies of King Charles I; similar issues of religion and royal authority provoked the Civil War in England and Scotland.

1649: Oliver Cromwell, who became Lord Protector of the Commonwealth that succeeded an executed Charles I, attempted to impose English authority and Protestant (Puritan) supremacy in Ireland, was defied and invaded.

1653: With resistance harshly crushed in Ireland, the confiscation of lands was resumed and, under the Act of Settlement, favourable treatment in their redistribution given to members of Puritan groups, especially in the northern counties.

1660: The monarchy was restored in the British Isles.

1688: James II, a Roman Catholic, was deposed and fled England, leaving the throne for the English Parliament to give to his daughter, Mary II, and her husband, the Dutch King, William of Orange (William III).

1690: James II led a revolt in Ireland; he and his supporters (Jacobites) were defeated by William III at the Battle of the Boyne.

1692: The Jacobite revolt was finally defeated after the siege of Limerick.

1704: A new Penal Code was enacted, which placed severe restrictions on the rights of Roman Catholics in education, politics, the military and public life.

1782: The Irish Parliament asserted itself as an independent legislative body, forcing the partial removal of restrictions on the rights of Roman Catholics; the British Parliament (which had united England and Scotland since 1707) was persuaded to recognize formal Irish independence (although, in effect, Ireland remained part of the British realm).

1796: The forces of revolutionary France made an unsuccessful attempt to invade Ireland. A rebellion led by Wolfe Tone, favourable to union with France, was subsequently defeated.

1801: The second Act of Union entered into force, incorporating the Kingdom of Ireland into the United Kingdom and dissolving the Irish Parliament.

1828: Daniel O'Connell, a Roman Catholic, was elected to the United British Parliament, but debarred on religious grounds; he was permitted to take his seat the following year, after the Catholic Emancipation Act was passed; other restrictions on Roman Catholic rights were also removed.

1845–48: The 'Great Famine' or the 'Irish Potato Famine' devastated the island, killing thousands and leading to the emigration of an estimated 1.1m. people (to the Americas, Australia and Great Britain, especially); the Famine, a result of poor harvest, administrative inactivity and a flawed system of land tenure, heightened discontent and ruined the economy.

1869: The Anglican (Protestant) Church of Ireland was disestablished; the Land Acts were passed, easing conditions for tenant farmers; deputies for Irish constituencies, led by Charles Stuart Parnell, campaigned for home rule.

1879: Irish leaders encouraged farmers to refuse rent to repressive landlords; the largely non-violent 'Land War' began.

1882: A refusal to pay rent to landlords led to the imprisonment of Parnell, but settlement of the 'Land War' was reached and Parnell released. The Secretaries of State for Ireland, Lord Frederick Cavendish and T. H. Burke, were assassinated in a Dublin park.

1886: The British Government made its first attempt to institute home rule in Ireland, but the proposed legislation split the ruling Liberal Party and was defeated in Parliament, leading to the fall of the Government.

1893: A further attempt to enact home rule gained wider support, but was, nevertheless, defeated in the upper house of Parliament.

1900: The nationalist party, Sinn Féin (Ourselves Alone), was founded.

1903: A new Land Act gave Irish tenant farmers the right to own land.

1914: At the third attempt, home rule was enacted, restoring an Irish Parliament, while retaining some Irish representation in the British Parliament. The implementation of the new legislation was delayed, however, by the outbreak of the First World War.

1916: In the so-called Easter Rising, a rebel group seized the General Post Office building in Dublin, demanding independence; the Rising was defeated and its leaders executed, but public opinion began to favour Irish separation from the British state.

1918: The extension of conscription to Ireland was opposed by Sinn Féin deputies in the Irish Parliament, who proclaimed an Irish Republic.

1919: The Sinn Féin deputies met as an Irish Assembly, the Dáil Eireann, and again proclaimed Ireland to be an independent republic, led by Eamonn De Valera.

1920: The Irish political parties rejected proposals to establish two parliaments in Ireland—one in Dublin, the other in Belfast (the latter to appease the mainly northern Protestants, who favoured continued Union with Great Britain). Unrest, led by the Irish Republican Army (IRA), resumed, with attempts to suppress it headed by a paramilitary police force.

1921: Ireland was partitioned by the Anglo–Irish Treaty: the Free State became an independent dominion of the British Crown; but six of the nine counties of Ulster, dominated by Protestants, remained within the United Kingdom, as the autonomous province of Northern Ireland.

1922: The Irish electorate endorsed dominion status, with an independent government and a bicameral parliament, but Sinn Féin rejected the result and there was a civil war in southern Ireland until 1924.

1937: A new Constitution was approved by referendum, declaring Éire to be a republic.

1938: Dr Douglas Hyde was elected to a seven-year term as President of Ireland.

1945: S. T. O'Kelly was elected President, in succession to Hyde; he was re-elected in 1952.

1949: Amendments to the Constitution were enacted, changing the country's name to the Republic of Ireland and formally severing all links with the United Kingdom and continuing the claim to the whole island of Ireland. The British Parliament enacted the Northern Ireland Act, confirming the six northern counties as a part of the United Kingdom of Great Britain and Northern Ireland, and the Ireland Act, which recognized the Republic as an independent state outside the British Commonwealth. In addition, Irish citizens were awarded full equal rights in the United Kingdom, including the right to vote, and British citizens subsequently received similar rights in the Republic.

1955: The Republic of Ireland became a member of the United Nations (UN).

1959: De Valera, the serving Prime Minister, resigned the premiership and was elected President, in succession to O'Kelly.

1969: A movement demanding improved civil rights for Roman Catholics in Northern Ireland gained support, but deteriorated into inter-communal violence, joined by a group known as the Provisional IRA (condemned by the British and Irish Governments as terrorists); British troops were sent to the province to maintain peace.

1970: Charles Haughey, the finance minister in the Fianna Fáil Government, was dismissed, along with another minister, after the two were charged in connection with a conspiracy to smuggle guns into Ireland. Both men were subsequently acquitted.

1973: Ireland joined the European Economic Community (later known as the European Union—EU), giving it access to important development funds; the United Kingdom joined at the same time. Erskine Childers was elected to the Presidency, in succession to De Valera. In Northern Ireland the British Government introduced constitutional changes, designed to improve Roman Catholic representation, and permitted a limited role for the Irish Government in the affairs of the province, provoking Protestant discontent.

1974: Childers died while in office. He was succeeded by Carroll O'Daly, an all-party nomination.

1976: Following the assassination of the British Ambassador to Dublin by Republican paramilitaries, the Irish Government introduced legislation to counteract paramilitary activity. O'Daly referred the legislation to the Supreme Court, to adjudicate on its constitutionality. Objections were raised by the Government to O'Daly's actions, and the President resigned; Patrick Hillery was nominated to succeed him, and was re-elected in 1983.

1979: Haughey gained leadership of Fianna Fáil and, consequently, the premiership.

1985: The Anglo-Irish Agreement was concluded between the British and Irish Governments, creating an Intergovernmental Conference and giving the Irish Government a consultative role in certain areas of policy in Northern Ireland; it also reaffirmed that Northern Ireland would remain under British control until such time as a majority of its inhabitants wished otherwise

1990: Mary Robinson was elected President, in succession to Hillery.

1991: Two Fianna Fáil members of the Government supported a motion demanding Haughey's removal as leader of Fianna Fáil, after allegations of misconduct were made against the premier. The two were dismissed and the motion defeated.

February 1992: Haughey resigned at the insistence of the Progressive Democrats, Fianna Fáil's partners in coalition, after further allegations of impropriety were made against him. Albert Reynolds, one of the two ministers dismissed the previous year for supporting the anti-Haughey motion, was elected to the leadership of the Party and, consequently, to the premiership.

November 1992: After its defeat in a motion of 'no confidence', the Government resigned; Fianna Fáil retained power after the ensuing general election, although its representation in the Dáil had been reduced, and it was forced to govern in coalition with the Labour Party.

October 1993: After more than 20 years of the 'Troubles' in Northern Ireland, the British and Irish Prime Ministers issued the framework for a negotiated peace settlement in the 'Downing Street Declaration'.

31 August 1994: The Provisional IRA declared a 'complete cessation of violence', followed by other paramilitary groups, beginning the process towards formal negotiations between all parties and even agreement on international involvement.

16 November 1994: The Labour Party withdrew from the governing coalition, following allegations that Reynolds had withheld information concerning delays in the extradition of an alleged criminal to Northern Ireland. The Government resigned the following day and, after protracted negotiations, Fine Gael and Labour were able to form a coalition Government, led by the former party's leader, John Bruton, which took office on 15 December.

May 1997: Further allegations of impropriety were made against Haughey, involving gifts made to him while Prime Minister.

6 June 1997: In the general election, Fine Gael lost seats and was unable to form a government. Fianna Fáil and the Progressive Democrats succeeded in forming an administration, led by Bertie Ahern.

19 July 1997: The Provisional IRA restored its cease-fire, after a bomb attack in London, the British capital, in the previous year, and Sinn Féin (the political wing of the Provisional IRA) were readmitted to the peace negotiations.

11 November 1997: Mary McAleese, a Roman Catholic from Northern Ireland, was inaugurated as President, becoming the first Irish head of state to be a British citizen.

April 1998: The so-called Good Friday Agreement between the political parties of Northern Ireland, brokered by the British and Irish premiers, provided the basis of a settlement which included the creation of a North–South ministerial council to co-operate on certain issues affecting the entire island. Under the terms of the agreement, provision was made for a change in the Irish Constitution, to abandon the direct territorial claim to Northern Ireland, and recognize that Northern Ireland could only form part of the Republic upon the consent of the majority of the province's people.

1 January 1999: Ireland and 10 other EU countries entered Stage III of the EU's programme of Economic and Monetary Union, introducing a new, common currency, the euro, intended to replace national currencies.

2 December 1999: Responsibility for the administration of Northern Ireland was transferred from the British Government to the newly created Northern Ireland Assembly and the elected Executive Committee.

11 February 2000: The Northern Ireland Assembly and the Executive Committee were suspended and direct rule over Northern Ireland by the British Government reimposed, following an ultimatum regarding the decommissioning of weapons held by the Provisional IRA.

30 May 2000: Administrative powers were again transferred to the Northern Ireland Assembly, following a commitment by the Provisional IRA to allow monitoring of its weapons storage sites for the purpose of ensuring that its arms were 'completely and verifiably beyond use'.

30 June 2000: The governing coalition defeated an opposition motion of 'no confidence' by just 84 votes to 80. The motion was prompted by allegations that Ahern and other senior Fianna Fáil members had withheld information earlier in the year from an independent judicial inquiry into political corruption.

31 January 2001: Fine Gael leader John Bruton resigned following a vote of 'no confidence' by party deputies; he was replaced by former Minister of Health, Michael Noonan.

Italy

753 BC: Traditional date for the foundation of Rome.

509 BC: The foundation of the Roman Republic, by which time the city was already a powerful state in Italy.

31 BC: Octavius Caesar, who adopted the name of Augustus, ended the civil wars which had raged throughout the Mediterranean Empire of Rome and established the Pax Romana and an imperial system of government.

AD 410: The sack of Rome by the Ostrogoths marked the disintegration of the Western Roman Empire and the Italian peninsula became fiercely contested by different peoples, powers and city states.

800: The Pope, Leo III, crowned Charles 'the Great' (Charlemagne), King of the Franks and conqueror of the Lombards of northern Italy, as Holy Roman Emperor, rejecting Eastern Roman ('Byzantine') suzerainty and being confirmed in possession of the Exarchate of Ravenna, the basis of the Papal States.

902: Muslim, Arab invaders conquered Sicily and contested possession of southern Italy with the Byzantines. The north was dominated by the Frankish Holy Roman Empire (except for nominally Byzantine Venice), with papal territory between.

1060: The Normans invaded Arab Sicily, having already fought the Byzantines in southern Italy, with papal support.

1130: The Norman ruler of Sicily adopted the royal title; his kingdom soon extended north to Naples and nearly to Rome. Northern Italy had developed autonomous, often republican, city states, over which Pope and Holy Roman Emperor vied for influence.

1183: By the Peace of Constance, the Holy Roman Emperor, Frederick I Barbarossa of the House of Hohenstaufen, recognized the partial independence of the Italian cities of the Veronese League (f. 1163) and the Lombard League (f. 1168) but retained some imperial privileges.

1186: Following an alliance between Milan and Frederick I, his son and heir, Henry, married Constance of Sicily, providing for the personal union of the two parts of Italy. However, papal opposition to imperial power, the fractious Italian states and dynastic rivalry in the German heartland of the Holy Roman Empire eventually prevented an imperial union of Italy.

1282: The Spanish Kingdom of Aragon obtained Sicily.

1284: The city-state of Genoa took possession of Corsica.

1309: The domicile of the Pope was transferred to Avignon in southern France; the election of a Roman Pope in 1378 resulted in a split, the Great Schism, within the Church (the French, Naples and Venice tended to support the Pope, the predominantly Germanic Empire, Florence, Genoa and Milan tended to favour the 'anti-Pope').

1326: Sardinia came under Aragonese control.

1381: Venice defeated Genoa, and extended its territory (known as *terra firma*) westward across northern Italy, mainly at the expense of the Duchy of Milan (these three city-states, in addition to Florence, were the most powerful in northern Italy).

1442: Aragon conquered Naples, which it united with Sicily.

1449: The Great Schism ended, a single Pope resuming residence in Rome.

1451: A series of disputes and conflicts between the more powerful Italian states was ended by the Peace of Lodi; an increasingly wealthy Italy was experiencing a period of considerable artistic and cultural achievement, influencing all of Western Europe, known as the Renaissance.

1494: The French claimed the Kingdom of Naples and invaded Italy, disrupting the political order in the peninsula and initiating a period of war and unrest, dominated by the rivalry of France and the Holy Roman Empire (now a hereditary possession of the House of Habsburg and personally united with Spain from 1519).

1559: By the Treaty of Cateau-Cambrésis, France was finally excluded from Italy, with the Spanish branch of Habsburgs the principal beneficiaries; the Austrian Habsburgs of the Empire retained considerable territory in the north. The curtailment of French intervention permitted the rise of the domain of the House of Savoy-Piedmont in the north-west.

1684: As part of a series of campaigns against Spain, France, led by Louis XIV, laid siege to Genoa, capturing it in the following year. Italian opposition to France was increasingly led by Victor Amadeus of the House of Savoy.

1713: The Treaty of Utrecht, which ended the War of the Spanish Succession, awarded the Spanish possessions in Italy (Mantua, Milan, Naples, Sardinia) to the Austrian Habsburgs, with the exception of Sicily, which went to Savoy (a French prince gained the Spanish throne).

1720: Austria ceded Sardinia to Savoy in exchange for Sicily.

1738: By the terms of the Peace of Vienna, which ended the War of the Polish Succession, Naples and Sicily (the Kingdom of the Two Sicilies) were awarded to a minor line of the Spanish Bourbons and Parma and Piacenza to a minor Austrian line.

1748: After defeat by Prussia in the second Silesian War, Austria was forced to cede Parma and Piacenza to Spain and parts of Milan to Savoy.

1792: Revolutionary France invaded and annexed Savoy, while King Victor Emmanuel retreated to Sardinia.

1797: Following a campaign by Napoleon Bonaparte, the French military leader, the terms of the Peace of Campo-Formio obliged Austria to cede its possessions in the peninsula, although it was awarded Venice (which had lost its republican independence). The French established several 'satellite republics' in Italy, notably the Cislapine (centred on Milan) and Ligurian (Genoa) Republics.

1802: Bonaparte reorganized Italy; the Cisalpine Republic became known as the Italian Republic, with Bonaparte himself as President; the Papal states, though much reduced in size, were restored, displacing a short-lived republic based in Rome; the Tuscan Republic became the Kingdom of Etruria (also based in Florence); and a Bourbon Kingdom was restored in Naples (ending the Parthenopean Republic).

1804: Bonaparte, now styled Napoleon I, Emperor of the French, proclaimed the Kingdom of Italy.

1806: Joseph Bonaparte, brother of Napoleon I, was declared King in both Spain and Sicily and Naples, displacing the Bourbons.

1808: Tuscany (Etruria) was annexed to the northern Kingdom of Italy; in the following year Rome was also annexed—Italian nationalism was increasing in reaction to arbitrary foreign domination and was shocked by Napoleon I's treatment of the popes.

1815: The Congress of Vienna settled the borders of post-Napoleonic Italy: the House of Savoy regained a realm in Piedmont and the north-west (known as the Kingdom of Sardinia), including Genoa; duchies were created in Lucca, Modena and Parma, and a Grand Duchy was created in Tuscany; the Papal States were restored, as was the Kingdom of the Two Sicilies in the greater part of southern Italy; and the Habsburgs of Austria were awarded territory in Lombardy and Venice. Austria effectively became the guarantor of this settlement, maintaining the *status quo* by force, if necessary, in all parts of Italy and, thereby, becoming a focus of nationalist resentment.

1832: Giuseppe Mazzini, a Genoese exiled for his nationalist views, formed the 'Young Italy' movement to bring about Italian unification.

1847: The influential nationalist newspaper, *Il Risorgimento* (The Resurgence), was founded in Turin by Camillo Count Benso di Cavour.

1848: Amid continued unrest, Naples, the Papal States and Tuscany received constitutions. Sardinia declared war on Austria, but was defeated after the Pope opposed the war. An uprising subsequently forced the Pope to leave Rome.

1849: A Roman Republic was declared, as part of the ongoing turbulence throughout Italy (particularly since the previous year), but this provoked French intervention to restore the Pope.

1852: Cavour became Prime Minister in Piedmont and Sardinia, intent on achieving Italian unification by using the power of the House of Savoy.

1856: Piedmont-Sardinia participated in the Crimean War, partly in order to draw attention to the desire for reunification. The National Society of Italy was founded, to work towards the same goal.

1859: France openly allied with the Kingdom of Sardinia against Austria, with the aim of forming a federation of Italian states; France gained Lombardy, but later ceded it to Sardinia, in exchange for Nice (Nizza) and Savoy.

1860: Plebiscites in Bologna, Modena, Parma and Tuscany showed a majority in favour of uniting under Piedmont-Sardinia. Giuseppe Garibaldi invaded Sicily with an army of committed patriots ('the thousand'), which soon defeated the Neapolitan monarchy and advanced north through Italy— Piedmont-Sardinia prevented Garibaldi from reaching French-protected Rome. Naples, Sicily, Umbria and the Marche all voted for unification.

1861: The Kingdom of Italy was proclaimed, under King Victor Emmanuel II of Piedmont and Sardinia. The capital was located in Florence until such a time as Rome formed part of the Kingdom.

1862: Garibaldi assembled a new army, intent on taking Rome, but was defeated at Aspromonte in Sicily.

1864: France agreed to withdraw from Rome, in exchange for an Italian commitment to protect the papal possessions.

1866: Italian support for Prussia during the Seven Weeks' War with the Habsburgs forced Austria, upon its defeat, to cede Venice to Italy.

1867: A third campaign on Rome by Garibaldi was defeated at Mentana, just outside the city, by French and papal forces.

1870: During the Franco-Prussian war, commitments elsewhere in Europe compelled France to withdraw its garrison from Rome; Italian troops eventually took the city, essentially completing the unification of Italy, of which it became the capital.

1871: A law defining relations between the Italian state and the Pope was enacted, guaranteeing the independence and territorial integrity of the Vatican.

1882: Italy formed the Triple Alliance with Austria-Hungary and Germany.

1887: Seeking to establish itself as a colonial power, Italy made advances in North Africa and annexed Eritrea.

1889: Italy annexed Somaliland and declared Abyssinia (now Ethiopia) a protectorate.

1896: Amid growing domestic discontent and after an unsuccessful war with Abyssinia, Italy withdrew from much of North Africa.

1911: Italy annexed the Ottoman territory of Tripolitania (west Libya), in North Africa, leading to war with the Ottoman Turks.

1912: Italian forces invaded the Dodecanese Islands in the Aegean Sea, which were under the control of the Turks; furthermore by the Peace of Lausanne, all of Libya became autonomous and, effectively, an Italian possession. Meanwhile, in domestic politics the 'revolutionary' group of the Socialist Party gained pre-eminence over the 'reformist' group; Benito Mussolini, a prominent member of the former, organized protests among disaffected urban and rural workers.

1914: A period of strikes and unrest known as the 'Red Week' saw the national authorities briefly lose control of a number of areas during June. Italy declared itself neutral in the First World War.

1915: Enticed by the promise of territorial gain, Italy agreed formally to repudiate the Triple Alliance. It declared war on Austria-Hungary soon after and, later, on Germany and the Ottomans.

1919: Groups of veteran soldiers, known as *fasci di combattimento* (combat squads), under the control of Mussolini, began to operate in Italian cities.

September 1919: By the Treaty of St Germain-en-Laye, Italy gained the Southern Tirol (Alto Adige), as well as Trieste and Istria from Austria.

1920: Socialist unrest in Milan and Turin was countered by the Fasci.

August 1920: Italy gained the Dodecanese Islands and Rhodes, by the Treaty of Sèvres with the Ottomans.

1921: The National Fascist Party (Partito Nazionale Fascista—PNF) was founded; attempted to undermine the authority of the bourgeois governments, by threat of force; with the support of corporate and military leaders, the nationalist movement, led by Mussolini, gained strength.

1922: Following Mussolini's 'March on Rome', the King empowered him to form a Government.

1923: A militia loyal to the PNF rather than to the King or state was formed.

1924: The PNF won an absolute majority of the seats in a general election, enabling Mussolini to pass legislation concentrating power in his hands.

1926: Opposition political parties were dissolved and the formation of new parties prohibited.

1927: Industrial and agricultural production were reorganized, in accordance with state needs; thus, the corporations began to gain power within Mussolini's system.

1928: An electoral law required a list of 400 deputies to be established, nominated by the corporations; the Fascist Grand Council was to select the deputies.

1929: The Lateran Treaty with the Vatican gave the Roman Catholic Church official status within Italy and recognized the sovereignty of the State of the Vatican City, an enclave within Rome, under the jurisdiction of the Pope.

1935: Italy invaded Abyssinia, through Somalia and Eritrea, and, in time, King Victor Emmanuel III was styled 'Emperor of Ethiopia'.

25 October 1936: A German-Italian pact established co-operation between the two nations, which became known as the Axis.

1939: Italy invaded and occupied Albania and signed the Pact of Friendship and Mutual Aid ('Pact of Steel') with Germany. When France and the United Kingdom declared war on Germany later that year, Italy became involved in the Second World War (although it did not declare war on the Allies until 1940).

1941: Italian forces in Abyssinia capitulated and continued to suffer reverses in North Africa and the Balkans.

25 July 1943: Mussolini was dismissed by Victor Emmanuel III and arrested; the PNF was dissolved and a non-Fascist Government was formed.

3 September 1943: Having already lost Sicily to Allied invasion, Italy signed an armistice, but the following week German forces occupied Rome and forced the Government to flee; Mussolini was released and formed an alternative government.

13 October 1943: The Italian Government declared war on Germany, but had to rely on Allied forces to liberate the country from German occupation in a hard-fought campaign.

28 April 1945: German forces in Italy surrendered. Mussolini was shot and killed by partisans while attempting to flee the country for neutral territory.

18 June 1946: The Italian Republic was proclaimed, Victor Emmanuel III having abdicated earlier in the month, responding to a referendum approving a republican constitution. The Christian Democratic Party (Partito della Democrazia Cristiana—DC) was to hold power unchallenged until 1963.

February 1947: Under the Paris Peace Treaties, Italy was forced to pay reparations and lost its colonies and Trieste.

1 January 1948: The Constitution of the Italian Republic entered into force.

1948: France and Italy formed a customs union.

1949: Italy became a member of the North Atlantic Treaty Organization (NATO).

1957: Italy signed the Treaty of Rome, becoming a founder member of the European Economic Community (known as the European Community—EC from November 1993, when a new European Union—EU was introduced).

1963: Following a general election the DC formed a coalition Government with the Italian Socialist Party (Partito Socialista Italiano—PSI); a succession of mainly coalition governments followed, comprising the DC and other major non-Communist parties.

1976: A new, minority DC-Government, under Giulio Andreotti, survived the vote of confidence only because of the non-participation of the Italian Communist Party (Partito Comunista Italiano—PCI). The PCI thereby established its importance as an opposition party.

June 1981: Giovanni Spadolini of the Italian Republican Party (Partito Repubblicano Italiano—PRI) became the first non-DC Prime Minister since 1946, after the previous DC-led Government resigned, owing to its involvement in a scandal concerning a masonic lodge, Propaganda Due (P-2), which had criminal connections.

June 1983: Bettino Craxi became Italy's first PSI Prime Minister.

1991: The Northern League (Lega Nord), an alliance of regionalist parties which denounced the Government's perceived southern bias and advocated federalism, was formed.

1992: A corruption scandal was uncovered which implicated government ministers in bribery and connections with organized crime. The anti-Mafia judicial investigations undermined the political establishment and eventually led to the collapse of the DC and the evolution of new parties.

28 May 1992: Oscar Luigi Scalfaro was inaugurated as President of the Republic.

April 1993: A referendum supported the amendment of the Constitution to allow the majority of the members of the Senate to be elected by a simple plurality. The Government, which had collapsed owing to the anti-Mafia judicial investigations into corruption, was replaced by a new coalition Government, with Carlo Azeglio Ciampi, a non-parliamentarian and former governor of the central bank, as Prime Minister. Ciampi undertook a programme of electoral reform and sought to resolve the country's economic problems and reduce the public debt.

March 1994: At legislative elections the Freedom Alliance (Polo per la Libertà e del Buon Governo) won a majority in the Chamber of Deputies (Camera dei Deputati) and Silvio Berlusconi of Come on, Italy! (Forza Italia), its dominant party, became Prime Minister.

January 1995: Following the collapse of Berlusconi's Government, a Government was formed by Lamberto Dini, formerly the Director-General of the central bank.

21 April 1996: As a result of the general election, the Olive Tree alliance (l'Ulivo), led by Romano Prodi, formed a Government.

June 1997: A parliamentary commission on constitutional reform announced recommendations for, among other things, a directly elected President with responsibility for defence and foreign policy and a reduction in the size of both houses of Parliament.

22 October 1998: A new Government (the country's 56th since the end of the Second World War) was announced, under the leadership of Massimo D'Alema of the Democrats of the Left (Democratici di Sinistra—DS, formerly the PCI).

1 January 1999: Italy was one of the first 11 participants in Stage III of the EU's Economic and Monetary Union (EMU), when a new, common European currency, the euro, was introduced.

March 1999: Prodi was nominated as the new President of the European Commission by EU heads of state and of government. The NATO bombardment of the Federal Republic of Yugoslavia began and Italian forces participated, but political support for the action was weaker than elsewhere in the Alliance.

13 May 1999: Carlo Azeglio Ciampi, the former central banker and premier, was elected President of the Republic, with the support of 707 of the 1,010 members of the electoral college; Ciampi was sworn in on 28 May.

18 December 1999: D'Alema resigned, following tensions within the ruling coalition. Two days later President Ciampi invited him to form a new government. Three of the 10 parties in the outgoing coalition withdrew their support, although they agreed not to oppose the new administration in a motion of 'no confidence' to be held on 23 December.

17 April 2000: Following regional elections in which the parties forming the governing coalition were decisively defeated by the opposition, the Government resigned.

26 April 2000: Giuliano Amato, formerly Minister of the Treasury and Budget in the outgoing administration, and Prime Minister from 1992–93, formed a new Government, which was endorsed by the Chamber of Deputies two days later.

21 May 2000: A series of referendums, one of which proposed the abolition of proportional representation in elections to the Chamber of Deputies, were invalidated owing to an insufficient participation rate. A similar referendum had been declared invalid for the same reason in April 1999.

24 October 2000: The Senate approved a bill to end compulsory military service for all males between the ages of 18 and 26 by 2006; conscription was to be replaced by a volunteer force.

9 March 2001: President Ciampi dissolved Parliament in preparation for elections scheduled to be held in May 2001.

Latvia

c. **2,000 BC:** The Balts, the ancestors of the Latvians (Letts), settled on the southern and south-eastern shores of the Baltic Sea.

AD 1201: Albert von Appeldern, the German Bishop of Livonia, founded the city of Rīga and established the crusading order of Sword Brethren.

1209: The German crusading order of the Teutonic Knights invaded Jersika, a town in southern Latvia controlled by a native ruler, Visvaldis, following his marriage to a pagan Lithuanian princess.

1290: The Teutonic Knights completed their conquest of Latvia with the capture of the kingdom of Zemgale. Latvia and Estonia were subsequently ruled by the Livonian Order of Teutonic Knights (formed in 1237 by an alliance of the German Order of Teutonic Knights and the Sword Brethren) under the name of Livonia.

1494: Serfdom was introduced in Livonia.

1524–34: Livonia renounced religious adherence to Rome and converted to Lutheranism.

1558: Ivan IV (the 'Terrible') of the Russian state of Muscovy attacked Livonia in an attempt to conquer part of the Baltic coast; his move instigated the Livonian War, which continued until 1582.

1561: The Livonian State of Teutonic Knights finally ceased to exist: northern Estonia fell under Swedish control, while the rest came under Polish–Lithuanian rule, with the kingdoms of Kurzeme and Zemgale becoming part of the autonomous Duchy of Courland (Kurland).

1629: Sweden conquered the Livonian territories of Poland.

1721: The Treaty of Nystad, concluded by Russia and Sweden, ended the Great Northern War and brought Estonia and much of Livonia under Russian rule.

1772: At the First Partition of Poland, Latgale, an eastern region of Livonia, was incorporated into the Russian Empire, as part of the Russian province of Vitebsk (now in Belarus).

1795: At the Third Partition of Poland the remainder of the Duchy of Courland became part of the Russian Empire.

1817–19: Serfdom was abolished in Latvia.

1901: The Latvian Social Democratic Party was established, which advocated greater territorial autonomy for Latvia.

October 1905: Two Latvian deputies were elected to the Duma (parliament), which was established in the tsarist capital of St Petersburg.

18 November 1917: A first National Council was elected in Valka, northern Latvia, at a meeting of the Rīga Democratic Bloc; the Council expressed its intention to establish Latvia as an independent sovereign state.

3 March 1918: Treaty of Brest-Litovsk: the Bolsheviks ceded large areas of western territory to Germany, including the Baltic regions.

18 November 1918: An independent Republic of Latvia was declared and a provisional administration, under the premiership of Kārlis Ulmanis, was formed.

3 January 1919: The Soviet Red Army captured Rīga, forcing the Provisional Government to flee to Kurzeme.

May 1919: With the aid of German troops, Latvian forces expelled the Red Army from Rīga.

8 July 1919: The Provisional Government returned to the capital and the Latvian National Council reconvened.

January 1920: The last Soviet troops were finally expelled from Latvia.

1 February 1920: The Latvian and Soviet Governments signed an armistice.

1 May 1920: At the first session of the Constituent Assembly (elections to which were held in the previous month) Jānis Čakste was elected President of the Assembly and of the Republic of Latvia.

11 August 1920: A Latvian–Soviet peace agreement, the Treaty of Rīga, was signed.

7 November 1922: Following the promulgation of a new Constitution, the first session of the new Saeima (Parliament) opened.

16 September 1923: The Saeima passed the Agrarian Reform Bill, initiating land reform in favour of the peasants.

May 1934: Ulmanis carried out a *coup d'état* and established a presidential dictatorship.

1936: Ulmanis became President of Latvia.

23 August 1939: The Treaty of Non-Aggression (the Nazi–Soviet Pact) was signed by the USSR and Germany; it included the 'Secret Protocols', which sanctioned the Soviet annexation of Latvia (as well as Eastern Poland, Estonia, Lithuania and Bessarabia).

17 June 1940: Red Army troops occupied Latvia. A pro-Soviet administration, headed by Augusts Kirchenšteins, was installed.

21 July 1940: The new parliament proclaimed the Latvian Soviet Socialist Republic (SSR) and requested to be admitted to the Soviet federation. The Latvian SSR was incorporated into the USSR on 5 August.

13–14 June 1941: The mass deportation of some 33,000 Latvians over a period of several months culminated in the expulsion from Rīga of 15,000 inhabitants overnight.

1 July 1941: German troops, which had invaded the USSR the previous week, reached Rīga.

13 October 1944: The Soviet army recaptured the Latvian capital and Courland.

24–27 March 1949: In a resumption of the process of sovietization, some 70,000 Latvians, mainly inhabitants of rural areas, were deported.

1952: The process of collectivization was completed.

1959: In purges of members of the Communist Party of Latvia (CPL) accused of Latvian nationalism, Jānis Kalnērziņš, First Secretary of the CPL since 1940, was dismissed and replaced by Arvīds Pelše.

1966: Augusts Voss succeeded Pelše as First Secretary and continued repressive policies of russification.

1984: Boris Pugo became First Secretary of the CPL. The Environmental Protection Club was established to protest against environmental damage.

July 1986: Under the more tolerant regime of the new Soviet leader, Mikhail Gorbachev, Helsinki-86 was established in Liepāja; the group aimed to monitor observance of the human-rights provisions of the Helsinki Final Act of 1975.

14 June 1987: A mass demonstration was organized by Helsinki-86 to mark the 1941 deportation of thousands of Latvian citizens. A further demonstration was held on 23 August to commemorate the signing of the Nazi–Soviet Pact.

June 1988: A resolution was adopted by Latvia's cultural unions demanding that Latvian become the official language, that the Secret Protocols of the Nazi–Soviet Pact of 1939 be published and that ecological damage be repaired.

September 1988: Jan Vigris replaced the conservative Pugo as First Secretary of the CPL.

29 September 1988: Latvian became the state language and the former Latvian flag and national anthem were declared no longer illegal (they were restored to official use in February 1990).

October 1988: The Latvian Popular Front (LPF) was formed by representatives of the opposition and radicals from the CPL; the new group resolved to seek sovereignty for Latvia within a renewed Soviet federation.

February 1989: The Latvian National Independence Movement (LNIM), which advocated full independence, held its first congress.

26 March 1989: In the elections to the all-Union Congress of People's Deputies, candidates supported by the LPF won 26 of the 34 seats contested.

28 July 1989: A declaration of sovereignty and economic independence was adopted by the Latvian Supreme Soviet (legislature).

December 1989: Candidates supported by the LPF won some 75% of the seats in local elections.

January 1990: The Latvian Supreme Soviet voted to end the Communist Party's monopoly of power.

15 February 1990: The Latvian Supreme Soviet condemned the 1940 request for admission to the USSR.

March–April 1990: In elections to the Latvian Supreme Soviet (subsequently renamed the Supreme Council), candidates endorsed by the LPF won 131 of the 201 seats contested; the CPL (including an anti-independence faction, Interfront) won some 59 seats and independent candidates gained 11 seats.

30 April–1 May 1990: A rival parliament, the Congress of Latvia, the members of which were elected only by citizens of pre-1940 Latvia and their descendants, convened; the Congress announced that Latvia was an occupied country and demanded full independence and the withdrawal of Soviet troops.

3 May 1990: Anatolijs Gorbunovs was elected Chairman of the Supreme Council, the republican head of state.

4 May 1990: The Supreme Council declared Latvia's incorporation into the USSR unlawful and announced the beginning of a transitional period towards full independence; Ivars Godmanis was elected premier of a new administration dominated by the LPF.

14 May 1990: A decree issued by President Gorbachev of the USSR annulled the declaration of independence of 4 May.

2 January 1991: Special units of the Soviet Ministry of Internal Affairs, which, the Latvian Government claimed, had been responsible for a series of explosions in Rīga in December, occupied the Rīga Press House.

20 January 1991: The 'Committee of Public Salvation', led by the First Secretary of the CPL, Alfrēds Rubiks, claimed authority in Latvia; his coup attempt eventually failed.

3 March 1991: In a referendum 73.7% of participants voted in favour of Latvian independence.

21 August 1991: Following the attempted *coup d'état* in Moscow (Russia—the Soviet capital), an emergency session of the Supreme Council was convened; the Council declared full independence and pronounced that the putschist State Committee for the State of Emergency was unconstitutional.

23 August 1991: Rubiks was arrested (in July 1995 he was sentenced to eight years' imprisonment) and the Communist Party of the Soviet Union (CPSU) was banned in Latvia.

6 September 1991: Latvia's independence was formally recognized by the State Council of the USSR.

17 September 1991: Latvia was admitted to the United Nations (UN).

15 October 1991: Legislation on citizenship was adopted by the Supreme Council; the law stipulated that all residents who were not citizens of pre-1940 Latvia or their descendants must apply for naturalization.

May 1992: The Latvian rouble was introduced for a transitional period until the country adopted its own currency, the lats, introduced as the only legal tender in Latvia on 18 October 1993.

5–6 June 1993: Elections were held to the new legislature (Saeima): Latvian Way, a political movement formed in February, won 36 of the 100 seats contested and formed a moderate right-wing coalition with the Latvian Farmers' Union (LFU), which won 12 seats. Later, Anatolijs Gorbunovs was elected Chairman and the Saeima voted to restore the Constitution of 1922. The new Government, headed by Valdis Birkavs, was approved by the Saeima on 21 July.

8 July 1993: Guntis Ulmanis of the LFU was inaugurated as President of Latvia, following three rounds of voting in the Saeima.

March 1994: The USA mediated an agreement on the withdrawal of Russian (former Soviet) troops from Latvia, according to which Russia was allowed use of the Skrunda base for a further four years, but all other troops were to leave by 31 August.

11 July 1994: The LFU withdrew from the ruling coalition, following disagreements over economic and agricultural policy, precipitating the Government's resignation.

22 July 1994: Following criticism of the law on citizenship and naturalization enacted in the previous month, but rejected by President Ulmanis, the Saeima removed the quota on the naturalization of non-ethnic Latvian residents.

15 September 1994: A new Government, again consisting mainly of Latvian Way members, assumed office, led by Māris Gailis.

February 1995: Latvia was admitted to the Council of Europe.

May 1995: The operations of Latvia's largest commercial bank, Banka Baltija, were suspended by the Government after several smaller commercial banks were declared insolvent. As a result of the continuing banking crisis the finance minister, Andris Piebalgs, resigned.

30 September–October 1995: In a general election nine parties and coalitions gained representation in the Saeima: the newly established Democratic Party Saimnieks (The Master—DPS) won the largest number of seats (18), followed by Latvian Way (17).

October 1995: Latvia submitted a formal application for full membership of the European Union (EU).

December 1995: The Saeima finally approved the formation of a new Cabinet of Ministers, consisting of members of most of the major parties, excluding the extreme right-wing People's Movement for Latvia (PML—Zigerists' Party), which had gained 16 seats; the coalition's Prime Minister was Andris Šķēle, who was without party affiliation.

18 June 1996: The Saeima re-elected Ulmanis as President.

12 July 1996: The dispute between Latvia and Estonia over fishing rights in the Gulf of Rīga was settled after the Governments concerned signed an agreement on the demarcation of their maritime borders.

January 1997: Šķēle resigned as premier, following criticism from President Ulmanis over a ministerial appointment; he was later reinstated and a new Cabinet formed on 13 February.

June 1997: A number of ministers resigned, following an investigation into compliance with a requirement for politicians to surrender all non-political offices.

25 July 1997: Šķēle announced the resignation of the Government, because of problems in the coalition; President Ulmanis invited Guntars Krasts, the outgoing Minister of the Economy and a member of the alliance of the Conservative Union for Fatherland and Freedom/Latvian National Independence Movement (LNNK), to form a new administration.

7 August 1997: The Saeima approved Krasts' proposal for a coalition of the largest political factions: the Conservative Union for Fatherland and

Freedom/LNNK, the DPS, Latvian Way, the LFU and the Christian Democratic Union of Latvia.

October 1997: Latvia and Russia agreed a treaty settling their common border.

5 November 1997: Rubiks was released from prison and announced his intention to resume political life.

16 January 1998: Latvia, Lithuania and Estonia signed a US–Baltic Charter of Partnership with the USA (the first meeting of the Partnership Commission was held on 8 July).

March 1998: Police action at a demonstration and, later in the month, a parade of Fascist veterans in Rīga provoked Russian condemnation.

3 April 1998: Atis Sausnitis, the Minister of the Economy, was dismissed, after he published a report on the probable impact of Russian sanctions, should relations continue to deteriorate. All of the ministers from his party, the DPS, resigned five days later.

30 April 1998: The Saeima approved a new coalition Government, comprising members of: the LFU; the Latvian Way; and an alliance of the Latvian National Reform Party and the Latvian Green Party.

22 June 1998: In compliance with advice from the Organization for Security and Co-operation in Europe (OSCE), the Saeima approved amendments to the citizenship law, easing requirements for nationalization. These amendments were deemed inadequate by the Russian Government, however, and the UFF collected enough signatures to force a referendum on the subject. This was held on 3 October, when 52.5% of votes cast approved the changes.

26 June 1998: Despite Saeima opposition, the Government voted to abolish the death penalty.

3 October 1998: At legislative elections the People's Party, led by the former Prime Minister, Šķēle, was the most successful, gaining 24 seats, followed by the Latvian Way with 21 seats, the Conservative Union for Fatherland and Freedom/LNNK with 17 seats and the New Party with eight seats.

14 October 1998: Latvia was admitted to the World Trade Organization (WTO), having completed negotiations on accession.

26 October 1998: The final citizenship law was formally promulgated, but, together with the later proposal of new legislation promoting the Latvian language in education and broadcasting, provoked some protest.

26 November 1998: A government coalition, headed by the former transport minister, Vilis Krištopans, and comprising the Latvian Way, the Conservative Union for Fatherland and Freedom/LNNK and the New Party, was formed. The Latvian Social Democratic Alliance joined the coalition in February 1999.

17 June 1999: Vaira Vike-Freiberga was elected as President, following seven rounds of voting in the Saeima. She took office on 8 July.

5 July 1999: Krištopans announced his Government's resignation following internal disagreements within the Latvian Way. President Vike-Freiberga asked Šķēle to form a new coalition Government comprising the People's Party, the Conservative Union for Fatherland and Freedom/LNNK and the Latvian Way.

14 July 1999: President Vike-Freiberga returned a language law, enforcing the use of Latvian in state and local government institutions and enterprises, to the Saeima for revision, after concerns that it infringed upon the rights of Latvians and violated European standards. The legislation had been severely criticized by the OSCE, the Council of Europe and the Russian Government, as well as by a large part of the population.

22 October 1999: Russia abandoned the last military post in the Baltic states, the Skrunda radar station.

9 December 1999: A revised version of controversial language legislation was passed, which allowed Russian to be spoken in business and private, while preserving and strengthening the Latvian language; the revision was nevertheless condemned by the Russian Government

10–11 December 1999: At the EU Heads of State and Government summit meeting in Helsinki (Finland) it was agreed that accession talks with six countries, including Latvia, would begin; formal negotiations commenced in February 2000.

21 January 2000: Vasiliy Kononov, an anti-Nazi resistance fighter during the Second World War, became the first person to be convicted of war crimes since the restoration of Latvian independence in 1991; he was sentenced to six years' imprisonment, following his conviction for the murder of nine Latvians during an attack on Macie Bati village in 1944.

February 2000: The Latvian Government was again criticized by Russia for what it perceived as anti-Soviet bias in the pursuit of criminal cases against individuals accused of war crimes, worsening bilateral relations; the former Russian President, Boris Yeltsin (1991–1999), refused a Latvian medal, to be awarded in recognition of the aid given by him in Latvia's independence process.

17 February 2000: Jānis Adamsons, the chairman of a parliamentary commission investigating a paedophilia scandal, alleged that witnesses had implicated the premier, Šķēle, the Minister of Justice and former premier, Valdis Birkavs, and the Director-General of the State Revenue Service, Andrejs Sonciks, in the affair.

12 April 2000: Šķēle resigned as premier following the withdrawal of the Latvian Way from the coalition, after a dispute over privatization.

25 April 2000: President Vike-Freiberga invited the former Mayor of Rīga, Andris Berzins (of the Latvian Way), to form a new administration. The new coalition Government of the People's Party, the UFF/LNNK, the Latvian Way and the New Party was approved by the Saeima on 5 May.

6 July 2000: Farmers ended a two-day blockade of Latvian border posts in protest at state agricultural policy, after the Government pledged to increase subsidies to the sector.

1 August 2000: The prosecutor investigating allegations of paedophilia made against Šķēle announced that no evidence had been found to support the allegations and the case would not proceed. Similar announcements had been made with regard to Birkavs and Sonciks the previous day.

Liechtenstein

4th–5th centuries: Germanic tribes migrated westwards, settling throughout western and central Europe. The area surrounding modern Liechtenstein was largely settled by the Alemanni.

6th–7th centuries: The Kingdom of the Alemanni was absorbed into the Frankish realm, the eastern part of which would later become the Holy Roman Empire.

1342: The County of Vaduz was formed within the Empire.

1499: The Swabian War was partly fought in and around the County of Vaduz.

1618–48: The Thirty Years' War was fought throughout the Empire, including in what is now Liechtenstein; the withdrawal of the Swiss from the Holy Roman Empire was acknowledged by the final peace settlement.

1699: Prince Johann Adam Andreas of the House of Liechtenstein purchased the Lordship of Schellenberg, and, in 1712, the County of Vaduz.

1719: Vaduz and Schellenberg were declared united by Emperor Charles VI and styled the Imperial Principality of Liechtenstein, still nominally within the Empire, but, effectively, independent, like many of the Germanic states.

1799: The French armies, under Napoleon Bonaparte I, invaded and occupied the Principality.

1806: Liechtenstein was compelled to join the French-established Confederation of the Rhine and the Holy Roman Empire was declared dissolved.

1813: The Confederation of the Rhine was, in turn, dissolved, as French influence over German states such as Liechtenstein ended.

1815: The German Confederation was established, the Principality joining at its foundation.

1852: A customs treaty was signed by the Principality and Austria.

1862: A new Constitution provided for the establishment of a Parliament.

1866: The dissolution of the German Confederation left Prussia to dominate northern Germany, uniting the southern states with it in a German Empire from 1871, but excluding Austria—Liechtenstein was a fragment isolated from the rest of the old Empire by Austrian territory, but itself not part of the Habsburg patrimony, leaving it effectively independent.

1868: Liechtenstein disbanded its army.

1914–18: The First World War imposed severe financial constraints on Liechtenstein, which remained neutral.

1919: Liechtenstein agreed that, henceforth, it would be represented by Switzerland in diplomatic affairs. The customs treaty with Austria was suspended.

1921: A new Constitution was enacted, vesting legislative power in the Prince and a unicameral Parliament and executive power in the Prince (assisted by a Government comprising five members of Parliament). A postal union was formed with Switzerland.

1923: Liechtenstein agreed to form a customs union with Switzerland, and upon the enactment of the treaty in the following year, the Swiss franc became the official currency.

1928: The Progressive Citizens' Party of Liechtenstein (Fortschrittliche Bürgerpartei Liechtensteins—FBPL) became the dominant political party in government.

1938: Franz-Jozef II was the first Prince to take up permanent residence in Liechtenstein.

1939–45: During the Second World War in Europe Liechtenstein once again remained neutral.

1960: Liechtenstein joined the European Free Trade Association (EFTA) as an associate member, by virtue of its customs union with Switzerland.

1969: The Constitution was amended to reduce the minimum voting age to 20 years.

1970: The Patriotic Union (Vaterländische Union—VU) replaced the FBPL as the main party in the coalition Government, following a general election.

1972: The agreement between the European Communities (which was to evolve into the European Union—EU) and Switzerland was extended to include Liechtenstein.

1974: The FBPL regained its majority, with Walter Kieber as the Head of Government.

1978: Liechtenstein became a member of the Council of Europe. The VU became the dominant party in government, under Hans Brunhart.

July 1984: A referendum approved amendments to the Constitution to extend suffrage to women over the age of 20 years, although women were not permitted to vote on communal affairs in three of Liechtenstein's 11 communes.

April 1986: Women were accorded the right to vote on communal affairs in the final three communes.

March 1989: The unicameral Parliament (Landtag) was increased in size from 15 members to 25.

November 1989: Prince Hans-Adam II succeeded Prince Franz-Josef II, upon his death.

September 1990: Liechtenstein joined the United Nations (UN).

May 1991: Liechtenstein became a full member of EFTA.

1992: The Constitution was amended to declare the equality of men and women. Liechtenstein's first referendum on membership of the European Economic Area (EEA—negotiated between the EU and EFTA) endorsed government and princely support for the move.

1993: Following a general election, the FBPL became the dominant party in the coalition once again. Markus Büchel was appointed Head of Government, but he was subsequently dismissed following a vote of 'no confidence'. A new election was held, and the VU regained its majority; Mario Frick became the Head of Government.

1 May 1995: Following approval in a referendum, Liechtenstein joined the EEA, despite continued opposition from its customs-union partner, Switzerland (which had itself rejected membership). The Principality subsequently joined the World Trade Organization (WTO).

April 1997: The FBPL withdrew from the Government, leaving a single party to govern alone for the first time since 1938.

29 November 1999: The European Court of Human Rights found that Prince Hans-Adam had restricted the right to free speech of Dr Herbert Wille, a senior judge who advocated that the Supreme Court and not the monarch decide constitutional issues, by refusing to reappoint him to his post in 1997, contrary to the wishes of the Landtag. Prince Hans-Adam was ordered to pay 100,000 Swiss francs in costs.

9–11 February 2001: In parliamentary elections, the FBPL won 14 of the 25 seats in the Landtag, the ruling VU won 11 seats and the Freie Liste (Free List—FL), one.

Lithuania

1231: Mindouh (Mindaugas), a regional chieftain, united Lithuanian tribes by founding the Grand Duchy of Lithuania (Litva) and Rus (many of the ruling class were Orthodox Slavs).

1386: The personal union between Lithuania and Poland was achieved by the marriage of the Lithuanian Grand Duke Jahaila (Jagiełło, baptized Władysław in 1386) and the Polish Queen Jadwiga (Hedwig). The following year Lithuania officially adopted Christianity.

1392–1430: Vytautas (Witold) the Great expanded Lithuanian power further east and towards the Black Sea, despite the Tatar victory at Vorskla in 1399.

1569: Lithuania (which included much of modern Belarus and, since the 15th century, the Samogitian lowlands of western Lithuania) surrendered its separate status by the Union of Lublin; the new Polish–Lithuanian Commonwealth was created to counter the threat from Sweden, the Russian state of Muscovy and the Turkish Ottoman Empire.

1795: At the Third Partition of Poland Lithuania was annexed by the Russian Empire.

1863: Following the additional rural hardships consequent to the emancipation of 1861, there was a revolt by the Lithuanian peasantry which was savagely repressed. A policy of russification was then instituted, although a strong nationalist movement emerged in the later decades of the century.

1915: Lithuania was occupied by German troops, following the outbreak of the First World War.

September 1917: A Lithuanian Conference was convened; the Conference adopted a resolution demanding the independence of the Lithuanian state and elected a Council of Lithuania, headed by Antanas Smetona.

16 February 1918: Lithuania's independence was formally declared by the Council of Lithuania. The declaration was contrary to the wishes of the German authorities, which had allowed the formation of the Council because they expected it to generate popular support for Germany's occupation of Lithuania.

1919: Lithuanian troops defended Lithuania's territory against invasion by Bolshevik, German and 'White' Russian forces.

April 1920: Elections were held to the Constituent Assembly.

12 July 1920: Lithuania's independence was recognized by Soviet Russia in the Treaty of Moscow.

9 October 1920: The Polish army captured Vilnius (Wilno) and its surrounding area. Poland did, however, subsequently recognize the independent state of Lithuania, with its capital at Kaunas.

1 August 1922: Lithuania's first Constitution was adopted, which declared Lithuania to be a parliamentary democracy.

1923: Lithuania occupied the former German territory of Klaipeda (Memel), which was under the jurisdiction of the League of Nations.

17 December 1926: Following the victory of the left wing in the May elections, Antanas Smetona, the leader of the Nationalist Party and former Chairman of the Council of Lithuania, seized power in a military coup and established authoritarian rule.

1938: Diplomatic relations with Poland were restored.

23 August 1939: In the 'Secret Protocols' to the Nazi–Soviet Pact (Treaty of Non-Aggression) Lithuania was assigned to Germany.

28 September 1939: The Treaty on Friendship and Existing Borders, agreed between Germany and the USSR, permitted the USSR to occupy Lithuania.

10 October 1939: Lithuania was compelled to sign a Treaty of Mutual Assistance with the USSR; the treaty forced Lithuania to accept the stationing of 20,000 Soviet troops on its territory, in return for which Vilnius (previously controlled by Poland) was returned. The city subsequently became Lithuania's capital.

15 June 1940: The Soviet Red Army invaded Lithuania; Smetona fled the country and a 'puppet' government was formed.

3 August 1940: Lithuania was formally incorporated into the USSR.

June 1941: Some 20,000 Lithuanians were deported to Siberia (Russia), shortly before the German invasion of the USSR and occupation of Lithuania, during which some 210,000 people were killed.

1944: With the defeat of Nazi Germany, Lithuania was recaptured by the Red Army. The collectivization of agriculture and a further series of deportations commenced. Organized partisan resistance to Soviet rule occurred throughout the country until 1952.

May 1972: Anti-Communist demonstrations took place in Kaunas.

August 1987: Dissident groups demonstrated on the anniversary of the signing of the Nazi–Soviet Pact.

February 1988: The security services prevented a celebration marking the 70th anniversary of Lithuanian independence.

3 June 1988: The Lithuanian Movement for Reconstruction (Sąjūdis) was formed by a group of intellectuals and writers.

August 1988: Aleksandr Yakovlev, a political ally of Mikhail Gorbachev (who had become the Soviet leader in 1985), visited Lithuania; his failure to condemn the actions of Sąjūdis served to strengthen the movement's position.

23 August 1988: At a mass rally in Vilnius the leaders of Sąjūdis denounced the Nazi–Soviet Pact and declared that the USSR had illegally occupied Lithuania.

October 1988: The First Secretary of the Communist Party of Lithuania (CPL), Ringaudas Songaila, was dismissed from his post and succeeded by Algirdas Brazauskas.

November 1988: As one of a number of concessions to Lithuanian nationalism, the Lithuanian Supreme Soviet recognized Lithuanian as the state language.

March 1989: In the elections to the all-Union Congress of People's Deputies Sąjūdis won 36 out of a total of 42 contested seats in Lithuania.

18 May 1989: The Lithuanian Supreme Soviet approved a declaration of Lithuanian sovereignty, which asserted the supremacy of Lithuania's laws over all-Union legislation.

20 December 1989: At a CPL Congress the Party declared its independence from the Communist Party of the Soviet Union (CPSU) and its support for multi-party democracy and independent statehood.

24 February 1990: Sąjūdis won an overall majority of seats in the elections to the Lithuanian Supreme Soviet.

11 March 1990: The Supreme Soviet (renamed the Supreme Council) declared the restoration of Lithuanian independence, the first of the Soviet republics to make such a declaration; on the same day it elected Vytautas Landsbergis, the leader of Sąjūdis, as its Chairman (*de facto* head of state). The legislature also restored the pre-1940 name of 'Republic of Lithuania', and suspended the USSR Constitution on Lithuanian territory.

17 March 1990: Kazimiera Prunskiene was appointed Prime Minister of Lithuania, the first woman premier of any of the Soviet territories.

April 1990: The USSR imposed an economic embargo on Lithuania, in retaliation for its declaration of independence; Soviet forces had also occupied CPL buildings in Vilnius and taken control of newsprint presses.

30 June 1990: Lithuania agreed to a six-month moratorium on independence. Discussions began in August, but were ended shortly afterwards by the Soviet Government.

January 1991: Prunskiene resigned as Prime Minister, following disagreements with Landsbergis on economic and foreign policy; she was replaced by Gediminas Vagnorius. Landsbergis announced the end of the suspension of the declaration of independence. Soviet troops fired on civilians gathered around the Vilnius television tower; 13 people were killed and 500 were injured. (In August 1999 six former officers of the CPL were convicted of complicity in attempts to overthrow the Government, and sentenced to between three and 12 years' imprisonment.)

9 February 1991: A referendum on independence took place in Lithuania: some 84% of the population participated, of which 90.5% voted in favour of independence. Lithuania refused to participate officially in the all-Union referendum on the future of the USSR in the following month.

August 1991: Military vehicles entered Vilnius during an attempted coup in the Soviet capital, Moscow. The Supreme Council joined in the condemnation of the coup and, upon its collapse, the Lithuanian Government ordered the withdrawal of Soviet forces from the republic.

6 September 1991: The State Council of the USSR formally acknowledged Lithuania's independence.

10 September 1991: Lithuania became a member of the Conference on Security and Co-operation in Europe (CSCE, renamed the Organization for Security and Co-operation in Europe—OSCE in December 1994); one week later the country was admitted to the United Nations (UN).

January 1992: Lithuania and Poland signed a Declaration on Friendly Relations and Neighbourly Co-operation (a formal treaty of friendship and co-operation was finally signed in April 1994); it guaranteed the rights of the respective ethnic minorities in each country and also recognized the existing border between the countries.

25 May 1992: A proposal to introduce an executive presidency was rejected in a referendum.

July 1992: A vote of 'no confidence' in Vagnorius won a majority in the Seimas (formerly the Supreme Council); Aleksandras Abišala replaced him as Prime Minister.

1 October 1992: Lithuania ceased to belong to the 'rouble zone'. A provisional monetary unit, the talonas, was introduced. It was replaced, on 25 June 1993, by the litas.

25 October 1992: The first round of voting in a general election took place. A new Constitution, which established a presidency, was overwhelmingly approved in a referendum; it was formally adopted on 6 November.

15 November 1992: The second round of voting in the parliamentary elections gave the former CPL, renamed the Lithuanian Democratic Labour Party (LDLP), a final total of 76 of the 141 seats in the Seimas; Sąjūdis won 49 seats.

December 1992: Bronislovas Lubys, a member of the Abišala Government, was appointed Prime Minister; a coalition Government was formed, including six ministers from the previous administration and only three LDLP members.

14 February 1993: Algirdas Brazauskas was elected President, securing some 60% of the votes cast (from December 1992 he had been acting head of state in his capacity as Chairman of the new Seimas).

March 1993: Adolfas Šleževičius, a member of the LDLP, was appointed Prime Minister.

May 1993: Lithuania became a full member of the Council of Europe.

31 August 1993: The last of the former Soviet (Russian) troops remaining on Lithuanian territory were withdrawn.

November 1993: Lithuania signed a number of bilateral agreements with Russia, including a 'most-favoured nation' treaty and social guarantees for ex-servicemen. Later disagreements over military transits delayed the implementation of the trade agreements.

January 1994: Lithuania joined the North Atlantic Treaty Organization's (NATO) Partnership for Peace programme of military co-operation. Lithuania had already expressed its intent to become a full member of NATO and had denounced Russian claims to be entitled to station troops on former Soviet territory.

20 December 1995: Lithuania's two largest commercial banks, the Lithuanian Joint-Stock Innovation Bank (LJIB) and Litimpex Bank, were declared insolvent and their operations suspended; senior officials from both banks were arrested on charges of fraud.

January 1996: The Ministers of Defence and Foreign Affairs tendered their resignations, when Prime Minister Šleževičius refused to resign following revelations that he had withdrawn funds from the LJIB just two days before the bank's operations were suspended. President Brazauskas refused to accept their resignations.

23 January 1996: Kazys Ratkevičius, the Chairman of the Bank of Lithuania, resigned. Six days later Romasis Vaitekūnas resigned as Minister of the Interior, following criticism of his handling of the banking crisis; it was revealed that he too had withdrawn funds from the LJIB just before its closure.

February 1996: The Seimas, by 94 votes to 26, approved a presidential decree dismissing Šleževičius from office (he also later resigned as leader of the LDLP and, in October, was charged with abuse of power while in office). Laurynas Mindaugas Stankevičius, previously Minister of Government Reforms and Local Governments, was appointed Prime Minister and chose a new cabinet.

June 1996: In what was hoped to be a move towards admission to the Central European Free Trade Area, Lithuania signed a free-trade agreement with Poland.

20 October 1996: The first round of voting in the general election was participated in by 53% of the electorate.

10 November 1996: Following the second round of the general election, participated in by 40% of the electorate, the Conservative Party (CP) had secured 70 seats in the Seimas and the Christian Democratic Party of Lithuania (CDPL) 16; the LDLP won only 12 seats, the nationalist Centre Union won 13 and the Lithuanian Social Democratic Party (LSDP) gained 12. The CP and the CDPL formed a coalition, supported by the Centre Union, and later in the month Landsbergis became parliamentary speaker and Vagnorius returned as premier (both were Conservatives). The Seimas confirmed Vagnorius as premier on 10 March 1998.

23 March 1997: In local elections the CP was the most successful party, securing some 33% of the total votes cast.

23–25 October 1997: President Brazauskas made the first official visit to Russia by a Baltic head of state since the collapse of the USSR. During the visit a state border delimitation treaty was signed and bilateral co-operation agreements reached. The treaty was ratified by the Seimas in October 1999.

21 December 1997: The two leading candidates in the presidential election were Arturas Paulauskas, a former prosecutor, who received 45.28% of the votes cast, and Valdas Adamkus, a retired environmental protection executive, who had mainly lived in the USA, who secured 27.9%.

4 January 1998: In the second round of the presidential election Adamkus received 50.37% of the votes cast, Paulauskas 49.63% (Adamkus was sworn in as President on 26 February).

16 January 1998: The Presidents of Lithuania, Estonia and Latvia met President Bill Clinton of the USA in Washington, DC (USA), and signed a Charter of Partnership, for the development of closer political and economic links.

22 September 1998: The Government adopted economic measures to protect Lithuanian industry from the effects of the financial crisis in Russia.

21 December 1998: In accordance with the European Convention on Human Rights and Fundamental Freedoms, the Seimas voted to abolish the death penalty.

21 April 1999: Following public criticism of his professional abilities by President Adamkus, Vagnorius survived a non-binding vote of confidence in the Seima.

3 May 1999: Vagnorius formally resigned as premier; Irena Degutiene was appointed interim Prime Minister.

18 May 1999: Following approval by the Seimas, the Mayor of Vilnius, Rolandas Paksas, was appointed Prime Minister; his Government, announced on 1 June, mainly comprised members of the CP and the CDPL.

27 October 1999: Paksas resigned as Prime Minister, following a dispute over the sale of the state-owned Mažeikiai NAFTA petroleum refinery to the US oil company, Williams International. Degutiene, who was once again appointed acting premier, declined the invitation to form a government. President Adamkus nominated the First Deputy Chairman of the Seimas, Andrius Kubilius, as Prime Minister; a new, largely unaltered, Government was appointed on 3 November.

11 December 1999: At a summit of European Union (EU) heads of government in Helsinki (Finland), Lithuania, which had applied for EU membership in 1995, was invited to begin accession negotiations from 28 March 2000. Lithuania hoped to achieve full membership of the EU by 2004.

19 March 2000: In local elections left-wing parties, notably the New Union, were the most successful; the CP had disappointing results, precipitating a division in the party.

26 April 2000: President Adamkus signed an amnesty law, releasing around 800–900 prisoners who met certain criteria, from overcrowded prisons.

9 May 2000: Following the announcement that a general election was to be held on 8 October, the two largest left-wing parties, the LDLP and the LSDP, announced the formation of an electoral alliance which, with the addition of two smaller parties, became known as the Social Democratic Coalition (SDC).

12 May 2000: A national energy strategy was approved, providing for the decommissioning of the first unit of the Ignalina nuclear power-station by 2005; the EU was to contribute €10m. to the project.

13 June 2000: The Seimas passed legislation claiming compensation from Russia for damage caused to the country during Soviet occupation; despite President Adamkus's opposition to the legislation, the Chairman of the Seimas, Vytautas Landsbergis, signed the law.

2 July 2000: The former premier, Gediminas Vagnorius, established the centre-right Moderate Conservative Union in preparation for the forthcoming legislative elections.

8 October 2000: In the legislative election the SDC gained 52 of the 141 seats in the Seimas; the Lithuanian Liberal Union (LLU), led by Rolandas Paksas, secured 34 seats and the New Union (NU), led by Arturas Paulauskas, 29. The CP won only nine seats, compared with 70 in the election held in October 1996.

12 October 2000: The LLU, NU, the Centre Union and the Modern Christian Democratic Union signed a coalition agreement, becoming known as the New Policy bloc. Agreements with several smaller parties ensured the bloc would have the support of a majority of deputies in the Seimas.

19 October 2000: Paulauskas was elected Chairman of the new Seimas.

26 October 2000: The Seimas approved a proposal by President Adamkus that Paksas be appointed Prime Minister. The President endorsed Paskas' Council of Ministers, comprising members of the LLU and NU, four days later and the Seimas gave its approval on 9 November.

13 November 2000: The LDLP and the LSDP announced that they would hold a congress to discuss a merger of the two parties in January 2001.

Luxembourg

3rd–6th centuries: Various Germanic tribes, migrating westwards, settled in the Roman province of Gaul. The area around modern Luxembourg was inhabited principally by the Alemanni, Franks and Goths. Eventually, the Franks gained pre-eminence in Gaul and, after the fall of the Western Roman Empire, a large part of the province was included in the Frankish realm.

925: The area that is now Luxembourg was absorbed into the German Holy Roman Empire.

963: A protégé of the Saxon emperors, Siegfried, who had substantial holdings of land in the region, signed the charter taking possession of the Lucilinburhuc Rock and a quantity of land overlooked by it, thereby founding the County of Luxembourg.

11th century: With the House of Luxembourg gaining prestige and power within the Empire, Henry, Count of Luxembourg, was granted the Duchy of Bavaria.

1194: Henry IV, Count of Namur-Luxembourg, lost the House's possessions to his nephew, Baldwin of Hainault—his daughter, Ermesind, inherited his title, but no lands as a result.

1196: Ermesind married, and acquired some of her lost patrimony; after her second marriage (contracted in 1221) she once more possessed the Counties of Luxembourg, Laroche and Durbuy, which her father had lost, as well as the Marquisate of Arlon.

1244: The town of Luxembourg received its charter.

1308: The Count of Luxembourg was elected to the imperial throne as Henry VII.

1313: John 'the Blind' of Luxembourg inherited the County of Luxembourg and the Kingdom of Bohemia; he sought to maintain his influence in the Empire, but impoverished the County.

1354: John the Blind's son, Emperor Charles IV, elevated Luxembourg to the status of a duchy.

1383: Emperor Wenceslas, the son of Charles IV, inherited the Counties of Luxembourg from another branch of the family; he financed his policies by pledging territory to foreign princes, with right of repurchase–Luxembourg was thus drawn into distant quarrels and became beset by unrest and lawlessness.

1411: Sigismund, Wenceslas' brother, became Emperor, but the Duchy of Luxembourg was pledged to Elizabeth of Görlitz.

1443: Luxembourg fell to Phillip the 'Good', Duke of Burgundy, who installed a governor and a governing council, and restored order.

1479: With the disintegration of Burgundy, Luxembourg fell to France, although the Burgundian titles passed to the Austrian Habsburgs. France laid siege to Luxembourg.

1542–44: The French occupation of the Duchy was ended by Imperial forces.

1556: Emperor Charles V, under whom Luxembourg had remained Roman Catholic, abdicated and left his Burgundian possessions in personal union with the Spanish Crown, to his son, Phillip II.

1624: The Duchy's customary laws were published for the first time in written form.

1635: France's entry into the Thirty Years' War brought hardship and French occupation to Luxembourg.

1659: Luxembourg secured a peace with France, at the expense of several of its major towns.

1698: Luxembourg, occupied by France in 1678–84 and then secured by treaty, reverted to Spain by the Treaty of Rijswijk.

1701–13: During the War of the Spanish Succession, French troops were stationed in the Duchy once again and there was considerable conflict in the area. The Treaty of Utrecht, which ended the War, awarded the Spanish Netherlands, including Luxembourg, to the Habsburgs.

1735: The Austrian administration undertook works to fortify Luxembourg against attack.

1769: An agreement was reached with France over mutual borders, which had been in dispute since the Treaty of Utrecht.

1795: Luxembourg, invaded by French revolutionary forces in the previous year, was declared a département of the French Republic.

1814: As the Napoleonic Empire declined, the French left Luxembourg and a provisional administration was established in the Duchy by the Allies.

1815: The Congress of Vienna established Luxembourg as a Grand Duchy and as a sovereign state within the newly created Germanic Confederation, but it was to be administered by King William I of the Netherlands.

1830–39: The Grand Duchy (apart from Luxembourg-Ville) was administered by the Belgian authorities. The Walloon (French-speaking) area in the west of the territory was annexed by Belgium and became the Belgian province of Luxembourg.

1839: The 'rump' of the Grand Duchy reverted to the Dutch monarchy and German association, becoming a member of the customs union (Zollverein).

1840: William II of the Netherlands established important organs of state in Luxembourg (government, constitution, code of laws and education system).

1848: A liberal, parliamentary Constitution, based on the Belgian model, was passed.

1856: William III removed many of the liberal elements of the Constitution.

1867: The London Congress declared Luxembourg to be an independent, neutral state, although the Dutch association did not end until the death of William III in 1890.

17 October 1868: The Constitution of 1848 was reintroduced; the garrison and all fortifications were dismantled, to emphasize the Grand Duchy's neutrality and demilitarized status.

1890: Luxembourg passed to the Duke of Nassau.

1914: At the outbreak of the First World War in Europe, German troops occupied Luxembourg, remaining there for the duration of the War.

1919: In a referendum, the people of Luxembourg confirmed the monarchic principle and Grand Duchess Charlotte succeeded to the throne. In addition, the Constitution was amended to vest sovereign power in the nation, to provide for universal male and female suffrage, and to introduce proportional representation for election to the Chamber of Deputies (Châmber vun Députéirten/ Chambre des Députés).

1921: Formation of the Belgium-Luxembourg Economic Union.

1940: During the Second World War, Germany annexed Luxembourg; a Government-in-Exile sat in London (United Kingdom) until liberation in 1944.

1941: In October only 3% of the electorate voted for incorporation into the German Reich and, later, an effective general strike against Nazi rule was organized.

1948: The Benelux Economic Union was formed by Belgium, Luxembourg and the Netherlands (the Union became effective in 1960 and a single customs area was established in 1970).

1949: Luxembourg was a founder member of the North Atlantic Treaty Organization (NATO).

18 April 1951: Luxembourg and four other countries established the European Coal and Steel Community (ECSC), the first institution of the European Community (EC), and established its headquarters in Luxembourg.

9 October 1956: Amendments to the Constitution were introduced to provide for a five-yearly general election to the Chamber of Deputies, replacing the older system of three-yearly partial elections.

1957: Luxembourg was a founder member of the European Economic Community (EEC) and the European Atomic Energy Community (EURATOM); Luxembourg-Ville was established as one of the three main bases of the Communities.

November 1964: Grand Duchess Charlotte abdicated in favour of her son, Prince Jean.

May 1974: At a general election the Christian Social Party (Parti Chrétien Social—PCS) lost its political dominance for the first time since 1919. A centre-left coalition Government was subsequently formed between the Socialist Worker's Party (Parti Ouvrier Socialiste Luxembourgeois—POSL) and the Democratic Party (Parti Démocratique Luxembourgeois—PDL).

July 1979: The PCS returned to power in a coalition Government, under the premiership of Pierre Werner, a former Prime Minister.

July 1984: Jacques Santer of the PCS became the new Prime Minister of another coalition Government.

June 1990: The Schengen Agreement (named after the town in Luxembourg where the accord was signed) of a number of EC countries compelled the abolition of internal border controls between the signatories.

12 December 1994: The Constitution was amended in accordance with the provisions of the Treaty on European Union.

January 1995: Santer took office as the President of the European Commission. He was replaced as Prime Minister by Jean-Claude Juncker.

12 July 1996: The Constitution was amended to introduce a Constitutional Court.

12 January 1998: The Constitution was amended further.

March 1998: Grand Duke Jean conferred wide-ranging constitutional powers on his son, Prince Henri, in what was seen as preparation for the succession.

1 January 1999: Luxembourg was one of the first group of countries to participate in Stage III of the European Union (EU)'s programme of Economic and

Monetary Union (EMU), whereby a new single European currency, the euro, was launched.

June 1999: Following a general election, Jean-Claude Juncker remained Prime Minister and a new coalition Government of the PCS and the PDL was formed.

7 October 2000: Prince Henri succeeded Grand Duke Jean as Head of State; his coronation was scheduled to be held in mid-2001.

November 2000: An agreement was reached with other EU member states that income from savings held in Luxembourg would be taxed from 2003, with 75% of revenue being transferred to the saver's country of residence. The agreement threatened the country's status as a tax haven.

Macedonia

6th century BC: The ancient kingdom of Macedon, with capitals at Pella and Aigai (Edessa), was established on the borders of the Hellenic territories.

336–323 BC: Reign of Alexander III ('the Great') of Macedon, the most famous of the ancient kings; he secured Macedon's hegemony over the Greeks and conquered the Persian Empire. His empire disintegrated after his death into a number of Hellenic kingdoms, of which Macedon became the territory of the Antigonid dynasty.

168 BC: Macedon was finally defeated by the Roman Empire and the kingdom was divided into four semi-autonomous territories.

148 BC: After an uprising the Roman province of Macedonia (an area which included large parts of modern-day northern Greece and western Bulgaria) was created.

AD 395: Following a division of the administration of the Roman Empire, Macedonia and Illyria to the north-west formally came under the authority of the Eastern Roman ('Byzantine') Emperor in Constantinople (now Istanbul, Turkey).

6th century: Southern Slav peoples began to move from Pannonia into the Balkans.

7th century: The ancestors of the Bulgars moved south of the Danube and merged with the Slavs and the autochthonous inhabitants of Macedonia.

865: Boris, the Khan of the Bulgars, converted to Eastern Orthodox Christianity following the missionary activity of the Byzantine brothers, SS Constantine (Cyril) and Methodius; a Slavonic liturgy (based on a dialect of the western Bulgar territory of Macedonia) was introduced with a written language, in the Cyrillic script which remains common to all the Eastern and Balkan Slavic peoples.

1014: Final defeat of the western Bulgarian, or Macedonian, realm under Samuel (Samuil) by the Byzantine Emperor, Basil II.

1187: The Emperor in Constantinople acknowledged Serb independence and the establishment of the second Bulgarian Empire (which was to include much of Macedonia and the surrounding territories).

1330: The Serbs defeated the Bulgarians and the Greek Byzantines at the Battle of Velbuzhde (Küstendil).

1346: Establishment of a Serbian patriarchate and the coronation of Stefan Dušan 'the Great' of Raška, who reigned (1331–55) as Tsar of the Serbs and Greeks, at Skopje; however, he failed in his ambition to conquer Constantinople (Carigrad).

1389: The Turkish Ottoman Empire secured its conquest of Macedonia and the region by its victory against the Serbian nobility at a battle on the plain of Kosovo Polje; the Ottoman Empire was administered by the confessional *millet* system, which placed the Orthodox of Macedonia (after 1453) under the jurisdiction of the Greek Ecumenical Patriarch in Constantinople.

1870: The Bulgarians declared an Exarchate for their Church—that is they proclaimed their autonomy from the Ecumenical Patriarchate and introduced the Slavonic liturgy; they contested with the Greek Church for adherents in the Macedonian region.

March 1878: The Treaty of San Stefano concluded the war between Russia, in support of the Orthodox Slavs, and the Ottomans; however, the Great Powers rejected the settlement, which created a 'Greater Bulgaria'.

July 1878: At the Congress of Berlin, Bulgaria was denied the annexation of Macedonia, while Serbia and Montenegro secured their independence; many Macedonians fled to Bulgaria after this treaty.

1893: Foundation of the Internal Macedonian Revolutionary Organization (IMRO), which opposed the partition of Macedonia, but supported the idea of a Southern Slav ('Yugoslav') federation.

1895: The foundation of the External Organization of Supremacists (based in Sofia, Bulgaria) divided Macedonian nationalism, as it favoured the incorporation of Macedonia into Bulgaria.

2 August 1903: The Ilinden Uprising against the Ottomans, in what is now Bulgarian (Pirin) Macedonia, was organized by IMRO and led by Gotse Delchev; the revolt was suppressed, but remains commemorated by both Macedonian and Bulgarian nationalists.

May 1913: The Peace of London concluded the First Balkan War, in which a league of Bulgaria, Greece, Montenegro and Serbia succeeded in removing the Turks from the bulk of their European possessions.

June 1913: Hoping to secure its claim to Macedonia, Bulgaria attacked Serbia, which had occupied Skopje (Usküb) after defeating the Ottomans at nearby Kumanovo (November 1912); Serbia was supported by Greece, Montenegro, Romania and the Turks.

August 1913: The Peace of Bucharest concluded the Second Balkan War; Bulgaria lost most of Macedonia, which was divided between Serbia (Vardar Macedonia or 'South Serbia') and Greece (Aegean Macedonia); Albanian independence was recognized.

28 July 1914: Habsburg Austria-Hungary declared war on Serbia; this started the First World War between the Central Powers, of Austria-Hungary and Germany, and the Entente Powers, of France, Russia, Serbia and the United Kingdom.

1915: Serbian Macedonia was occupied by Bulgaria, which joined the Central Powers in the conquest of Serbia.

4 December 1918: Proclamation of the Kingdom of Serbs, Croats and Slovenes, which united Serbia (including Vardar Macedonia) and Montenegro with the former Habsburg lands, under the Serbian monarchy.

3 October 1929: Following the imposition of a royal dictatorship, the country was formally named Yugoslavia.

March 1941: A *coup d'état* reversed previous policies and aligned Yugoslavia with the Allied Powers of the Second World War.

April 1941: German and Italian forces invaded Yugoslavia, which was partitioned; Macedonia was again occupied by Bulgaria, which lost much local support to the Communists.

29 November 1945: Following elections for a Provisional Assembly, the Federative People's Republic of Yugoslavia was proclaimed, with Tito (Josip Broz, leader of the Communist resistance forces) as prime minister. By this time a Macedonian alphabet and orthography had been prepared and accepted by the Communist authorities, who wished to foster a distinct Macedonian identity.

January 1946: A Soviet-style Constitution established a federation of six republics and two autonomous regions in Yugoslavia; one of the republics was Macedonia; this was not only an acknowledgement of Macedonian nationalism, but an attempt to resolve the competing claims of Serbia and Bulgaria (until 1948 Tito had ambitions of a greater federation including the latter).

1958: The archdiocese of Ohrid, an ancient see, was established, despite the protests of the Serbian Orthodox hierarchy which resented the move towards separation.

April 1963: A new Constitution changed the country's name to the Socialist Federal Republic of Yugoslavia (SFRY).

18 July 1967: The autocephaly of the Macedonian Orthodox Church was declared, but the Serbian Church refused to acknowledge it and was backed by the Ecumenical Patriarch and the other established Orthodox Churches.

November 1968: Demonstrations in Tetovo by ethnic Albanians, present in large numbers in western Macedonia, demanded the creation of a seventh federal republic, for the Albanians of Yugoslavia.

4 May 1980: Tito died; his responsibilities were transferred to the collective State Presidency and to the Presidium of the ruling League of Communists of Yugoslavia (LCY).

1981: Protests by Albanians in the neighbouring Serbian Autonomous Province of Kosovo (officially renamed Kosovo and Metohija from September 1990) provoked measures by the Macedonian authorities against Albanian nationalism.

1988: There were further demonstrations in the republic, not only about economic conditions and in favour of reform, but also by Albanian students.

1989: The Communist regime amended the republican Constitution to allow a multi-party system; however, ethnic tension increased when further amendments declared that Macedonia was a 'nation-state' of the ethnic Macedonians, omitting mention of the Albanian minority.

February 1990: The Movement for All-Macedonian Action (MAMA) was founded; although a nationalist party, it disclaimed any territorial ambitions for the republic.

June 1990: The Internal Macedonian Revolutionary Organization—Democratic Party for Macedonian National Unity (IMRO—DPMNU), a more extreme nationalist party, was founded and elected Ljubiša (Ljubčo) Georgievski as leader.

July 1990: Ante Marković, the federal prime minister, formed the Alliance of Reform Forces (ARF), an all-Yugoslav party which supported his Government and advocated Western-style reforms.

November 1990: Two rounds of elections to a new, unicameral 120-seat Assembly (Sobranje) were held in Macedonia.

9 December 1990: The final round of voting in Macedonia produced an inconclusive result, with the nationalist opposition, IMRO—DPMNU, winning the largest number of seats (37); the League of Communists of Macedonia—Party of Democratic Reform (LCM—PDR, the former ruling Communists) won 31 seats, the republican ARF 19 (subsequently the Liberal Party) and the two predominantly Albanian parties, the Party of Democratic Prosperity (PDP) and the People's Democratic Party, together, 25.

7 January 1991: The IMRO—DPMNU, the LCM—PDR and the Macedonian ARF agreed on a coalition administration (subsequently Stojan Andov of the ARF was elected President of the Sobranje and, eventually, Kiro Gligorov of the LCM—PDR President of the Republic, with Georgievski of the IMRO—

DPMNU as Vice-President); however, an administration under Milo Djukanović did not satisfy the competing demands of the parties.

25 January 1991: The Sobranje unanimously adopted a declaration of Macedonia's sovereignty, including a statement of its right to secede from the SFRY.

March 1991: Nikola Kljušev became premier of a new administration, composed of non-political 'experts'.

7 June 1991: The Sobranje changed the state's name to the Republic of Macedonia; among other constitutional amendments and against a background of increasing tension in Croatia and Slovenia, which were attempting to secede from the federation, the Sobranje declared Macedonian neutrality and also provided that it alone could authorize a state of emergency (this was done on 4 August).

8 September 1991: Some 95% of the two-thirds of eligible voters who participated in the referendum were in favour of an independent and sovereign Macedonia; the large ethnic Albanian minority boycotted the poll.

October 1991: Croatia and Slovenia declared their final independence. The IMRO—DPMNU announced that it was to leave the Government, following the resignation of Georgievski as Vice-President. Later, the Macedonian Government announced that more than 60% of federal bases in the republic had been evacuated; the total withdrawal of federal troops was completed in March of the following year.

17 November 1991: The new Constitution was enacted, despite opposition from the majority of the ethnic Albanian deputies and three of the IMRO—DPMNU deputies; with the promulgation of the new Constitution Macedonia was declared to be an independent country.

January 1992: An unofficial referendum conducted among the ethnic Albanian population resulted in a 99.9% vote in favour of territorial and political autonomy for the Albanian population. The Commission of the European Community (EC—known as the European Union, EU, from November 1993) acknowledged that Macedonia fulfilled the requirements for official recognition; however, Greek objections to the use of the name 'Macedonia' and the use of the Star of Vergina (an emblem associated with Alexander the Great) on the Macedonian national flag ensured that EC recognition for Macedonia was not forthcoming; nevertheless, on 16 January, Bulgaria became the first country officially to recognize Macedonia; Turkey followed suit early in the following month.

April 1992: The new Constitution of the Federal Republic of Yugoslavia (FRY) referred only to Serbia and Montenegro, effectively acknowledging the secession of Macedonia. Diplomatic relations were established with Croatia.

June 1992: Negotiations between the Macedonian Minister of Foreign Relations and the Greek Prime Minister, Konstantinos Mitsotakis, ended in failure.

July 1992: Following a vote of 'no confidence' passed in the Sobranje, and after demonstrations by more than 100,000 people in the capital protesting at its failure to gain recognition for an independent Macedonia, the Government resigned.

September 1992: Branko Crvenkovski, leader of the Social Democratic Alliance of Macedonia (SDAM, known as the LCM—PDR until 1991), was appointed Chairman (Prime Minister) of a new coalition Government.

October 1992: A new citizenship law stipulating a 15-year residency requirement prior to granting citizenship came into effect, angering many ethnic Albanians.

December 1992: The UN Security Council authorized the dispatch of troops, civilian police and military observers to Macedonia in order to monitor the inter-ethnic tensions, following an increase in sometimes violent unrest.

April 1993: Macedonia was admitted to the United Nations (UN) despite Greek objections, but under the name of the 'Former Yugoslav Republic of Macedonia'.

May 1993: A new currency, the new Macedonian denar, was introduced.

September 1993: Negotiations between Macedonia and Greece, held in New York (USA) under UN auspices, failed to resolve the dispute over the former Yugoslav republic's name.

December 1993: The United Kingdom established full diplomatic relations with Macedonia, followed, in a co-ordinated move, by France, Germany and the Netherlands before the end of the year.

16 February 1994: Greece suspended diplomatic relations with Macedonia and prohibited the country from using the Greek port of Thessaloníki, except for humanitarian aid.

17 February 1994: The PDP split, with the more radical faction later forming the Party of Democratic Prosperity of the Albanians in Macedonia (PDPAM).

16 October 1994: Kiro Gligorov, a candidate of the Alliance for Macedonia (consisting of the SDAM, the Liberal Party and the Socialist Party of Macedonia—SPM) was re-elected to the presidency by an overwhelming majority (78.37% of votes valid cast). His only opponent in the election was Ljubiša Georgievski, representing IMRO—DPMNU. The first round of voting in the general election was also held; a second round of voting, held on 30 October, was boycotted by IMRO—DPMNU which, having won no seats in the first round, made allegations of widespread fraud.

13 November 1994: A third round of legislative elections was held in some constituencies, owing to irregularities in earlier rounds; final results confirmed that the Alliance for Macedonia had won the majority of seats (of which 58 went to the SDAM, 29 to the Liberals and eight to the SPM); the PDP won 10 seats. The Sobranje subsequently approved an SDAM-led administration, again headed by Crvenkovski and including the PDP.

17 February 1995: Violent disturbances occurred in Tetovo, following the opening of an 'illegal' Albanian-language university, resulting in the death of an Albanian. A few days later the rector of the institution, Fadil Sulejmani, was arrested and was subsequently sentenced to two-and-a-half years' imprisonment.

31 March 1995: The Macedonian contingent of UN peace-keeping forces in the former Yugoslavia was named the UN Preventive Deployment Force (UNPREDEP); it became an independent command in February 1996 and its mandate was eventually extended until February 1999.

13 September 1995: Macedonia and Greece signed an agreement establishing diplomatic relations and economic ties between the two countries: Greece was to lift its embargo in return for Macedonia relinquishing its claim to the Star of Vergina for its national flag.

3 October 1995: President Gligorov was seriously injured in a car-bomb attack.

12 October 1995: Macedonia was accepted into the Organization for Security and Co-operation in Europe (OSCE), with the ending of Greek objections; the country had become a member of the Council of Europe earlier in the month.

23 February 1996: A new Government, in which the Liberal Party was unrepresented, was approved by the Sobranje, following the collapse of the Alliance for Macedonia.

8 April 1996: Macedonia and the FRY established full diplomatic relations in an accord on normalizing relations and promoting co-operation; both countries recognized the other's sovereignty, independence and territorial integrity.

July 1996: Parliamentary and popular protests were made by ethnic Albanian deputies over the status of the Albanian-language university at Tetovo, culminating in a demonstration outside Tetovo prison where the rector, Sulejmani (whose sentence had been reduced to one year), was incarcerated (he was released on 1 February 1997); sporadic protests continued.

October 1996: The outbreak of an unidentified illness in Tetovo, to which hundreds of ethnic Albanian children succumbed, provoked Albanian demonstrations and allegations of deliberate poisoning by the Macedonian authorities.

17 November 1996: In the first round of voting in local elections, the SDAM received the greatest number of votes, followed by the IMRO—DPMNU-led alliance and then the PDP; the PDPAM and the People's Democratic Party (which were to merge in 1997) gained an increased proportion of the ethnic Albanian vote.

January 1997: Government proposals to adopt Albanian as the language of instruction at the teacher-training faculty of the University of Skopje provoked outrage among Macedonian students. However, parliament refused to provide for the use of Albanian in the legislature, leading to pressure from within the PDP to withdraw from the ruling coalition.

February 1997: Further municipal elections in Tetovo (where voting had to be repeated) resulted in victory for the PDPAM, prompting renewed displays of nationalist sentiment by ethnic Albanians.

9 April 1997: An increase in civil unrest in neighbouring Albania led to additional troops being deployed on the Macedonian–Albanian border.

22 May 1997: The Constitutional Court forbade the use of the Albanian flag in Macedonia, causing protests by ethnic Albanians.

29 May 1997: The Sobranje approved Crvenkovski's new Government, which remained led by the SDAM, but including the PDP and the SPM.

8 July 1997: The Sobranje adopted legislation stipulating that the use of the Albanian flag, and flags of other nationalities, would only be permitted on national holidays, with the Macedonian flag being displayed at the same time; government officials forcibly removed Albanian flags displayed at municipal buildings in Gostivar and Tetovo, leading to violent clashes between protesting ethnic Albanians and security forces, which resulted in three deaths and the arrests of 500 protesters.

17 September 1997: The mayor of Gostivar was sentenced to almost 14 years' imprisonment after being found guilty of inciting ethnic tension and rebellion in the July flag troubles; the leader of the municipal council was sentenced to three years' imprisonment for failing to obey the Constitutional Court's May ruling (both men's sentences were reduced on appeal, to seven and two years, respectively).

5–6 March 1998: Some 50,000 ethnic Albanians attended a rally in Skopje in support of the ethnic Albanians in the neighbouring Serbian province of Kosovo and Metohija and to demand international intervention in the region; at the demonstration an Albanian flag was hoisted and the Albanian national anthem was played—ethnic Albanian leaders were later charged with inciting ethnic unrest.

13 April 1998: The Democratic Party of Albanians (DPA—formed in 1997 by the merger of the PDPAM and the People's Democratic Party) announced that it was to withdraw its members from all government institutions in protest at the continuing imprisonment of Rufi Osmani, the former mayor of Gostivar.

31 August 1998: The PDP and the DPA announced the establishment of a political co-operation agreement, including an electoral alliance, to promote the cause of ethnic Albanians in Macedonia.

26 September 1998: Macedonia signed an agreement with Albania, Bulgaria, Greece, Italy, Romania and Turkey on the establishment of multinational forces in South-Eastern Europe, to operate under UN auspices.

18 October 1998: In the first round of voting in elections to the Sobranje, the IMRO—DPMNU won 26.9% of the valid votes cast, followed by the SDAM with 23.8%; the alliance of ethnic Albanian parties won 19.6% of the votes cast, while the newly-formed Democratic Alternative (DA) won 10.8%, the Liberal-Democratic Party (LDP—the Liberal Party had merged with the Democratic Party of Macedonia in 1996) 6.9% and the Movement for Cultural Tolerance and Civic Co-operation, a coalition of the SPM and five parties representing various ethnic minorities, 4.1%.

1 November 1998: After a second round of voting the 'For Changes' alliance (which comprised the IMRO—DPMNU and the DA) gained 58 seats in the Sobranje, followed by the SDAM with 29 and the PDP-DPA grouping with a total of 24. A further round of voting in two electoral districts was held on 15 November, in which For Changes and the PDP-DPA each won a further seat.

23 November 1998: Georgievski was invited to form a coalition Government; his Cabinet, appointed in early December, comprised 14 representatives from the IMRO–DPMNU, eight from the DA and five members from the DPA; following its inclusion in the administration the DPA reversed its decision to withdraw its representatives from government institutions.

7 December 1998: A 2,300-strong North Atlantic Treaty Organization (NATO) 'extraction force' was deployed in Macedonia to assist in the evacuation of OSCE monitors in Kosovo in the event of a large-scale conflict there.

29 December 1998: The Sobranje approved legislation providing for the early release of some 8,000 prisoners, including Osmani; however, on 5 January 1999 President Gligorov refused to approve the amnesty, claiming it was unconstitutional.

4 February 1999: The legislature approved the amnesty law for a second time, overriding the presidential veto; Osmani was released two days later.

26 February 1999: The People's Republic of China vetoed a UN Security Council resolution to extend the UNPREDEP mandate for a further six months, following a decision by the Macedonian Government to recognize China (Taiwan), which had prompted the People's Republic of China to suspend diplomatic relations with Macedonia. UNPREDEP formally ended its six-year mission on 1 March.

7 March 1999: Local elections were held in Gostivar and Tetovo. No candidate was elected in Gostivar, owing to low voter turn-out. Murtezan Ismaili of the DPA was elected mayor of Tetovo.

April 1999: Following an escalation in the conflict in neighbouring Kosovo, about 14,000 further NATO troops were deployed near the Macedonian–Serbian border; the number of forces was further increased, to 16,000, in June, when the border was repeatedly closed to prevent further influxes of refugees.

19 May 1999: A reorganization of cabinet portfolios took place; among the changes was the appointment of a new Minister of Economy, Mihailo Tolevski.

20 June 1999: Following the FRY Government's acceptance of a peace plan the end of NATO's air campaign, the return of refugees from Macedonia to Kosovo began.

12 August 1999: The UN High Commissioner for Refugees (UNHCR) agreed to give Macedonia US$4m. in compensation for expenses incurred during the Kosovo crisis.

31 October and 14 November 1999: In the first round of the presidential election, Tito Petkovski, the candidate of the SDAM, gained 32.7% of the votes cast, while the IMRO—DPMNU nominee, Boris Trajkovski, won 20.8% and the DA leader, Vasil Tupurkovski, 16%. As nobody secured a majority, a second ballot took place on 14 November between the two leading candidates, which Trajkovski won, with 52.8% of votes cast. The SDAM disputed the results, claiming widespread malpractice, particularly in the western regions where the population of ethnic Albanians was high. The accusations were supported by the OSCE.

27 November 1999: The Supreme Court upheld a legal appeal by the SDAM against the election results and ruled that a further ballot should take place in some regions in the west of the country.

5 December 1999: A partial round of elections took place for 10% of the electorate. The overall results were virtually unchanged; Trajkovski won with 52.9% of votes cast. The SDAM continued to claim irregularities; nevertheless, on 15 December, Trajkovski was inaugurated as President.

14 December 1999: Macedonia and Greece signed an agreement on military co-operation.

22 December 1999: Following negotiations between the leaders of the three parties that made up the government coalition, a redistribution of cabinet portfolios was effected; the new Government, which contained seven new ministries, including Tupurkovski, who became a Deputy Prime Minister, was approved by the Sobranje five days later.

23 February 2000: Macedonian troops were placed on alert at the border with Kosovo, owing to concern over increasing violence in the region.

5 April 2000: Representatives of the Macedonian Government and the EU met in Brussels (Belgium) to discuss regional co-operation; Macedonia hoped to sign an association agreement with the EU in 2000.

14 April 2000: The Sobranje approved legislation making compulsory the return of property expropriated under the Communist regime.

17 June 2000: Following several incidents on the Macedonia–Kosovo border, including one in which two Macedonian soldiers were shot, intensive talks on border security were held in Skopje between President Trajkovski, the Minister of Defence, Nikola Kljusev, and the Commander of the NATO-Russian peace-keeping force in Kosovo (K-FOR), Juan Ortuno.

19 June 2000: The Macedonian Minister of Internal Affairs, Dosta Dimovska, and her Bulgarian counterpart signed a co-operation agreement on control of their common border.

25 June 2000: The Government decided to reduce the number of ministries from 21 to 15.

10 September 2000: Municipal elections were held throughout Macedonia. International observers criticized the conduct of the elections and 27 of the 123 municipalities required a repeated first ballot.

24 September 2000: The second ballots and, where required, repeated first ballots of the municipal elections were held. Electoral irregularities were also reported in this round and repeated ballots were scheduled to continue in individual municipalities for several months. Final results, where available, showed that the governing coalition, known as 'For the Good of Everyone', won approximately one-half of the country's municipalities, principally in rural areas. The opposition coalition ('For Macedonia—Together', comprising the SDAM, the LDP, the SPM and several smaller parties) secured control of most of the larger cities, while the DPA was successful in areas where the majority population was of ethnic Albanian origin.

6 November 2000: Tensions between two of the partners in the governing coalition were resolved when the IMRO—DPMNU and the DA agreed on a programme of alterations to electoral legislation and increased DA participation in negotiations with international institutions.

30 November 2000: The DA formally abandoned its coalition with the IMRO—DPMNU, although three individual members of the party chose to remain in the reconstituted governing coalition, with IMRO—DPMNU, the DPA and numerous members of smaller parties and independents. The new coalition had the support of 63 of the 120 members of the Sobranje. Georgievski appointed five new ministers to the vacancies created by the defection of the DA. A motion of 'no confidence' in the President of the Sobranje, Savo Klimovski, proposed by the new coalition was carried. Klimovski resigned and Stojan Andov was elected to succeed him.

13 December 2000: The principal border crossing between Macedonia and Greece was reopened. Representatives of both countries' governments held negotiations aimed at improving bilateral relations.

29 December 2000: President Trajkovski visited the capital of the FRY, Belgrade, for a meeting with the federal President, Vojislav Kostunica. A number of bilateral agreements were signed and both countries emphasized the necessity to improve their bilateral relations.

6 March 2001: National armed forces launched a heavy assault on Kosovo-Albanian separatist guerrillas near the Macedonian border village of Tanusevci. The Government appealed for assistance in combating the rebels from KFOR, the joint NATO-Russian peace-keeping force in Kosovo. The following day US KFOR troops shot and wounded two Albanian fighters near Tanusevci and, two days after the request for help, 300 US troops stationed in Kosovo were transferred to the border region.

Malta

c. **800 BC:** Phoenician seafarers colonized the island of Malta.

218 BC: Titus Sempronius led a Roman army to a successful invasion of Malta and the Maltese islands were incorporated within the Roman Empire. The Maltese enjoyed a certain degree of autonomy in this arrangement.

AD 869: Malta was captured by Muslim Arabs, whose influence in the Maltese language can still be detected today.

1090: Under Count Roger of Sicily, the Normans invaded Malta; following negotiations the Arabs continued to govern the islands, in return for an annual tribute.

c. **1123:** The Maltese islands were formally incorporated into the Sicilian Crown (under King Roger II, 1105–54), also governed by the Normans.

1194: After the death of King William II (1154–94), his aunt, Constance, wife of the Holy Roman Emperor, Henry IV, inherited the Kingdom of Sicily.

1266: The papacy reasserted its overlordship of the Kingdom of Sicily and granted it to the French House of Anjou—French rule proved unpopular in Sicily and it (and Malta) fell to the Spanish Kingdom of Aragon, leaving Naples and the mainland Italian territories to the Angevins.

23 March 1530: Emperor Charles V, also King of Spain, ceded the islands of Malta and Gozo to the sovereign, military Order of the Hospital of St John of Jerusalem ('Hospitallers').

1565: A five-month siege on Malta of the Ottoman Turks, using 200 vessels and 40,000 men, was successfully resisted.

1798: During his Egyptian campaign, Napoleon Bonaparte of France captured Malta and expelled the Hospitallers.

1814: By the Treaty of Paris, Malta was ceded to the United Kingdom by France, thereby becoming a British crown colony.

1835: A Council of Government was established, consisting only of members nominated by the British authorities.

1849: A new Constitution established a Council of Government consisting of 10 nominated members and eight elected members.

1887: The Council of Government was enlarged to 20 members, 14 of whom were to be elected.

1914–18: During the First World War, Malta acted as a hospital base and a naval base.

1921: Malta was granted its first self-governing Constitution (known as the Amery-Milner Constitution); the island's role as an imperial fortress was managed by the United Kingdom, while domestic affairs were put under the control of a Senate and Legislative Assembly.

1930: A power struggle between the political élite (represented by the Prime Minister, Gerald Strickland), and the local Roman Catholic Church began, and the Constitution was suspended (until 1932).

1933: Executive powers of government and administration in Malta were returned to the governor-general, an appointment of the British government.

1939–45: During the Second World War Malta was heavily bombarded—the first air raids commenced in June 1940 and in March–April 1942 twice as many bombs were dropped on Malta as in one year on London (United Kingdom) at the height of the 'Blitz'; in July 1943 the Allied invasion of Sicily, leading to the surrender of the Italian naval fleet, was launched from Malta.

September 1947: Following the recommendations of a constitutional committee three years earlier, a legislature was established with 40 members elected by proportional representation; Dr Paul Boffa became the first Prime Minister of the governing Malta Labour Party (MLP—Partit tal-Haddiema).

1949: Boffa resigned over disagreements within the MLP over the conduct of negotiations with the British concerning the management of the naval dock-yard; he subsequently formed a new political party.

1950–53: In three successive elections the Nationalist Party (Partit Nazzjonalista—PN) was brought to power under the leadership of Dr Giorgio Borg Olivier, in coalition with the party of Boffa.

1955: Elections returned the MLP to power with an overall majority of 23 seats, under the leadership of Dominic (Dom) Mintoff, against the 17 seats of the PN.

February 1956: A referendum showed Malta to be in favour of integration with the United Kingdom, although 71% of the votes were abstentions.

30 December 1957: The House of Representatives, the Maltese legislature, voted to sever links with the United Kingdom.

1958: The MLP Government resigned in protest at the United Kingdom's continued dominance of Malta.

1962: In an election to the enlarged legislature the PN secured 26 seats, the MLP 16 seats and the Democratic Nationalist Party, the Christian Worker's Party and the Progressive Constitutional Party together gained eight seats.

21 September 1964: Malta became an independent, sovereign state within the Commonwealth, retaining the British monarch as its own; the United Kingdom signed the Mutual Defence and Assistance Agreement, which ensured financial recompense by the British, in return for the use of Malta's military facilities.

1966: In the first general election since independence the PN was returned to power with 28 seats, under the leadership of Borg Olivier; the MLP was the only other party to gain representation, with 22 seats.

1970: An Association Agreement was signed with the European Economic Community (EEC), by means of which aid was provided for development and infrastructure projects in Malta.

1971: The MLP, led by Dom Mintoff, took power after winning the general election with 29 seats to the PN's 26 seats.

1972: The Mutual Defence and Assistance Agreement with the United Kingdom was replaced by a new seven-year agreement.

13 December 1974: The Constitution was amended and Malta was declared a republic, still within the Commonwealth; Sir Anthony Mamo, a former Governor-General, was elected by the House of Representatives as the first President.

1976: In a general election the MLP was returned to power with a three-seat majority in the legislature, which had been enlarged to 65 seats; Dr Anton Buttigieg was subsequently elected President by the legislature.

31 March 1979: With the expiry of the agreement made in 1972, British troops were withdrawn from Malta.

1980: Italy agreed to guarantee Malta's neutrality and to provide financial and technical aid over five years.

1981: An agreement guaranteeing Malta's neutrality was signed with the USSR.

December 1981: The MLP secured a majority of three seats in the House of Representatives with only 49.1% of the votes cast; the PN, which had received 50.9% of the votes cast, refused to accept the result and refused to take its seats in the House, organizing a campaign of civil disobedience.

February 1982: Agatha Barbara was elected President by the legislature.

1984: Mintoff retired, to be succeeded by his deputy, Dr Karmenu (Carmelo) Mifsud Bonnici, after two years of increasingly controversial government in which there had been a dispute over Church land and education, accusations of repression and a number of significant foreign-policy initiatives.

1985: The Government reached an agreement with the Roman Catholic Church providing for the phased introduction of free education in Church schools, but guaranteeing their autonomy.

January 1987: The Constitution was amended to ensure that a party which received more than 50% of the total votes cast in a general election would obtain a majority of seats in the legislature. At the general election the PN obtained 50.9% of the votes cast but won only 31 of the 65 seats in the House of Representatives, while the MLP, with 48.9% of the votes cast, won the remaining 34 seats; thus, four seats were added to the PN's total, giving a majority of one; the leader of the PN, Dr Edward (Eddie) Fenech-Adami, became Prime Minster.

1989: Vincent Tabone was elected President by the legislature (in succession to Paul Xuereb, who had been Acting President since 1987).

1992: In the general election the PN secured 34 seats compared to the 31 seats of the MLP.

1994: Dr Ugo Mifsud Bonnici, the cousin of the former premier and leader of the MLP, was elected President.

1996: The PN Government, seeking to confirm its mandate to pursue the goal of full membership of the European Union (EU—formal application made in 1990), arranged a general election; the MLP won 50.7% of the votes cast and 31 seats, while the PN won 47.8% of the votes cast and the remaining 34 seats. Following the award of four additional seats to the MLP, it was able to form a Government, led by Dr Alfred Sant, the MLP leader; the new administration immediately withdrew Malta's application for full membership of the EU.

1997: The Government announced the initiation of a 'national discussion' of proposals to legalize divorce.

5 September 1998: At the general election the PN, led by Fenech-Adami, secured 51.8% of the votes cast and 35 seats, compared to the 48.0% and 30 seats obtained by the MLP. Upon taking office as Prime Minister, Fenech-Adami declared his intention to resume negotiations for EU entry.

4 April 1999: Prof. Guido Marco, former Deputy Prime Minister and Minister of Foreign Affairs, took office as President.

13 October 1999: A report published by the European Commission stated that Malta had already achieved the economic criteria for accession to the EU.

15 February 2000: Formal negotiations on Malta's accession to the EU began.

Moldova

106: Emperor Trajan made Dacia a province of the Roman Empire (by 118 Rome had secured its hegemony over an area including much of modern Moldova).

270: Rome abandoned Dacia to Visigothic invaders, the first of many incursions by peoples from the north and east.

***c.* 1359:** According to tradition, a Transylvanian prince, Dragoş, became the first lord, or domn, of the region between the Carpathians and the Dnestr (a region which takes its name from the river Molda). Other independent principalities emerged at this time, on the borders of Hungarian territory—the dominant peoples of these Moldovan (Moldavian) and Wallachian lands were Orthodox Christians speaking a Latinate tongue.

1457: Ştefan III ('the Great') came to power in Moldova, ruling until his death in 1504; under Ştefan, Moldova reached the height of its political and military power, and gained control of the lands stretching from the Carpathians to the Dnestr (Nistru) and the Black Sea.

1512: Moldova became a dependency of the Turkish Ottoman Empire.

1612: The Ottomans regained control of Moldova from Sigismund III of Poland.

1711: Following periodic uprisings by local nobles (boieri) in Moldova, the territory's autonomous status within the Ottoman Empire was revoked, and directly appointed Turkish administrators, Phanariots, were introduced; these Phanariots made Greek the official language and the Romanian Orthodox Church fell under Hellenic influence.

1768–74: The first Russian–Turkish war took place; the Ottomans were assisted by the Habsburg Empire in resisting a Russian attempt to occupy Moldova and Wallachia.

1806–12: In another Russian–Turkish conflict, Russian forces gained control of the lands between the Prut and the Dnestr rivers; the war was ended by the Treaty of Bucharest, under which Moldova was divided; the part west of the

Prut remained in the Ottoman Empire, while the eastern territory of Bessarabia (between the Prut and the Dnestr, extending to the Black Sea) became an autonomous region within the Russian Empire.

1815: The annexation of Bessarabia by Tsar Alexander I (1801–25) was approved by the Congress of Vienna.

1828: Bessarabia's autonomy was abolished and it became an imperial district (oblast); the use of the Romanian language in public pronouncements was suspended.

1854: Russian was made the official language of Bessarabia.

1871: Bessarabia became a province (guberniya) of the Russian Empire, by which time western Moldova (Moldavia) and Wallachia had been united in a single Romanian state (the Ottomans recognized its independence in 1878).

1905: The first Romanian-language publications appeared in Bessarabia, during a revolutionary threat to tsarist authority.

1917: With the collapse of tsarist authority in the 1917 Revolutions, revolutionary committees of soldiers and peasants quickly established a parliament (Sfatul Ţării) in the Bessarabian capital, Chişinău (Kishinev), and declared a Bessarabian Democratic Moldovan Republic.

27 March 1918: The Sfatul Ţării, having declared Bessarabia's independence on 24 January, voted for union with Romania (to counter threats from Bolshevik, 'White' Russian and Ukrainian interests).

1 December 1918: The unification of Romania was declared, after Transylvania and northern Bucovina had also voted to join the Romanian kingdom.

28 October 1920: The union of Bessarabia with Romania was recognized in the Treaty of Paris.

1924: A Moldovan Autonomous Soviet Socialist Republic (ASSR) was established in Soviet Ukraine, in territory to the east of the Dnestr river; the USSR claimed that the Romanians, in occupying Bessarabia, had violated Moldova's right to self-rule.

23 August 1939: The Treaty of Non-Aggression (the Nazi–Soviet or Molotov–Ribbentrop Pact), which was signed by the USSR and Germany, included the 'Secret Protocols', sanctioning territorial gains for the USSR in Bessarabia.

28 June 1940: The Soviet Red Army entered Bessarabia.

2 August 1940: Bessarabia officially became part of the USSR; parts of annexed Moldova were united with the existing ASSR, and the resulting Moldovan Soviet Socialist Republic (SSR) was declared a Union Republic of the USSR; two Bessarabian counties on the Black Sea, one county in the north and more than one-half of the counties of the former Moldovan ASSR were apportioned to Ukraine.

1941–44: The introduction of a Cyrillic alphabet for the 'Moldovan' language was interrupted by the Romanian occupation of Bessarabia, following the German invasion of the USSR; the Romanians were expelled towards the end of the Second World War.

1950–52: Leonid Brezhnev (Soviet leader 1964–82) was First Secretary of the Communist Party of Moldova (CPM).

1961: Ivan Ivanovich Bodiul became First Secretary of the CPM.

1982: Bodiul was succeeded as Moldovan leader by Semion Kuzmich Grossu, who held the post for seven years.

May 1989: The pro-Romanian Popular Front of Moldova (PFM) was established; among its aims were the abolition of the use of the Cyrillic script and the return to a Latin one, and the acceptance of Romanian as the country's state language.

31 August 1989: The Moldovan Supreme Soviet adopted laws which returned Moldovan to the Latin script, made it the state language of the republic and recognized its unity with the Romanian language. After protests by the Slav population, Russian was to be retained as the language of inter-ethnic communication.

November 1989: Grossu, a conservative, was finally replaced as First Secretary of the CPM by the more reformist Petru Lucinschi, an ethnic Romanian, following rioting in Chişinău.

25 February 1990: Elections to the Moldovan Supreme Soviet were held; the PFM won the largest number of seats.

April 1990: The new Moldovan Supreme Soviet convened; Mircea Snegur, a CPM member supported by the PFM, was re-elected Chairman of the Supreme Soviet. The legislative later adopted a modified version of the Romanian tricolour as Moldova's national flag.

May 1990: Petr Paskar's Government resigned after losing a vote of 'no confidence'; Mircea Druc was appointed Chairman of a Council of Ministers (Prime Minister) dominated by radical reformers; the new Government immediately undertook a series of political reforms, including revoking the CPM's constitutional monopoly of power.

23 June 1990: The Moldovan Supreme Soviet adopted a declaration of sovereignty which asserted the supremacy of Moldova's Constitution and laws throughout the republic; the 1940 annexation of Bessarabia by the USSR was declared to have been illegal and, on the following day, thousands of Moldovans and Romanians assembled at the border in commemoration of the

50th anniversary of the occupation. The Supreme Soviet also specified the name of the Republic to be 'Moldova', rather than the russified 'Moldavia'.

19 August 1990: Five counties (raione) in southern Moldova, largely populated by ethnic Gagauz (Orthodox Christian Turks), declared a separate 'Gagauz SSR' (Gagauzia).

2 September 1990: Slavs in the territory east of the Dnestr river proclaimed their secession from Moldova and the establishment of a 'Dnestr SSR', which was based at Tiraspol.

September 1990: Snegur was elected by the Supreme Soviet to the newly instituted post of President of the Republic.

25 October 1990: Elections to a 'Republic of Gagauzia' Supreme Soviet were held, despite the opposition of some 50,000 armed Moldovan nationalists, who were prevented from violence only by Soviet troops.

February 1991: The Moldovan Supreme Soviet resolved not to conduct the all-Union referendum on the future of the USSR, but to endorse proposals for a confederation of states without central control.

May 1991: Mircea Druc was replaced as Prime Minister by Valeriu Muravschi, having lost support in the legislature, which later renamed the state the Republic of Moldova and the Supreme Soviet was renamed the Moldovan Parliament.

27 August 1991: Following the attempted coup in the Soviet capital of Moscow, Russia, Moldova declared its independence from the USSR and the CPM was banned. Romania recognized Moldova's independence and diplomatic relations between the two countries were established.

8 December 1991: The first popular presidential elections in Moldova took place; Snegur, the only candidate, received 98.2% of the votes cast.

21 December 1991: Moldova, as well as 10 other former Union Republics, signed the Almaty (Alma-Ata) Declaration, by which was formed the Commonwealth of Independent States (CIS). In the same month armed conflict broke out in the Transdnestr region (Transnistria) between the Slavic 'Dnestr Guards' and government troops.

February 1992: The PFM re-formed as the Christian Democratic Popular Front (CDPF).

June 1992: The CDPF-dominated Government resigned; Andrei Sangheli was appointed Prime Minister and, over the following two months, negotiated a new coalition administration. The pro-Romanian minority in Parliament (including the CDPF) remained able to prevent the enactment of basic or constitutional legislation (which required a two-thirds majority).

21 July 1992: A peace agreement accorded Transnistria 'special status' within Moldova; Russian, Moldovan and Dnestrian peace-keeping forces were deployed in the region to monitor the cease-fire.

January 1993: Alexandru Moşanu was replaced as Chairman of the Moldovan Parliament by Lucinschi, the former First Secretary and now leader of the Agrarian Democratic Party (ADP), which dominated the Government and enjoyed strong support in mainly rural Moldova.

August 1993: The Moldovan Parliament failed to secure the necessary majority for ratification of the Almaty Declaration and to formalize the country's entry into the CIS. Nevertheless, President Snegur continued to sign CIS documents, including a treaty on economic union in September.

January 1994: The President of the 'Dnestr Republic' (the 'Transdnestrian Moldovan Soviet Socialist Republic'), Igor Smirnov, declared a state of emergency in Transnistria, until 1 March, in an attempt to prevent the inhabitants of the region from participating in the forthcoming Moldovan general election.

27 February 1994: Multi-party elections to the new, 104-member, unicameral Moldovan Parliament took place; the ADP emerged as the largest party (winning 43.2% of the votes cast and 56 seats), followed by the Slav-dominated former Communists, the Socialist Party, in alliance with the Yedinstvo (Unity) movement (28 seats). Pro-unification groups shared the remaining 20 seats: the Peasants' Party of Moldova/Congress of Intelligensia alliance (11) and the CDPF alliance (nine).

March 1994: In a national referendum on Moldova's statehood, more than 95% of those who voted were in favour of the country's continuing independence. Andrei Sangheli and Petru Lucinschi were re-elected Prime Minister and Chairman of Parliament, respectively.

April 1994: The Moldovan Parliament finally ratified membership of the CIS by 76 votes to 18. Later in the month Sangheli appointed a new Council of Ministers, consisting solely of members of the ADP.

28 July 1994: Parliament adopted a new Constitution, which described Moldova as a sovereign, independent, unitary and indivisible state. The official state language was described as 'Moldovan', although that was acknowledged to be identical to Romanian. The Constitution proclaimed the country's neutrality and provided for a 'special autonomous status' for Transnistria and Gagauzia within Moldova (the exact terms of which were to be determined at a later date).

21 October 1994: Following two years of negotiations, Moldova and the Russian Federation signed an agreement on the future of the 15,000-strong Russian 14th Army deployed in Transnistria, by which Russia pledged to withdraw the troops within three years. The withdrawal of the Army's weapons and ammunitions began in the following June, although the process was subsequently suspended on a number of occasions.

December 1994: The Moldovan Parliament adopted legislation on the special status of Gagauz-Eri (Gagauzia): the region was to enjoy a considerable degree of autonomy; Gagauz was to be one of three official languages; and legislative power was to be vested in a regional assembly, the Halk Toplusu, while a directly elected bashkan was to hold a quasi-presidential position. This law entered into force in February 1995.

March–April 1995: Local elections in the 'Transdnestrian Moldovan Soviet Socialist Republic' confirmed the popularity of the Union of Patriotic Forces, which had led the self-proclaimed republic for the previous four years. In a referendum, some 91% of those who voted were against the agreed withdrawal from the region of the 14th Army. President Snegur declared both the elections and the referendum illegal.

May–June 1995: The ADP and the Moldovan Party of Communists (MPC) won a majority of seats in elections to the 34-member Halk Toplusu of Gagauz-Eri. Gheorghe Tabunshchik, the First Secretary of the Comrat branch of the MPC, emerged as the victor in an election to the post of Bashkan.

June 1995: In response to the rejection by Parliament of his proposal to make Romanian (rather than Moldovan) the country's official language, President Snegur resigned his membership of the ADP and established, in the following month, the Party of Revival and Accord of Moldova (PRAM), with the support of 11 rebel ADP deputies.

24 December 1995: A new bicameral legislature was elected in Transnistria. At the same time, two referendums were held in the region; 82.7% of the electorate endorsed a new constitution which proclaimed Transnistria's independence, while 89.7% voted for the region to become a member of the CIS as a sovereign state.

February 1996: Parliament again rejected, by 58 votes to 25, a proposal that Romanian replace Moldovan as the state language.

March 1996: President Snegur accused the Government of incompetence and corruption and dismissed Pavel Creangă, the Minister of Defence. In April, however, Parliament declared the dismissal was unconstitutional, because it was without the consent of the Prime Minister and, following the upholding of the declaration by the Constitutional Court, Creangă was reinstated.

21 July 1996: Officials from the Moldovan and Transnistrian legislatures initialled a memorandum on the principles for a peace settlement, which envisaged Transnistria as having 'special status' within a Moldovan confederation; President Snegur declared his opposition to the memorandum and announced that any decision on the issue be postponed until after the presidential election.

17 November 1996: In the first round of the presidential election Snegur received 38.7% of the votes cast, while his closest rival, the parliamentary speaker, Lucinschi, gained 27.7%; the MPC candidate, Vladimir Voronin, won 10.2% of the ballot.

1 December 1996: As no candidate in the presidential election had received more than one-half of the votes cast, the two leading candidates contested a second round of voting: Lucinschi gained 54.1% of the ballot, compared with Snegur's 45.9%.

10 January 1997: Smirnov, who had been re-elected for a second term as President of the 'Dnestr Republic' in December 1996, with more than 70% of the votes cast, was formally inaugurated.

15 January 1997: Lucinschi was inaugurated as President of Moldova. The next day he nominated Ion Ciubuc, Chairman of the State Accounting Chamber, as Prime Minister; Ciubuc was confirmed as premier later in the month.

8 May 1997: The memorandum of understanding on the normalizing of relations between Moldova and Transnistria was signed by President Lucinschi and Smirnov in Moscow, Russia; the memorandum committed both sides to further negotiations on the status of the region; Russia, which was willing to withdraw troops from Transnistria, and Ukraine were guarantors of the agreement.

July 1997: Dumitriu Diacov, leader of the pro-Lucinschi Movement for a Democratic and Prosperous Moldova (MDPM), was dismissed from his post as deputy speaker of Parliament by the legislature, as relations between the President and Parliament deteriorated.

14 October 1997: Representatives of the Government of Moldova and the 'Dnestr Republic' resolved a number of issues, including an agreement to monitor military manoeuvres in the security zone of Transnistria and a reduction in the size of this zone.

10 November 1997: Ciubuc and Smirnov signed a document designed to foster economic and social co-operation between Moldova and the 'Dnestr Republic'.

17 February 1998: At a meeting sponsored by the Organization for Security and Co-operation in Europe (OSCE), President Lucinschi and Smirnov signed protocols on economic co-operation in Tiraspol; following the meeting President Lucinschi declared that the 'Dnestr Republic' remained an integral part of Moldova, but Smirnov stressed the partnership of two equal states.

17 March 1998: The Moldovan Supreme Court nullified a resolution by the legislature of Gagauz-Eri to hold a referendum on a constitution for the region. A 10-year economic co-operation programme with Russia was agreed.

20 March 1998: At a meeting in Odessa, Ukraine, representatives of Moldova, the 'Dnestr Republic', Russia and Ukraine agreed a reduction in Moldovan and Transnistrian peace-keeping forces; Russian troops were to remain in Transnistria until a final political settlement had been reached.

22 March 1998: In a general election the MPC won the largest number of seats (40) in the 104-seat Parliament, while the Democratic Convention of Moldova (CDM), an alliance which included the PRAM and the CDPF, gained 26 seats and the pro-Lucinschi MDPM came third with 24 seats; the Moldovan Party of Democratic Forces won 11 seats.

21 April 1998: The CDM, the MDPM and the Party of Democratic Forces agreed to form a parliamentary alliance, led by former President Snegur; the MPC, therefore, was excluded from all major parliamentary and government posts. Two days later Diacov of the MDPM was elected speaker of the legislature.

21 May 1998: Parliament approved a new Government, again led by Ciubuc, a member of the Democratic Convention of Moldova; the cabinet included other members of the Convention and its parliamentary allies.

4 August 1998: Moldova and Ukraine agreed a border delineation so as to facilitate Moldova's construction of a petroleum terminal on the Danube; the two countries also agreed to draft a 10-year economic co-operation treaty.

26 August 1998: The Joint Moldovan–Transnistrian Monitoring Mission approved a plan to allow Ukrainian peace-keepers to patrol in the security zone on the Dnestr.

10 December 1998: A parliamentary commission found that Lucinschi, Ciubuc and Ion Sturza had violated the law on privatization, through the sale of military and civilian aircraft to the USA, which had caused substantial financial losses for Moldova.

1 February 1999: Prime Minister Ion Ciubuc resigned, as, subsequently, did the parliamentary leader, Snegur, when his candidate for the premiership was rejected.

12 March 1999: Ion Sturza was confirmed as premier.

23 May 1999: A referendum on presidential government was held. The Constitutional Court later deemed it to be valid, despite the rate of participation being below the stipulated threshold of 60%, but not a binding plebiscite.

May 1999: Following local elections in Moldova, both Transnistria and Gagauzia were to be designated autonomous entities, responsible for supporting themselves financially.

10 November 1999: Ion Sturza's Government was dismissed following a vote of 'no confidence' by Parliament.

20 December 1999: Parliament approved a new Government under Dumitru Braghis, ending six weeks of political crisis, in which two previous nominees had failed to attract a sufficient number of votes.

March 2000: An agreement was signed between the 'Transdnestrian Supreme Soviet' and the Moldovan Parliament, to the effect that Transnistrian deputies would, henceforth, participate in the work of international parliamentary organizations as part of the Moldovan delegation.

17 April 2000: Up to 20,000 students protested against the withdrawal of their right to free public transport, a result of the budget for 2000 and advice from the International Monetary Fund (IMF), leading to rioting and clashes with police over several days.

18 April 2000: Parliament refused to approve the privatization of the wine and tobacco industries for a second time and, consequently, the IMF suspended lending to Moldova for the remainder of the year.

22 June 2000: The 'Transdnestrian Supreme Soviet' was converted to a unicameral parliament, reduced in number from 67 to 43 deputies, with more clearly defined fields of responsibility.

21 July 2000: Parliament overturned a veto imposed by the President on a law that introduced parliamentary rule to Moldova, permitting Parliament to elect the Head of State; Lucinschi had favoured a national constitutional referendum. Meanwhile, the President of the 'Dnestr Republic', Igor Smirnov, dismissed his Government the next day, and introduced a form of presidential rule; a new cabinet was to be instated to act as a consultative body.

28 July 2000: Constitutional amendments transforming Moldova into a parliamentary state were enacted.

12 August 2000: The first sitting of the Moldovan, Russian and Ukrainian state commissions for a Transnistrian settlement took place in Moscow, where the implementation of decisions reached at a summit meeting of the OSCE, held in Istanbul, Turkey, in November 1998, was discussed, including the deployment of peace-keeping units in the security zone.

22 September 2000: Parliament approved a change in the law on presidential electoral procedure and an alteration to the electoral code.

23 November 2000: The Minister of Foreign Affairs, Nicolae Tebekaru, was dismissed and replaced by Nicolae Cernomaz, hitherto ambassador to several countries in Central Europe. The Minister of Education and Science, Ion Gutu, resigned and was succeeded by Ilie Vancea.

4 December 2000: The first election for the presidency to be held under the new legislation took place, following the annulment of the ballot held three days previously owing to procedural irregularities. The MPC candidate, Vladimir Voronin, was supported by 50 of the 101 parliamentary deputies, his opponent, the Chairman of the Constitutional Court, Pavel Barbalat, received 35 votes, while the other 13 ballot papers returned were deemed invalid. As neither of the candidates reached the level of support required to be elected (three-fifths of the 101 deputies, or 61 votes), a second round of voting was scheduled for 6 December.

6 December 2000: The second ballot for the presidency proved inconclusive, Voronin receiving 59 votes and Barbalat 35. The electoral law required that nominations for candidates be reopened and a new election held within 15 days.

10 December 2000: Parliamentary elections were held in Transnistria. Of the 43 seats, 25 were won by independent candidates; the Yedinstvo (Unity) movement emerged as the largest single party, with nine seats, the pro-Government Obnovleniye (Renovation) bloc secured seven seats and the Power to the People! bloc, one. The election was cancelled in one constituency owing to revelations of electoral malpractice on the part of both candidates.

21 December 2000: A further round of voting for the presidency, between the same two candidates, proved inconclusive after a number of centre-right deputies boycotted the parliamentary session. The next ballot was delayed until 16 January 2001, but President Lucinschi announced that he would ask the Constitutional Court to permit him to dissolve Parliament before that date, so that a new legislature could elect his successor.

26 December 2000: The Constitutional Court supported President Lucinschi's proposal to dissolve Parliament and obliged him to do so. Five days later the President signed a decree dissolving Parliament with effect from 12 January 2001 and providing for parliamentary elections on 25 February.

25 February 2001: In parliamentary elections, the MPC won 71 of 101 seats and the Braghis Alliance centrist electoral bloc won 19 seats.

Monaco

5th century: After the fall of the Western Roman Empire, Germanic tribes migrated throughout Western Europe. The town of Monaco, which had been a port of some significance in Greek and Roman times, formed part of the Ostrogoth kingdom, based in modern Italy.

6th century: The region was conquered by the Eastern Roman Empire.

7th century: The Lombards invaded and conquered northern Italy, and launched a series of campaigns against Frankish Provence. The old town of Monaco was destroyed in one of these campaigns, c. 640.

8th century: The Franks conquered the region, and absorbed it into the Carolingian Empire. Coastal areas fell victim to maritime attack and piracy, attributed to both Vikings and Moors.

10th century: The region formed part of the Kingdom of Burgundy, administered from Arles.

1162: The German Emperor, Frederick I, at the time also ruler of the greater part of Italy, placed the Ligurian coast (including Monaco) under the suzerainty of the city of Genoa.

1191: Genoese suzerainty of Monaco was confirmed by Emperor Henry VI and the construction of a fortress began.

1209: Monaco was invaded and conquered by Provence. Genoa restored its authority in the town soon after, although the coastal strip was effectively isolated by Provençal territory.

1297: The Grimaldi family, seeking refuge from the Genoese civil wars (1270–1419), first occupied Monaco, holding it as a hereditary possession.

1330: Charles Grimaldi was officially granted the town of Monaco, although Genoa occupied the town again after his death.

1419: The Grimaldis returned to power in Monaco, under Jean I, with increasingly nominal Genoese suzerainty—its emergence as a *de facto* independent city-state was permitted by the rival jealousies of the surrounding states.

1456: France and Genoa signed a treaty prohibiting attack on Monaco; subsequent agreements between France and the Grimaldis permitted French ships to use Monaco as a base, in exchange for French protection from attack.

1506: Genoa laid siege to Monaco.

1525: Under the terms of the Treaty of Tordesillas, Monaco became a Spanish protectorate. This status was confirmed in 1542.

1614: Honoré II of Monaco took the title of Prince.

1641: An alliance with France was signed, providing for the establishment of a garrison of French troops, under the Prince's control; the Spanish troops departed, Monaco issued its own currency and was widely accepted as an independent state. The rest of Honoré II's reign and that of his grandson and successor, Louis I (to 1701), is known as Monaco's 'Grand Siècle'.

1678: Louis I codified the Principality's laws, publishing what became known as the *Code Louis*.

1714: The Treaty of Utrecht deprived Monaco of the coastal area to the east.

1746: An eight-month blockade by Austrian and Sardinian troops began, owing to suspicion of Monaco's neutrality during the War of the Austrian Succession (Monaco was also neutral in the Seven Years' War of 1756–63).

1760: Monaco lost its western extremities and was confined to its present borders.

1789: The French Revolution concentrated opposition to absolute monarchy; Prince Honoré III established a Council, consisting of members nominated by him, and elected by heads of families.

1793: Occupied by French revolutionary troops in the previous year, the Grimaldis were declared deposed and a republic was proclaimed; Monaco was then declared part of France.

1814: The Grimaldi family returned to Monaco upon the first fall of Napoleon I, the French Emperor, and restored the old regime.

1815: With the final defeat of Napoleon I, the Grimaldis again returned, but the principality was placed under Sardinian protection.

1848: Prince Florestan I was obliged to sign a charter introducing a constitutional monarchy to Monaco, providing for a Council of State and an elected assembly.

1854: A trade agreement was signed with France, followed by a customs treaty in 1865.

1861: Monaco's current status, under French protection, was established; the so-called 'Belle Époque' of Monaco, which lasted until the outbreak of the

First World War, saw independence confirmed and institutions of state established.

1866: Monte Carlo was founded, with the aim of attracting wealthy foreign tourists to spend money in the Principality; public services were largely financed by income from the state monopoly on gambling.

January 1911: The Constitution of the Principality of Monaco was promulgated.

1914: The outbreak of the First World War, in which Monaco remained neutral, occasioned the suspension of the Constitution (a revised version was reintroduced in 1917).

1918–19: New agreements with France included provision for the incorporation of Monaco into the French Republic should the ruling Prince die without a male heir.

1929: The Constitution was again suspended, during a period of global economic recession (a revised version was reintroduced in 1933).

1942: During the course of the Second World War, Monaco was occupied by Italian troops (replaced by German troops in 1943).

1944: Monaco was bombarded during the Allied invasion of southern France and liberated soon after. A new series of treaties with France, signed in the following year, largely restored the *status quo ante*.

1949: Rainier III succeeded to the throne of Monaco.

1959: The Constitution was suspended.

December 1962: The revised Constitution established the principle of the divine right of monarchy and established a National Council (Conseil National) with executive and legislative power.

1963: A new series of treaties and conventions were signed with France, following a crisis in French-Monegasque relations, occasioned by disagreement over the control of a regional broadcasting organization the previous year. In the general election, the National and Democratic Union (Union Nationale et Démocratique—UND), a group of candidates supportive of Prince Rainier III, won 17 of the 18 seats on the National Council.

1968: The UND won all 18 seats on the National Council.

1973: In the general election, the UND won 16 of the 18 seats available, two opposition parties gaining one seat each.

1978: The UND again won all 18 seats on the National Council in the general election. The group also won all the seats in the general elections held in 1983 and 1988.

1993: The UND did not field a list in the general election. The two lists contesting the election, the Liste Campora and the Liste Médecin, named after their respective leaders, won 15 and two seats respectively, an independent winning the remaining seat.

1998: The UND, led by Jean-Louis Campora, won all 18 seats on the National Council.

31 October 2000: Prince Rainier threatened to seek an end to the French Government's control over the principality, following reports by the French authorities that Monaco's laws relating to banking and money laundering were inadequate.

The Netherlands

3rd–5th centuries: After the fall of the Roman Empire the region which now forms the modern Netherlands was invaded by Germanic tribes, which migrated from the east. The Franks settled in the south and the Saxons in the east. The Frisians, a people whose presence in the region pre-dated the Roman era, remained relatively undisturbed in the north.

922: Land round Haarlem was granted to a Viking nobleman by the French king, although three years later the area which became the province of Holland moved under the jurisdiction of the Holy Roman Empire (it had previously fallen under the middle kingdom of the Carolingian Franks) as part of the Duchy of Lower Lorraine.

8th–9th centuries: The Franks conquered the northern areas of the region, and under Charles 'the Great' (Charlemagne), subsequently gained the Saxon areas. The Frankish Kingdom, which encompassed much of Western Europe, was later divided, the region that is now the modern Netherlands becoming part of the eastern Kingdom.

10th–11th centuries: The eastern Frankish Kingdom became the German (later the Holy Roman) Empire, and the northern Low Countries, including the modern Netherlands, were subject to imperial rule as Friesland and as part of the Duchy of Lower Lorraine.

12th century: Imperial authority was continually eroded by the leaders of smaller divisions within the Empire. Within the Low Countries, these included Brabant, Geldern, Hainault, Holland, Limburg, Namur and Zeeland, as well as the bishopric of Utrecht. The cities of the Low Countries were among the wealthiest in the Empire, a result of the flourishing trade markets for textiles and other goods.

1256: William II, Count of Holland, died prior to his planned departure for Rome to be crowned Holy Roman Emperor—Holland had by now largely subdued Frisia and was vying for influence in the Low Countries with the prince-bishops of Liège and Utrecht, the duchies of Lorraine and Brabant and, above all, the wealthy cities of the County of Flanders.

1323: Holland and Zeeland were unified, creating a dominant force in the Low Countries.

1345: The Wittelsbach family, based in Bavaria, took possession of Friesland, Hainault and Holland.

1355: Brabant came under the control of the Luxembourg family, which at that time was dominant within the Empire.

1382: Following the Battle of Roosbeeke the Low Countries were subjected to the Duchy of Burgundy.

1477: Burgundy was united with the Habsburg dynasty by marriage, by which time it had gained most of the southern provinces, and it later gained the northern provinces.

1515: The Duchy of Burgundy was inherited by Charles of Habsburg; in the following year he became King of Spain and in 1519 he was crowned Holy Roman Emperor (as Charles V).

1551: Charles V formally vested the 17 variegated territories of the Imperial Circle of Burgundy (including the Netherlands) in the Spanish Crown.

1556: Charles V abdicated, and was succeeded in the Spanish and Burgundian possessions by his son, Phillip II; each province of the Netherlands was, essentially, autonomous, with a governor appointed by the King; overall local control rested with the Governor-General and the States-General (assembly of the provinces).

1566: The Dutch Calvinist Church, which would later become the established state church of the Netherlands, was founded.

1568: After years of unrest, provoked by the rise of Calvinism in the north, the Low Countries rose in revolt against Spain; the rebels were led by William of Orange and relied on naval superiority—the conflict known variously as the War of Dutch Independence, the Eighty Years' War or the Revolt of the Netherlands had begun.

1576: The provinces of the Netherlands formed the Pacification of Ghent, which opposed the perceived brutality of Spanish forces.

1579: The northern provinces formed the Union of Utrecht, in defiance of the previous year's Union of Arras in the south, which had accepted the restoration of Spanish authority—the Low Countries were, therefore, essentially divided between the Catholic, Latinate south (which would become modern Belgium) and the Protestant, Germanic north (Netherlands).

1581: The Union of Utrecht declared itself independent from Spain, once more acknowledging only the jurisdiction of the Empire; it was organized as the United Provinces of the Netherlands, under the chairmanship of Holland.

1584: The United Provinces of the Netherlands enacted the Constitution of the Dutch Republic. The decision in the following year to attack the overseas possessions of Spain and Portugal (in union 1580–1640) marked the beginnings of a colonial empire.

1602: The Dutch East India company was founded to exploit the wealth of the new colonies and to gain control of the valuable world spice trade.

1621: Hostilities with Spain were resumed after a 12-year truce, albeit on a lesser scale.

1648: The Treaty of Westphalia concluded the Thirty Years' War and the United Provinces left the Empire, gaining complete independence. The separate Peace of The Hague forced Spain to recognize the Dutch Republic.

1651: Jan de Witt succeeded in keeping vacant the office of stadholder (chairman of the federal executive), normally held by a member of the House of Orange; the quasi-monarchy was restored with de Witt's death in 1672.

1688: The Stadholder, William III of Orange, was summoned to the English throne to preserve Protestant rule; he ruled jointly with his wife, Mary, daughter of the previous English king, James II, until her death in 1694, and alone until his death in 1702.

1713: The Treaty of Utrecht, concluding the War of the Spanish Succession, ceded the Dutch several fortresses on the border with the Spanish (now Austrian) Netherlands.

1787: There was popular unrest in the Austrian Netherlands, provoked by the reforms of Emperor Joseph II and his predecessor.

1789: The Austrian Netherlands (Belgium) seceded from Habsburg control as the 'Republic of the United Belgian Provinces'; however, the revolt was quickly defeated.

1795: Revolutionary France supported the establishment of a Batavian Republic in the United Provinces of the Netherlands, which ceded Dutch territory south of the Rhine to France.

1806: The French Emperor, Napoleon I, dissolved the Batavian Republic and established a Kingdom of the Netherlands for his brother, Louis Bonaparte.

1814–15: The Congress of Vienna, which ended the European wars with revolutionary France, created a new Kingdom of the United Netherlands, with the former Austrian Netherlands and Luxembourg coming under Dutch administration as the Kingdom of the United Netherlands. The throne was granted to the son of the last Stadholder-General of the House of Orange, as King William I.

1830: An uprising against Dutch rule in Brussels resulted in a declaration of Belgian independence, which was supported by France and the United Kingdom.

1839: Under the terms of the Treaty of London, the Netherlands recognized Belgian independence and inviolability, and ceded the greater part of Luxembourg to the new state.

1848: Amid revolutionary fervour elsewhere in Europe, William II of the Netherlands agreed to a new Constitution, creating a constitutional monarchy.

1867: Luxembourg declared its independence; final recognition of its independence by the Dutch was obtained in 1890.

1914–18: The Netherlands remained neutral throughout the First World War.

1920–28: A series of rebellions erupted in the Dutch East Indies; a People's Council of the territories had been formed in 1918, although the movement towards autonomy and eventual independence was criticized for its perceived slow rate of progress.

1940: Following the outbreak of the Second World War in Europe, the Netherlands was invaded and annexed by German troops; a Government-in-Exile was established in London (United Kingdom).

1942: Japanese troops occupied the Dutch East Indies.

1945: The Netherlands were liberated from German occupation and it became a founder member of the United Nations (UN). Japan left the Dutch East Indies, where a Republic of Indonesia was proclaimed.

1948: The Netherlands formed the Brussels Treaty Organization, with Belgium and Luxembourg. (The Organization became effective in 1960 as the Benelux Economic Union and a single customs area was established in 1970.)

1949: The Netherlands was a founder member of the North Atlantic Treaty Organization (NATO).

27 December 1949: The Dutch East Indies (except West New Guinea, now Irian Jaya, which remained under Dutch control until 1963) formally seceded from the Union of the Netherlands, to form the United States of Indonesia.

18 April 1951: The Netherlands and five other countries formed the European Coal and Steel Community (ECSC), the first institution of the three European Communities.

December 1954: Queen Juliana I signed the Charter for the Kingdom of the Netherlands, declaring the Dutch possessions in Europe (Netherlands) and the Caribbean (Suriname—Dutch Guiana and the Netherlands Antilles) to be a single realm under the House of Orange-Nassau.

1963–73: Support for the traditional 'confessional' Catholic and Protestant parties and 'progressive' Liberal and Socialist parties began to diminish.

May 1973: A left-of-centre coalition Government was formed under the premiership of Dr Johannes (Joop) den Uyl of the Labour Party (Partij van de Arbeid—PvdA).

25 November 1975: Suriname gained its independence.

December 1977: Following the collapse of the previous Government, a new centre-right coalition was formed, led by Andries van Agt of the Christian Democratic Appeal (Christen-Democratisch Appèl—CDA), an alliance of the three traditional confessional parties, which formally merged in 1980.

September 1981: A new centre-left Government was formed, also led by van Agt; however, it collapsed in the following year.

September 1982: Rudolphus (Ruud) Lubbers of the CDA formed a centre-right coalition Government.

17 February 1983: A new Constitution came into force.

1 January 1986: Aruba, part of the Netherlands Antilles, was granted separate status within the Kingdom of the Netherlands.

October 1989: Lubbers formed a new centre-left coalition Government.

November–December 1992: The two legislative chambers ratified the Treaty on European Union, which had been signed by European Community (EC, known as the European Union—EU from November 1993) heads of state and of government at Maastricht in December 1991.

1992–93: The Government debated and approved legislation enabling euthanasia to be practised when repeatedly requested by a terminally ill patient.

August 1994: Willem (Wim) Kok of the PvdA was appointed Prime Minister of a coalition Government, also comprising members of the Volkspartij voor Vrijheid en Democratie (People's Party for Freedom and Democracy—VVD) and Democrats 66 (Democraten 66—D66).

August 1996: Conscription to the armed forces was terminated.

1 January 1999: The Netherlands was one of the first group of 11 countries to participate in Stage III of the EU's Economic and Monetary Union (EMU), involving the introduction of a common European currency, the euro.

Norway

7th–8th centuries: Various Viking (Norse) kingdoms were established in Norway, some by Vikings expelled from Sweden.

795: Viking raids on Europe by Danish, Norwegian and Swedish warriors began, primarily on coastal settlements and along navigable rivers; the attacks continued for 200 years and spanned from Italy to the Shetland Islands (now part of the United Kingdom).

860: Iceland was discovered by Viking explorers sailing from Norway.

872: Harold Fairhair (died *circa* 933) completed his conquest of Norway from his base in the east, breaking the power of the nobles and prompting many of them to emigrate to Iceland when colonization began in 874.

930: The rule of law was established in Norway, and the first assembly (Ding) was formed.

995: King Olaf I Trygvasson, while on campaign in England, was baptized and, upon his return, forced the acceptance of Christianity in Norway.

1000: Olaf I was defeated by his former ally, King Sweyn (*circa* 960–1014) of Denmark, and Norway came under the latter's rule.

1015: Olaf II Haraldson restored Norwegian independence and allied himself with King Anund of Sweden against the Danes.

1028: Swedish–Norwegian naval forces were crushed by the Danes, led by King Knud (Canute) II 'the Great', at Helgeaa and Norway was reconquered.

1035: With the death of Knud, the Danes were expelled from Norway by Magnus I, son of Olaf II.

1164: At the Diet (Assembly) of Bergen, during a time of dynastic civil wars, the bishops of Norway attempted to establish an elective monarchy.

1177: Sverrir Sigurdsson, a Faroe Islander, landed in Norway and, by 1184, had overcome ecclesiastical opposition to be crowned King—he sought to strengthen the monarchy and establish the hereditary principle.

1262: Iceland came under Norwegian rule.

1266: By the Treaty of Perth, Norway sold the Isle of Man and ceded the Hebrides to Scotland—although both were recent acquisitions (Norwegian ambitions in Ireland had failed).

1319: Magnus VII Ericsson, already King of Norway, was elected King of Sweden, uniting the two thrones.

1355: Magnus VII's son, Haakon VI, inherited Norway (his brother inherited Sweden) and later married Margrethe, the daughter of the King of Denmark.

1380: Olaf, the son of Haakon VI and Queen Margrethe, was elected King in both Denmark and Norway (this led to the Union of Kalmar, with Norway, and Greenland and Iceland, under the Danish Crown which, later, was in personal union with the Crown of Sweden); his mother acted as regent.

1533: Norway was granted self-government.

1536: The Diet of Copenhagen established Lutheranism as the state religion of the Danish realm.

1645: Following one of several wars between Denmark and Sweden, the Peace of Brömesboro awarded former Norwegian territory in central Scandinavia to Sweden.

1658: Sweden defeated Denmark, which had allied with Poland and Russia, and took the area around the Norwegian city of Trondheim, adjacent to the territory gained in 1645.

1814: Under the terms of the Treaty of Kiel, Denmark, which had supported France during the Napoleonic wars, relinquished sovereignty over Norway to Sweden; after a brief struggle for independence, Norway accepted the Swedish union, but was permitted to retain its own constitution and parliament.

1905: After continual political disputes, Sweden accepted the independence of Norway—a Danish prince assumed the throne as Haakon VII.

1914–18: Norway maintained neutrality during the First World War.

1920: A system of proportional representation was introduced for parliamentary elections. The League of Nations awarded the island of Spitsbergen (Svalbard) to Norway (Sweden renounced its claim on the island five years later).

1935: The Norwegian Labour Party (Det norske Arbeiderparti—DnA) was elected to government (apart from the period of German occupation and one month in 1963, it remained in power until 1965).

1940: Norway, despite its declared neutrality in the Second World War, was invaded by Germany, which established an administration under Vidkun

Quisling; the King and a broad coalition of political parties formed a Government-in-Exile in the United Kingdom.

1945: German forces surrendered and Norway was liberated. A provisional administration, led by Einar Gerhardsen of the DnA, won an absolute majority in elections a few months later. Norway became a founder member of the United Nations (UN).

1949: Norway became a founder member of the North Atlantic Treaty Organization (NATO).

1952: Constitutional reforms ended the arrangement whereby two-thirds of the Storting (Parliament) were elected by rural constituencies; the Agrarian Party, therefore, changed its name to the Centre Party (Senterpartiet—Sp). Norway joined Denmark, Iceland and Sweden in founding the Nordic Council (Finland joined in 1955).

1960: Norway joined the European Free Trade Association (EFTA) as a founder member. A subsequent application to join the European Economic Community (EEC, part of what became known as the European Community— EC and then, from 1993, the European Union—EU) was withdrawn after the United Kingdom was refused membership.

1961: Dissent within the DnA regarding Norway's membership of NATO had become the basis for a new party, the Socialist People's Party (Socialistisk Folkeparti—SF), gains for which in the general election were sufficient to deprive the DnA of its overall majority.

1965: A coalition of non-socialist parties, which had held power for four weeks in 1963, defeated the DnA Government of Einar Gerhardsen at the general election, forming an administration under Per Borten of the Sp.

1966: Norway's first trial drilling for petroleum took place in its waters over the continental shelf.

1969: Norway's third application to join the EEC provoked political debate and division on the subject of membership.

March 1971: Borten resigned following revelations that he had deliberately disclosed confidential details of Norway's negotiations with the EEC to a prominent opponent of membership; his coalition was succeeded by a minority DnA Government, led by Trygve Bratteli.

1972: In a consultative referendum on membership, a narrow majority rejected Norway's entry to the EEC; Bratteli resigned, and a coalition of the Liberals (Venstre), the Sp and the Christian Democrats' Party (Kristelig Folkeparti— KrF) was formed, with Lars Korvald (KrF) as Prime Minister.

1973: A general election enabled Bratteli to form another minority DnA Government, dependent on the support of a socialist alliance known from 1975 as the Socialist Left Party (Socialistisk Venstreparti—SV); a new anti-tax party, renamed in 1977 as the Progress Party (Fremskrittspartiet—FrP), established itself in this election.

1976: Odvar Nordli succeeded Bratteli as Prime Minister of the DnA minority Government.

1981: Nordli resigned for reasons of ill health and was succeeded by Gro Harlem Brundtland, Norway's first female Prime Minister. In the general election, however, the DnA lost support to centre-right groups and a minority administration, led by Kåre Willoch, became Norway's first Conservative (Høyre) Government since 1928.

1985: Elections returned Willoch's Government (joined in coalition by the Sp and the KrF in 1983) to power, although without an overall majority.

1986: Willoch resigned when the Storting narrowly rejected a proposal to increase taxation on petrol (gasoline); as the Constitution did not allow for a general election before the expiry of the Storting's term (1989), King Olaf V invited Brundtland to form a minority DnA administration. The new Government devalued Norway's currency, the krone, by 12% and a revised budget was approved by the Storting.

1989: At the general election, both the DnA and the Conservative Party lost support to more radical parties—the SV were returned with 17 seats in the Storting (gaining nine) and the FrP were returned with 22 seats (gaining two), despite the latter attracting allegations of racism during the campaign. The Sámi (Lapps) of northern Norway elected 39 representatives for a new Sameting (consultative assembly) to be based in Karasjok. A new coalition of the Conservatives, the Sp and the KrF, led by Jan Syse (Conservative leader since 1988), formed a minority Government dependent upon the support of the FrP.

1990: The DnA formed another minority Government, led by Brundtland, following the collapse of the centre-right coalition.

1992: After Brundtland, the DnA and the Storting had all previously declared their support, Norway again applied to join the EC. Brundtland resigned the Labour leadership (but not the premiership) and was replaced by the DnA's Secretary-General, Thorbjørn Jagland.

1993: At the general election, the DnA increased its representation from 63 to 67 seats, the Sp (which was vocal in opposition to EC membership) increased its representation from 11 to 32 seats (becoming the second-largest party in the Storting), while the Conservative Party won 28 seats, losing nine.

1994: A national referendum narrowly rejected Norway's negotiated entry into the EU (52.4% of participants opposing membership), although the country was participating in the European Economic Area (which had taken effect at the beginning of the year).

1996: Brundtland resigned as Prime Minister and was succeeded by Jagland, who promised continuity of policy, but suffered some political scandal in the Government later in the year.

16 September 1997: At the general election, the DnA retained 65 seats (35.0% of the votes cast), the FrP won 25 seats (15.3%), the KrF won 25 seats (13.7%) and the Høyre won 23 seats (14.3%).

October 1997: Jagland resigned from the leadership of the DnA, fulfilling a promise to stand down if the party lost any of its percentage share of the vote. Kjell Magne Bondevik (parliamentary leader of the KrF) formed a minority coalition of the KrF, the Sp and the Liberals.

November 1997: A series of long-running disputes over territorial waters and fishing rights was settled when an accord on the disputes in the Arctic Sea was signed by the Governments of Greenland, Iceland and Norway.

November 1998: The Government was obliged to abandon proposed tax increases in order to secure the support of the FrP (and thus parliamentary approval) for the 1999 budget.

March 1999: The Storting approved compensation valued at US $57.5m. for Norway's Holocaust victims and their descendants.

9 March 2000: Bondevik resigned following his defeat in a motion of 'no confidence' brought during a debate on the construction of new power stations.

17 March 2000: Jens Stoltenberg, the leader of the DnA, took office as Prime Minister, leading a single-party minority government (the DnA controlled 65 of the 165 seats in the Storting).

Poland

966: The first historical ruler of Poland, Prince Mieszko I, converted to Latin Christianity.

1320: Lidisław I was crowned King of a reunited Poland.

1386: The Grand Duke of Lithuania became King, as Władysław II, by marriage to Jadwiga of Poland; they founded the Jagiellonian dynasty (1386–1572) and established a personal union of Poland with Lithuania.

1493: A two-chamber Sejm (parliament) was established.

1569: Under Sigismund II a permanent union with Lithuania was established, by the Union of Lublin, which was to last until the final dismemberment of the Polish–Lithuanian Commonwealth in 1795.

1764: Election of Stanisław II, who ruled until 1795.

1772: The First Partition of Poland, between Russia, Prussia and Austria, took place.

1791: Stanisław II created Europe's first modern constitution.

1793: The Second Partition of Poland.

1795: The Third Partition extinguished the Polish state.

1807: The Grand Duchy of Warsaw was established by Napoleon I of France.

1815: The 'Congress Kingdom of Poland' was formed under Russian patronage.

1905–07: Revolution in Russian Poland.

1915: The Russian occupation was ended by German victory on the eastern front in the First World War.

1916: Restoration of an 'independent' Kingdom of Poland by Germany.

3 June 1918: The Entente Governments recognized the principle of Polish independence.

11 November 1918: Józef Piłsudski assumed power in Warsaw; Poland was declared an independent republic.

28 June 1919: The Treaty of Versailles recognized Polish independence.

13–19 August 1920: Soviet forces were defeated at the Battle of Warsaw.

18 March 1921: The Treaty of Rīga was signed by Poland, Ukraine and Soviet Russia, formally concluding the Soviet–Polish war and defining the frontiers in the region.

1922: Stanisław Wojsiechowski was elected Head of State.

12 May 1926: Piłsudski seized power in a *coup d'état*.

25 January 1932: A non-aggression pact was signed with the USSR.

26 January 1934: A non-aggression pact was signed with Germany.

23 March 1935: A new Constitution was enacted.

12 May 1935: Death of Piłsudski.

31 March 1939: France and the United Kingdom announced guarantees of Poland's independence, in response to German territorial demands.

23 August 1939: The Nazi–Soviet Pact was signed, including a secret agreement between the USSR and Germany to partition Poland.

1 September 1939: Germany invaded Poland, which caused the start of the Second World War.

17 September 1939: The USSR invaded Poland.

30 September 1939: A Government-in-Exile was formed in Paris (France) under Gen. Władysław Sikorski, moving to London (United Kingdom) in 1940.

22 June 1941: Germany invaded the USSR; all of Poland was occupied by Nazi forces.

5 January 1942: The Polish Workers' Party (PWP) was founded.

April 1943: The Warsaw Ghetto uprising was suppressed by German troops.

25 April 1943: German investigators discovered, at Katyn in the USSR, the bodies of 4,000 Polish officers, who had been murdered by Soviet secret police in 1940 (the USSR only admitted its responsibility in April 1990).

4 July 1943: Gen. Sikorski, Prime Minister of the Government-in-Exile, died in an air crash.

23 July 1944: The Polish Committee of National Liberation (Lublin Committee—PKWN) was established under Soviet auspices.

1 August–2 October 1944: The Warsaw Rising was eventually suppressed by German troops.

February 1945: German forces withdrew from Warsaw. The British, Soviet and US leaders, Winston Churchill, Stalin (Iosif V. Dzhugashvili) and Franklin D. Roosevelt, met in the Crimean town of Yalta (now in Ukraine): the 'Curzon line' was agreed as Poland's eastern border; Stalin promised 'free and unfettered elections' in Poland after the War.

21 April 1945: A Soviet–Polish Treaty of Friendship was signed.

6 July 1945: The USA and the United Kingdom formally recognized the 'Provisional Government of National Unity', which was dominated by members of the Soviet-backed PKWN, but included Stanisław Mikołajczyk and a few others from the Government-in-Exile.

17 July–2 August 1945: The Potsdam Conference: the Allies agreed to give former German territories east of the Oder–Neisse line to Poland.

19 January 1947: Elections to the Sejm were won by the Democratic Bloc, a grouping dominated by the PWP and led by Władysław Gomułka; the United Kingdom and the USA complained that the elections did not meet the requirements agreed at Yalta.

6 February 1947: The People's Republic of Poland was declared; Bolesław Bierut took office as President.

October 1947: Mikołajczyk fled to London after threats to his life.

September 1948: Gomułka was forced to admit 'political errors' and was dismissed as Party leader.

December 1948: The founding congress of the Polish United Workers' Party (PZPR) took place after the PWP merged with the Polish Socialist Party; Bierut was appointed Party First Secretary.

1949: Gomułka was arrested, accused of 'rightist and nationalist deviations'.

22 July 1952: A new Soviet-style Constitution was adopted.

1954: Bierut was succeeded by Józef Cyrankiewicz as Chairman of the Council of Ministers, but remained Party First Secretary.

14 May 1955: The Treaty of Warsaw founded the Soviet bloc military organization known as the Warsaw Pact.

28–29 June 1956: Seventy-four people died in riots in Poznań protesting against food price rises.

October 1956: Władysław Gomułka was appointed First Secretary by the Eighth Party Plenum and began to introduce some political liberalization.

March 1968: Nation-wide anti-government student protests took place, followed by a Party-inspired campaign against Jews and intellectuals.

April 1968: Marshal Marian Spychalski was appointed Head of State.

November 1968: The Soviet leader, Leonid Brezhnev, announced the 'Brezhnev Doctrine' (declaring the right of the USSR to intervene in the affairs of its Warsaw Pact allies) in Warsaw.

December 1970: Gomułka and Spychalski resigned after workers were killed when police suppressed strikes and protests in the Baltic ports; Piotr Jaroszewicz replaced Józef Cyrankiewicz (who became Head of State) as Chairman of the Council of Ministers; Edward Gierek was appointed First Secretary.

7 December 1970: A treaty was signed by Poland and the Federal Republic of Germany (West Germany), confirming the post-1945 Polish western border.

1972: Gierek launched a 'modernization programme' of large-scale investment funded chiefly by Western banks.

June 1976: Strikes and demonstrations prevented planned food price rises from being implemented.

September 1976: The Workers' Defence Committee (KOR) was formed after striking miners were arrested at Radom.

16 October 1978: Cardinal Karol Wojtyła, Archbishop of Kraków, was elected head of the world-wide Roman Catholic Church as Pope John Paul II.

February 1980: Piotr Jaroszewicz was replaced as Chairman of the Council of Ministers by Edward Babiuch at the Party Congress.

July 1980: Food price rises led to strikes and workers' protests; unofficial strike committees were formed to press for pay increases and, subsequently, for political demands to be met.

14 August 1980: Some 17,000 workers at the Lenin Shipyards in Gdańsk (formerly Danzig) went on strike and issued a list of economic and political demands; the strike spread to Szczecin (formerly Stettin) one week later and involved over 150,000 workers.

24 August 1980: Babiuch resigned and was replaced by Józef Pińkowski as Chairman of the Council of Ministers.

31 August 1980: Following negotiations with Lech Wałęsa and other union delegates, the Gdańsk and Szczecin agreements were signed: the Government agreed to the unions' demands, including the right to form free trade unions and the right to strike.

5 September 1980: Gierek was replaced as First Secretary by Stanisław Kania.

17 September 1980: Representatives from some 35 independent trade-union committees met to form the independent trade union, Solidarity (Solidarność).

10 November 1980: Solidarity was officially recognized.

1 January 1981: The Central Council of Trade Unions was dissolved.

10–11 February 1981: Pińkowski was replaced as Chairman of the Council of Ministers by Gen. Wojciech Jaruzelski.

October 1981: Jaruzelski replaced Kania as Party First Secretary.

13 December 1981: Jaruzelski declared martial law; a Military Council of National Salvation was established; Wałęsa and other Solidarity activists were arrested and imprisoned.

October 1982: With major demonstrations in May and August, the authorities took further action against the opposition by outlawing independent trade-union activity.

13 December 1982: Martial law was suspended (Wałęsa had been released from gaol the previous month).

22 July 1983: Martial law was formally lifted; the Military Council of National Salvation was dissolved.

5 October 1983: Lech Wałęsa was awarded the Nobel Peace Prize.

October 1984: Jerzy Popiełuszko, a pro-Solidarity priest, was murdered by security forces.

October 1985: Some multi-candidate ballots were allowed in legislative elections; Solidarity urged a boycott and, later, challenged the results.

6 November 1985: Jaruzelski resigned as the Chairman of the Council of Ministers, becoming President of the Council of State (Head of State); he was succeeded by Prof. Zbigniew Messner.

November 1987: A referendum on radical government plans for reform failed to achieve the necessary majority, partly owing to a Solidarity-backed boycott.

June 1988: Only 55% of the electorate participated in local elections after Solidarity urged a boycott, following months of continuing civil and industrial unrest.

19 September 1988: Zbigniew Messner's Government resigned; Dr Mieczysław Rakowski became Chairman of a more reformist Council of Ministers.

31 October 1988: Large-scale protests took place after the Government announced the closure of the Lenin Shipyards in Gdańsk.

6 February 1989: 'Round-table' negotiations between the Government and opposition leaders, headed by Lech Wałęsa, opened in Warsaw. Following two months of talks, a negotiated agreement was reached: Solidarity was to be re-legalized; partly free elections were to be held; and economic reforms were promised. Two days later appropriate constitutional amendments were adopted, including the creation of a new, bicameral National Assembly; 65% of seats in the lower chamber (Sejm) were to be reserved for Communists.

17 May 1989: Full legal status was granted to the Roman Catholic Church (diplomatic relations with the Holy See were restored in July) and freedom of conscience guaranteed.

June 1989: Elections to the National Assembly took place (in two rounds): Solidarity won 99% of the freely elected seats.

28–29 July 1989: Jaruzelski, having been narrowly elected President on 19 July, resigned all Party posts; he was replaced as First Secretary by Mieczysław Rakowski.

August 1989: Solidarity having refused a coalition with the Communists the previous month, Lt-Gen. Czesław Kiszczak was chosen as premier, but he failed to form a government. President Jaruzelski then accepted Solidarity's earlier proposal of a coalition with the United Peasants' Party and the Democratic Party; Tadeusz Mazowiecki was asked to lead a new, multi-party administration.

29–30 December 1989: The National Assembly approved amendments to the Constitution, including an end to the PZPR's monopoly of power, and the restoration of the official name and flag of pre-war Poland. Finance minister Leszek Balcerowicz's economic reform plan (already approved by the International Monetary Fund—IMF) was approved by the Sejm.

November 1990: Poland's western border was confirmed by the signature of a treaty with the reunified Germany.

25 November 1990: The presidential election took place: Wałęsa received some 43% of the votes cast, but premier Mazowiecki was forced into third place by a maverick candidate, Stanisław Tymiński; Mazowiecki's Government resigned the next day.

9 December 1990: Wałęsa won the second round of the presidential election with 74% of the vote.

January 1991: Jan Bielecki was approved as Chairman of the Council of Ministers by the Sejm, and his proposed Government was also accepted. The Citizens' Parliamentary Club (the group of Solidarity deputies in the National Assembly) was split by the formation of the Democratic Union (UD).

March 1991: The 'Paris Club' of 17 Western creditor governments cancelled 50% of Poland's US $33,000m. foreign debt.

4 April 1991: The first of the 50,000 Soviet troops remaining in Poland were withdrawn.

30 August 1991: The Bielecki Government offered its resignation after repeated obstruction by the Sejm of its policies for economic reform; parliament rejected the resignation the following day, but also, later, rejected a request for special economic powers for the Government.

27 October 1991: Only 43.2% of the electorate participated in Poland's first fully free elections to the Senat (the upper house of the National Assembly) and the Sejm; a total of 29 parties won representation in the Sejm: the largest, with 62 of the 460 seats (12.3% of the votes cast), being the UD; the Democratic Left Alliance (SLD), led by the Social Democracy of the Republic of Poland (SRP, as the PZPR was known from 1990), won 60 seats (11.9%).

December 1991: Following weeks of negotiations, Jan Olszewski of the Centre Alliance was appointed Chairman of the Council of Ministers (Prime Minister).

June 1992: Following its lack of progress with economic reform, and disputes with President Wałęsa, a motion of 'no confidence' in the Government was passed by the Sejm. The leader of the Polish Peasant Party (PSL), Waldemar Pawlak, was appointed premier, but failed to form a government.

July 1992: Hanna Suchocka of the UD became Prime Minister and formed a seven-party coalition to govern.

8 December 1992: An interim Constitution, the 'Small Constitution', entered into force while a comprehensive revision of the 1952 Constitution was in progress.

28 May 1993: As a result of continuing dissatisfaction over government economic and social policies, a vote of 'no confidence' in the Suchocka Government was passed in the Sejm; however, President Wałęsa refused to accept the Prime Minister's resignation and dissolved parliament.

19 September 1993: A general election took place, under a new electoral law designed to minimize the fragmentation of parliamentary representation; the SLD and the PSL, also dominated by former Communists, gained the most number of votes cast (20.4% and 15.4%, respectively) and between them took 303 of the 406 seats.

October 1993: The PSL leader, Pawlak, was appointed Prime Minister and formed a Government of SLD and PSL members, plus one Union of Labour member and an independent.

April 1994: Wałęsa threatened to dissolve parliament when some SLD and PSL deputies proposed a constitutional amendment removing responsibility for ratifying government appointments from the President, following President

Wałęsa's rejection of a nomination for a new finance minister. Poland formally applied for membership of the European Union (EU).

October 1994: President Wałęsa demanded the resignation of the Minister of National Defence, Adm. Piotr Kolodziejczyk, owing to his failure to implement military reforms; the Prime Minister, Pawlak, accepted the resignation in November, but the President and Government failed to agree on a successor.

February 1995: Relations between President Wałęsa and the Government deteriorated further as the former demanded Pawlak's resignation. This achieved, Józef Oleksy of the SLD, the speaker of the Sejm and a former Communist minister, was appointed premier and formed a new Government in early March.

July 1995: President Wałęsa vetoed privatization legislation, claiming that it gave the state too large a role; the presidential veto was overturned by the Sejm, but the Constitutional Tribunal ruled against the legislation in November.

5 and 19 November 1995: The first round of the presidential election was contested by 13 candidates; Aleksander Kwaśniewski, Chairman of the SRP, gained 35.1% of the votes cast, and Wałęsa 33.1%. In the second round of voting Kwaśniewski won 51.7% of the votes cast and Wałęsa 48.3%.

23 December 1995: After the Supreme Court dismissed claims of electoral malpractice against him by supporters of Wałęsa, Aleksander Kwaśniewski took office as President.

January 1996: Oleksy resigned as Prime Minister, to be elected leader of the SRP, in succession to Kwaśniewski. The President appointed Włodzimierz Cimoszewicz, a former Minister of Justice, as premier.

18 February 1996: A referendum was held on the constitutionality of the mass privatization scheme (initiated the previous November); it was, however, inconclusive, as less than the required minimum of 50% of the electorate participated.

November 1996: Poland became a full member of the Organisation for Economic Co-operation and Development.

6 March 1997: The announcement that 3,000 Gdańsk shipyard workers were to lose their jobs followed months of industrial unrest and provoked demonstrations and pickets of government offices throughout the country.

2 April 1997: The National Assembly approved a new Constitution, which slightly reduced presidential powers and committed the country to a social market economy; it was endorsed in the following month by 52.7% of votes cast in a national referendum and took effect on 17 October.

8 July 1997: Poland was formally invited by the North Atlantic Treaty Organization (NATO) to begin accession negotiations, with the aim of extending membership to it, the Czech Republic and Hungary by April 1999.

21 September 1997: In the general election the Solidarity Election Action, a coalition comprising 36 parties, emerged as the strongest grouping, securing 201 seats in the Sejm and 51 in the Senat; the SLD retained 164 seats in the Sejm and 28 in the Senat, while the PSL retained only 27 and three, respectively; the third party, therefore, was the Freedom Union (UW), with 60 deputies and eight senators.

15 October 1997: Jerzy Buzek, a member of Solidarity since its formation, was nominated as Prime Minister and eventually agreed a coalition with the UW later in the month.

December 1997: Marian Krzaklewski, the leader of the AWS alliance, whose rejection of the opportunity to become Prime Minister was seen as confirmation of his intention to contest the presidential election of 2000, announced the formation of a new political party, the Social Movement of Solidarity Election Action (RS AWS).

8 January 1998: The National Assembly ratified the Concordat, an agreement governing relations between the State and the Roman Catholic Church, which had been reached in 1993 but approval of which had been repeatedly delayed by the previous SLD-led coalition Government.

24 May 1998: Poland's share of funding from the EU Poland and Hungary Assistance for Economic Restructuring (PHARE) programme was reduced by €34m., owing to a number of errors, including financial mismanagement, by the Polish delegation; the EU-integration minister, Ryszard Czarnecki, was subsequently demoted.

24 July 1998: Six AWS deputies withdrew their support for the Government, in protest at the decision to sell the bankrupt Gdańsk shipyard, birthplace of the Solidarity movement. This followed the ruling coalition's loss of nine other deputies in preceding weeks, who left to register their disapproval of the hardship caused by the Government's economic reforms.

1 September 1998: The death penalty was abolished.

11 October 1998: Local government elections indicated continuing support for the ruling AWS-led coalition, although the SLD secured the largest number of seats in nine of the 16 voivodships.

4 December 1998: Some 6,000 farmers demonstrated in Warsaw to demand an increase in government expenditure in the agricultural sector; unrest in various industrial sectors continued throughout the month.

18 December 1998: The Institute of National Remembrance Act, which allowed citizens access to secret-service files compiled on them in the

Communist era, was enacted, after the Sejm voted to discount a presidential veto; the act came into effect in January 1999.

20 January 1999: The deputy health minister, Jacek Wutzow, was dismissed after the introduction of health-care reform at the beginning of the month had led to protests and strikes and the threat of the UW's withdrawal from the governing coalition.

12 March 1999: Poland was formally admitted to NATO, along with the Czech Republic and Hungary.

25 March 1999: Prime Minister Buzek effected a reorganization of the Council of Ministers; among the changes were the appointments of new Ministers of Agriculture and of Health, following the unrest in both sectors.

19 August 1999: An estimated 80 people were injured in Bartoszyce, in northern Poland, when violence erupted between police and farmers at a demonstration against government agricultural policy and the low price of grain.

2 September 1999: The Deputy Prime Minister and Minister of the Interior, Janusz Tomaszewski, resigned after he was accused of failing to disclose his associations with the country's security forces in the 1980s; in a government reshuffle in early October he was succeeded as interior minister by Marek Biernacki.

24 September 1999: In one of the largest protests since the fall of Communism, some 35,000 people demonstrated in Warsaw against health, education and pension reform; the protesters, which included opposition leaders, demanded the resignations of the premier and the deputy premier and minister of finance, Leszek Balcerowicz.

11 December 1999: Solidarity announced that it was to withdraw from politics and become an 'organization of employees'; the movement's voting rights within the AWS were transferred to the RS AWS, now led by Buzek.

22 January 2000: The Minister of the Treasury, Emil Wąsacz, narrowly survived a vote of 'no confidence' in the Sejm, following widespread dissatis-faction with the Government's privatization plan.

12 April 2000: All foreign-exchange controls on the złoty were lifted and the 'crawling-peg' mechanism (which progressively reduced the value of the złoty against a 'basket' of Western currencies, including the US dollar) was aban-doned.

18 April 2000: Jacek Wolski was appointed the new Minister of European Integration; the post had been vacant for more than a year, leading to accusa-tions that the Government was not fully committed to gaining EU accession.

19 May 2000: The Prime Minister, Buzek, suspended the Government of Warsaw's central commune (a coalition of the Freedom Union and the SLD), replacing it with a centrally appointed commissioner; leaders of the Freedom Union demanded Buzek's resignation and threatened to withdraw the party from the Government.

29 May 2000: Following internal disagreement, the UW announced its withdrawal from the Government, in protest at parliamentary opposition to its proposals on tax reform by a number of AWS deputies; Buzek refused to accept the resignations, which included that of his deputy prime minister, Balcerowicz, and the foreign minister, Bronisław Geremek.

8 June 2000: Negotiations aimed at maintaining the governing coalition ended in failure, and the withdrawal of the UW from the Government was formalized; Buzek subsequently formed a minority Government comprising AWS members.

11 July 2000: President Kwaśniewski became the first Polish head of state since the collapse of Communist rule in 1989 to make an official visit to Russia; both countries pledged to improve bilateral relations.

13 July 2000: Fearing a deterioration in relations with Poland's south-eastern neighbour, Ukraine, government ministers criticized a project by the Russian natural-gas company, Gazprom, to construct a natural-gas pipeline from that country to Slovakia via Poland, avoiding Ukraine; President Kwaśniewski was also criticized, having previously expressed both approval and disapproval of the plan.

17 July 2000: The Minister of National Education, Mirosław Handke, resigned; he was replaced by Edmund Wittbrodt.

10 August 2000: A court investigating allegations of collaboration by public figures with the Communist-era security forces acquitted Kwaśniewski of any such involvement; Wałęsa was acquitted on similar charges the following day.

16 August 2000: Emil Wąsacz resigned, as a result of continuing criticism of his leadership of the privatization programme among members of the Sejm; he was replaced by Andrzej Chronowski.

8 October 2000: Kwaśniewski was re-elected to the presidency, receiving 53.9% of the votes cast. Andrzej Olechowski (an independent and former minister in Solidarity and AWS Governments) obtained 17.3% of the ballot, Marian Krzaklewski (the official AWS candidate) 15.6% and Jarosław Kalinowski of the PSL, 6.0%.

22 October 2000: Hanna Gronkiewicz-Waltz, the President of the National Bank of Poland, announced her resignation, with effect from 1 January 2001, in order to take up a post with the European Bank for Reconstruction and Development.

29 November 2000: The Governments of Poland and Hungary began negotiations on a potential alliance between the partially state-owned petroleum concerns, PKN Orlen and MOL.

8 December 2000: Leszek Balcerowicz, who had resigned the leadership of the UW, received the presidential nomination for the vacancy as head of the National Bank. The Sejm approved Balcerowicz's candidacy on 22 December.

17 December 2000: The UW elected Bronisław Geremek as leader, in succession to Balcerowicz.

23 December 2000: Five of the largest parties in the AWS coalition agreed to merge formally into a single party, to be led by Buzek.

7 March 2001: The National Assembly voted in favour of reinstating or providing compensation for property seized from Polish citizens by the State between 1944 and 1989. President Kwaśniewski, however, expressed the reservations that this would exclude Jewish claimants who fled Poland during or after the Second World War, and would also place the nation under considerable financial strain.

Portugal

***c.* 490:** As the Western Roman Empire disintegrated, several Germanic tribes, including the Vandals, Suevi, Quadi and Alani migrated to Iberia; the Suevi settled in modern-day Galicia and northern Portugal, the Vandals settled further south, before continuing into the Maghreb.

575: The Suevi realm was conquered by the Visigoths.

711: The Kingdom of the Visigoths was conquered by the Arabs, following the battle of Jerez de la Frontera; most of Iberia came under the control of the Emirate (Caliphate from 929) of Cordoba.

1094: The region around Oporto, previously disputed by the Christian Kingdom of Castile to the north and the Muslim Caliphate of Cordoba to the south, obtained independence under a Christian Lord.

1139: After victory in the Battle of Ourique Alfonso I, the ruler of Oporto, proclaimed himself King of Portugal—the kingdom covered approximately one-half of the modern state's territory, but was engaged in southward expansion.

1148: During the Second Crusade an English fleet captured Lisbon from the Arabs and gave it to the Kingdom of Portugal.

1179: Portugal received papal recognition as an independent, Christian Kingdom.

1254: The Assembly (Cortes), comprising representatives of the principal towns, first met.

1267: Portugal was awarded suzerainty of the Algarve, following a dispute with Castile.

1340: Portugal and Castile allied to defeat Arab invasion at Rio Salado.

1383: John II of Castile obtained the Portuguese throne through marriage, leading to unrest in Portugal.

1385: The Portuguese deposed John II and proclaimed the son of Pedro I, the previous Portuguese monarch, King John I. Portugal subsequently defeated Castile at Aljubarrota, confirming continued Portuguese independence.

1415: Expansion into North Africa led to the conquest of Ceuta.

1419: Madeira, which had originally been discovered (but not charted) by Portuguese sailors in the 14th century, was rediscovered and claimed for Portugal.

1420–30: Portuguese sailors, often sponsored by the third son of King John I, Henry 'the Navigator', began to make expeditions along the western coast of Africa.

1445: Discovery of the Cape Verde Islands.

1455: A papal bull awarded Portugal sole rights to exploration in Africa.

1471: Tangiers was captured from the Moors.

1482: Portuguese explorers settled on the Gold Coast of West Africa.

1486: The Portuguese discovery of Angola—expeditions to settle in the territory began in 1491.

1487: Explorers reached the Cape of Good Hope at the southern extremity of Africa.

1493: Pope Alexander VI decreed the division of the newly discovered lands into Spanish and Portuguese possessions, along a north–south line 100 leagues (about 560 km) west of the Azores (the Portuguese having exploration rights to the east of the line)—confirming Portugal's monopoly on African development established in the papal bull of 1455 and giving Spain similar rights in the Americas.

1494: The Treaty of Tordesillas redefined the division line as being 370 leagues west of Cape Verde.

1495: The Jews were expelled from Portugal.

1498: An expedition led by Vasco da Gama arrived in India.

1500: Brazil (east of the treaty line) was claimed for Portugal by Pedro Alvares Cabral, who had sailed away from storms in the Atlantic Ocean while bound for India.

1509: The Portuguese defeated Egyptian and Gujurati fleets at Diu, enabling Portugal to establish its first land post in India. Portugal claimed Sumatra.

1510: Goa was conquered.

1529: A further division line was drawn to the east of the Moluccas (the 'Spice Islands', now Indonesia—claimed for Portugal in 1511, effectively dividing the earth into two hemispheres, one (mainly Africa, Asia and the East Indies) for Portuguese exploration and control, the other (the Americas, excluding Brazil) for the Spanish.

1580: Phillip II of Spain enforced his inheritance of Portugal.

1606: The Spanish and Portuguese fleets were defeated by the Dutch in the East Indies and the Dutch took control of many Portuguese possessions in the region.

1635–37: The Dutch ousted the Portuguese from trading posts in Formosa (now Taiwan), Ceylon (Sri Lanka) and the Gold Coast (Ghana).

1640: The Portuguese seceded from their union with Spain, proclaiming their own King, John IV.

1661: After some years of conflict with the Dutch (which had included a damaging naval blockade of all Portuguese harbours in 1658), a peace treaty ceded Ceylon and the East Indies in return for the Dutch renouncing any claim to Brazil.

1668: Spain recognized the independence of Portugal.

1750: Sebastão, the Marquis of Pombal, gained political power in Portugal, with economic and administrative reform his priority.

1807: France, having conquered Spain, occupied Portugal and the three countries united under the Treaty of Fontainbleu; the Portuguese royal family fled to Brazil.

1811: After two years of fighting, British troops helped to drive the French out of Portugal.

1815: The process towards Brazilian independence began.

1822: King John VI, who had returned from Brazil the previous year, accepted the liberal Constitution enacted by the Assembly. Brazil declared itself an independent Empire under John VI's immediate heir, Pedro, who did not return to Portugal with the rest of his family.

1825: Portugal recognized Brazilian independence under Pedro I.

1826: Death of John V; he was succeeded by his grand-daughter, Maria II da Gloria, although his son, Miguel (who had led the reaction against the liberal Constitution—annulled in 1823—and Assembly) disputed the succession.

1828: Miguel was appointed Regent, but then declared himself King, provoking civil war.

1834: Maria was accepted as Queen and civil conflict ended, although some unrest continued among Miguel's supporters.

1906: João Franco was elected premier; his authoritarian style was assisted by King Carlos I's removal of parliamentary supremacy.

1910: Revolution deposed King Manuel II and a republic was proclaimed, with a Constitution enacted the following year.

1911–26: During this period of political instability there were eight Presidents, some 22 governments and numerous attempted revolutions and *coups d'état*, problems compounded by involvement in the First World War in 1916–18.

1926: Gen. Gomes da Costa took power in a military uprising, the Constitution was suspended, and Parliament dissolved. Gen. Carmona took power and was elected President (to 1951). Dr António de Oliveira Salazar was offered the post of finance minister, although he only accepted the appointment in 1928, after the powers of the office were extended.

1932: Salazar became premier and set about a radical transformation of the state's Constitution and administration.

1933: The Constitution of the New State (Estado Novo), providing for a directly elected President and a unicameral National Assembly, was enacted the following year.

1934: At the general election, only one list of candidates was presented, that of the National Union, a grouping which supported the Constitution and the leadership.

1961: Portugal lost its possessions in India and suffered violent unrest in its African colonies.

1968: Salazar resigned the premiership owing to ill health.

1974: The Government was overthrown in a bloodless *coup d'état* (known as the 'Revolution of Carnations'); a new military administration was installed, with Gen. António de Spinola at the head of a Committee (Junta) of National Salvation, which promised a return to democracy. Portugal recognized the independence of Guinea-Bissau and the legitimacy of India's occupation of Goa.

1975: Free elections to a new Constituent Assembly were held, after a period of some turbulence. Angola, the Cape Verde Islands, Mozambique and São Tomé and Príncipe declared independence. Portugal withdrew from Portuguese (East) Timor.

1976: A new Constitution came into force and elections to a new Assembly of the Republic were held. The Socialist Party (Partido Socialista—PS) won the greatest number of seats in the Assembly, without securing an absolute majority. The army chief of staff, Gen. António Ramalho Eanes, was subsequently elected President by a consensus of the parties in the Assembly. Eanes asked Dr Mário Lopes Soares, leader of the PS, to form a government.

1977: Soares' minority Government was unable to sustain power and the PS entered into a coalition with the rightist Social Democratic Centre (Centro Democrático Social—CDS).

1978: Eanes dissolved the Government; a series of interim governments was installed.

1979: A centre-right coalition known as the Democratic Alliance (Aliança Democrática—AD), comprising the CDS, the Social Democratic Party (Partido Social Democrata—PSD) and the People's Monarchist Party (Partido Popular Monárquico) won an absolute majority at the general election, and Dr Francisco Sá Carneiro became Prime Minister.

1980: A further general election, required by the Constitution, was also won by the AD, and Sá Carneiro retained the premiership; Eanes was re-elected to the presidency. Sá Carneiro was subsequently killed in an air crash, later believed to have been caused by a bomb. Dr Francisco Pinto Balsemão became Prime Minister.

1982: The 1976 Constitution was revised, abolishing the Council of the Revolution and indirectly replacing it with the Council of State, and moderating the powers of the President.

1983: At the general election held in April, the PS won the most seats in the Assembly of the Republic, but was unable to obtain an absolute majority. A coalition was formed with the PSD and Soares returned to the premiership.

1985: The PSD left the coalition and the Government collapsed. After the general election the PSD was the largest party in the Assembly of the Republic and it formed a minority Government, led by Prof. Aníbal Cavaco Silva.

1986: Portugal, together with Spain, joined the European Community (known as the European Union from 1993). Soares was elected President, in succession to Eanes.

1987: Cavaco Silva's Government collapsed. In the subsequent general election, the PSD won over 50% of the votes cast and an absolute majority of seats. Cavaco Silva retained the premiership.

1989: Further amendments were made to the Constitution, removing explicitly Marxist elements.

October 1991: The PSD retained its absolute majority after the general election and Cavaco Silva remained Prime Minister.

1 October 1995: At the general election, the PS won 112 of the 230 seats in the Assembly of the Republic, and was able to form a minority administration, led by António de Oliveira Guterres.

14 January 1996: Jorge Fernando Branco de Sampaio, of the PS, was elected President, in succession to Soares.

1 January 1999: Portugal participated in the third stage of the EU's Economic and Monetary Union programme, including the introduction of a new currency, the euro, designed to replace national currencies from 2002.

10 October 1999: In a general election, the PS won 44.0% of the votes cast and 115 seats in the Assembly of the Republic, exactly one-half of the total; the PSD obtained 32.3% of the votes cast and 81 seats, the United Democratic League (Coligação Democrática Unitária—CDU, a coalition of left-wing parties) and the Partido Popular each secured 15 seats, and the Partido Ecologista Os Verdes and the Bloco Esquerda each won two. Guterres formed a new administration.

20 December 1999: The territory of Macau, first established as a Portuguese trading post with China in 1557 and under Portuguese administration continuously since that date, reverted to Chinese sovereignty.

14 January 2001: Sampaio was re-elected President for a second term, receiving 55.8% of the valid votes cast.

5 March 2001: The Minister of Infrastructure, Jorge Coelho, resigned after a road bridge over the River Douro collapsed, killing 70 people. Guterres launched an investigation when it was revealed that the local council had been campaigning for repairs to the bridge for more than a decade.

ROMANIA

106: Emperor Trajan made Dacia a province of the Roman Empire.

270: Rome abandoned Dacia to Visigothic invaders, the first of many incursions by peoples from the north and east.

1365: Emergence of independent principalities in Moldavia (now north-east Romania and parts of Moldova and Ukraine) and Wallachia (now south-west Romania), having formerly been Hungarian banates or border lordships.

1394: Wallachia became a dependency of the Ottoman Empire.

1457–1504: Reign of Ştefan III ('the Great') of Moldavia.

1512: Moldavia recognized Ottoman overlordship.

1593–1601: Reign of Mihail ('the Brave') of Wallachia, who briefly united Moldavia and Transylvania with his realm.

April 1856: Under the terms of the Treaty of Paris the principalities of Wallachia and Moldavia were unified, but remained under Turkish suzerainty; the Moldavian Bojar, Cuza, became the ruler.

1866: A prince of the House of Hohenzollern-Sigmaringen replaced the ousted Cuza as Carol I of Romania.

13 July 1878: By the Treaty of Berlin Romania was recognized as an independent state and was ceded part of the Dobrogea.

27 March 1881: Romania was recognized as a kingdom.

1916: Romania entered the First World War after generous promises of territory by the Entente Powers; however, much of the country was occupied by the Axis Powers.

1919–20: Following the post-First World War peace treaties, Romania received Bessarabia, Bucovina, Transylvania, the Banat and Crisana-Maramureş.

1938: King Carol II established a royal dictatorship, suspending the Constitution and banning political parties.

27 June 1940: Romania ceded Bessarabia and Northern Bucovina to the USSR.

August 1940: Romania ceded southern Dobrogea to Bulgaria and northern Transylvania to Hungary.

September 1940: Carol II abdicated in favour of his son, Michael (Mihail), after having appointed Gen. Ion Antonescu as Prime Minister.

22 June 1941: Romania joined the German invasion of the USSR.

23 August 1944: Antonescu was arrested and Romania became a supporter of the Allied cause.

31 August 1944: Soviet troops entered Bucharest.

6 March 1945: The Soviets installed a 'puppet' government under Petru Groza.

November 1946: Elections were held and won by the Communist-led National Democratic Front.

30 December 1947: The Romanian People's Republic was proclaimed following the abdication of King Michael under pressure from the ruling Romanian Workers' Party (RWP).

24 September 1952: A new Constitution, based on the Soviet model, was approved by the Grand National Assembly.

30 November 1952: Elections were held for the Grand National Assembly. Gheorghe Gheorghiu-Dej, First Secretary of the RWP, became absolute leader.

March 1965: Following Gheorghiu-Dej's death, Nicolae Ceaușescu was elected First Secretary of the RWP.

June 1965: The RWP changed its name to the Romanian Communist Party (RCP).

August 1965: A new Constitution was adopted; the country's name was changed to the Socialist Republic of Romania.

December 1967: Ceaușescu became President of the State Council.

1968: Romania refused to join in the Warsaw Pact's suppression of the 'Prague Spring' revolt in Czechoslovakia.

1971: Romania was admitted to the General Agreement on Tariffs and Trade (GATT—known as the World Trade Organization, WTO, from January 1995).

1972: Romania was admitted to the International Monetary Fund (IMF) and the International Bank for Reconstruction and Development (World Bank).

March 1974: Ceaușescu became President of the Republic.

15 November 1987: Thousands of workers in Braşov demonstrated against the Government's economic policy; the local RCP headquarters was sacked.

December 1987: Protests took place in Timişoara and other cities. Following a three-day conference of the RCP, Ceauşescu announced improvements in food supplies and wage increases.

March 1988: Ceauşescu announced plans for the complete 'systematization' of the country by 2000.

June 1988: Following a demonstration by 50,000 Hungarians outside the Romanian embassy in Budapest, the Romanian Government ordered the closure of the Hungarian consulate in Cluj-Napoca.

March 1989: In an open letter to the President, six retired RCP officials questioned Ceauşescu's uncompromising policies, accusing him of disregard for the Constitution.

15–17 December 1989: Mounting protests in Timişoara over attempts to arrest László Tőkes, an ethnic Hungarian pastor, culminated in the army opening fire on demonstrators.

21 December 1989: Ceauşescu was interrupted by hostile chanting during a speech in the centre of Bucharest. During a subsequent demonstration the police and army shot dead many of the protesters.

22–25 December 1989: Ceauşescu and his wife fled Bucharest, but were later captured near Târgovişte, summarily tried by a military tribunal and executed. Meanwhile, anti-Ceauşescu forces seized control of the radio and television stations, and a Council of the National Salvation Front (NSF) was formed.

26 December 1989: Ion Iliescu was declared President and Petre Roman was made Prime Minister.

27 December 1989: A final Securitate (secret police) assault on the television station was driven back by the army.

28 December 1989: The name of the country was changed by decree to Romania.

1 January 1990: The NSF Council abolished the Securitate.

24–29 January 1990: Following an announcement that the NSF would contest the elections which were to be held in May, anti-NSF demonstrations were held; these were dispersed by NSF loyalists, who later attacked the offices of parties opposed to the NSF.

February 1990: The NSF and opposition parties agreed on the formation of a 253-seat Provisional National Unity Council (PNUC), which elected a 21-member Executive Bureau with Iliescu as its President. A demonstration against Iliescu and the NSF was followed by one in support of the NSF by miners from the Jiu valley.

March 1990: Opposition groups led by George Serban drew up the Timişoara Declaration, which urged the banning of former Communists from office and democratic reforms. There were disturbances between ethnic Hungarians and nationalist Romanians.

22 April 1990: Opposition supporters began an occupation of University Square in Bucharest.

20 May 1990: The NSF won decisively in the first free elections since 1937. Ion Iliescu was elected President with over 85% of the votes cast.

13–15 June 1990: Police forcibly removed the opposition supporters who had been occupying University Square, prompting unrest in which the police head-quarters was set on fire and there was an attempt to take over the television station. Miners from the Jiu valley were transported to the capital by the Government, and later attacked anyone in Bucharest suspected of being an anti-government sympathizer; at least six people were killed.

20 June 1990: Ion Iliescu (who later resigned the leadership of the NSF) was sworn in as President and appointed Petre Roman to head a new Government.

August 1990: Anti-government demonstrations resumed in University Square, but the Mayor of Bucharest subsequently declared an indefinite ban on meetings and demonstrations in Bucharest's squares.

November 1990: The Prime Minister, Roman, was granted special powers by the National Assembly to rule by decree and hasten the reforms for the free-market economy, following the introduction of emergency economic measures in the previous month. There were various demonstrations, in Bucharest and elsewhere, against the Government's economic policies, against the re-emergence of the RCP as the Socialist Labour Party and demanding reunification with Soviet Moldova.

December 1990: President Iliescu met union leaders in an attempt to avoid a general strike being called over worsening living conditions; the Government agreed to demands that the second stage of its price liberalization programme be postponed.

26 December 1990: The former sovereign, King Michael, was expelled from the country during a 24-hour visit.

February 1991: Trading in foreign currencies commenced at six authorized Romanian banks. Land-reform legislation came into effect, returning between 0.5 and 10 hectares of arable land to agricultural workers, according to the size of the family plot nationalized by the Communists.

1 April 1991: The second stage of the Government's price liberalization programme began; individual income tax was introduced; the leu was devalued against the US dollar by 72%. The National Assembly subsequently passed legislation allowing direct foreign investment in Romanian enterprises and the IMF approved financial support for one year.

29–30 April 1991: Nine ministers were dismissed in a reshuffle of the Council of Ministers; three non-NSF members were appointed ministers; however, the National Assembly vetoed the appointment of two radical ministers, including one non-NSF member.

14 August 1991: The Privatization Law was approved, providing for the distribution of 30% of the capital of state commercial companies by voucher to the general public, and for the sale of the remaining 70%; overall some 47% of state capital was to remain under government control.

27 August 1991: The Government announced its recognition of Moldova immediately after its parliament had declared its independence from the USSR; however, the following day President Iliescu referred to the inevitability of Moldova and Romania being reunited.

23–26 September 1991: Coal-miners in the Jiu valley went on strike over pay and conditions; when they demonstrated in Bucharest (as they had done in June, but relatively peacefully) violence broke out. The Roman Government resigned to enable the creation of a government of 'national opening'.

October 1991: Theodor Stolojan (former Finance Minister and President of the National Privatization Agency), at the invitation of President Iliescu, formed a new Government, which included members of the NSF, the National Liberal Party (NLP), the Agrarian Democratic Party and the Romanian Ecological Movement.

8 December 1991: A referendum approved the new Constitution, passed by the legislature in November.

March 1992: Local elections in February–April confirmed the decline in the popularity of the NSF and provoked a split in the ruling party: a pro-Iliescu wing formed the Democratic National Salvation Front—DNSF, while a 'rump' NSF retained Roman as leader.

27 September 1992: Legislative and presidential elections were held. The DNSF won the greatest number of seats, with 117 of the 328 elective seats in the Assembly of Deputies, the lower chamber of Parliament, and 49 of the 143 seats in the Senate; the Democratic Convention of Romania (DCR), an opposition alliance, won 82 seats in the Assembly of Deputies and 34 seats in the Senate. Ion Iliescu narrowly failed to win the required majority for immediate election as President.

11 October 1992: In a second round of voting, Iliescu, with 61% of the votes cast, defeated Emil Constantinescu, of the DCR, to be elected President.

November 1992: After extended negotiations, Nicolae Văcăroiu, a nominally independent bureaucrat, formed a Government consisting of equal numbers of DNSF members and independents.

May 1993: Price subsidies for many basic commodities and services were abolished, precipitating renewed industrial unrest. Minimum wages in the public sector were increased by about 75%.

9–10 July 1993: At its second national conference, the DNSF changed its name to the Romanian Social Democratic Party (RSDP) and merged with several left-wing parties.

7 October 1993: After its application for membership had been rejected earlier in the year owing to its poor civil-liberties record, Romania was finally admitted to the Council of Europe (Hungary abstained from voting).

26 January 1994: Romania became the first former Communist country to sign a Partnership for Peace agreement with the North Atlantic Treaty Organization (NATO).

March 1994: Against a background of further economic restructuring, the appointment of new ministers marked a failure of the PSDR's attempts to broaden its coalition.

18 August 1994: Two members of the ultra-nationalist Romanian National Unity Party (RNUP) were appointed to the Council of Ministers. In January 1995 the extreme nationalist parties in Parliament, the RNUP, the Greater Romania Party and the Socialist Labour Party (SLP), formally agreed to co-operate with the ruling PSDR.

May 1995: Romania ratified the Council of Europe's Framework Convention, which was that organization's first-ever legally binding instrument devoted to the general protection of national minorities. The Director of the National Agency for Privatization was arrested and charged with fraud.

June 1995: Following an increase in widespread dissatisfaction with the Government's economic record, workers in the energy sector, supported by the coal-miners and railway employees, held a three-day strike in order to demand salary increases. Meanwhile, Romania formally applied for membership of the European Union (EU), with the backing of all political parties.

1 August 1995: The mass privatization scheme was instigated, with each Romanian over 18 years of age receiving vouchers worth 975,000 lei, which could be exchanged for shares in the 4,000 state-owned enterprises that were to be sold.

December 1995: The Minister of Commerce, Petru Crisan, resigned following accusations of inappropriate business transactions.

June 1996: The ruling PSDR won the largest number of mayoral and council posts in local elections; however, there were allegations of electoral malpractice.

16 September 1996: Romania and Hungary signed a treaty of historic reconciliation, the Treaty of Understanding, Co-operation and Good Neighbourliness, in Timişoara, under which Hungary renounced claims to parts of Transylvania while Romania guaranteed a range of rights to its ethnic Hungarian population.

3 November 1996: In the general elections, the DCR won 122 of the 328 elective seats in the lower house and 53 of the Senate's 143 seats, while the PSDR took 91 and 41 seats, respectively, and the recently formed Social Democratic Union (SDU—a merger of the Democratic Party–DP, as the NSF was now known and the Romanian Social Democratic Party) gained 53 deputies and 23 senators. In the first round of the simultaneous presidential election Iliescu won 32.3% of the ballot, while his closest rival, Constantinescu, who was again the DCR's candidate, took 28.2%.

17 November 1996: In a second round of voting in the presidential election Iliescu was defeated by Constantinescu, who gained 54.4% of the valid votes cast.

19 November 1996: The former trade unionist and Mayor of Bucharest, Victor Ciorbea, was nominated as Prime Minister. He later announced a radical economic reform programme, which aimed to reduce the budget deficit, lower inflation, accelerate the privatization programme and liberalize foreign-exchange markets.

12 December 1996: A coalition Government dominated by the DCR, but also including representatives of the SDU and the Hungarian Democratic Union of Romania (HDUR), was sworn in.

January 1997: A National Council for Action against Corruption and Organized Crime (NCACOC) was established, to be headed by President Constantinescu. Meanwhile, the Government lost the support of Romania's Alternative Party and the RNUP, the latter protesting the lack of progress in the introduction of economic and social-welfare reforms.

14 April 1997: Parliament approved legislation providing for the privatization of six state-owned banks; such reforms contributed to what was regarded as IMF approval later in the month, when a new stand-by credit was granted.

8 August 1997: Some 20,000 workers took part in nation-wide demonstrations against the announcement of the closure of 17 loss-making state enterprises (involving 29,000 jobs).

11 August 1997: Several leading members of the PSDR, who had resigned from the party in the previous month, following disagreements over party policy, formed a new, centre-left party, the Alliance for Romania (AFR), led by a former foreign minister, Teodor Melescanu; the AFR held 13 seats in the lower house and two in the Senate.

19 November 1997: A rally in Bucharest organized by trade unions as part of an ongoing protest at increasing poverty was attended by some 40,000 people; in the previous month some 5,000 people demonstrated in the capital to demand the Government's resignation.

2 December 1997: In an effort to contain growing discontent within the governing coalition over policy, Ciorbea reorganized the cabinet; Daniel Daianu, an independent technocrat, replaced Mircea Ciumara as finance minister.

23 December 1997: The Minister of State and Minister of Foreign Affairs, Adrian Severin, resigned after a judicial investigation failed to uphold his allegation that a number of politicians and newspaper editors were collaborating with foreign intelligence services.

29 December 1997: Traian Basescu, a member of the DP and Minister of Transport, was forced to resign after criticizing the Government for its slow pace of reform. Ciorbea's refusal to reinstate the minister led the DP to threaten to withdraw from the coalition.

7 February 1998: Ciorbea announced the formation of a new Council of Ministers, which included members of the DCR as well as the HDUR and five independents; however, the DP refused to support the administration until Ciorbea was removed from office.

30 March 1998: Following increasing pressure from within the coalition, as well as continued social unrest, Ciorbea resigned as premier; President Constantinescu appointed the interior minister, Gavril Dejeu, as an interim Prime Minister.

15 April 1998: Radu Vasile, Secretary-General of the Christian Democratic National Peasants' Party (CDNPP—part of the DCR alliance), was confirmed as the new premier; his proposed coalition cabinet and his programme for accelerated market reform were also approved by the legislature.

25 June 1998: The Senate voted to forbid former secret police agents from holding public office; consequently, the Minister of Health, Francisc Baranyi, was dismissed from the Council of Ministers after admitting that he had collaborated with the Securitate.

23 September 1998: Daniel Dăianu, the Minister of Finance, was dismissed from the cabinet, after the NLP withdrew its support for him; he was replaced by Decebal Traian Remes.

3 October 1998: The HDUR withdrew their threat to leave the governing coalition after the Government agreed to establish a Hungarian- and German-language university in Romania.

19 October 1998: The Minister of Privatization and Chairman of the State Property Fund, Sorin Petru Dimitriu, resigned from his post, following criticism over the slow pace of the privatization process.

27 November 1998: The agriculture minister, Dinu Gavrilescu, was dismissed, after the coalition parties agreed to restructure the Government; the plan, which envisaged a reduction in the number of ministries, was approved by the Chamber of Deputies on 16 December.

4 January 1999: Miners in the Jiu valley went on strike, demanding a 35% pay increase and the reversal of a decision to close two coal mines. Following the Vasile's refusal to negotiate over the issue, 10,000–20,000 miners marched on Bucharest; however, violent clashes broke out between marchers and the security forces.

21 January 1999: Amid severe criticism of the security forces' management of the protest, the Minister of the Interior, Gabril Dejeu, was forced to resign, to be replaced by Constantin Dudu Ionescu. The following day an agreement was reached between the premier and the miners' leader, Miron Cozma, ending the strike.

15 February 1999: Cozma was sentenced *in absentia* to 18 years' imprisonment for his role in the miners' protests of 1991; in response, Cozma led a protest march of up to 4,000 miners; again, violence ensued between protesters and security forces, during which one miner died and more than 100 people injured; several hundred protesters, including Cozma, were arrested.

17 April 1999: Ciorbea and other members of the CDNPP resigned from the party in order to form the Christian Democratic National Alliance.

24 May 1999: A general strike was organized by trade unions in protest at austerity measures and legislative changes; it was estimated that only 8% of union members participated in the strike; however, labour unrest intensified in the following month.

31 May 1999: The Chamber of Deputies approved amendments to the electoral law, increasing the threshold for parliamentary legislation from 3% to 5%, with alliances required to gain a further 3% for each member party. Legislative and presidential elections were scheduled for late 2000.

19 June 1999: The Chamber of Deputies voted in favour of allowing the public access to the files of the Securitate; the legislation was promulgated by the President in December.

16 July 1999: In a controversial ruling, the Supreme Court of Justice sentenced Gen. Victor Athanasie Stănculescu and Gen. Mihai Chițac to 15 years' imprisonment for ordering the security forces to open fire on protesters during the Timișoara uprising in 1989; an appeal against the sentences was rejected in February 2000.

10 December 1999: Romania was one of six countries invited to begin negotiations on entry into the EU. Formal accession talks commenced on 15 February 2000, when Romania announced its intention to join the EU by 2007.

13 December 1999: Amid continuing social unrest, President Constantinescu dismissed Vasile, after all seven CDNPP ministers and three NLP ministers had resigned from the cabinet, withdrawing their support for the premier; the Minister of Labour and Social Protection, Alexandru Athanasiu, was appointed interim Prime Minister.

17 December 1999: Constantinescu nominated the Governor of the National Bank of Romania, Mugur Isărescu, as Prime Minister. The legislature subsequently approved his appointment and that of a new Council of Ministers, largely unchanged, but with a new Minister of State and President of the Economic-Financial Co-ordination Council, Mircea Ciumara and a new Minister of State and of Foreign Affairs, Petre Roman.

27 January 2000: The education minister, Andrei Marga, submitted his resignation after teachers conducted a national strike; he later agreed to remain in office after measures to alleviate the crisis in the education sector were agreed.

30 January 2000: A cyanide spill at the Baia Mare gold mine released approximately 22m. gallons of the chemical into the Lapus river, poisoning the ecological system of the Tisza river and 2,000 km of the Danube. In February a joint Hungarian–Romanian committee of experts was formed with the EU, to evaluate the ecological damage caused by the accident. Following an investigation, the plant accepted full responsibility for the disaster and compensation was demanded.

3 February 2000: Following his expulsion from the CDNPP, Vasile established the far-right Romanian People's Party.

14 March 2000: Sorin Frunzaverde was appointed Minister of National Defence after Victor Babiuc resigned from the DP and, consequently, from his ministerial post.

March 2000: A US $21m. plan to clear the wreckage of three bridges across the river Danube (Dunav), destroyed during NATO air strikes against Yugoslavia in April 1999 was announced; the blockage had resulted in financial losses of around $800m. in 1999. In the same month an agreement was also reached between Romania and Bulgaria on the position of the new bridge on the Danube, to be funded by the EU-led Stability Pact for South-East Europe.

5–10 April 2000: Extensive flooding in the west of the country caused seven deaths and severe damage to transport, communications, crops and some

10,000 homes; the European Commission granted 20,000m. lei in aid to alleviate the crisis.

25 May 2000: The largest investment fund in Romania, the Fondul National de Investitii, suspended operations after it was unable to meet refunding demands, causing widespread public protests; the Fund's administrator, Ana Maria Vlas, disappeared. On 2 June Stefan Boboc, the former head of National Securities Commission, was arrested on charges of abuse of his position within the Commission with regard to the Fund.

18 June 2000: The PSDR won the largest number of mayoral and council posts in local elections, gaining 36.7% of the votes cast, followed by the DP, with 12.7% and the DCR, with 11.1%.

27 June 2000: Following his election as Mayor of Bucharest, Traian Basescu, hitherto Minister of Transport, was replaced by Anca Boangiu.

16 July 2000: Decebal Traian Remes tendered his resignation as Minister of Finance following a disagreement over strategy for the forthcoming legislative elections, but Isărescu declined to accept the resignation.

August 2000: Remes resigned from the National Liberal Party, citing a perceived leftward shift in the party's policies.

26 November 2000: Legislative and presidential elections were held in Romania. Ion Iliescu of the PSDR (who was President from 1990–96) received 36.4% of the votes cast in the first ballot of the presidential election, compared with 28.4% received by the second-placed candidate, Corneliu Tudor of the right-wing Greater Romania Party (GRP). In the legislative election, the PSDR won 155 seats in the Chamber of Deputies and 65 in the Senate, the GRP won 84 in the Chamber of Deputies and 37 in the Senate, with the DP and the NLP each gaining 30 deputies and 13 Senate mandates.

10 December 2000: In the second ballot of the presidential election, Iliescu received 66.8% of the valid votes cast, compared with 33.2% gained by Tudor. Iliescu assumed the presidency on 20 December and subsequently invited Adrian Nastase of the PSDR to form a minority government.

28 December 2000: Nastase's proposed Government was endorsed by the legislature, agreements having been signed with a number of opposition parties, although not the GRP. The new administration was sworn in on 3 January 2001.

The Russian Federation

c. **878:** Kievan Rus, the first unified state of the Eastern Slavs, was founded, with Kiev (Kyiv) as its capital.

c. **988:** Vladimir (Volodymyr) I ('the Great'), ruler of Kievan Rus, converted to Orthodox Christianity.

1237–40: The Russian principalities were invaded and conquered by the Mongol Tatars.

1462–1505: Reign of Ivan III of Muscovy (Moscow), who consolidated the independent Russian domains into a centralized state.

1480: Renunciation of Tatar suzerainty.

1533–84: Reign of Ivan IV ('the Terrible'), who began the eastern expansion of Russian territory.

1547: Ivan IV was crowned 'Tsar of Muscovy and all Russia'.

1552: Subjugation of the Khanate of Kazan.

1556: Subjugation of the Khanate of Astrakhan.

1581: The Russian adventurer, Yermak Timofeyev, led an expedition to Siberia, pioneering Russian expansion beyond the Ural Mountains.

1645: A Russian settlement was established on the Sea of Okhotsk, on the coast of eastern Asia.

1654: Eastern Ukraine came under Russian rule as a result of the Treaty of Pereyaslavl.

1679: Russian pioneers reached the Kamchatka Peninsula and the Pacific Ocean.

1682–1725: Reign of Peter (Petr) I ('the Great'), who established Russia as a European Power, expanded its empire, and modernized the civil and military institutions of the state.

1703: St Petersburg was founded at the mouth of the River Neva, in north-west Russia.

1721: The Treaty of Nystad with Sweden ended the Great Northern War and brought Estonia and Livonia (now Latvia and parts of Estonia) under Russian rule. Peter I, who was declared the 'Tsar of all the Russias', proclaimed the Russian Empire.

1762–96: Reign of Catherine (Yekaterina) II ('the Great'—Princess Sophia of Anhaldt-Zerbst), who expanded the Empire in the south, after wars with the Ottoman Turks, and in the west, by the partition of Poland.

1772: Parts of Belarus were incorporated into the Russian Empire at the First Partition of Poland.

1774: As a result of the Treaty of Kuçuk Kainavci with the Turks, the Black Sea port of Azov was annexed and Russia became protector of Orthodox Christians in the Balkans.

1783: Annexation of the Khanate of Crimea.

1793: Second Partition of Poland; acquisition of western Ukraine and Belarus.

1795: Third Partition of Poland.

1801–25: Reign of Alexander (Aleksandr) I.

1801: Annexation of Georgia.

1809: Finland became a possession of the Russian Crown.

1812: Bessarabia was acquired from the Turks. Napoleon I of France invaded Russia.

1815: The Congress of Vienna established 'Congress Poland' as a Russian dependency (annexed 1831).

1825: On the death of Alexander I, a group of young officers, the 'Decembrists', attempted to seize power; the attempted *coup d'état* was suppressed by troops loyal to the new Tsar, Nicholas (Nikolai) I.

1825–55: Reign of Nicholas I.

1853–56: The Crimean War was fought, in which the United Kingdom and France aided Turkey against Russia, after the latter had invaded the Ottoman tributaries of Moldavia (including modern Moldova) and Wallachia; the War was concluded by the Congress of Paris.

1855–81: Reign of Alexander II, who introduced economic and legal reforms.

1859: The conquest of the Caucasus was completed, following the surrender of rebel forces.

1860: Acquisition of provinces on the Sea of Japan from China and the establishment of Vladivostok.

1861: Emancipation of the serfs.

1867: The North American territory of Alaska was sold to the USA for US $7m.

1868: Subjugation of the Khanates of Samarkand and Bukhara.

1873: Annexation of the Khanate of Khiva.

1875: Acquisition of Sakhalin from Japan in exchange for the Kurile Islands.

1876: Subjugation of the Khanate of Kokand.

1881: Assassination of Alexander II.

1881–94: Reign of Alexander III, who re-established autocratic principles of government.

1891: Construction of the Trans-Siberian Railway was begun.

1894–1917: Reign of Nicholas II, the last Tsar.

1898: The All-Russian Social Democratic Labour Party (RSDLP), a Marxist party, held a founding congress in Minsk (now in Belarus). In 1903, at the Second Congress in London (United Kingdom), the party split into 'Bolsheviks' (led by Lenin—Vladimir Ilych Ulyanov) and 'Mensheviks'.

1904–05: Russia was defeated in the Russo–Japanese War.

22 January 1905: Some 150 demonstrators were killed by the Tsar's troops, in what came to be known as 'Bloody Sunday'.

17 October 1905: Strikes and demonstrations in the capital, St Petersburg, and other cities forced the Tsar to introduce limited political reforms, including the holding of elections to a Duma (parliament).

January 1912: At the Sixth Congress of the RSDLP the Bolsheviks formally established a separate party, the RSDLP (Bolsheviks).

1 August 1914: Russia entered the First World War against Austria-Hungary, Germany and the Ottoman Empire (the Central Powers).

2 March (New Style: 15 March) 1917: Abdication of Tsar Nicholas II after demonstrations and strikes in Petrograd (as St Petersburg was renamed in 1914); a Provisional Government, led by Prince Lvov, took power.

9 July (22 July) 1917: In response to widespread public disorder, Prince Lvov resigned; he was replaced as Prime Minister by Aleksandr Kerenskii, a moderate socialist.

25 October (7 November) 1917: The Bolsheviks, led by Lenin, staged a *coup d'état* and overthrew Kerenskii's Provisional Government; the Russian Soviet Federative Socialist Republic (RSFSR or Russian Federation) was proclaimed.

6 January (19 January) 1918: The Constituent Assembly, which had been elected in November 1917, was dissolved on Lenin's orders. A civil war between the Bolshevik Red Army and various anti-Communist leaders (the 'Whites'), who received support from German and from Entente or Allied forces, was by now under way and lasted to 1921.

14 February (Old Style: 1 February) 1918: First day upon which the Gregorian Calender took effect in Russia.

3 March 1918: Treaty of Brest-Litovsk: the Bolsheviks ceded large areas of western territory to Germany, including the Baltic regions, and recognized the independence of Finland and Ukraine. Belarus, Georgia, Armenia and Azerbaijan subsequently proclaimed their independence.

6–8 March 1918: The RSDLP (Bolsheviks) was renamed the Russian Communist Party (Bolsheviks)—RCP (B).

9 March 1918: The capital of Russia was moved from Petrograd (renamed Leningrad in 1924) to Moscow.

10 July 1918: The first Constitution of the RSFSR was adopted by the Fifth All-Russian Congress of Soviets.

18 July 1918: Tsar Nicholas II and his family were murdered in Yekaterinburg (Sverdlovsk 1924–91) by Bolshevik troops.

11 November 1918: The Allied Armistice with Germany (which was denied its gains at Brest-Litovsk) ended the First World War.

4 March 1919: Establishment of the Third Communist International (Comintern).

8–16 March 1921: At the 10th Party Congress of the RCP (B), the harsh policy of 'War Communism' was replaced by the New Economic Policy (NEP), which allowed peasants and traders some economic freedom.

18 March 1921: A rebellion by Russian sailors in the island garrison of Kronstadt was suppressed by the Red Army. Signing of the Treaty of Rīga between Russia, Ukraine and Poland, which formally concluded the Soviet–Polish War of 1919–20, with territorial gains for Poland.

3 April 1922: Stalin (Iosif V. Dzhugashvili) was elected General Secretary of the RCP (B).

18 April 1922: The Soviet–German Treaty of Rapallo was signed, which established diplomatic relations between the two powers.

30 December 1922: The Union of Soviet Socialist Republics (USSR) was formed at the 10th All-Russian (first All-Union) Congress of Soviets by the RSFSR, the Transcaucasian Soviet Federative Socialist Republic (TSFSR), the Ukrainian SSR (Soviet Socialist Republic), the Belarusian SSR, and the Central Asian states of the Khorezm People's Socialist Republic and the People's Soviet Republic of Bukhara.

6 July 1923: Promulgation of the first Constitution of the USSR.

21 January 1924: Death of Lenin.

31 January 1924: The first Constitution of the USSR was ratified by the Second All-Union Congress of Soviets.

October 1927: Expulsion of Trotskii (Lev Bronstein) and other opponents of Stalin from the Communist Party.

1928: The NEP was abandoned; beginning of the First Five-Year Plan and forced collectivization of agriculture, which resulted in widespread famine, particularly in Ukraine.

November 1933: Recognition of the USSR by the USA.

18 September 1934: The USSR was admitted to the League of Nations.

1 December 1934: Sergei Kirov, a leading member of the Political Bureau (Politburo) of the Communist Party, was shot in Leningrad, allegedly on the orders of Stalin; following the shooting, Stalin initiated a new campaign of repression.

25 November 1936: The anti-Comintern Pact was signed between imperial Japan and Nazi Germany.

26 September 1936: Nikolai Yezhov replaced Genrikh Yagoda as head of the security police, the People's Commissariat for Internal Affairs; a series of mass arrests and executions, which came to be known as the 'Great Purge' or the 'Yezhovshchina', began.

5 December 1936: The second Constitution of the USSR (the 'Stalin' Constitution) was adopted; two new Union Republics (the Kyrgyz and Kazakh SSRs) were created, and the TSFSR was dissolved into the Georgian, Armenian and Azerbaijani SSRs.

March 1938: Nikolai Bukharin, Aleksei Rykov and other prominent Bolsheviks were sentenced to death at the Moscow 'Show' Trials.

23 August 1939: Signing of the Treaty of Non-Aggression with Germany (the Nazi–Soviet Pact), including the 'Secret Protocols', which sanctioned territorial gains for the USSR in eastern Poland, the Baltic states (Estonia, Latvia and Lithuania) and Bessarabia (then Romania, now Moldova).

17 September 1939: Soviet forces invaded eastern Poland.

28 September 1939: The Treaty on Friendship and Existing Borders was signed by Germany and the USSR, by which the two powers agreed that the USSR should annex Lithuania.

30 November 1939: The USSR invaded Finland.

14 December 1939: The USSR was expelled from the League of Nations.

June 1940: The Baltic states and Bessarabia were annexed by the USSR.

21 August 1940: Trotskii was murdered in Mexico by a Soviet agent.

22 June 1941: Germany invaded the USSR in Operation Barbarossa.

2 February 1943: German forces surrendered at Stalingrad (now Volgograd), marking the first reverse for the German Army. Soviet forces began to regain territory.

15 May 1943: The Comintern was dissolved.

8 May 1945: German forces surrendered to the USSR in Berlin and Germany subsequently capitulated; most of Eastern and Central Europe had come under Soviet control.

26 June 1945: The USSR, the USA, the United Kingdom, China and 46 other countries, including the Belarusian and Ukrainian SSRs, signed the Charter of the United Nations.

8 August 1945: The USSR declared war on Japan and occupied Sakhalin and the Kurile Islands.

September 1947: The Communist Information Bureau (Cominform) was established, to control and co-ordinate Communist Parties that were allied to the USSR.

25 January 1949: The Council for Mutual Economic Assistance (CMEA or Comecon) was established, as an economic alliance between the USSR and its Eastern European allies.

14 July 1949: The USSR exploded its first atomic bomb.

5 March 1953: Death of Stalin; he was replaced by a collective leadership, which included Georgii Malenkov and Nikita Khrushchev.

17 June 1953: Soviet troops suppressed demonstrations in Berlin.

September 1953: Khrushchev was elected First Secretary of the Central Committee of the Communist Party of the Soviet Union (CPSU).

14 May 1955: The Warsaw Treaty of Friendship, Co-operation and Mutual Assistance was signed by Albania, Bulgaria, Czechoslovakia, the German Democratic Republic (GDR—'East' Germany), Hungary, Poland, Romania and the USSR. The Treaty established a military alliance between these countries, known as the Warsaw Treaty Organization (or the Warsaw Pact).

14–25 February 1956: At the 20th Party Congress, Khrushchev denounced Stalin in the 'secret speech'.

17 April 1956: The Cominform was abolished.

26 August 1956: The first Soviet inter-continental ballistic missile (ICBM) was launched.

4 November 1956: Soviet forces invaded Hungary to overthrow Imre Nagy's reformist Government.

June 1957: Malenkov, Molotov and Kaganovich (the so-called 'Anti-Party' group) were expelled from the CPSU leadership after attempting to depose Khrushchev.

4 October 1957: The USSR placed the first man-made satellite (Sputnik I) in orbit around the earth.

March 1958: Khrushchev consolidated his position in the leadership by being elected Chairman of the Council of Ministers (premier), while retaining the office of CPSU First Secretary.

August 1960: Soviet technicians were recalled from the People's Republic of China, as part of the growing dispute between the two countries.

12 April 1961: The first manned space flight was undertaken by Maj. Yurii Gagarin on the Vostok I spacecraft.

3–4 June 1961: The US President, John F. Kennedy, met Khrushchev for official talks in Vienna, Austria.

30 October 1961: Stalin's body was removed from its place of honour in the mausoleum in Red Square, in Moscow.

18–28 October 1962: The discovery of Soviet nuclear missiles in Cuba by the USA led to the 'Cuban Missile Crisis'; tension eased when Khrushchev announced the withdrawal of the missiles, following a US blockade of the island.

5 August 1963: The USSR signed the Partial Nuclear Test Ban Treaty.

13–14 October 1964: Khrushchev was deposed from the leadership of the CPSU and the USSR and replaced as First Secretary by Leonid Brezhnev and as premier by Aleksei Kosygin.

20–21 August 1968: Soviet and other Warsaw Pact forces invaded Czechoslovakia to overthrow the reformist Government of Alexander Dubček.

12 August 1970: A non-aggression treaty was signed with the Federal Republic of Germany (FRG—'West' Germany).

May 1972: The US President, Richard Nixon, visited Moscow, thus marking a relaxation in US–Soviet relations, a process which came to be known as *détente*.

1 August 1975: Signing of the Helsinki Final Act by 32 European countries, plus the USA and Canada, committing all signatories to approve the post-1945 frontiers in Europe and to respect basic human rights.

16 June 1977: Brezhnev became Chairman of the Presidium of the Supreme Soviet (titular head of state).

7 October 1977: The third Constitution of the USSR was adopted.

24 December 1979: Soviet forces invaded Afghanistan (the last troops were not to be withdrawn until February 1989).

October 1980: Kosygin was replaced as premier by Nikolai Tikhonov.

10 November 1982: Death of Leonid Brezhnev; Yurii Andropov, former head of the Committee for State Security (Komitet Gosudarstvennoi Bezopasnosti—KGB), succeeded him as General Secretary of the CPSU.

9 February 1984: Death of Andropov; Konstantin Chernenko succeeded him as General Secretary.

10 March 1985: Death of Chernenko; he was succeeded as General Secretary by Mikhail Gorbachev.

2 July 1985: Andrei Gromyko was replaced as Minister of Foreign Affairs by Eduard Shevardnadze; Gromyko became Chairman of the Presidium of the Supreme Soviet.

27 September 1985: Nikolai Ryzhkov replaced Tikhonov as Chairman of the Council of Ministers.

24 February–6 March 1986: At the 27th Congress of the CPSU, Gorbachev proposed radical economic and political reforms and 'new thinking' in foreign policy; emergence of the policy of *glasnost* (meaning a greater degree of freedom of expression).

26 April 1986: An explosion occurred at a nuclear reactor in Chernobyl (Chornobyl), Ukraine, which resulted in discharges of radioactive material.

July 1986: Soviet troops begin their withdrawal from Afghanistan.

October 1986: A summit took place in Reykjavík, Iceland, attended by Gorbachev and the US President, Ronald Reagan, at which the issue of nuclear disarmament was discussed.

December 1986: Andrei Sakharov, the prominent human-rights campaigner, returned from internal exile in Gorkii (now Nizhnii Novgorod); rioting occurred in Alma-Ata (Almaty), Kazakhstan.

January 1987: At a meeting of the CPSU Central Committee, Gorbachev proposed plans for the restructuring (*perestroika*) of the economy and some democratization of local government and the CPSU.

21 June 1987: At local elections, the CPSU nominated more than one candidate in some constituencies.

21 October 1987: Boris Yeltsin, who had been appointed First Secretary of the Moscow City Party Committee in 1985, resigned from the Politburo.

8 December 1987: In Washington, DC, the USA, Gorbachev and President Reagan signed a treaty to eliminate all intermediate-range nuclear forces (INF) in Europe.

27–29 February 1988: In the first serious inter-ethnic conflict under Gorbachev, 32 people died in attacks on Armenians in Sumgait, Azerbaijan.

5–17 June 1988: A millennium of Christianity in Russia was celebrated with official approval.

1 October 1988: As the pace of reform quickened, Andrei Gromyko resigned as Chairman of the Presidium of the Supreme Soviet to be replaced by Mikhail Gorbachev.

1 December 1988: The all-Union Supreme Soviet approved constitutional amendments creating a new legislative system, consisting of the Congress of People's Deputies and a full-time Supreme Soviet (a number of wide-ranging reforms, including partly free elections, had been agreed by the Party earlier in the year).

6 December 1988: In a speech at the UN, Gorbachev outlined his 'new thinking' on foreign policy and announced troop withdrawals from Eastern Europe.

25 March 1989: Multi-party elections to the newly established Congress of People's Deputies took place; several prominent 'hardliners' were defeated by radical candidates.

9 April 1989: Twenty people were killed in Tbilisi, Georgia, when soldiers dispersed a demonstration.

25 May 1989: The Congress of People's Deputies convened for the first time; Gorbachev was elected to the new post of Chairman of the USSR Supreme Soviet (executive President).

27 May 1989: Congress elected an all-Union Supreme Soviet, which would act as a full-time legislature, but there were protests when only a few radicals managed to gain seats.

6 December 1989: After issuing declarations of political and economic sovereignty in May, the Supreme Soviet of Lithuania abolished the Communist Party's constitutional right to power, thus establishing the first multi-party system in the USSR. Lithuanian independence was declared on 11 March 1990.

January 1990: A state of emergency was declared in Baku, Azerbaijan, following widespread disturbances. Later in the month Democratic Platform, a reformist faction within the CPSU, held its founding conference.

4 February 1990: Some 150,000 people joined a pro-reform march in the centre of Moscow. Three days later the CPSU Central Committee approved draft proposals to abolish Article 6 of the Constitution, which had guaranteed the CPSU's monopoly of power.

4 March 1990: Elections took place to the local and republican soviets of the Russian Federation; reformists made substantial gains in the larger cities, notably Moscow and Leningrad (elections to the Supreme Soviets of Belarus, Estonia, Kazakhstan, Kyrgyzstan, Latvia, Lithuania, Moldova, Tajikistan, Ukraine and Uzbekistan also took place in February–March, producing overtly nationalist majorities in the Baltic republics and Moldova).

15 March 1990: Congress approved the establishment of the post of President of the USSR and elected Mikhail Gorbachev to that office.

29 May 1990: Boris Yeltsin was elected as Chairman of the Supreme Soviet of the Russian Federation. Two weeks later Congress adopted a declaration of Russian sovereignty within the USSR.

5 June 1990: More than 500 people were killed in inter-ethnic violence in Kyrgyzstan, as protests increased throughout the USSR.

16 July 1990: The Supreme Soviet of Ukraine declared Ukraine to be a sovereign state, with the right to maintain its own armed forces.

22 August 1990: Turkmenistan declared itself to be a sovereign state.

24 August 1990: Tajikistan declared itself to be a sovereign state.

3 September 1990: Boris Yeltsin announced a 500-day programme of economic reform to the Supreme Soviet of the Russian Federation.

1 October 1990: In New York, the USA, France, the United Kingdom, the USA and the USSR, the four Occupying Powers of Germany, formally recognized the full sovereignty of a unified Germany.

October 1990: Legislation allowing freedom of conscience and the existence of other political parties, apart from the CPSU, was adopted by the all-Union Supreme Soviet. It also approved a reform programme designed to establish a market economy. In Georgia pro-independence parties won an overall majority in the Supreme Soviet.

25 October 1990: Kazakhstan declared itself to be a sovereign state and outlawed the storing or testing of nuclear weapons on its territory.

30 October 1990: Kyrgyzstan declared itself to be a sovereign state.

December 1990: Despite further constitutional changes and proposals for a new Union Treaty, Eduard Shevardnadze resigned as Minister of Foreign Affairs (on 21 December), claiming that the country was moving towards dictatorship. Later in the month Congress granted Gorbachev extended presidential powers. Ryzhkov was succeeded as Soviet premier by Valentin Pavlov, while Gennadii Yanayev was eventually endorsed as Vice-President.

13 January 1991: Thirteen people died when Soviet troops occupied radio and broadcasting buildings in Vilnius, Lithuania. One week later four people died in Rīga, Latvia, when Soviet troops occupied government buildings.

22 February 1991: Some 400,000 people demonstrated in Moscow, in support of Boris Yeltsin, who had demanded Gorbachev's resignation, and reform.

17 March 1991: In an all-Union referendum on the issue of the future state of the USSR, some 75% of participants approved Gorbachev's concept of a 'renewed federation' (several republics did not participate.

23 April 1991: Gorbachev and the leaders of nine Union Republics, including Yeltsin, signed the 'Nine-Plus-One Agreement'.

12 June 1991: Yeltsin was elected President of the Russian Federation in direct elections, with Aleksandr Rutskoi, a former general in the Afghan war, as Vice-President; residents of Leningrad voted to change the city's name back to St Petersburg.

1 July 1991: The USSR, together with the other member countries of the Warsaw Pact, signed a protocol which formalized the dissolution of the alliance. Eduard Shevardnadze and Aleksandr Yakovlev, together with other reformists, announced the formation of a new reformist movement, later known as the Movement for Democratic Reforms.

31 July 1991: The USSR and the USA signed the first Strategic Arms' Reduction Treaty (START 1).

16 August 1991: Yakovlev resigned from the CPSU (which a few weeks previously had abandoned Marxism-Leninism), warning of the possibility of a coup against Gorbachev.

18–21 August 1991: With Gorbachev placed under house arrest in his Crimean dacha (summer residence), the self-proclaimed State Committee for the State of Emergency in the USSR (SCSE), under Vice-President Yanayev, attempted to seize power in a *coup d'état*. Thousands of people demonstrated against the coup in St Petersburg and in Moscow, where people gathered at the White House, the seat of the Russian Federation's administration. Yeltsin demanded the restoration of Gorbachev to power and, amid increasing institutional opposition, the coup attempt collapsed and Gorbachev was reinstated. Estonia declared independence on 20 August and Latvia the next day.

23 August 1991: Gorbachev, replacing supporters of the coup attempt, appointed Vadim Bakatin Chairman of the KGB, Gen. Yevgenii Shaposhnikov Minister of Defence and Viktor Barannikov Minister of Internal Affairs. Aleksandr Bessmertnykh was dismissed as Minister of Foreign Affairs. Yeltsin suspended the activities of the Russian Communist Party (RCP) and the publication of six CPSU newspapers (the RCP was formally banned in November).

24 August 1991: Gorbachev resigned as General Secretary of the CPSU, nationalized the Party's property, demanded the dissolution of the Central Committee and banned party cells in the Armed Forces, the KGB and the police. The Supreme Soviet of Ukraine adopted a declaration of independence, pending approval by referendum on 1 December (90% of the participating voters were to approve the decision).

25 August 1991: Gorbachev established an interim government, headed by Ivan Silayev. The Supreme Soviet of Belarus adopted a declaration of independence.

27 August 1991: The Supreme Soviet of Moldova proclaimed the republic's independence.

30 August 1991: The Supreme Soviet of Azerbaijan voted to 're-establish' the independent status the country had enjoyed until 1920.

31 August 1991: The Supreme Soviets of Uzbekistan and Kyrgyzstan adopted declarations of independence.

6 September 1991: The newly formed State Council, which comprised the supreme officials of the Union Republics, recognized the independence of Estonia, Latvia and Lithuania.

9 September 1991: The Supreme Soviet of Tajikistan adopted a declaration of independence.

23 September 1991: Armenia declared its independence, following a referendum two days previously.

27 September 1991: Ivan Silayev officially resigned as Prime Minister of the Russian Federation, following his appointment as Soviet Prime Minister; he was one of a number of reformers promoted by Gorbachev.

5 October 1991: The USSR was officially admitted as an associate member of the International Monetary Fund (IMF).

18 October 1991: A treaty, which established an Economic Community between its signatories, was signed by representatives of the Russian Federation and Armenia, Belarus, Kazakhstan, Kyrgyzstan, Tajikistan, Turkmenistan and Uzbekistan; four other republics had earlier agreed to some form of economic co-operation.

21 October 1991: The first session of the newly established all-Union Supreme Soviet was attended by delegates of the Russian Federation, Belarus,

Kazakhstan, Kyrgyzstan, Tajikistan, Turkmenistan and Uzbekistan. Representatives of Azerbaijan and Ukraine attended as observers.

27 October 1991: Following a referendum, Turkmenistan declared its independence. An election was held in the Chechen-Ingush Autonomous Republic to the presidency of the self-proclaimed 'Chechen Republic' (Chechnya) and was won by Gen. Dzhokhar Dudayev.

November 1991: President Yeltsin announced the formation of a new Russian Government, with himself as Chairman (Prime Minister) and Gennadii Burbulis as First Deputy Chairman.

8 December 1991: The leaders of the Russian Federation, Belarus and Ukraine, meeting at Belovezhskaya Pushcha near Brest, Belarus, agreed to form a Commonwealth of Independent States (CIS) to replace the USSR, as stated in the so-called Minsk Agreement.

16 December 1991: Kazakhstan declared its independence, following a decision by it and the four other Central Asian republics to join a Commonwealth.

21 December 1991: At a meeting in Almaty, the leaders of 11 former Union Republics of the USSR signed a protocol on the formation of the new CIS. Georgia did not sign, but sent observers to the meeting.

25 December 1991: Mikhail Gorbachev formally resigned as President of the USSR, thereby confirming the effective dissolution of the Union.

30 December 1991: The 11 members of the CIS agreed, in Minsk, Belarus, to establish a joint command for armed forces (this arrangement was formally ended in 1993); use of nuclear weapons was to be under the control of the Russian Federation's President, after consultation with other Commonwealth leaders and the agreement of the presidents of Belarus, Kazakhstan and Ukraine.

2 January 1992: A radical economic reform programme was introduced, under which most consumer prices were liberalized.

31 March 1992: Eighteen of the 21 autonomous republics of the Russian Federation, the leaders of the Russian administrative regions and the mayors of Moscow and St Petersburg signed the Russian Federation Treaty; representatives from the Chechen Republic and Tatarstan did not participate.

15 May 1992: At a meeting of the CIS Heads of State in Tashkent, Uzbekistan, a Five-Year Collective Security Agreement was signed by Armenia, Kazakhstan, Russia, Tajikistan, Turkmenistan and Uzbekistan.

15 June 1992: Yeltsin appointed Yegor Gaidar, an economist and supporter of radical market reform, as acting Prime Minister (he had been joint First Deputy Prime Minister since May).

269

1 October 1992: The Government's privatization programme was initiated, with the issue of a 10,000-rouble privatization voucher to every Russian citizen.

30 November 1992: The Constitutional Court announced its verdict concerning Yeltsin's ban on the CPSU and the RCP of November 1991: the Court upheld the abolition of the national structures of the two parties and the decision to confiscate Communist properties, but declared the ban on local party branches illegal.

9 December 1992: The Congress rejected Yeltsin's nomination of Gaidar as Prime Minister; Yeltsin subsequently appointed Viktor Chernomyrdin to the post.

3 January 1993: President Yeltsin and the US President, George Bush, signed START 2, which envisaged a reduction in the strategic nuclear weapons of both powers. It was ratified by the Russian legislature on 14 April 2000, and signed into law on 4 May.

11 March 1993: Congress attempted to reduce the powers of President Yeltsin by granting itself the right to suspend any presidential decrees that contravened the Constitution, pending a ruling by the Constitutional Court.

20 March 1993: Following the rejection by Congress of his proposal to hold a referendum on the issue of the respective powers of the presidency and the legislature, Yeltsin announced his intention to rule Russia by decree until such a referendum could take place.

28 March 1993: A proposal to impeach President Yeltsin was narrowly defeated; however, a majority of deputies also voted against the dismissal of the parliamentary Chairman, Ruslan Khasbulatov, who was one of Yeltsin's leading opponents.

25 April 1993: Some 65.7% of the registered electorate participated in a referendum, of which 57.4% endorsed President Yeltsin and 70.6% voted in favour of early elections to the Congress of People's Deputies.

12 July 1993: At the Constitutional Conference, a proposed compromise constitution, based on the presidential and parliamentary drafts, was approved by 433 of a total 585 delegates.

24 July 1993: In an attempt to control inflation in Russia, all rouble notes printed between 1961 and 1992 were withdrawn from circulation and replaced with new ones; no new notes were issued to any other country until January 1994, when Tajikistan agreed, effectively, to surrender control of its monetary policy to Russia; Belarus agreed to similar conditions in April 1994—despite various wider agreements on expanding the 'rouble zone', in practice it remained confined to these two countries.

31 August 1993: Following a series of meetings in Moscow, the heads of administration from 58 constituent parts of the Russian Federation and 45 heads of regional legislative bodies approved President Yeltsin's proposal for the establishment of a Federation Council, which convened in mid-September.

21 September 1993: Yeltsin issued a decree On Gradual Constitutional Reform (Decree 1,400), which suspended the powers of the legislature with immediate effect and set the date for elections to a new bicameral legislature, the Federal Assembly. An emergency session of the Supreme Soviet appointed Rutskoi acting President, although the Constitutional Court ruled against this.

23 September 1993: As the institutional crisis continued, an emergency session of the Congress of People's Deputies was convened.

24 September 1993: At a meeting of the CIS Council of Heads of State, in Moscow, an agreement was reached on a framework for economic union, including the gradual removal of tariffs and a currency union; nine states signed the agreement, and Turkmenistan and Ukraine agreed to be associate members of such a union.

26 September 1993: Some 10,000 demonstrators attended a rally outside the White House, the seat of the Supreme Soviet, in support of the legislators.

28 September 1993: An unarmed militia-man was killed in disturbances in the centre of Moscow, as a crowd of several thousand supporters of Khasbulatov and Rutskoi attempted to break through the police cordon around the White House.

3 October 1993: Negotiations between the Government and parliament, mediated by the Russian Orthodox Church, broke down. A state of emergency was declared in Moscow after a group of anti-Yeltsin demonstrators stormed the office of the Mayor of Moscow and the Ostankino television building. Rutskoi was formally dismissed from office, and he and Khasbulatov issued an 'appeal to the people' to defend parliament.

4 October 1993: The White House was shelled by government forces and severely damaged by fire, and over 100 people were reported to have been killed. Later that day Khasbulatov and Rutskoi surrendered and the perpetrators of the violence were arrested.

7 October 1993: The Constitutional Court was suspended, pending the adoption of a new constitution and the election of new judges.

15 October 1993: The Constitutional Convention opened. Yeltsin decreed that a nation-wide plebiscite be held on the draft constitution. The leaders of the anti-Government insurrection were charged with incitement to riot.

12 December 1993: The proposed new Constitution was approved by 58.4% of participating voters in a referendum. On the same day elections to the new Federal Assembly (consisting of the Federation Council and the State Duma) were held, producing an unexpected number of votes for Vladimir Zhirinovskii's radical nationalist Liberal Democratic Party of Russia (LPDR), which obtained approximately 22.8% of votes cast, and for the Communists (with some 12.4%).

January 1994: Parliamentary representatives of the Communist Party established a conservative bloc with the Democratic Party and the Agrarian Party; this bloc controlled 115 seats out of a total of 450 in the State Duma, while the liberal bloc occupied some 196 seats and the LDPR 64 seats.

February 1994: The State Duma granted an amnesty to the members of the SCSE of the 1991 coup attempt and to the organizers of the parliamentary resistance of September–October 1993.

22 June 1994: Russia became a signatory to the Partnership for Peace co-operation programme drawn up by the North Atlantic Treaty Organization (NATO). A broader accord with NATO also came into effect.

30 July 1994: Against a background of armed raids by rebel Chechens on Russian towns, Yeltsin declared his support for an 'Interim Council' in Chechnya. The Council, headed by Umar Avturkhanov, had proclaimed itself the rightful Government of Chechnya, in opposition to the administration of President Dudayev, which, within a fortnight, ordered mobilization in Chechnya.

3 September 1994: Armed conflict broke out in Argun, east of Groznyi, the capital of Chechnya, between supporters of Dudayev and opposition troops.

11 October 1994: The rouble collapsed, losing almost one-quarter of its value against the US dollar and resulting in the resignation of several ministers and the Chairman of the Central Bank, Viktor Gerashchenko.

26 November 1994: Groznyi was attacked by warplanes, allegedly operating from a federal airbase. Opposition forces had attacked the city earlier in the month with Russian tanks.

11 December 1994: Following the collapse of peace negotiations earlier in the month, Yeltsin ordered the invasion of Chechnya by some 40,000 federal ground troops.

19 January 1995: After a bitterly fought resistance, Dudayev fled Groznyi and established his headquarters at Galanchezh, to the south-west.

March 1995: The Russian Government installed the 'Government of National Revival' in Chechnya, chaired by Salambek Khadzhiyev; this existed alongside the Provisional Council, now largely discredited, but was replaced in November by a new Government, under Doku Zavgayev.

14 June 1995: The militant Chechen leader, Shamil Basayev, took over 1,000 people hostage in the town of Budennovsk (Stavropol Krai). After a few days, to secure the release of the captives, the Prime Minister, Chernomyrdin, intervened in the negotiations and agreed to resume peace talks with the Chechen rebels.

21 June 1995: A vote of 'no confidence' in the Government was overwhelmingly passed in the State Duma over the crisis in Chechnya.

12 July 1995: An impeachment motion against the President was defeated, largely owing to the fact that Yeltsin was hospitalized at the time, having just suffered a heart attack.

30 July 1995: A military accord was signed on the gradual disarmament of the Chechen rebels, in return for the partial withdrawal of federal troops from Chechnya; it remained in effect until October.

17 December 1995: A total of 43 political parties and electoral blocs took part in the election to the State Duma, in which an estimated 64.4% of eligible voters participated. The Communist Party of the Russian Federation (CPRF) achieved the greatest success, winning 22.7% of the votes cast; the LDPR won 11.2% of the votes, Our Home is Russia (a centre-right electoral bloc headed by Viktor Chernomyrdin) 10.1% and Yabloko (headed by the liberal, Grigorii Yavlinskii) 6.9%.

9 January 1996: Chechen rebels, led by Salman Raduyev (the 'Lone Wolf'), held some 2,000 civilians captive in the Dagestani town of Kizlyar. Some hostages were later released, while others were taken in convoy to the nearby village of Pervomaiskoye. The village was bombarded for several days by federal air and ground troops, resulting in the release of the captives at the expense of many casualties.

25 January 1996: Russia was admitted to the Council of Europe.

15 March 1996: Some five years after the all-Union referendum on the fate of the USSR, the Communist-dominated State Duma declared the Minsk Agreement null and void, although this motion was not endorsed by any other state bodies and officials stated that there was no implicit threat to the sovereignty of other former Soviet states.

2 April 1996: The Russian President signed a treaty with President Lukashenka of Belarus establishing a 'Community of Sovereign Republics'. The treaty envisaged closer integration, with a view to the eventual creation of a confederation. Four days previously, the two Presidents had signed the so-called Quadripartite Treaty with Kazakhstan and Kyrgyzstan, envisaging closer economic and infrastructural co-operation.

21 April 1996: Dzhokhar Dudayev, the Chechen rebel leader, was reportedly killed in a Russian missile attack. He was succeeded by his erstwhile Deputy President, Zemlikhan Yandarbiyev.

27 May 1996: A cease-fire agreement was concluded between Yeltsin and Yandarbiyev (in effect from 1 June).

16 June 1996: Eleven candidates contested the presidential elections; Yeltsin secured the greatest number of votes (35%), followed by the leader of the CPRF, Gennadii Zyuganov (32%); retired Lt-Gen. Aleksandr Lebed won an unexpectedly high level of support, with 15% of the votes cast, and was later appointed to the Government.

3 July 1996: Amid increasing speculation about his health, Boris Yeltsin won the second round of voting in the presidential election with 53.8% of the votes cast. Yeltsin was inaugurated as the first democratically elected President of post-Soviet Russia on 9 August.

31 August 1996: Following a successful attack by Chechen forces on Groznyi, Lt-Gen. Lebed, the newly appointed Secretary of the Security Council, negotiated a cease-fire with the rebel chief of staff, Col Khalid 'Aslan' Maskhadov; the basic principles of the peace agreement included postponing a solution to the issue of Chechen sovereignty until 2001.

16 October 1996: Despite his success in negotiating a peace deal in Chechnya, Aleksandr Lebed was dismissed; this followed several months of open conflict between Lebed and the interior minister, Anatolii Kulikov.

6 November 1996: Less than one day after undergoing major heart surgery President Yeltsin reassumed his presidential powers, temporarily transferred to the Prime Minister, Chernomyrdin.

2 April 1997: A Treaty of Union was signed by the Presidents of Russia and Belarus, without consultation with their respective legislatures; the following month a Charter of the Union of Belarus and Russia was concluded, committing the two countries to closer integration but stopping short of advocating full union.

27 May 1997: At a NATO summit meeting in Paris, France, a Founding Act on Mutual Relations, Co-operation and Security between NATO and the Russian Federation was signed, which provided Russia with equal status with the Alliance in peace-keeping operations and enhanced its consultative rights.

28 May 1997: The Russian–Ukrainian dispute over ownership of the Soviet Black Sea Fleet was finally resolved: Russia would lease part of the naval base at the Crimean port of Sevastopol (Sevastopil) for 20 years and provide financial compensation for ships and equipment received from Ukraine; a few days later a Treaty on Friendship, Co-operation and Partnership was signed by the Presidents of the two countries.

20 November 1997: Anatolii Chubais, a First Deputy Prime Minister and the Minister of Finance, and one of several high-ranking government and administrative officials to admit to accepting advance payments for a book about Russia's privatization programme, lost his finance portfolio; although not implicated in the scandal, Boris Nemtsov, a former Governor of Nizhnii

Novgorod Oblast, was replaced by Sergei Kiriyenko as Minister of Fuel and Energy.

November 1997: During a visit by President Yeltsin to the People's Republic of China, it was agreed to end a long-running border dispute and allow for the implementation of a 1991 accord demarcating the entire 4,300-km frontier.

1 December 1997: The Partnership and Co-operation Agreement between Russia and the European Union (EU) of 1994 took effect; the accord was to provide a permanent forum for trade and politics and to aim to remove restrictions on exports and extend Russia's 'most-favoured nation' status.

17 January 1998: A reallocation of cabinet portfolios, at the expense of Chubais and Nemtsov, indicated a further erosion of reformist influence in government, to the satisfaction of a critical parliament.

27 March 1998: Following the dismissal of Chernomyrdin and his Government a few days before, Sergei Kiriyenko was nominated as premier; a new Government was gradually appointed over the following month. Kiriyenko was confirmed as premier by the State Duma on 24 April, his nomination having been rejected twice earlier in the month.

17 July 1998: Following the approval, four days earlier, of an IMF loan of US $22,600m., the State Duma rejected two of the main tax proposals in the government programme of emergency fiscal measures demanded by the Fund. The remains of Tsar Nicholas II and members of his family and household were buried in St Petersburg on the 80th anniversary of their murder.

17 August 1998: Following an escalating financial crisis, and in a complete reversal of its monetary policies, the Government announced a series of emergency measures, which included the effective devaluation of the rouble.

21 August 1998: The State Duma reconvened for an extraordinary plenary session to debate the financial and economic crisis in Russia; a resolution was passed urging the voluntary resignation of President Yeltsin. Two days later, allegedly at the behest of powerful industrial figures, President Yeltsin dismissed Kiriyenko's administration and reappointed Chernomyrdin premier.

11 September 1998: Following the State Duma's second overwhelming rejection of Chernomyrdin's nomination as Prime Minister, a compromise candidate, the foreign minister, Yevgenii Primakov, was confirmed as premier by the State Duma; the same day two conservatives were appointed to key economic posts—Yurii Maslyukov (who had briefly held the trade and industry portfolio) became deputy prime minister responsible for economic policy, and Viktor Gerashchenko returned as Chairman of the Central Bank, after the resignation of Sergei Dubinin four days previously.

5 November 1998: The Constitutional Court ruled that Boris Yeltsin was ineligible to seek a third presidential term in 2000.

8 December 1998: The bodies of three British citizens and one New Zealander, who had been kidnapped in the previous month, were discovered in Chechnya; the motive for the murders remained unclear. When, three months later, a representative of the Russian Ministry of the Interior was kidnapped in Chechnya, all Russian officials withdrew from the republic.

4 March 1999: Boris Yeltsin dismissed Boris Berezovskii as Executive Secretary of the CIS, prompting protests that the decision had not been approved by the Commonwealth's Council of Heads of State.

8 March 1999: One day after the Federation Council had refused to accept the resignation of the Prosecutor-General, Yurii Skuratov, whose investigation into the activities of the Central Bank had allegedly uncovered incidences of official corruption, compromising footage of him was broadcast on state-run television. The following month he was suspended from his post by a presidential decree. In November the Constitutional Court upheld the President's action, pending the commencement of criminal proceedings.

21 March 1999: The Chechen President and Chairman of the Council of Ministers, Aslan Maskhadov, escaped injury in an assassination attempt in the republic's capital.

24 March 1999: Russia condemned NATO airstrikes against Yugoslav targets, initiated in response to the repression of ethnic Albanians in the Serbian province of Kosovo and Metahija, and suspended relations with the Organization.

16 April 1999: The Duma voted overwhelmingly in favour of the Federal Republic of Yugoslavia's admission to the Union of Russia and Belarus. Political leaders assessed the measure to be of enormous symbolic significance, but of little real practical impact.

12 May 1999: The unexpected dismissal of Primakov and his Government was effected by Yeltsin, who cited their failure dramatically to improve the economic situation and appointed Sergei Stepashin, hitherto First Deputy Prime Minister and Minister of the Interior, as acting premier; he was approved by the State Duma one week later.

15 May 1999: The State Duma's impeachment attempt failed, as none of the five counts brought against the President, including that of bringing about 'genocide' through economic reforms that resulted in a lower birth-rate and a reduced life expectancy, succeeded in securing the necessary majority of two-thirds of the chamber's membership.

12 June 1999: Russian troops entered Kosovo, ahead of NATO forces. The Serbs had capitulated three days earlier, aided by the mediation efforts of Russia special envoy to the Balkans conflict, the former Prime Minister, Viktor Chernomyrdin. International negotiations took place throughout the month on the role to be undertaken in the region by Russian peace-keeping forces.

14 July 1999: It was revealed that Swiss prosecutors had opened a criminal investigation into Pavel Borodin, the head of the Presidential Administrative Office, and 22 others alleged to have been involved in money 'laundering' (the processing of illegally obtained funds into legitimate accounts) and the payment of bribes to a Swiss company, Mabetex, which had been awarded the contract for the lavish renovation of the Kremlin. A warrant for Bodin's arrest was issued by the Swiss authorities in January 2000.

28 July 1999: The Executive Board of the IMF approved a US\$4,500m. standby credit, to be released in instalments. The disbursement of the funds, which were designated for existing debt repayments, was suspended in February 2000, owing to concerns about the extent of economic reform in Russia.

7 August 1999: Armed Chechen guerrillas invaded neighbouring Dagestan and seized control of two villages. Russian troops retaliated and claimed, by the end of the month, claimed to have quelled the rebel action.

9 August 1999: In an unforeseen move, Prime Minister Sergei Stepashin was dismissed by Yeltsin, and replaced by Vladimir Putin, hitherto the Secretary of the Security Council and head of the FSB.

31 August 1999: Over 30 people were injured in a bomb explosion in a shopping centre in Moscow. Four further explosions, which targeted residences in Moscow and elsewhere, occurred in September, killing hundreds.

23 September 1999: Russia initiated major airstrikes against Chechnya, officially in retaliation for the bombings, which were suspected of having been perpetrated by Chechen rebel extremists. However, a small minority alleged the Russian Government to have been responsible for the bomb attacks, in order to justify the offensive and, as a result, increase the Government's popularity prior to legislative and presidential elections.

6 December 1999: Following the full-scale invasion of Chechnya at the beginning of November, Russian forces warned residents of the capital, Groznyi, to evacuate the city by 11 December or face attack, resulting in strong international disapproval. A ground offensive against the city subsequently commenced.

8 December 1999: The signature of the Union Treaty of Russia and Belarus took place in Moscow. The Treaty entered into force on 26 January 2000, following its ratification by the Russian executive.

19 December 1999: A total of 29 parties and blocs contested the election to the State Duma, in which 62% of the electorate participated. The Chechen constituency remained vacant, as the conflict made it impossible to hold elections there. The CPRF secured the most seats, with 113. Unity (Yedinstvo), formed by 31 leaders of Russia's regions, performed extremely well, taking 72 seats. The Fatherland—All Russia bloc did not do as well as expected, obtaining 67 seats. The Union of Rightist Forces, led by Sergei Kiriyenko, obtained 29 seats, Yabloko took 21, and the Zhirinovskii bloc won 17. Yurii Luzhkov won the Moscow mayoral election, which took place concurrently, defeating both Kiriyenko and Pavel Borodin.

31 December 1999: Boris Yeltsin unexpectedly resigned as President. Vladimir Putin assumed the role in an acting capacity, and a presidential election, under the terms of the Constitution required within three months of Yeltsin's resignation, was scheduled for 26 March 2000.

14 January 2000: A new national security concept was published, which lowered the threshold for the use of nuclear weapons, in an attempt to contain the threat from the West's perceived attempts to achieve global domination. The document also prepared the way for greater domestic state control and protectionism.

18 January 2000: The Duma reconvened, and the ideologically dissimilar CPRF and Unity factions formed an alliance. In protest at the move, which was seen as a cynical attempt to divide the decisive positions in the Duma among themselves, the Fatherland—All Russia, Yabloko and Union of Rightist Forces factions, together with the newly formed Russia's Regions group of deputies, agreed to a boycott. The situation was resolved after eight days, following Putin's intervention and the reallocation of committee chairmanships, together with the appointment of an additional Deputy Chairman. In the following month further appointments were made to appease the protesters.

9 February 2000: A Treaty of Friendship, Neighbourliness and Co-operation was signed between Russia and the Democratic People's Republic of Korea, replacing a 1961 agreement, which had been abolished following the establishment of diplomatic relations between the then-USSR and the Republic of Korea in 1990.

26 March 2000: Fourteen candidates contested the presidential election. Vladimir Putin achieved a clear victory in the first round, with 52.9% of the votes cast. Of the 68.9% of the electorate who participated, 29.2% voted for the Communist candidate, Gennadii Zyuganov.

6 April 2000: The Parliamentary Assembly of the Council of Europe voted to suspend Russia's membership unless progress were made to end human-rights abuses in Chechnya.

5 May 2000: Putin decreed that, henceforth, Chechnya was to come under direct federal, rather than direct presidential, rule. Aslan Maskhadov was no longer to be recognized as President of the republic, and on 19 June a new administrative leader for Chechnya, Mufti Akhmad Kadyrov, was inaugurated.

7 May 2000: Vladimir Putin was inaugurated as President of the Russian Federation. He subsequently relinquished the post of premier and formed a new Government headed by the former First Deputy Prime Minister, Mikhail Kasyanov.

13 May 2000: The President issued a decree dividing Russia's 89 constituent regions and republics between seven federal districts. Each district was to come under the control of a presidential envoy, who was to oversee local regions' compliance with federal legislation and receive funding from Moscow, in order to prevent local governors from acting in contravention of central policy. Of the new presidential envoys, who were appointed a few days later, only two were civilians, the rest being senior officers of the security services or the military.

31 May 2000: Three pieces of legislation, proposed by Putin to extend the powers of the President and curtail those of the regional governors, were passed by the State Duma. The first proposed that regional governors should lose their seats in the Federation Council, and be replaced by representatives elected from regional legislatures; following its ratification by the Federation Council in July, all existing Council members were to be replaced by the beginning of 2002. The second bill accorded the President the right to dismiss regional governors, and the third allowed governors to remove from office elected officials who were subordinate to them.

13 June 2000: In what was seen as a challenge to the so-called 'oligarchs', Vladimir Guzinskii, the Chairman of the Media-Most holding company, was arrested and charged with fraud in connection with his acquisition of a state-run video company in 1998. All charges were withdrawn on 27 July.

8 August 2000: A bomb exploded in central Moscow, resulting in 11 deaths and some 90 injuries. Following the explosion, suspected to have been perpetrated by extremists, security measures in the city were increased.

12 August 2000: The Russian nuclear submarine, Kursk, sank after an explosion, during exercises in the Barents Sea. The Russian authorities attracted criticism, owing to delays in responding to the crisis, and international rescue efforts were unsuccessful; all 118 sailors on board the vessel perished.

20 August 2000: Tsar Nicholas II and his family were canonized by the Patriarch of the Russian Orthodox Church, Aleksei II.

27 August 2000: Television broadcasts were disrupted by a fire at the Ostankino television tower in the capital. Chechen rebels later claimed responsibility for the fire, although the Russian authorities denied that there was any evidence of sabotage.

12 September 2000: It was revealed that Vladimir Putin had been the target of a failed assassination plot during a CIS conference held in the previous month.

19 September 2000: The General Staff issued an order specifying a reduction of some 350,000 in the strength of the Russian armed forces; the reductions were expected to take place in the period 2001–03. On 9 November the Security Council voted to reduce the overall strength of the Russian armed forces by 600,000 (approximately one-fifth of 2000 levels) by 2005.

20 September 2000: The Minister for the Press, Broadcasting and Mass Media, Mikhail Lesin, admitted that he had approved a document stating that criminal charges against Guzinskii would be dropped in return for the sale of Guzinkskii's media interests to the partially state-owned gas company, Gazprom.

October 2000: Relations with Afghanistan were strained, following the arrest of a number of Afghan citizens for alleged violations of Russia's borders. The Taliban Government accused Russia of supporting the Afghan opposition and of military activity hostile to Afghanistan in neighbouring states. Russia claimed that Afghanistan was training and harbouring alleged Islamic terrorists.

10 October 2000: President Putin and the Presidents of Belarus, Kazakhstan, Kyrgyzstan and Tajikistan signed a treaty creating a new customs union, to be known as the Eurasian Economic Community.

30 October 2000: An agreement was signed between Russia and the EU, providing for greater co-operation on energy and security matters.

13 November 2000: A federal arrest warrant was issued for Guzinskii, on charges of fraud relating to loans granted to his companies. International assistance in the pursuit of Guzinskii was sought on 4 December.

15 November 2000: Boris Berezovskii, former Executive Secretary of the CIS, who had refused to return to Russia to answer questions concerning the alleged embezzlement of US$970m. from the state airline, Aeroflot, accused Putin of having accepted some of the money in question from Swiss companies under his own control to finance his presidential campaign. The accusations against Putin and his Yedinstvo party were strongly denied.

23 November 2000: The State Council, a body comprising the President and the territorial governors and formed as part of the reforms of the Federation Council in May, convened for the first time.

30 November 2000: Draft legislation proposed by President Putin to grant permanent immunity from prosecution for any acts committed by a President during his or her period of office received initial approval from the State Duma; it required approval on two further occasions to become law. Putin's opponents criticized the legislation, claiming that it contravened the constitutional principle of equality of all citizens before the law. In a meeting with President Alyaksandr Lukashenka of Belarus, President Putin signed an agreement on the introduction of a common currency unit for the two countries by 2008.

13 December 2000: Vladimir Guzinskii was arrested and imprisoned in Spain.

7 March 2001: The State Duma voted to adopt a bill proposing new words for the national anthem, which dated from the Soviet era.

14 March 2001: The Duma was scheduled to vote on a Communist-proposed motion of 'no confidence' in the Government.

San Marino

301: A small Christian community was founded on Mount Titano (according to legend, by Marinus, a stone-cutter from Dalmatia). After the fall of the Roman Empire in the West the community evolved into a free city, dedicated to Marinus, and was later styled the Republic of San Marino (it claims to be Europe's oldest state). Government was carried out by an assembly of the heads of families, known as the Arengo.

1243: Two Captains-Regent (Capitani-Reggenti) were elected to assume executive power; the twice-yearly election of the joint heads of state and of government remains a feature of the Sammarinese political system.

1463: San Marino joined an alliance with Pope Pius II against the lord of nearby Rimini and was rewarded by being granted additional territory, encompassing the towns of Fiorentino, Montegiardino and Serravalle.

1503: Forces loyal to Cesare Borgia, the son of Pope Alexander VI, occupied San Marino, but left after his death.

1631: The independence of San Marino was acknowledged by the Pope, whose territory surrounded the republic.

1739: An Italian Cardinal, Alberoni, occupied San Marino; an appeal to the Pope led to the restoration of the Republic's independence.

1797: Napoleon Bonaparte, the leader of revolutionary France's military expansion, declined to conquer San Marino while in Italy and even offered to increase the Republic's territory—the Sammarinese refused the offer.

1862: Despite declining membership of a unified Italian state, San Marino signed a treaty of friendship and co-operation with Italy; (this treaty was subsequently renewed in 1939 and revised in 1971) and prospered as a tax haven for wealthy Italians.

1957: The left-wing coalition, led by the San Marino Communist Party (Partito Comunista Sammarinese—PCS) which had ruled San Marino since the end of the Second World War, collapsed, and was replaced by a Government led by the San Marino Christian Democrat Party (Partito Democratico Cristiano Sammarinese—PDCS).

1974: The Manuscript of Rights was promulgated, acting with earlier statutes as the basis of a constitution.

1978: The PDCS, its grip on government loosening since 1973, was unable to form a coalition and a PCS-led coalition came to power.

1986: The PDCS returned to government, initially in coalition with the PCS, and its leadership persisted into and throughout the 1990s.

1988: San Marino was admitted to the Council of Europe.

1992: San Marino became a member of the United Nations (UN).

1998: The PDCS (losing one seat in the general election, to keep 25 of the 60 seats in Parliament) and the San Marino Socialist Party (Partito Socialista Sammarinese—PSS), who retained their 14 seats, renewed their coalition, first formed in 1992; the former PCS won 11 seats.

1 January 1999: By virtue of Italy's participation in Stage III of the EU's programme of European and Monetary Union (EMU), San Marino adopted the new common currency, the euro.

Slovakia

5th–7th centuries: Slavic tribes migrated to central Europe from the eastern plains.

830: The Great Moravian Empire was established, eventually including Slovakia and Bohemia.

907: The Hungarians destroyed the Moravian forces at the Battle of Bratislava (Pressburg).

11th century: Slovakia was incorporated into the Kingdom of Hungary, although parts were subsequently claimed by the Kingdom of Bohemia.

1491: The Peace of Pressburg acknowledged Habsburg claims to the throne of Hungary.

1526: The Austrian Habsburgs inherited their claim to Hungary upon the death of Louis II, at the battle of Mohács. The Kingdom was partitioned between the victorious Ottomans, the principality of Transylvania and the Habsburgs, who retained control of the Slovak territories; Pressburg became the capital of Hungary, and Hungarian monarchs were crowned there for the next three centuries.

1781–85: Serfdom was abolished in both the Czech and Slovak lands.

1844: The first grammar of the Slovak language, written by L'udovít Stur, was published.

1848: There was an unsuccessful Slovak rebellion against Hungarian rule.

1861: A National Congress of Slovaks issued the Memorandum of the Slovak Nation, which demanded autonomy for Slovakia.

1867: The *Ausgleich* (Compromise) creating the Habsburg Dual Monarchy of Austria-Hungary restored full Hungarian control over Slovakia; a policy of 'magyarization' soon commenced, contributing to a high rate of emigration.

30 May 1918: The Pittsburgh Agreement, which provided for the creation of a common Czech-Slovak state, was signed between Slovak and Czech exiles in the USA.

28 October 1918: The Republic of Czechoslovakia was proclaimed (for details on Czechoslovakia, see chapter on the Czech Republic).

29 September 1938: The Munich Agreement between the United Kingdom, France, Italy and Germany permitted the cession of the Czechoslovak territories known as Sudetenland to Germany. This also caused the collapse of the Czechoslovak First Republic.

October 1938: Slovakia and Carpatho-Ruthenia (after 1945 part of the USSR—Ukraine) gained autonomy; the Hlinka Slovak National People's Party (HSNPP), under the pro-fascist leadership of Mgr Jozef Tiso, was declared the only authorized party in Slovakia.

2 November 1938: Hungary annexed parts of southern Slovakia.

14 March 1939: The day before Nazi Germany began the occupation of the Czech Lands Adolf Hitler, the German leader, agreed to a separate Slovak state.

1941: The Tiso regime adopted a Jewish Code that enabled it to begin a policy of extermination of Jews.

29 August 1944: An uprising against HSNPP rule began in Slovakia. By the end of October it had been suppressed by German troops.

April 1945: The Government-in-Exile returned to Czechoslovakia; it agreed to some limited Slovak autonomy.

16 May 1946: In national elections the Czechoslovak Communist Party (CPCz) won 38% of the votes cast; in Slovakia, however, it won only some 30%, with the Democratic Party winning 62%.

1947: Gustáv Husák organized a Communist 'coup' in Slovakia, by accusing many members of the Democratic Party of being sympathetic to the HSNPP.

February–June 1948: The Communists effectively seized power in the whole country and introduced a new Constitution.

1954: Husák and other prominent Slovak Communists, accused of 'Slovak nationalism', were the latest victims of the purges in the CPCz.

1960: A new Constitution formally limited Slovak autonomy, dissolving the local executive and removing legislative authority from the Slovakian National Council.

January 1968: Alexander Dubček, leader of the Communist Party of Slovakia (CPS), became First Secretary of the CPCz and initiated the so-called 'Prague Spring' reforms.

August 1968: After a meeting in Bratislava the countries of the Warsaw Pact (except Romania) sent troops to invade Czechoslovakia; Dubček and other government and Party leaders were abducted.

1 January 1969: A federal system of government was introduced, despite the ending of other reforms, with the country comprising the Slovak and Czech Socialist Republics.

April 1969: Husák, rehabilitated in the early 1960s, replaced Dubček as First Secretary of the CPCz.

1975: Ludvík Svoboda resigned as President and was replaced by Husák.

1 January 1977: A group of Czechoslovak dissidents published the 'Charter 77' manifesto, which demanded an end to the abuse of civil and political rights.

1987: Miloš Jakeš replaced Husák as leader of the CPCz.

1988: Towards the end of the year large anti-government demonstrations began to occur and this escalated in 1989.

November 1989: Opposition activists formed an anti-government coalition known as Public Against Violence (PAV—the Czech equivalent was Civic Forum). The leadership of Civic Forum and PAV began discussions with the Communist leadership, as protests continued to increase throughout the country. At the end of the month the Federal Assembly abolished the CPCz constitutional monopoly on power.

December 1989: Demonstrations in Prague, Bratislava and other cities continued. A new federal Government was announced, with a majority of non-Communist members. Dubček was elected Chairman of the Federal Assembly. Husák resigned as President and was replaced by the dissident Czech play-wright, Václav Havel.

April 1990: As part of a continuing process of reform and liberalization the name of the country was changed to the Czech and Slovak Federative Republic.

June 1990: Elections to the Federal Assembly took place; PAV (in Slovakia) and Civic Forum (in Bohemia and Moravia) won an overall majority. In elections to the Slovakian National Council, the republican legislature, PAV emerged as the largest party, with some 35% of the votes cast and 48 of the 150 seats; Vladimír Mečiar of PAV was elected premier of Slovakia.

December 1990: Constitutional changes delimited the powers of the federal, Czech and Slovakian Governments.

March 1991: Mečiar, the premier of the Slovak Republic, left PAV over the issue of Czech–Slovakian relations and his advocacy of more autonomy. There were also large demonstrations in favour of independence; President Havel was attacked by crowds when he visited Bratislava.

April 1991: Mečiar and seven members of his cabinet were dismissed by the Presidium of the Slovakian National Council, because of their defection from the disintegrating PAV; Jan Čarnogurský, leader of the Christian Democratic Movement (CDM), was appointed as premier instead.

June 1991: Mečiar was elected Chairman of the newly formed Movement for a Democratic Slovakia (MDS).

September 1991: A group of Slovakian politicians, mostly members of the MDS and the Slovak National Party (SNP), formed the Initiative for a Sovereign Slovakia (mainly as an attempt to forestall a referendum authorized by the Federal Assembly in June).

5–6 June 1992: Elections to the federal and republican legislatures took place; the MDS emerged as the dominant Slovakian party, winning some 37% of the votes cast and 74 seats in the Slovakian National Council. The former Communists, the Party of the Democratic Left (PDL), won 29 seats, the CDM 18 and the SNP 15. The remaining 14 seats were won by a coalition of Hungarian parties; Mečiar was elected to lead an MDS-dominated Slovakian Government.

17 July 1992: The Slovakian National Council overwhelmingly approved a declaration of sovereignty and the dissolution of the federation came to appear inevitable.

1 September 1992: The Slovakian National Council adopted a new Constitution for the Republic, which was to come into effect upon the dissolution of Czechoslovakia.

October 1992: Slovakia, without the agreement of Hungary, started to divert the River Danube into a newly constructed canal, part of the Gabčíkovo dam scheme.

November 1992: At the third attempt, and by only three votes, the Federal Assembly approved the legislation which would end the federation, despite opposition even from Slovakian deputies.

1 January 1993: With the dissolution of all federal structures, the Slovak Republic became a sovereign nation, as did the Czech Republic.

February 1993: Separate Slovakian and Czech currencies (both called koruna) were introduced. The parliament, the National Council of the Slovak Republic, finally elected a President for the country, Michal Kováč, deputy leader of the MDS and a former Chairman of the Czechoslovak Federal Assembly.

June 1993: Slovakia became a member of the Council of Europe and finalized its association agreement with the European Community (EC—known as the European Union from November).

October 1993: The MDS and the SNP (which had left the previous coalition in March) agreed to form a new coalition Government.

March 1994: Following a number of splits in the ruling parties a motion of 'no confidence' in Mečiar's Government was passed in the National Council. A new Government was formed, with Jozef Moravčík (leader of the newly formed Democratic Union of Slovakia—DUS) as Prime Minister, which included representatives of six former opposition parties and groupings.

30 September–1 October 1994: In the general election the MDS was the most successful party, winning, in alliance with the Farmers' Party of Slovakia, some 35% of the votes cast and a total of 61 seats. Of the remaining seats the Common Choice bloc (an alliance of left-wing parties, led by the PDL) secured 18, a coalition of Hungarian parties 17, the CDM 17, the DUS 15, the newly formed Association of Workers of Slovakia (AWS) 13 and the SNP nine.

December 1994: After protracted negotiations Mečiar and the MDS formed a new government coalition, with the nationalist SNP and the left-wing AWS.

19 March 1995: Slovakia signed a Treaty of Friendship and Co-operation with Hungary, which guaranteed the existing border between the two countries and the rights of their ethnic minorities.

May 1995: With increasing tension between the President and the Government, a parliamentary vote of 'no confidence' in Kováč was passed, but failed to acquire the three-fifths majority required to depose him.

August 1995: The President's son, also called Michal Kováč, was abducted and taken to Austria, before being detained in that country on an international arrest warrant issued by a court in Munich (Germany) investigating charges of embezzlement; President Kováč claimed that there was evidence to suggest Slovak Intelligence Service (SIS) involvement in his son's abduction; the Austrian courts eventually decided against his extradition to Germany and he was permitted to return to Slovakia in February 1996.

15 November 1995: A law was passed restricting the official use of any language other than Slovak, provoking domestic and international criticism, notably from Hungarians.

March 1996: Parliamentary approval of the friendship treaty with Hungary required significant amendments to the document and, as a condition of co-operation by the more radical members of the government coalition, a Law on the Protection of the Republic (controversial anti-subversion legislation eventually rejected by parliament in February 1996).

May 1996: After several months of mutual accusations by the President and Prime Minister, Kováč filed libel charges against Mečiar; this followed the latter's public claim that the President had been personally involved in an alleged fraud which had led to the German demands for his son's extradition.

June 1996: Following SNP criticism of the extension of MDS control into non-political areas, Mečiar held unsuccessful negotiations with opposition parties, in an attempt to form a new coalition.

January 1997: A civic movement, Charter 97, was formed to monitor observance of the Constitution and of civil rights.

23–24 May 1997: A referendum on membership of the North Atlantic Treaty Organization (NATO) and the reform of presidential elections was declared invalid, owing to insufficient voter participation (this was believed to be because of a boycott protesting an interior ministry decision to omit an opposition-sponsored proposal for a direct election to the presidency).

10 July 1997: The Slovak Democratic Coalition (SDC), a new grouping of five opposition parties including the CDM and the DUS, demanded Mečiar's resignation after announcements that, for failing to fulfil political criteria, Slovakia would not be among the first former Communist countries to join NATO or the EU.

30 September 1997: The National Council rejected an opposition motion for the reinstatement of František Gaulieder, a former MDS deputy whose parliamentary mandate was unconstitutionally revoked when he resigned from the party. Subsequently, the European Parliament adopted a resolution appealing for the restoration of Gaulieder's mandate and questioning the Slovak parliament's commitment to democracy and the rule of law; the MDS rejected the resolution.

10 December 1997: The Constitutional Court ruled that the President's five-year term of office would end on the anniversary of his inauguration rather than of his election, as advocated by Mečiar.

29 January 1998: The National Council failed to obtain the three-fifths' majority required to elect a new President; the MDS had not nominated a candidate to succeed Kováč, leading to opposition allegations that Mečiar deliberately sought to leave the presidency vacant; further attempts to elect a President in the following month also failed.

21 February 1998: President Kováč announced a new referendum on direct presidential elections (scheduled for April), following a ruling by the Constitutional Court that the interior minister had acted unlawfully over the May 1997 referendum.

2 March 1998: President Kováč's term expired without a replacement having been elected; Mečiar, as Prime Minister, constitutionally assumed most of the functions of head of state (he used these powers to cancel the rescheduled referendum and halt all criminal proceedings relating to the previous one, provoking considerable protest).

22 April 1998: Three parties of the Hungarian minority merged to form the Party of the Hungarian Coalition (PHC), following government proposals to legislate for representation in parliament to be limited only to those parties gaining more than 5% of the votes cast.

20 May 1998: Despite strong opposition from the SDC and the PHC, the National Council approved the amended electoral legislation. Later that month multi-party negotiations to end the constitutional *impasse* collapsed when agreement could not be reached on a non-political candidate for the presidency.

8 June 1998: The Mochovce nuclear power plant in western Slovakia was activated, despite an adverse safety report and international concern (particularly from neighbouring Austria).

14 August 1998: The Supreme Court rejected an MDS petition to bar the SDC from participating in the general election (on the grounds that its party registration was illegal, as it remained a coalition rather than a party).

15 September 1998: Televize Markiza, Slovakia's principal independent broadcaster, was acquired by a company believed to have links with the MDS—there were also rumours of SIS involvement; Televize Markiza was subsequently fined 3.5m. koruny (US $100,520) for the violation of a law, introduced in May, prohibiting political broadcasts (live coverage of a rally protesting the station's takeover) in the approach to an election.

25–26 September 1998: The MDS emerged from the general election as the largest party, with 27.0% of the votes cast (43 seats); the SNP won 9.1% of the votes cast (14 seats) and the AWS failed to reach the 5% threshold. Four opposition parties secured representation: the SDC (26.3%—42 seats), the PDL (14.7%—23 seats), the PHC (9.1%—15 seats) and the Party of Civic Understanding (PCU—8.0%—13 seats).

30 October 1998: The new Government, a coalition of the SDC (nine ministerial seats), the PDL (six), the PHC (three) and the PCU (two), was appointed, with the SDC's Mikuláš Dzurinda as Prime Minister.

14 January 1999: The National Council approved a constitutional amendment introduced by the new Government, providing for direct election of the President.

8 April 1999: The head of the SIS during Mečiar's premiership, Ivan Lexa, was divested of his immunity from prosecution in respect of charges made in February connected with the abduction of the former President Kováč's son and other offences, alleged to have been committed by the SIS under his leadership; Lexa was arrested and detained on 15 April.

15 May 1999: In the first direct presidential election the governing coalition's candidate, Rudolf Schuster (the mayor of Košice and chairman of the PCU), obtained 47.4% of the votes cast, Mečiar 37.2%; in the second round of voting two weeks later, Schuster received 57.2% of the votes cast and was duly elected President.

July 1999: The Constitutional Court ruled that the Government's revocation of amnesties granted by Mečiar to those allegedly involved in the abduction of Michal Kováč, junior, and those facing charges connected with the May 1997 referendum, was unlawful; proceedings against Lexa and others were subsequently halted.

9 August 1999: The Minister of Transport, Posts and Telecommunications, Gabriel Palacka, resigned following allegations of irregularities in the privatization of the state telecommunications company; he was replaced by Josef Macejk.

19 October 1999: After public protests in Bratislava at worsening economic consitions, the Minister of the Economy, L'udovit Cernak, resigned; he was succeeded by L'ubomir Harach.

17 January 2000: Dzurinda announced the formation of a new political party, the Slovak and Democratic Christian Union (SDCU), to contest the legislative election scheduled for 2002, after failing to concentrate the SDC into a single party; several other members of the Government announced their intention to leave their parties to join the SDCU in February.

13 April 2000: A motion of 'no confidence' in the Government, proposed by the MDS, was defeated, although a number of PDL deputies supported the motion, despite their party's membership of the governing coalition; motions of 'no confidence' in several individual ministers were also defeated in April.

20 April 2000: Mečiar was arrested and charged with fraud and abuse of power, relating to payments made to members of his Government while he was premier; he was also fined for refusing to give evidence in the investigation into the abduction of Michal Kováč, junior.

27 April 2000: A further motion of 'no confidence' in the Minister of the Interior, Ladislav Pittner, over the means used to detain Mečiar, was proposed by MDS deputies, but was defeated.

10 May 2000: The MDS began a boycott of the parliamentary session, in protest at the supposed politicization of the judicial process, including the investigations into Lexa and Mečiar; the boycott ended on 6 June.

22 May 2000: Dzurinda and his Czech counterpart, Miloš Zeman, signed an agreement formally resolving disputes over the division of Czechoslovak property between the two successor states upon the dissolution of Czechoslovakia at the end of 1992; the agreement provided for the cancellation of a disputed Slovakian debt for the sum of one Czech koruna and the transfer of 4 metric tons of gold from the Czech Republic to Slovakia.

19 June 2000: President Schuster underwent emergency surgery for an abdominal complaint. He required a second operation the following week and remained in a coma for several days, having been transported to Austria for specialist medical attention.

3 July 2000: Dzurinda and the Chairman of the National Council, Jozef Migaš, signed an agreement providing for an emergency division of presidential powers during Schuster's incapacity, there being no procedure identified in the Constitution for the temporary replacement of an indisposed President. Dzurinda represented Slovakia abroad and controlled the armed forces, while Migaš controlled the presidency's legislative assent. On the same day, Schuster began to regain consciousness.

4 July 2000: The Minister of Health, Tibor Šagát, resigned following criticism of his conduct in a report into the treatment received in Slovakia by President Schuster. Šagat was subsequently replaced by Roman Kováč.

21 July 2000: Authorities investigating the activities of Ivan Lexa, who had not been seen in Slovakia since September 1999, confirmed reports that he had unsuccessfully sought residency in Grenada in that month and was outside Slovakia, despite a statement issued by Lexa's lawyers claiming that he had remained in the country.

31 July 2000: President Schuster made his first public appearance following his illness and officially resumed his presidential powers.

24 August 2000: Parliament voted to remove Lexa's immunity from investigation and to allow the issue of an international arrest warrant.

11 November 2000: A referendum on the holding of early legislative elections, proposed by the MDS after a petition was signed by 600,000 citizens, was declared invalid as fewer than 50% of the electorate voted. The participation rate was 20.3%, of whom 92.4% supported the motion and 4.8% opposed it.

27 November 2000: Lexa was charged *in absentia* with the abduction of Michal Kováč, junior.

2 January 2001: Pavol Kanis resigned from his post as Minister of Defence, following allegations of corruption. He was replaced by Jozef Stank, a former ambassador to the Czech Republic.

Slovenia

168 BC: Illyria (in the north of which lay the territory which is now Slovenia) was annexed by the Roman Empire.

AD 395: Following a division of the administration of the Roman Empire, Illyria was ruled by the Eastern Roman ('Byzantine') Emperor in Constantinople (now Istanbul, Turkey).

5th century: Southern Slav peoples began to move from Pannonia into Illyria and the Balkans.

7th century: Western Slavic tribes associated themselves with the Slavic Duchy of Carinthia (based in modern Austria), while Western Christian missionaries from Salzburg were active among these ancestors of the Slovenes, introducing the Latin script and a Western cultural orientation.

745: Carinthia fell under the influence of the Frankish (German) empire, becoming a mark or marcher lordship in 788; the Slav conversion to Christianity was, therefore, secured.

812: By the Treaty of Aix-la-Chapelle (Aachen), the Byzantine Emperor, Michael I, acknowledged the Frankish ruler, Charles ('the Great'—Charlemagne), as Emperor in the West; German influence over the Slovene-inhabited areas of Carinthia and Carniola was thus established, although Byzantine (and Venetian) influence remained on the Istrian coast.

869–74: Kocelj briefly established a Slovene principality in Lower Pannonia (southern Hungary).

1335: Carniola and Carinthia became hereditary possessions of the Austrian House of Habsburg, within the Holy Roman Empire.

1490: Death of the Hungarian King, Matthias I Corvinus, who had, temporarily, conquered the Habsburg lands.

1551: A minister of the Protestant (Calvinist) Church of Carniola, Primož Trubar, published a catechism which was the first book in the Slovene language.

1584: Jurij Dalmatin translated the Bible into Slovene and Adam Bohorič wrote a Slovene grammar.

1599: The Counter-Reformation secured the Slovenes for Roman Catholicism by the final extinction of the Church of Carniola, the writings of which, however, had already provided the basis of Slovene literature.

1815: The Congress of Vienna confirmed Austrian rule over Istria and Dalmatia, which were formerly Venetian.

1848: A group of Slovene intellectuals formulated the first political manifesto advocating a united Slovenia.

1867: The *Ausgleich* or Compromise created, in the Habsburg territories, the 'Dual Monarchy' of Austria-Hungary; the Slovenes were found in four of the 15 Austrian crownlands: Carniola (where they formed a majority); Carinthia; Styria; and the Coastal Lands around Trieste (ancient Aquileia).

28 June 1914: The heir to the Habsburg throne, Archduke Francis Ferdinand, and his wife were assassinated in Sarajevo (Bosnia and Herzegovina), which led to the start of the First World War.

July 1917: Prominent Slovenes, together with other Southern Slavs (excluding the Bulgarians), declared their intention to form a unitary state, under the Serbian monarchy.

29 October 1918: Following the defeat and dissolution of the Danubian Dual Monarchy, the Southern Slav (Yugoslav) peoples separated from the Austro-Hungarian system of states (a Southern Slav republic was established on 15 October); Carniola and parts of the Coastal Lands, Styria and Carinthia, among other territories, were subsequently ceded formally to the new state.

4 December 1918: Proclamation of the Kingdom of Serbs, Croats and Slovenes, which united the former Habsburg lands with Serbia and Montenegro.

3 October 1929: Following the imposition of a royal dictatorship, the country was formally named Yugoslavia.

1937: Josip Broz (Tito) became General-Secretary of the Communist Party of Yugoslavia (CPY), which was to become the main partner in the Partisan (National Liberation Army) resistance to the German invasion.

April 1941: German and Italian forces invaded Yugoslavia, which was dismembered, with Germany annexing Lower Styria and parts of Carinthia, and Italy annexing Ljubljana (Laibach) and Istria; the Liberation Front, which was to become the Slovene wing of the Partisan movement, was founded.

29 November 1945: A Provisional Assembly proclaimed the Federative People's Republic of Yugoslavia, elections having taken place after fighting ended in Carinthia and Styria in May.

January 1946: A Soviet-style Constitution, establishing a federation of six republics (including a Socialist Republic of Slovenia) and two autonomous regions, was adopted.

November 1952: The Communist Party was renamed the League of Communists of Yugoslavia (LCY) and several liberal reforms were adopted.

1954: Istria was partitioned between Italy (which gained the city of Trieste) and Yugoslavia (most of the territory was awarded to Slovenia, which thereby gained a coastline, but the southern Istrian peninsula became part of Croatia).

April 1963: A new Constitution changed the country's name to the Socialist Federal Republic of Yugoslavia (SFRY).

1971: Following the granting of the rights of autonomy to the federal units, Tito introduced a system of collective leadership and the regular rotation of posts; a collective State Presidency for Yugoslavia was established, with Tito as its head. However, later in the year, there was a purge of 'nationalist' liberals throughout Yugoslavia.

1975: The Treaty of Osimo formally established the Yugoslav–Italian borders.

4 May 1980: Tito died; his responsibilities were transferred to the collective State Presidency and to the Presidium of the LCY.

1988: Against a background of increasing dissatisfaction with the state of the economy, the military trial of journalists on *Mladina* magazine and of an army officer provoked the first demands for Slovenian independence.

27 September 1989: With rising dissatisfaction throughout Yugoslavia, the Slovenian Assembly reaffirmed the sovereignty of their Republic and declared its right to secede from the SFRY.

December 1989: Serbian enterprises were instructed to sever all links with Slovenia, which retaliated by closing its borders to Serbian goods and implementing reciprocal economic sanctions. Six of the main opposition parties united in the Democratic Opposition of Slovenia (DEMOS), which advocated economic independence.

20–23 January 1990: At its 14th (Extraordinary) Congress, the LCY voted to abolish its leading role in society, but rejected Slovenian proposals to restructure the federal Party; the Slovenian delegation withdrew from the Congress and the League of Communists of Slovenia suspended its links with the LCY.

4 February 1990: A conference of the League of Communists of Slovenia renounced its links with the LCY and decided to change its name to the Party of Democratic Reform.

8 March 1990: The Slovenian Assembly renamed the territory the Republic of Slovenia.

April 1990: The opposition DEMOS coalition won the direct elections to the Assembly's main Socio-Political Chamber (gaining 47 of the 80 seats); and emerged as the winner in the Chamber of Municipalities (the Chamber of Associated Labour was elected on a non-party basis). At the second round of voting Milan Kučan, the leader of the former Communists, was elected President of the republican Presidency. The following month Lojze Peterle, leader of the Slovenian Christian Democratic Party (a member of DEMOS), was elected President of the Executive Council (Premier).

2 July 1990: The Assembly proclaimed the full sovereignty of Slovenia.

28 September 1990: The Assembly asserted its jurisdiction over the Slovenian Territorial Defence Force; the move was denounced by the federal authorities, which, in January 1991, ordered that all 'unauthorized' armed units should surrender their weapons.

23 December 1990: A referendum, in which an overwhelming majority voted in favour of secession, was held in Slovenia, despite federal warnings of unconstitutionality and economic sanctions.

20 February 1991: The Slovenian Assembly adopted a resolution initiating its process of 'dissociation' from Yugoslavia, although it declared its willingness to negotiate on the federation's future as well as the details of secession.

8 May 1991: With the failure of various attempts to negotiate a new federation, Slovenia announced that it would secede from Yugoslavia by 26 June, resulting in tension between the Territorial Defence Force and the federal Yugoslav People's Army (YPA). Slovenia subsequently formed a new Slovenian Territorial Army.

25 June 1991: The Slovenian and Croatian Assemblies declared the independence and sovereignty of their Republics, formally beginning dissociation from the federation.

27 June 1991: The YPA began military operations in Slovenia, mobilizing to secure the international borders of the SFRY and bombing Ljubljana airport. Fighting continued intermittently over the next few weeks, despite European Community (EC) efforts to negotiate a cease-fire.

7–8 July 1991: The EC mediated a cease-fire in the former Yugoslavia and a three-month moratorium on further implementation of the Slovenian and Croatian declarations of dissociation.

2 October 1991: The Slovenian Assembly resolved to end all involvement in Yugoslavia after 7 October, the last day of the EC-negotiated moratorium. The last YPA troops left Slovenia, by sea, on 26 October.

23 December 1991: The Slovenian Constitution was enacted, providing for a bicameral legislature, with elections scheduled for 1992. In the same month the DEMOS coalition was dissolved.

15 January 1992: Slovenia was officially recognized by the EC (known as the European Union—EU after November 1993), having been recognized by Germany the previous month. The USA recognized the country in April and, on 22 May, it was admitted to the UN.

May 1992: As a result of a vote of 'no confidence' by the National Assembly (Državni Zbor), Lojze Peterle resigned as Prime Minister. His successor was Dr Janez Drnovšek, leader of the Liberal Democratic Party (LDP) and a former President of the SFRY State Presidency.

6 December 1992: The first presidential and parliamentary elections since Slovenian independence were held; Kučan, the incumbent head of state, was elected President of the Republic and Drnovšek was confirmed as Prime Minister, leading a coalition government composed mainly of members of the LDP (which later merged with three other parties to form the Liberal Democracy of Slovenia—LDS), the Slovenian Christian Democrats (SCD) and the United List alliance (subsequently known as the United List of Social Democrats—ULSD).

February 1993: Slovenia began negotiations with Italy to revise the Treaty of Osimo of 1975.

23 July 1993: Arms illegally destined for Bosnia and Herzegovina were discovered at Maribor airport; several leading Slovenian politicians were implicated in the scandal, including the Minister of Defence, Janez Janša.

April 1994: The Social Democratic Party of Slovenia (SDPS) left the coalition in protest at the dismissal from the cabinet of its President, Janša, the previous month.

September 1994: Following the appointment of Jožef Školjč of the LDS to the presidency of the Državni Zbor, Peterle resigned as foreign minister, claiming that the LDS was gaining too much power at the expense of its coalition partners.

June 1995: A meeting between the premiers of Croatia and Slovenia resolved most of the border dispute between them, but not the question of the outstanding obligation of the old Ljubljanska Banka to Croatian citizens (negotiations resumed in September).

November 1995: Slovenia recognized the Federal Republic of Yugoslavia (FRY—Serbia and Montenegro) following agreements on peace in the former SFRY.

1 January 1996: Slovenia was formally admitted to the Central European Free Trade Agreement (CEFTA), as its fifth member.

26 January 1996: The ULSD became the second party to withdraw from the coalition, considerably limiting the Government's power to enact legislation.

10 June 1996: Having reached an accord with Italy, which had previously objected to Slovenia's application, the country finally signed an association agreement (Europe Agreement) with the EU. Later that month it was admitted, as an associate partner, to the Western European Union defence organization.

10 November 1996: Legislative elections were held; the Liberal Democracy of Slovenia (LDS) gained 25 seats in the 90-seat Državni Zbor, and subsequently increased its parliamentary bloc to 45, after securing the support of the ULSD, the Democratic Party of Pensioners of Slovenia (DESUS), the Slovenian National Party (SNP) and the two deputies of the Hungarian and Italian minorities; however, an electoral alliance, known as the Slovenian Spring, comprising the Slovenian People's Party (SPP), the SDPS and the SCD, also gained 45 seats.

28 November 1996: Parliament began its constituent session, but Drnovšek of the LDS-led bloc failed to be confirmed as premier by the newly convened legislature.

8 December 1996: A referendum on reforms to the electoral system was held, in which only 37.7% of the electorate participated; none of the proposed reforms received the requisite number of votes for endorsement.

9 January 1997: Following protracted negotiations over the nomination of a Prime Minister, which ended only when an SCD deputy defected from the Slovenian Spring to become an independent deputy and agreed to support Drnovšek's candidacy, the new Državni Zbor re-elected Drnovšek to the premiership; a coalition Government was approved in late February.

14 July 1997: In order to meet the requirements for ratification of the Europe Agreement, signed in June 1996, the Državni Zbor voted in favour of amending Article 68 of the Constitution, to allow foreigners to purchase land in Slovenia (despite fears of a return of Italian families who had left Slovenia after the Second World War).

31 July 1997: Zoran Thaler, again Minister of Foreign Affairs, resigned his post following opposition claims that Slovenia's accession to the EU would be on less favourable terms than other states.

23 November 1997: In a presidential election Kučan won a second (and final) term of office by an overwhelming majority, with 55.6% of the votes cast; his nearest rival, Janez Podobnik, the President of the Državni Zbor, gained 18.4% of the ballot.

26 November 1997: A new, 40-member National Council (Državni Svet—parliament's upper house) was indirectly elected by an electoral college for a five-year term.

25 February 1998: The Minister of Defence, Tit Turnšek, resigned following an incident involving two military intelligence agents arrested in Croatian territory in January (relations were already tense because of the December 1997 amendment of the Croatian Constitution, removing Slovenes as a recognized minority).

25 August 1998: Slovenia and Croatia agreed to begin negotiations on the future status of the jointly-owned Krško nuclear power-station, which Slovenia had privatized in the previous month. In November it was announced that the dispute would be resolved on the basis of co-ownership.

20 October 1998: After having been accused of corruption by members of the Democratic Party of Slovenia and the SCD, the Minister of Defence, Alojz Krapež, resigned. He was replaced, on 4 February 1999, by Franci Demšar.

10 November 1998: Accession negotiations on Slovenia's full EU membership began. The first meeting of the EU–Slovenia Association Council was held on 22 February 2000. Slovenia hoped to gain EU membership in 2003.

16 February 1999: The Minister of Internal Affairs, Mirko Bandelj, lost a vote of 'no confidence' in the Državni Zbor and was relieved of his position; he was succeeded, on 24 March, by the hitherto Secretary-General of the Government, Borut Šuklje.

3 March 1999: The Minister of Economic Affairs, Metod Dragonja, resigned from his post for personal reasons; he was replaced, on 20 April, by Dr Tea Petrin.

25 March 1999: Following Šuklje's appointment as Minister of Internal Affairs, Nevenka Črešnar-Pergar was appointed Secretary-General of the Government.

28 May 1999: The Minister of Agriculture, Forestry and Food, Ciril Smrkolj, was accused by the ULSD of abusing his position; however, the proposal for his dismissal was rejected by a large parliamentary majority.

22 June 1999: The Minister for Education and Sport, Slavko Gaber, announced his resignation. He was replaced the following month by the State Secretary for Higher Education, Dr Pavel Zgaga.

21 January 2000: The Minister of Foreign Affairs, Boris Frlec, resigned, following criticism of his failure to resolve long-standing disputes between Slovenia and Croatia, and controversial statements made by him during an official visit to the People's Republic of China; he was replaced by the Ambassador to the USA, Dimitrij Rupel, on 2 February.

February 2000: Following a disturbance in the disputed Slovenian–Croatian border village of Hotiza, a bilateral expert commission was established to resolve the problem.

15 March 2000: It was announced that the nine ministers belonging to the SPP were to resign their posts in mid-April, after which the SPP would merge with the SCD.

3 April 2000: Drnovšek attempted to form a new Government, nominating eight independents to replace the SPP ministers; however, his proposals were defeated in the Državni Zbor five days later and, no longer enjoying a parliamentary majority, he was obliged to resign.

3 May 2000: Andrej Bajuk, the nominee of Coalition Slovenia, an alliance formed by the new SPP–SCD party and the SDPS, narrowly won (by 46 votes to 44) endorsement as premier in the Državni Zbor in a third round of voting.

7 June 2000: Bajuk's proposed administration was endorsed by parliament; the new Government was to govern until legislative elections were held later in the year.

4 August 2000: Bajuk was elected chairman of a new political party, having resigned from the SPP. The new party would contest the legislative election as New Slovenia—Christian People's Party.

15 October 2000: In the general election the LDS obtained 36.2% of the votes cast, equating to 34 seats in the Državni Zbor; the SDPS received 15.8% of the ballot (14 seats), the ULSD 12.1% (11 seats) and the SPP–SCD 9.5% (nine seats); Bajuk's New Slovenia won eight seats, while DESUS, the Slovenian National Party (SNP) and the Party of Young People each secured four.

1 December 2000: The Državni Zbor endorsed the appointment of a new coalition Government led by Drnovšek and supported by the LDS, the ULSD, the SPP–SCD and DESUS.

22 February 2001: Representatives of the member states of the former SFRY met in Ljubljana to discuss the distribution of joint assets and future economic co-operation.

Spain

5th century: Iberia (a Roman province for nearly 600 years) was invaded by Germanic tribes, migrating from central Europe—the Suevi settled in the north-west of the peninsula, the Vandals in the west and south.

6th century: The Visigoths (who had adopted the Christian Arian heresy) expanded their kingdom from southern France (Gaul) and then throughout Iberia, forcing the Vandals to flee to their lands in the Maghreb, and conquering the Suevi by 585.

711: The Iberian peninsula was invaded by Arabs, who inflicted a series of defeats on the Visigoths (who had now adopted Roman Christianity), compelling them to retrench in an area of north-western Iberia, known as Asturias.

732: The Arab advance into Western Europe was terminated by the Franks at Poitiers; Arab domination north of the Pyrenees was, therefore, prevented and, as the Franks and the Christian princes reasserted some independence, Arab power was later confined to the area south of the River Ebro in north-eastern Iberia.

756: The Arab Emirate of Cordoba was founded by a prince of the Umaiyad dynasty.

795–97: The Franks established the Spanish March south of the Pyrenees—this stabilized the Christian border, gradually pushing back Arab overlordship, founding the County of Barcelona and strengthening the lords of what became the kingdoms of Aragon, Navarre and Castile and aiding the King of Asturias (later Leon).

912–61: Under Abd al-Rahman, Cordoba dominated most of Iberia and claimed the caliphate of the whole Muslim world.

1031: The Almoravid dynasty took control of the remaining lands of Cordoba after the old caliphate had been rent by 23 years of civil wars.

1037: The kingdoms of Castile and Leon were united and the *reconquista* (reconquest) of Arab lands in Iberia gathered pace, notably under Alfonso VIII, at the end of the century, and his lieutenant, Rodrigo Díaz ('El Cid').

1137: Aragon and the County of Barcelona (Catalonia) united.

1157: Castile and Leon separated upon the death of Alfonso VII, although the *reconquista* continued, further aided by the foundation of military orders in the following year.

1212: A Castilian victory at Navas de Tolosa helped dissolve the Arabic Almohad empire and Arab power was confined to the south, primarily in Granada.

1213–76: The reign of James I 'the Conqueror' saw Aragon acquire Valencia and the Balearics.

1217–52: The reign of Ferdinand III 'the Saint' of Castile saw reunion with Leon (1230) and considerable expansion, although the kingdom descended into turmoil thereafter.

1234: The small Kingdom of Navarre acquired a French ruling house, but maintained a precarious independence.

1282: Peter III of Aragon gained the Crown of Sicily, but the power behind the acquisition was a cohesive noble class, the strength of which was recognized five years later when the Privilege of Union permitted the nobility armed resistance to infringement by the monarch of their rights.

1340: Castilian victory in Salado against the Moors (a mixed Arab and Berber people from North Africa) was the first in almost one century, the kingdom having been afflicted by a fractious nobility (Castile had even lost territory to the Moors, namely Gibraltar in 1333)—under Alfonso XI expansion resumed, even crossing to North Africa.

1442: Alfonso V of Aragon added Naples and southern Italy to his Sicilian Crown.

1479: The Peace of Alcacovas united Aragon and Castile under the 'Catholic Monarchs', Ferdinand (III of Aragon, which he had just inherited, and I of Spain) and Isabella I, married 10 years previously (who had inherited Castile in 1474).

1492: Against a background of state-sponsored religious zealotry, the Spanish forces of Aragon and Castile conquered Granada and expelled the Muslims, and then the Jews, from Spain. Meanwhile, Christopher Columbus, a Genoese navigator in the service of Castile, 'discovered' the Americas by landing on Hispaniola.

1512: Most of the territory of the Kingdom of Navarre was conquered, essentially giving peninsular Spain its modern borders.

1516: The kingdoms of Spain (personally united in a single Crown) were inherited by the grandson of Ferdinand and Isabella, Charles, who was also the heir of the Austrian Habsburgs and who became Holy Roman Emperor (Charles V) in 1519.

1521: Mexico was conquered by Spanish troops, under Hernán Cortés.

1529: Peru was conquered by Francisco Pizarro.

1556: Charles V, having exhausted his vast realm in war against France and the new threat of Protestantism, abdicated: he left his Spanish (including Sicily and Naples) and Burgundian (including the Low Countries) inheritances to his son, Phillip II; and his Austrian Habsburg birthright (and the imperial title) to his brother.

1571: An ongoing conflict with the Ottoman Turks was settled by victory at the naval Battle of Lepanto, which established Spanish domination of Mediterranean shipping.

1580: Portugal was united with Spain.

1581: The northern provinces of the Netherlands seceded from Spain (there had been open revolt for 14 years, and Dutch independence was not recognized until 1648).

1610: The Moors and Moriscos (converted Muslims), who controlled much of Spain's commercial wealth, were again expelled.

1640: Spain, weakened by war and embroiled in a long-running series of disputes with France, had to suffer the secession of Catalonia (to 1652) and of Portugal (permanently).

1700: Charles II, the last Spanish Habsburg, died and left the throne to Phillip of Anjou, a French prince—the prospect of a union between France and Spain alarmed other European powers.

1703: The Grand Alliance of other European countries against France, engaged in the War of the Spanish Succession since 1701, proclaimed Archduke Charles of Austria King of Spain.

1704: British forces seized Gibraltar.

1713–14: By the Treaty of Utrecht, the French House of Bourbon was left in possession of Spain and its non-European colonies (although the union of French and Spanish thrones was prohibited), while Austria gained the southern Netherlands, Savoy took Sicily and the United Kingdom acquired Gibraltar and Minorca.

1805: At the Battle of Trafalgar, off south-western Spain, the Spanish fleet was destroyed, along with the greater part of the French fleet, by the British navy (conflict with the United Kingdom had prompted Carlos—Charles—IV of Spain to ally with Napoleon Bonaparte, revolutionary France's leader and then Emperor).

1808: French troops in Iberia, for an offensive against Portugal, obliged the Spanish Bourbons to renounce their throne in favour of Napoleon I's brother, Joseph Bonaparte. British troops landed in the Iberian peninsula to support Portugal and encourage Spanish civil war to the detriment of the French.

1811: Spain's American colonies (Louisiana had been ceded to France in 1800) began to fight for their independence.

1813: Ferdinand VII, son of Carlos IV, regained the throne, and installed a reactionary regime.

1833: With the death of Ferdinand VII, his daughter, Isabella II, succeeded under a regency; her rights were challenged by supporters of her father's brother, Don Carlos, who favoured absolutism. The legitimists prevailed, but were constantly challenged by 'Carlists' and, increasingly, republicans, and the Government alternated between liberal and conservative constitutions.

1868: Isabella II was finally deposed by the military and a republic was proclaimed; rivalries for the vacant throne, between the French-backed Bourbons and the Hohenzollerns, led to the Franco-Prussian War in 1870 (despite a compromise candidate, the Savoyard, Amadeus, Duke of Aosta, being awarded the Spanish Crown in that year).

1873: Amadeus, who had also endured Carlist revolt, abdicated and a new Republic was proclaimed.

1874: The conservative general, Martínez Campos, oversaw the restoration of the Bourbon monarchy, in the person of Alfonso XII—a constitutional monarchy was gradually established.

1898: With domestic unrest prevalent, Spain lost a war with the USA and its remaining non-African colonies.

1923: A military uprising was led by Gen. Miguel Primo de Rivera, who deposed King Alfonso XIII, suspended the Constitution and established a non-political, military Government.

1930: Primo de Rivera, who had restored constitutional rule and become Prime Minister in 1925, resigned.

1931: Republicans won the general election and Alfonso XIII left the country; a progressive, liberal Constitution was enacted, with the separation of Church and state, and autonomy for the Basque country and Catalonia.

1933: Right-wing parties won the elections, with political instability and civil unrest following. The nationalist Falange party was founded by the son of Primo de Rivera.

1936: The Popular Front (a disparate coalition of left-wing and republican groups) gained power in the elections, but amid growing unrest, the monarchist politician Calvo Sotelo was assassinated. A powerful military uprising, supported by the Roman Catholic Church, the Falange and the monarchists, and led by Gen. Francisco Franco y Bahamonde, then precipitated the Spanish Civil War.

1939: Franco, recognized as head of state and actively supported by Germany and Italy since 1936, accepted the surrender of the republican Government—meanwhile, he refused to join in the Second World War.

1947: A referendum favoured the re-establishment of the monarchy, but was ignored by Franco.

1955: Spain, which had been barred from admission to the United Nations (UN) in 1946, was allowed to join.

1968: Serious unrest, beginning on the university campuses, and attracting some Church support, was suppressed by the military.

1969: Franco nominated Juan Carlos de Borbón (Bourbon), grandson of Alfonso XIII, as his successor.

1975: Franco died and Juan Carlos I became King, presiding over the establishment of a democratic regime.

1977: A general election was held, an overall majority in the new legislature being won by the Union of the Democratic Centre (Unión de Centro Democrático—UCD), a coalition led by Adolfo Suárez González, the incumbent Prime Minister.

1978: The leading political parties agreed a Constitution, formally establishing a bicameral Parliament (as elected the previous year) in a unitary state composed of 'autonomous communities'.

1979: Suárez retained an overall majority after a general election.

1981: Lt-Col Antonio Tejero led an unsuccessful *coup d'état*—popular, as well as royal support for the Constitution was confirmed.

1982: Spain, which had opposed membership of the North Atlantic Treaty Organization since its transition to democracy, reversed its policy and agreed to join. The Spanish Socialist Workers' Party (Partido Socialista Obrero Español—PSOE) won an absolute majority in the Congress of Deputies (Congreso de los Diputados) at the general election, and formed a Government led by Felipe González Márquez.

1986: Spain became a member of the European Community (EC, later known as the European Union—EU). The PSOE retained its absolute majority in the general election held in June.

1989: Following a general election, the PSOE was returned to power. Allegations of electoral irregularities, however, led to the eventual reduction in the number of PSOE seats to 175 of the available 350. To retain power, the party entered into an alliance with three smaller parties.

1993: At the general election held in June, the PSOE won only a relative majority, with 159 of the 350 seats. After the failure of coalition negotiations with the nationalist parties, González led a minority administration, with the informal support of the regional parties.

3 March 1996: The centre-right People's Party (Partido Popular—PP), led by José María Aznar López, emerged from the general election as the largest party in the Congress of Deputies, with 156 of the 350 seats, the PSOE winning only 141. The PP signed agreements gaining it the support of the Basque, Canary Island and Catalan regional parties, enabling it to govern with an effective majority.

July 1998: Two ministers of the Socialist Government of the late-1980s and early 1990s were imprisoned for having subsidized an illegal paramilitary group opposed to Basque Homeland and Liberty (Euskadi ta Askatasuna—ETA).

16 September 1998: ETA, which had been conducting an armed struggle against Spanish institutions, declared an end to military activity.

16 October 1998: The former military leader of Chile, Gen. Augusto Pinochet Ugarte, was detained in London (United Kingdom) on an arrest warrant issued by a Spanish court investigating allegations of murder and torture committed during his period in power. Following a protracted series of legal hearings, the British authorities permitted Pinochet to return to Chile in March 2000, proceedings for his extradition to Spain having been abandoned on medical grounds.

1 January 1999: Spain participated in Stage III of the EU's programme of Economic and Monetary Union, introducing a new currency, the euro.

28 November 1999: ETA announced the end of its cease-fire; terrorist activity attributed to ETA subsequently resumed.

12 March 2000: At a general election the PP secured an absolute majority in the Congress of Deputies, with 183 seats, having increased its proportion of the votes cast from 38.8% to 44.6%. The PSOE obtained 125 seats, the Catalan alliance Convergència i Unió 15, the left-wing coalition Izquierda Unida eight and the Basque Nationalist Party (Partido Nacionalista Vasco) seven. The PP also increased its strength in the Senate.

27 April 2000: Aznar formed a new Government, with the support of a number of deputies from regional parties.

22 July 2000: The opposition PSOE elected José Luis Rodriguez Zapatero as its new leader.

Sweden

7th–8th century: The Viking kings of Svear, whose seat was at Uppsala, expanded their territory, initially to cover much of modern Sweden, then to other, non-Viking territories in the Baltic region (Courland, Finland, Prussia).

9th century: Swedish Vikings (Varangions) campaigned and traded in central and eastern Europe, appearing in Constantinople and, in Novgorod and Kiev under Rurik and his sons, establishing the first significant states of the Eastern Slavs.

1008: Olaf Skutkonnung, a king of the Uppsala dynasty, was baptized, but upon his death there followed a prolonged power struggle between Christian and non-Christian factions.

1319: Magnus VII Ericsson of Norway was also elected King of Sweden.

1355: Norway and Sweden were divided between two sons of Magnus VII, with Erik gaining Sweden.

1387: Noblemen opposing King Albert of Sweden invited the joint Danish and Norwegian forces into Sweden.

1389: Albert was captured at the battle of Åsle. Stockholm was besieged, but eventually fell in 1395.

1397: Sweden joined the unified Denmark and Norway in the Union of Kalmar, with the Swedish throne to be occupied by the Danish monarch.

1471: The Danes were defeated by Swedish forces at the battle of Brunkeberg. Unrest at Danish rule continued, despite the establishment of a representative assembly in the previous decade.

1520: A riot against the coronation of yet another Danish monarch as King of Sweden led to a general revolt under Gustavus Eriksson Vasa.

1523: Vasa was elected to the Swedish throne as Gustavus I, his capital being established in Stockholm, which was taken from the Danes with German Hanseatic help.

1561: In the secularization and partition of the State of Teutonic Knights, Estonia was awarded to Sweden.

1592: Sigismund I Vasa inherited the crown of Sweden, but was also elected to the Polish throne (as an heir of the Jagiellons)—he was a champion of the Roman Catholic cause, although Lutheranism became the state religion of Sweden in the following year.

1598: Sigismund was defeated at the Battle of Stangebro and declared deposed by the Swedish Parliament.

1604: The union with Poland was dissolved and Sigismund's uncle, Charles of Södermanland, was elected (as Charles IX) to start a Protestant Vasa dynasty on the Swedish throne.

1611: Accession to the throne of Gustavus II Adolphus, supported by the nobility.

1613: The Peace of Knäred ended the War of Kalmar with Denmark.

1617: According to the Peace of Stolbovo, Sweden gained Karelia and Ingermanland from the Muscovite Russian state.

1621: The legislature enacted the Articles of War, which made military service compulsory for peasants, thereby creating a large, modern army—Gustavus II Adolphus' armies captured Livonia from Poland-Lithuania.

1630: Swedish armies intervened in the German Thirty Years' War and landed in Mecklenburg, later taking control of Mecklenburg and Pomerania.

1631: The Treaty of Bärwalde was concluded with France, under the terms of which France gave subsidies to Sweden in exchange for assistance in the Thirty Years' War.

1645: The Peace of Brömseboro ended war with Denmark, with Sweden gaining territory in central Scandinavia (from Norway) and southern Sweden (from Denmark), as well as the previously Danish islands of Gotland and Ösel.

1648: The Peace of Westphalia ended the Thirty Years' War: Sweden maintained a presence at Osnabrück and gained Hither Pomerania and the Duchy of Bremen, thereby giving it control over a number of Baltic and North Sea river mouths.

1654: Sweden invaded Poland under Charles X Gustavus, with the assistance of Brandenburg (the war lasted to 1660).

1658: The Peace of Roskilde ended war with Denmark and Sweden gained the remaining Danish territory in southern Sweden and the Trondheim region of Norway.

1675: Sweden, increasingly dependent on the French subsidy, was compelled to attack Brandenburg by France, but was defeated.

1700: The Great Northern War began, with Denmark, Poland and Russia allied against Sweden which, under Charles XII, was initially successful.

1709: Sweden campaigned in Russia and Ukraine, ending with heavy defeat at the Battle of Poltava; Charles XII and the remnants of his army fled to Turkey.

1721: By the Treaty of Nystad, Sweden was humbled by its Russian-led enemies, displaced from Baltic pre-eminence and confirmed in its losses: Livonia, Finland and the Åland Islands were ceded to Russia; while Denmark, Hanover and Prussia gained Swedish possessions in Germany.

1772: Threatened by Denmark, Prussia and Russia, the new King, Gustavus III, reasserted the absolute strength of the monarchy and Sweden subsequently attacked Russia and regained Finland.

1809: The Treaty of Fredrickshamn awarded Finland to Russia. Sweden, again humiliated, then displaced its King, Gustavus IV Adolphus, in favour of a marshall of the imperial army of France, Jean-Baptiste Bernadotte (King Charles XIV), in a constitutional but (from 1810) hereditary monarchy.

1814: Norway, hitherto a possession of the Danish crown, was to retain its own constitution, but the Swedish King occupied its throne.

1855: An Anglo-French treaty guaranteed the contemporary borders of Scandinavia, owing to the perceived threat of Russian expansionism.

1905: The Union between Norway and Sweden was dissolved peacefully— Oscar II declined the Norwegian throne for a member of his family and it was awarded to a Danish prince.

1909: A system of proportional representation was introduced.

1917: A parliamentary system of government was adopted.

1921: Universal adult suffrage was introduced.

1932–76: The Swedish Social Democratic Labour Party (Sveriges Socialdemokratiska Arbetareparti—SAP) first entered government (it was to lead Sweden, alone or in a coalition, and apart from a short period in 1936, until 1976).

1946: Sweden became a member of the United Nations (UN), having been neutral throughout the Second World War (as in the First World War).

1949: The Freedom of the Press Act was passed.

1952: Sweden was a founding member of the Nordic Council, a body promoting co-operation between the Nordic states in a number of policy areas.

1960: Sweden was a founding member of the European Free Trade Association (EFTA).

January 1971: The bicameral legislature (Riksdag) was replaced by a unicameral model, with a rigid system of proportional representation.

1 January 1975: A new Constitution came into effect, which, among other things, removed the monarch's power to appoint the premier.

September 1976: The first post-war Government led by a party other than the SAP came to power, with Thorbjörn Fälldin of the Centre Party (Centerpartiet—CP) as Prime Minister.

1979: The Act of Succession was amended to enable female succession ahead of younger male siblings.

March 1980: A referendum on nuclear power approved the progressive elimination of the nuclear-power programme by 2010.

September 1982: The SAP returned to Government, after a general election.

February 1986: The Prime Minister, Olof Palme, was assassinated in Stockholm; he was replaced by Ingvar Carlsson.

October 1991: A new, non-SAP coalition Government, led by Carl Bildt of the Moderate Party (Moderata Samlingspartiet—MS), came to power.

October 1994: Carlsson formed a new minority SAP Government, after a general election in which the SAP obtained 161 seats and 45.3% of the votes cast.

13 November 1994: In a referendum on Sweden's proposed membership of the European Union (EU), 52.2% of the votes cast supported its membership (accession took place on 1 January 1995).

March 1996: Carlsson retired from his position as Prime Minister; he was replaced by Göran Persson.

September 1998: Following a general election, the SAP remained the principal political party, but the number of parliamentary seats held by it declined by some 19%.

28 September 2000: Persson proposed the abandonment of Sweden's commitment to neutrality, while retaining its non-aligned status.

1 January 2001: Sweden assumed the EU Presidency.

Switzerland

3rd–6th centuries: Germanic tribes migrated from the east into western and central Europe. The area of modern Switzerland was settled initially by the Alemanni and Lombards, later by the Burgundians and, in the south, the Italian Ostrogoths.

534: The Burgundian and Ostrogoth possessions in the area were conquered by the Franks.

880: The Treaty of Ribemont, which formalized divisions of the Carolingian Empire (into which the Frankish realm had evolved), partitioned modern Switzerland between Upper Burgundy and the East Frankish Kingdom, a small area in the south of the country falling to the Kingdom of Italy.

1033: Upon the death of its King, Rudolph III, the Kingdom of Burgundy was deeded to the Germanic Empire. The Holy Roman Empire, therefore, came to contain the whole of present-day Switzerland.

11th century: Emperor Henry IV granted the Dukes of Zähringen control over the greater part of modern Swiss territory.

1218: The extinction of the Zähringen dynasty led to their lands being fragmented; of the small entities which resulted, several reverted to direct imperial rule.

1278: The Habsburgs, who were a rising dynasty within the Holy Roman Empire, encountered popular resistance to imperial rule in Schwyz and Uri, two of the directly administered territories.

1291: Schwyz, Uri and Unterwalden, known as the three 'original cantons', joined an Eternal Union to protect their interests and liberties from the Empire; the Confederation received support from German princes opposed to imperial dominance, as well as from external enemies of the Empire.

1315: The Confederation successfully defeated a Habsburg attack at the Battle of Morgarten.

1332: The canton of Lucerne joined the Confederation.

1353: Berne, Glarus, Zug and Zürich joined the original states and Lucerne to form the Confederation of the Eight Cantons.

1415: The Confederation conquered Aargau, previously a Habsburg possession.

1440–46: A dispute between Schwyz and Zürich led to a conflict in which the latter received French and Habsburg assistance.

1450: Zürich renounced its alliance with Habsburg Austria; it rejoined the Confederation the following year—the Confederation subsequently conquered the greater part of the Habsburg territories in Switzerland.

1481: The Compact of Stans regulated the network of mutual alliances (Confederation, alliances, associated leagues, protectorates, etc.) which comprised the Swiss Union. It was prompted by the accession of Fribourg, a free city of Savoy, and of Solothurn, an imperial free city and Swiss ally since 1385.

1497: The Rhaetian leagues of the south-east became allies of the Confederation—the League of God's House had been formed in 1367, the Oberbund or Mountain League in 1399 and the League of 10 Jurisdictions in 1436.

1499: The Confederation, having rejected proposals made by the Emperor, Maximilian I, for an Empire-wide tax, fought in the Swabian War—the Peace of Basle granted recognition and effective independence to the Swiss, with the proviso that the country remain 'related to the Empire'.

1501: Schaffhausen, an imperial city and Swiss ally for 48 years, and Basle, an episcopal city, joined the Confederation.

1513: With the accession of Appenzell (a protectorate since 1411 and ally since 1452), the Confederation was further enlarged, to 13 cantons, each effectively autonomous in internal matters.

1515: The Confederation was encouraged by France to participate in the wars against Italy. At the end of the campaign the allies signed the Treaty of Fribourg, known as the Perpetual Peace, which also guaranteed the French King the right to raise an army within the cantons, in exchange for an annual payment.

1523: Ulrich Zwingli, a Zürich priest, presented his objections to the power of the Roman Catholic Church; accepted in the city, Zwingli soon gained adherents to his form of Protestantism in other cantons and in neighbouring areas of France and Germany.

1531: Zwingli was killed in a conflict between Roman Catholic and Protestant cantons.

1536: John Calvin published his rejections of Roman Catholicism in Geneva, which had become a formal ally of the Confederation that same year (Calvin was expelled from the city in 1538, but returned to found his church in 1541).

1549: The Calvinist Genevan Church and that of Zwingli were united—the Genevan doctrine began to spread through Europe.

1648: By the Treaty of Westphalia (the Swiss had remained neutral throughout the Thirty Years' War, despite French offers of alliance), all ties between the Confederation and the Empire were severed.

1685: An influx of Protestant refugees from France, after Protestant worship was prohibited there, disturbed the balance between the Protestant and Roman Catholic cantons, and a series of minor conflicts developed (these were resolved in 1712), but distaste for other denominations also served to reinforce cantonal autonomy.

1797: The allied Rhaetian leagues were annexed by the French satellite state, the Cisalpine Republic.

1798: A civil war in Switzerland, accelerated by ideas inspired by the revolutionary events in France, resulted in the proclamation of the Helvetic Republic—it included all 13 cantons, as well as four other Swiss territories. The Jura, associated with Basle since 1579, was transferred to Berne.

1803: The Helvetic Republic gave way to a restored Confederation, in which the four new cantons were also included: Aargau; Ticino, a former subject territory (since 1440); Thurgan, a subject territory since 1460; and St Gall, an associated abbatial state since the 1450s. France annexed Basle, Geneva (as the département of Léman) and, in 1810, the bishopric of Sion (a Swiss ally since 1416, as the département of Simplon).

1815: The Congress of Vienna restored Swiss federative independence, returned territory lost during French dominance and established a permanent guarantee of Swiss neutrality. Five cantons were formally admitted as full members of the Swiss Confederation: Neuchâtel (an ally since 1406, a possession of the Hohenzollerns since 1701—remaining so until 1857—but annexed by France in 1798); Vaud (subject territory since 1536); Geneva; Valais (Sion); and Graubunden or Grisons (Rhaetian leagues).

1830: Ten cantons replaced their constitutions with liberal drafts, removing aristocratic privileges in government, and instituting a degree of democracy; several uprisings supporting a democratic republic for the entirety of Switzerland were defeated in the following years.

1838: The remaining cantons liberalized their constitutions, but conflict arose over whether to maintain Switzerland as a Confederation of autonomous states or whether it should become a federal, unitary state.

1845: The Sonderbund, an alliance of conservative and Roman Catholic states (Schwyz, Uri, Unterwalden, Lucerne, Fribourg and Valais), was formed to resist further centralization; the Assembly of the Confederation demanded that the Sonderbund be dissolved.

1847: The Sonderbund was forcibly dissolved by the army of the Confederation.

1848: A new Constitution was enacted, providing for an elected National Council, and a Council of Estates to represent the cantons on the national level; these two bodies collectively nominated the executive, the Federal Council, from which the federal President was chosen; the cantons retained a high degree of autonomy in internal matters, although 'external' issues, such as foreign, transport, currency and customs policy were to be dealt with at the national level.

1859: Swiss citizens were prevented from serving as mercenaries in foreign armies, a hitherto common practice.

1864: Henri Dunant, a Genevan, founded the Red Cross organization.

1874: The Constitution was revised, providing for legislative decisions to be approved or rejected by referendum.

1920: The League of Nations began meetings in Geneva, Switzerland having firmly established its neutrality.

1960: Switzerland was a founder member of the European Free Trade Association (EFTA).

1961: Switzerland applied for membership of the European Economic Community (EEC, later known as the European Community—EC), but withdrew the application, amid fears that the political aspect of the Community might have compromised its neutrality.

1963: Switzerland became a full member of the Council of Europe.

February 1971: The enfranchisement of women in federal elections was approved at a referendum.

1979: Following a campaign by French-speaking residents of the Jura region, the first new canton since 1815 was formed, seceding from the predominantly German-speaking canton of Bern.

October 1984: The Federal Assembly elected Switzerland's first female cabinet minister, Dr Elisabeth Kopp, as Head of the Federal Department of Justice and Police.

1986: At a referendum, 75.7% of voters rejected a proposal to join the United Nations (UN) as a full member, despite support for membership by the Government.

December 1988: Kopp was elected by a large majority in the Federal Assembly to the post of Vice-President. In the same month she announced her resignation from her post as Head of the Federal Department of Justice and Police following allegations that she had violated regulations concerning official secrecy.

February 1989: Kopp was replaced as Vice-President; one year later she was acquitted of the charges brought against her by the Federal Supreme Court.

March 1990: As a consequence of the investigations into allegations against Kopp, it emerged that the authorities held about 900,000 secret files on some 200,000 Swiss citizens and foreigners, a revelation which provoked popular unrest and prompted the Government to concede a reform of state security and to open the files to public scrutiny.

1991: In elections to the National Council, the trend of declining support for the long-ruling government coalition continued: the coalition (comprising the Social Democratic Party, the Radical Democratic Party, the Christian Democratic People's Party and the Swiss People's Party) obtained 149 seats; and the Green Party increased its number of seats from nine to 14.

1992: Government proposals to join the International Monetary Fund (IMF) and the World Bank were approved in a referendum.

1992: Following an agreement to create the European Economic Area, a free-trade zone encompassing the EC (known as the European Union—EU from November 1993) and EFTA member states, the required legislation had been subsequently approved by Parliament; the Swiss electorate, however, rejected ratification of the agreement by 16 cantons to seven.

1995: The ruling coalition increased its representation in elections to the National Council to 162 seats; the Green Party won nine seats.

April 1996: The Federal Council approved the construction of two new Alpine tunnels for rail freight transport as part of the Neue Eisenbahn-Alpen-Transversale (NEAT) project.

December 1996: It was agreed that the requirement of work permits for citizens of EU member states would be phased out over a period of six years.

December 1998: Switzerland and the EU concluded a bilateral trade agreement, having settled the lengthy dispute over the level of tolls to be imposed on road freight traffic through Switzerland. The agreement was ratified by referendum on 22 May 2000.

24 October 1999: Elections to the National Council were held, in which the ruling coalition gained 163 of the 200 seats. The election was notable, however, for the strong performance of the Swiss People's Party, which gained the greatest number of votes of any one party and increased its representation in the National Council to 44 seats, compared with the 29 it obtained in the previous election. The Green Party won nine seats and the Liberal Party six.

1 January 2000: Adolf Ogi, of the Swiss People's Party, assumed the Presidency of the Swiss Confederation.

24 September 2000: A proposal to impose a limit of 18% on the proportion of non-Swiss nationals who may reside in Switzerland was defeated in a national referendum.

18 October 2000: Ogi announced his resignation from the Federal Council, with effect from the expiry of his term of office as federal President on 31 December.

6 December 2000: Samuel Schmid, of the Swiss People's Party, was elected to the National Council to replace Ogi. Moritz Leuenberger, of the Social Democratic Party, was elected to succeed Ogi as President from 1 January 2001.

4 March 2001: Following a poll in which the Swiss public rejected by 77% the motion that the Government should begin negotiations to join the EU, the Government stated that it remained committed in principle to future membership.

Ukraine

c. 878: The Eastern Slavs founded the state of Kievan Rus, with Kiev (Kyiv or Kiyev) as its capital.

c. 988: Kievan Rus officially converted to Orthodox Christianity, following the baptism of its ruler, Volodymyr I (Vladimir 'the Great').

1237–40: As a result of internecine feuds over succession, the defenceless Kievan state was captured by invading Mongol Tatars and Kiev burned to the ground.

1475: Establishment of the Crimean Khanate of the Tatars.

1596: By the Union of Brest a number of Orthodox bishops, mainly in what is modern Western Ukraine and Belarus, acknowledged the primacy of the Roman Catholic spiritual leader, the Pope.

1648: Bohdan Khmelnitsky led a rebellion by Ukrainian Cossacks against their Polish overlords, which resulted in the formation of a Cossack state in eastern Ukraine.

1654: Eastern Ukraine came under Russian rule by the terms of the Treaty of Pereyaslav.

1667: Ukraine was divided between the Polish–Lithuanian Commonwealth (which gained the western region) and the Russian Empire (which gained Ukrainian territory east of the Dnieper—Dnipro).

1709: Ivan Mazepa, Hetman (ruler) of the Ukrainian Cossack state, supported Charles XII of Sweden in his invasion of Ukraine; the Russian army defeated the Swedes and the Cossack state was incorporated into the Russian Empire.

1783: The Crimean Khanate was acquired by Russia.

1793: At the Second Partition of Poland the regions of Galicia and Bukovyna (Bukovina) were acquired by the Habsburgs (who had acquired Transcarpathia—Carpatho-Ruthenia in the 11th century), while the rest of Western Ukraine came under Russian rule.

1839: The 'Uniate' Church, formed by the Union of Brest, was suppressed in eastern (Russian) Ukraine.

1861: Emancipation of the serfs throughout the Russian Empire.

1876: The use of the Ukrainian language was banned in the tsarist territories, in reinforcement of a decree of 1863.

1917: Following the collapse of the Russian Empire, Ukrainian nationalists formed a Central Rada (council or soviet) in Kiev.

9 January 1918: The Rada proclaimed a Ukrainian People's Republic.

9 February 1918: The Central Powers (Germany and Austria-Hungary) recognized the independence of the new country in a peace treaty.

April 1918: Following the signing of the Treaty of Brest-Litovsk in March, under which the Bolshevik Russian authorities ceded Ukraine to Germany, the Government of the Ukrainian People's Republic was replaced by a pro-German administration, headed by Hetman Pavlo Skoropadsky.

December 1918: With the defeat of Germany, Skoropadsky was deposed and a liberal Directorate Government was established in Ukraine.

January 1919: The Ukrainian People's Republic was united with the Western Ukrainian People's Republic (formed in Galicia and Bukovyna after the collapse of the Habsburg Monarchy the previous year).

December 1920: A Ukrainian Soviet Socialist Republic (SSR) was proclaimed in eastern Ukraine, following the occupation of the area by the Soviet Red Army; later that month (20 December) the Republic signed a Treaty of Alliance with the Bolshevik administration in Russia.

18 March 1921: The Soviet–Polish War was formally ended by the signing of the Treaty of Rīga; the Treaty provided for the division of Western Ukraine according to the provisions of earlier international agreements between Poland (which gained Volhynia and Galicia), Czechoslovakia (Transcarpathia or Carpatho-Ruthenia) and Romania (Bukovyna—Romania had also acquired the previously Russian territory of Bessarabia).

30 December 1922: At the 10th All-Russian (first All-Union) Congress of Soviets the Union of Soviet Socialist Republics (USSR) was proclaimed; the Ukrainian SSR was a founding member.

1928: The New Economic Policy (NEP), in effect since 1921 and under which Ukraine had thrived, was abandoned by the all-Union Government; it was replaced by a system of forced collectivization of agriculture.

1929: The right-wing Organization of Ukrainian Nationalists (OUN) was founded in Galicia.

1932–33: The Great Famine, the direct result of Stalin's (Iosif V. Dzhugashvili) policy of collectivization, resulted in the deaths of some 6m.–7m. Ukrainian peasants.

1933: Mykola Skrypnyk, the moderate leader of the Communist Party of Ukraine (CPU), committed suicide; Stalin appointed a close political ally, Lazar Kaganovich, to replace him.

1936–38: Large numbers of the Ukrainian cultural and political élite suffered in what came to be known as the 'Great Purge', a series of mass arrests and executions by the Soviet security police, the NKVD (People's Commissariat for Internal Affairs), under the leadership of Nikolai Yezhov.

June 1941: The German army invaded Ukraine, as part of 'Operation Barbarossa'. Later in the year, in Lviv (Lvov) the OUN declared independence from the Soviet Government.

1942: The Ukrainian Insurgent Army was established by the OUN; the partisans continued to carry out attacks against the Communist Government into the early 1950s.

9 May 1945: Following Germany's unconditional surrender, the Second World War ended in Europe; Ukraine had suffered considerable damage during the conflict and some 6m. inhabitants were estimated to have died. The hitherto Czechoslovak region of Transcarpathia subsequently became part of the Ukrainian SSR; southern Bessarabia (a Romanian territory between the World Wars) became part of Ukraine; and some of the territories on the Dniester, taken to form a Moldovan (Moldavian) autonomous region in 1924, were regained. (Northern Bukovyna had become part of the Ukrainian SSR in 1944.)

26 June 1945: The Ukrainian SSR was one of 50 countries to sign the Charter of the United Nations.

1954: During Nikita Khrushchev's period as Soviet leader Ukraine gained the territory of Crimea, a peninsula on the Black Sea previously controlled by Russia. Crimea's Tatar population had been deported to Central Asia by Stalin in 1944.

1963: Petro Shelest became First Secretary of the CPU; during his time in office a nationalist intellectual movement developed in Ukraine and many independent (*samizdat*) publications were produced.

1972: Shelest was replaced as Communist leader by Volodymyr Shcherbytsky, a politician loyal to the all-Union Government. There was widespread repression of dissidents.

1976: The Helsinki Group was founded in Ukraine to monitor the effects in the Republic of the Helsinki Final Act (the human-rights final agreement signed by 32 European countries, Canada and the USA in Finland the previous year).

The Group was subsequently suppressed, but re-emerged as the Ukrainian Helsinki Union in 1988.

26 April 1986: A serious explosion took place at the Chornobyl (Chernobyl) nuclear power-station in northern Ukraine; large quantities of radioactive material were discharged, but information concerning the accident was suppressed.

1987: Mikhail Gorbachev, the Soviet leader, granted amnesty to a large number of Ukrainian political prisoners.

November 1988: The Ukrainian People's Movement for Restructuring (Rukh) was founded in Kiev.

September 1989: Rukh, headed by Ivan Drach, held its founding conference. On 28 September Volodymyr Shcherbytsky resigned, following his failure to control the opposition movement and the miners' unrest in the Donbas (Donbass) region; Volodymyr Ivashko replaced Shcherbytsky as First Secretary.

December 1989: Gorbachev granted official recognition to the Ukrainian Uniate Church (users of the Roman Catholic Byzantine Rite), after a meeting with Pope John Paul II.

4 March 1990: Elections were held to the Ukrainian Supreme Soviet; Rukh, participating as a member of the Democratic Bloc electoral coalition, won 108 of a total of 450 seats.

June 1990: Ivashko was elected Chairman of the republican Supreme Soviet and subsequently resigned as First Secretary of the CPU. He was succeeded by Stanislav Hurenko.

16 July 1990: The Ukrainian Supreme Soviet adopted a declaration of sovereignty, which asserted the right of Ukraine to possess its own military forces and proclaimed the supremeacy of republican law on its territory. In the same month Ivashko was appointed Deputy General Secretary of the Communist Party of the Soviet Union (CPSU).

23 July 1990: Leonid Kravchuk, formerly Second Secretary of the CPU, was elected Chairman of the Ukrainian Supreme Soviet in succession to Ivashko.

17 October 1990: Vitaliy Masol, Chairman of the Council of Ministers (Prime Minister), was forced to resign, following two weeks of protests by students in Kiev. Vitold Fokin was elected to replace him the following month.

20 January 1991: In a referendum the inhabitants of Crimea voted to restore to the region the status of an autonomous republic.

17 March 1991: In an all-Union referendum on the issue of the future status of the USSR, 70.5% of Ukrainian participants approved Gorbachev's concept of a 'renewed federation'; an additional question on Ukrainian sovereignty gained support from 80.2% of the electorate; a third question on outright independence, which was held only in parts of Western Ukraine, was supported by 88.4% of voters.

24 August 1991: Following the attempted *coup d'état* in Moscow (the Russian and Soviet capital), the Ukrainian Supreme Soviet adopted a declaration of independence, by 346 votes to one, pending approval by referendum on 1 December.

30 August 1991: The CPU was declared illegal (it was permitted to reform in June 1993 and the ban was lifted in October 1994).

1 December 1991: Presidential elections were held simultaneously with a referendum on Ukraine's declaration of independence, in which 90.3% of participants voted in favour; Leonid Kravchuk was elected to the new post of executive President of the Republic, with 61.3% of the votes cast.

8 December 1991: At a meeting in Belarus, the leaders of Ukraine, Belarus and the Russian Federation agreed to form a Commonwealth of Independent States (CIS) to replace the USSR.

21 December 1991: At a meeting in Almaty, Kazakhstan, a protocol on the formation of the Commonwealth was signed by the leaders of 11 former republics of the USSR; the resignation of Gorbachev as Soviet President on 25 December confirmed the dissolution of the Union.

5 May 1992: The Crimean parliament voted to declare independence from Ukraine. The resolution was annulled the following week by the Ukrainian legislature and rescinded by the Crimean parliament, following threats of an economic blockade and direct rule from Ukraine. The following month however, Ukraine granted Crimea full autonomy.

30 September 1992: Fokin's Government resigned, having been heavily defeated in a vote of 'no confidence'; the premier was held responsible for the worsening economic situation.

13 October 1992: Leonid Kuchma was approved as Prime Minister by the Verkhovna Rada; several members of Rukh and New Ukraine, a grouping of parliamentary deputies whose aim was to promote radical economic reform, were appointed to the new Government.

13 November 1992: The rouble ceased to be legal tender in Ukraine; it was replaced by the karbovanets, a currency coupon, intended as a transitionary stage to the introduction of a new currency.

21 November 1992: The Verkhovna Rada granted Kuchma emergency powers to rule by decree for a period of six months, in order to implement economic reforms.

20 May 1993: Following the Verkhovna Rada's refusal to extend his emergency powers, and a bid by President Kravchuk to head the Government (now known as the Cabinet of Ministers) himself, Kuchma tendered his resignation. The following day both Kuchma's resignation and President Kravchuk's request were refused by parliament. In the previous two months the influence of the reformists in the Government had been curtailed and President Kravchuk had expressed dissatisfaction with the economic programme.

16 June 1993: An emergency committee, headed by Kuchma, was established to deal with the critical political and economic situation in Ukraine, following widespread industrial action in the east.

9 September 1993: Kuchma resigned for the third time in four months, in protest at continued parliamentary opposition to his economic programme. The premier's resignation was accepted by the Verkhovna Rada two weeks later, which simultaneously passed a vote of 'no confidence' in the entire Cabinet.

22 September 1993: President Kravchuk appointed Yuhym Zvyahilsky, a proponent of increased state involvement in the economy, acting premier. Five days later President Kravchuk assumed direct leadership of the Cabinet of Ministers.

25 October 1993: Ukraine agreed with the USA that it would dismantle its ex-Soviet nuclear warheads, in return for US economic aid. Three months later the USA promised further aid and security guarantees in a nuclear-disarmament agreement with Ukraine and Russia, whereby Ukraine would transfer its remaining warheads to Russia. This process was completed in June 1996.

8 December 1993: The Cabinet of Ministers declared a state of emergency in Ukraine, owing to the critical economic situation.

30 January 1994: The final round of voting in the Crimean presidential elections was held; Yuriy Meshkov secured 72.9% of the votes cast.

8 February 1994: Ukraine became a signatory to the Partnership for Peace programme, proposed by the North Atlantic Treaty Organization (NATO).

27 March 1994: Elections were held to the all-Ukrainian and Crimean parliaments; in Crimea pro-Russian parties won the majority of the seats. At the same time, in a referendum held in Crimea, some 70% of participants supported greater autonomous powers for the peninsula.

April 1994: Following a second round of voting in elections to the Verkhovna Rada, the Communists won the largest proportion of the seats (86), with their allies, the Peasants' Party of Ukraine and the Socialist Party of Ukraine (SPU), gaining 18 and 14 seats, respectively; Rukh secured 20 seats. A total of 112 seats remained unfilled; subsequent rounds of voting gradually reduced this number.

May 1994: Oleksandr Moroz, the leader of the SPU, was elected Chairman of the Verkhovna Rada. The Crimean Supreme Council voted overwhelmingly to restore the region's Constitution of May 1992, a move that was denounced by the all-Ukrainian Government.

June 1994: Vitaliy Masol, who served as Prime Minister between 1987 and 1990, was re-elected to the post. The first round of voting in the presidential election was contested on 26 June.

10 July 1994: The second round of voting in the election to the presidency was contested by the two most successful candidates in the first ballot, President Kravchuk and the former premier, Leonid Kuchma; Kuchma was elected President, securing 52.1% of the votes cast.

8 August 1994: President Kuchma placed himself directly in charge of government and subordinated all local councils to the presidency. He subsequently implemented a wide-ranging programme of economic reform.

16 November 1994: The Treaty on the Non-Proliferation of Nuclear Weapons was ratified by the Verkhovna Rada, thus finally enabling the implementation of the first Strategic Arms Reduction Treaty (START 1), the protocols to which had been signed in May 1992.

1 March 1995: Masol resigned as Prime Minister, allegedly over differences with President Kuchma relating to economic policy; he was replaced, initially in an acting capacity, by Yevgeniy Marchuk, who was confirmed as premier in June.

17 March 1995: The all-Ukrainian parliament voted to abolish the Crimean Constitution of May 1992 and the republic's presidency. The following month President Kuchma imposed direct rule in Crimea, which remained in force until 28 August.

4 April 1995: The Verkhovna Rada passed a vote of 'no confidence' in the Cabinet of Ministers, in protest against its radical economic policies; however, the Government failed to resign.

May 1995: Following the refusal of the Supreme Council to grant him additional executive powers, President Kuchma ordered a nation-wide referendum of confidence in the presidency and the legislature. The Supreme Council vetoed this decree, whereupon Kuchma revoked the Council's veto.

8 June 1995: As a compromise solution to the growing constitutional crisis, the President and parliament signed a Constitutional Agreement; this provided for increased presidential powers in return for the cancellation of the proposed referendum.

3 July 1995: President Kuchma appointed a new Government under Marchuk, in which the reformist Viktor Pynzenyk's jurisdiction over economic reform was effectively removed. In the same month Yevhen Suprunyuk, a pro-Ukrainian, was elected Chairman of the Crimean Parliament.

July 1995: The dispute between two of Ukraine's rival Orthodox churches (the Kievan and the Moscow Patriarchates), begun in the early 1990s, escalated into violence at the funeral of Patriarch Volodymyr of the Kievan Patriarchate; mourners, supported by members of a radical nationalist group, were involved in clashes with the security forces, which prompted the resignation of the Minister of Justice.

9 November 1995: Ukraine was admitted to the Council of Europe.

27 May 1996: Marchuk was dismissed, owing to the growing economic crisis; he was succeeded by Pavel Lazarenko, whose appointment was confirmed by parliament on 11 July. A new Cabinet of Ministers was subsequently formed.

28 June 1996: After continuing debate and following an ultimatum by President Kuchma that included the threat of a referendum, the Verkhovna Rada finally adopted a new Constitution.

July 1996: An agreement providing for the settlement of wage arrears was reached between the Government and miners, following a reprise of widespread industrial action in the coal-mining industry; a structural reorganization of the industry began. An assassination attempt on Lazarenko shortly afterwards was linked by some to his role in resolving the dispute.

2 September 1996: A new currency, the hryvnya, was introduced.

6 February 1997: Kiselev, who had replaced Suprunyuk as Chairman of the Crimean parliament in October 1996, was dismissed; he was replaced by Anatoliy Hrytsenko on 13 February.

2 April 1997: Pynzenyk resigned, following months of political obstruction to economic reforms, which included a delay in approving the 1997 budget (finally adopted in June).

28 May 1997: An agreement on the division of the Soviet Black Sea Fleet, control over which had been disputed with Russia since 1992, and on the status of the naval base of Sevastopil was signed by President Yeltsin of Russia and President Kuchma. Three days later, in a Treaty of Friendship, Co-operation and Partnership, Russia recognized for the first time the sovereignty of Ukraine; the Treaty was ratified by Ukraine on 14 January 1998.

19 June 1997: President Kuchma removed Lazarenko from office, ostensibly owing to illness, but reportedly because of his failure to expedite economic reform; there were also persistent allegations of government corruption. Vasyl Durdynets was appointed acting Prime Minister.

16 July 1997: Valeriy Pustovoytenko, formerly a Minister without Portfolio, was narrowly approved by the legislature as Prime Minister.

22 October 1997: A new electoral law, providing for a combination of proportionally and directly elected seats was finally approved by President Kuchma.

19 March 1998: Criminal proceedings were initiated against the former premier, Lazarenko, on charges of embezzlement. He was subsequently charged with money laundering in Switzerland. He sought asylum in the USA, but was detained in that country in February 1999 and indicted on similar charges.

29 March 1998: Of the 30 parties and electoral blocs that contested the general election, eight parties gained the 4% of the votes necessary for representation in the Supreme Council; the CPU secured a total of 123 seats; of the 225 directly elected seats, the greatest number (136), were won by independent candidates; the results in several constituencies were later declared invalid (repeat elections began in mid-August). In Crimea, where elections were held simultaneously at the demand of the Ukrainian legislature, the CPU secured 40 of the 100 seats, and independent candidates gained 44.

14 May 1998: Leonid Hrach, the leader of the Communist Party in Crimea, was elected Chairman of the Crimean Supreme Council.

7 July 1998: The Verkhovna Rada finally succeeded in electing a speaker, appointing Oleksandr Tkachenko, a former Communist Party official, to the position.

12 January 1999: A new Crimean Constitution came into effect, establishing relations between Kiev and Crimea, and giving Crimea the right to draft a budget and to manage its own property.

15 January 1999: The Supreme Council approved a law on presidential election. Under the law, adopted on 22 March, presidential candidates were to be supported by 1m. signatures from members of the public who were eligible to vote. A candidate was to require over 50% of the votes cast in order to win in the first round, whereas a simple majority was to suffice to secure victory in subsequent rounds.

9 February 1999: A new trading band for the hryvnya was announced, effectively devaluing the currency; in August, however, it declined in value, to lie outside the new exchange-rate margin, which was to have remained in place until the end of the year.

2 March 1999: Following his replacement as Chairman of Rukh, Vyacheslav Chornovil registered a new, breakaway faction; however, he was killed in a car accident one month later.

2 October 1999: One of the candidates in the presidential election, Nataliya Vitrenko of the Progressive Socialist Party, was injured by a grenade attack during a regional campaign meeting.

31 October 1999: None of the 13 candidates achieved an overall majority in the presidential election, in which 67% of the electorate participated. Kuchma won 36.5% of the votes cast, and the Communist candidate, Petro Symonenko, obtained 22.2%. International observers criticized media bias in Kuchma's favour.

14 November 1999: Leonid Kuchma won the second round of the presidential elections with 57.7% of the votes cast. Symonenko obtained 37.8% of the votes,which was, notably, the highest share achieved by a Communist candidate since the Soviet era. Kuchma was inaugurated as President on 30 November.

22 December 1999: The nomination as Prime Minister of Viktor Yushchenko, hitherto the Chairman of the National Bank of Ukraine, was endorsed by the legislature, following the earlier rejection of the incumbent Prime Minister, Valeriy Pustovoytenko. A new Cabinet of Ministers was subsequently appointed, and the number of ministries reduced.

13 January 2000: A parliamentary majority faction, formed by deputies from 11 centre-right parties and the group of independents, and led by Leonid Kravchuk, petitioned for the removal from office of the Supreme Council Chairman, Oleksandr Tkachenko, and his deputy, Adam Martynyuk. Despite left-wing opposition, eight days later the majority faction voted unanimously to remove Tkachenko and Martynyuk from office. In early February it elected Ivan Plyushch, who had held the post in 1994, Chairman; Stepan Havrysh was appointed as his deputy. The left-wing 'rump' denied the majority access to the Supreme Council for some days, but later that month the majority appeared to have won control of the legislature.

31 January 2000: Viktor Yushchenko denied allegations by Pavlo Lazarenko that large amounts of International Monetary Fund (IMF) funds had been diverted from the central bank into Ukrainian government securities in December 1997. In February the IMF decided to initiate an investigation and suspended further lending to Ukraine.

11 March 2000: An explosion at the Barakova coal mine in the Donbass region resulted in the deaths of 82 workers, and drew attention to the sector's poor safety record.

22 March 2000: A law was promulgated, which abolished the death penalty.

29 March 2000: The Government agreed to close the Chornobyl reactor by December of that year, following the offer of additional funds from the Group of Seven (G-7) industrialized countries. The sole operable unit at Chornobyl had been restarted in November 1999, in order to cope with increased demand for power supplies during the winter.

16 April 2000: Some 81% of the electorate participated in a referendum on constitutional change, of whom 85% were in favour of the dissolution of the Supreme Council for non-approval of the budget within three months of its submission, almost 90% agreed that the number of deputies should be reduced from 450 to 300, some 89% supported limiting deputies' immunity and some 82% voted to introduce a bicameral legislature.

1 June 2000: The Supreme Council rejected proposals for the partial privatization of the state-owned telecommunications company, Ukrtelecom.

2 June 2000: Lazarenko, who remained in detention in the USA, was charged by the Ukrainian Prosecutor-General with ordering three murders.

15 June 2000: The Minister of Fuel and Energy, Serhiy Tulub, resigned; he was subsequently replaced by Serhiy Yermilov.

25 June 2000: The Minister of the Economy, Serhiy Tyhypko, resigned following his election to the Supreme Council. Vasyl Rohoviy, who had previously held the position from April 1998–January 2000, assumed the portfolio on 9 August.

29 June 2000: A Swiss court convicted Lazarenko *in absentia* and imposed an 18-month suspended prison sentence, in addition to the confiscation of some US $6.6m. from his Swiss bank accounts.

13 July 2000: Following requests made by Ukraine, the Polish government agreed not to support the construction by the Russian natural-gas company, Gazprom, of a new natural-gas pipeline from the Russian Federation across Poland, Slovakia and Hungary, avoiding Ukraine. Gazprom had previously alleged that gas was being abstracted from its existing pipeline across Ukraine.

21 September 2000: Kravchuk resigned as leader of the majority group in the Supreme Council and was replaced by Oleksandr Karpov.

29 September 2000: The Minister of Foreign Affairs, Borys Tarasyuk, was dismissed. He was subsequently replaced by Anatoliy Zlenko, who had previously held the position from December 1991–July 1994.

17 November 2000: A settlement was agreed regarding Ukraine's debts to the Russian Federation arising from the supply of natural gas and the alleged abstraction of gas from the pipeline crossing Ukraine.

28 November 2000: Following the discovery earlier in the same month of a body believed to be that of journalist Heorhiy Honhadze, SPU leader Oleksandr Moroz announced that he had taken possession of recordings in which a voice purported to be that of President Kuchma was heard ordering the killing of Honhadze. President Kuchma strongly denied the allegations and the presidential administration began legal action against Moroz on 2 December.

14 December 2000: A committee of the Supreme Council examined the recordings provided by Moroz.

15 December 2000: The last operational reactor at the Chornobyl site was removed from service. On 8 December the European Bank for Reconstruction and Development had granted Ukraine a loan of some US $215m. in order to complete two power stations designed to replace Chornobyl.

7 March 2001: President Kuchma dismissed the Minister of Fuel and Energy, Serkiy Yermilov, replacing him with Stanislav Stashevskiy, former mayor of Kiev.

The United Kingdom

5th century: With the disintegration of the Roman Empire in the West, the province of Britain was invaded by the Angles, Jutes and Saxons. The Romano-Celtic Britons were expelled or subdued, although independent territories persisted in the north and west.

6th century: The heptarchy—seven territorial kingdoms within 'England'—was established.

7th century: Christianity was introduced into England.

685: The Picts, who had never been subdued by Rome, defeated Northumbria in battle, asserting independence from the heptarchy for their realm and that of the Scots.

8th century: Raids on coastal settlements by Danish Vikings began, with Viking kingdoms developing in Scotland, Ireland and York.

843: The Pictish and Scottish realms united as Scotland, chiefly in order to repel Viking attacks.

9th century: Viking incursions continued, and England effectively came under Danish control.

878: The Danes were defeated by Alfred the Great of Wessex, the predominant English kingdom. England was divided along a Roman road running north-west from London, the eastern portion remaining under Danish control (Danelaw).

937: King Athelstan of Wessex, who ruled over most of England, defeated an alliance of Danes, Scots and Welsh forces.

959: Edgar, who had been supported by the liberated northern kingdoms against his predecessor, Edwy, acceded to the throne of Wessex, and was thus crowned as the first King of England.

1013: The Danish conquest of England was completed. Sweyn was declared King of England.

1014: Sweyn died, and was succeeded by Canute. Ethelred returned from exile and defeated Canute, causing a dispute over the crown.

1042: Edward 'the Confessor' restored an Anglo-Saxon monarchy after the exhaustion of Canute's line.

1066: England was conquered by William, Duke of Normandy.

1072: William I of England invaded Scotland; the King, Malcolm, paid homage to William.

1090: The Norman invasion of Wales was defeated.

1097: The Scottish throne, which had been divided between Malcolm's brother and eldest son, was seized by his third son, Edgar; the country was reunited, but became dependent on England (which had seized Cumberland in 1092).

1099: William II died, and was succeeded by his younger brother, Henry, who united the Norman and Saxon lines in England by marrying the daughter of Malcolm III of Scotland.

1106: The Channel Islands became a possession of the English Crown.

1153: After a period of dynastic dispute, the House of Plantagenet, under Henry, ascended to the English throne, thus reuniting Normandy and England, and giving the English Crown extensive holdings elsewhere in France.

1175: Henry claimed the Lordship of Ireland, having already extended his influence in Wales and forced Scotland to be held by its Kings as an English fief.

1209–13: King John, who had lost considerable territory in France, invaded both Scotland and Wales, making peace in both countries, but, in confrontation with the Church, was forced to make England and Ireland papal fiefs.

1215: The nobility forced John to sign the Magna Carta, a charter limiting royal power, establishing the rule of law, and creating the basis of England's unwritten constitution.

1259: The Peace of Paris defined the English estates in France, but forced Henry III to pay homage to the King of France in their respect. A peace was agreed with the Welsh, though this was short-lived, a border war erupting three years later.

1264: The restive baronage, led by Simon de Montfort, defeated Henry III at Lewes, compelling him to call a Parliament, or King's Council, with territorial representatives from the nobility and clergy, and burgesses from towns.

1267: Henry recognized Llewellyn as Prince of Wales.

1275: Edward I passed the Statute of Westminster, increasing the independence of the judiciary.

1277: Llewellyn of Gwynedd, who had refused to recognize Edward as his superior, was defeated by the King, and his power reduced.

1282: Llewellyn was killed in battle; his brother took up the struggle and was executed the following year.

1284: The Statute of Wales formalized the country's passing to the English Crown.

1290: Scotland came under increased English influence. The Isle of Man passed to England, but was returned to Scotland in 1293.

1300: Edward again invaded Scotland, and proposed that his son and heir be styled Prince of Wales.

1323: After a series of conflicts, notably Scottish victory at Bannockburn (1314), peace was signed between the two British kingdoms, confirming Scotland's independence.

1332: The English Parliament sat as two houses for the first time.

1335: Edward III invaded and occupied Scotland.

1337: Edward III claimed the French throne, by right of his mother, and proclaimed himself 'King of France'; a defeat of Flanders, hitherto allied with France, effectively began the conflict known as the Hundred Years' War.

1341: The division of Parliament into two houses, of Commons and Lords, was formalized.

1347: English forces captured Calais, which was to remain in English hands until 1559. A truce was subsequently signed, which was renewed annually until 1555.

1353: The Statute of Praemunire forbade appeals to Rome on matters decided in English courts. Scotland and France renewed their alliance.

1399: King Richard II, whose rule was perceived as absolutist by Parliament, was usurped by Henry of Lancaster (Henry IV).

1400–05: Henry IV was beset by internal unrest among nobles, a Scottish declaration of war, and an insurrection in Wales, led by Owen Glendower. France supported both Wales and Scotland.

1404: After the capture of Harlech Castle by Glendower's forces, a Welsh Parliament was convened at Machynlleth.

1406: A plan among Glendower and some English nobles to conquer and partition England was confounded by Henry IV's victory over the Welsh; he regained control in Wales by 1409.

1415: The Hundred Years' War with France was resumed, with dramatic success under Henry V.

1420: The Treaty of Troyes confirmed English possessions in France, and Henry V married the daughter of the King of France, but was killed in 1422.

1430: Henry VI was crowned King of France; Joan of Arc was tried for witchcraft and executed the following year, but English power was on the wane.

1449: England retained only Calais of its French possessions, and the Hundred Years' War ended four years later, leaving England to descend into a dynastic civil war, known as the Wars of the Roses.

1485: Richard II, of the House of York, was defeated at Bosworth by the heir of the Lancastrian dynasty, Henry Tudor—he ascended the throne as Henry VII, later marrying Elizabeth of York and, by reconstructing state power, confirmed the end of the Wars of the Roses.

1521: Henry VIII was awarded the title 'Defender of the Faith' by the Pope, for his pamphlet refuting Martin Luther's 'Protestant' theses.

1534: By the Act of Supremacy, Henry was declared Supreme Head of the Church in England, severing the ecclesiastical link with Rome.

1536: Wales was formally incorporated into England.

1547: Edward VI, son of Henry and Jane Seymour, ascended the throne, proceeding to make the Church of England more Protestant in doctrine. England again invaded Scotland, captured Edinburgh, and exiled Mary, Queen of Scots, to France.

1553: The accession of Mary I, sister of Edward VI, brought about renewed links with the Roman Church and the persecution of Protestants.

1558: England lost Calais in a war with France. Mary I died, to be succeeded by her half-sister, Elizabeth. Elizabeth I established a moderately Protestant Church of England, with the monarch as Supreme Governor, earning the enmity of Roman Catholic nobles and foreign powers (notably Spain), who then championed the cause of Mary, Queen of Scots.

1569: Mary Stuart was forced to abdicate as Queen of Scotland. She took refuge in England—her claim to the throne and her Catholicism led to her execution in 1586.

1584: The first English overseas colony was established in Virginia.

1588: The English fleet defeated the Spanish Armada, which had been sent to destroy England's naval capability.

1600: The East India Company was founded, to improve England's position in trade with the Far East.

1603: Elizabeth I died and was succeeded by James VI of Scotland (James I of England), who had been brought up in Calvinist Scotland, thereby uniting the two British monarchies.

1607: Those born in England or Scotland after the accession of James I were granted common citizenship. However, the English Parliament rejected complete union of the two countries.

1639: Having ruled without the English Parliament since 1629, Charles I dissolved the Scottish Parliament and attempted to enforce his introduction of Anglicanism into Calvinist Scotland.

1640: Difficulties in Scotland forced Charles I to recall the English Parliament; though this body was also dominated by Puritans and opposed to royal absolutism.

1642: Continuing constitutional and religious problems in all three kingdoms (England, Ireland and Scotland) provoked Civil War.

1648: The Scots, now allied to Charles I, invaded England and were defeated by the parliamentary forces under Oliver Cromwell.

1649: Charles I was executed by the victorious Cromwell, who became Lord Protector of the republican Commonwealth and later re-established republican authority in Ireland.

1651: The Stuart heir, Charles, was crowned King of Scotland as Charles II. He subsequently invaded England in order to reclaim the throne, but was defeated by Cromwell and fled to France.

1653–60: Cromwell dissolved Parliament, and ruled as Lord Protector, with the assistance of a Council of State.

1660: Parliament supported the restoration of the monarchy and Charles II regained all the British Crowns.

1679: The Habeas Corpus Act forbade imprisonment without trial and arbitrary arrest.

1685: James (II of England, VII of Scotland) succeeded to the throne upon his brother's death; a Roman Catholic, he immediately sought to weaken Parliament by attempting to discard standing laws and reopening public offices to other Catholics.

1688: Parliament invited William of Orange, brother-in-law of James and Stadholder of Protestant Holland, to claim the English throne, in response to James II's increasingly absolutist tendencies. In the so-called 'Glorious Revolution', James II fled to France upon William's arrival in England. William was subsequently crowned as William III.

1689: The Declaration of Rights was issued, ensuring equitable taxation and personal liberty.

1690: William III suppressed Irish Catholic revolt at the Battle of the Boyne.

1701: The Act of Succession established the German House of Hanover as the heirs to the throne. England formed part of the Grand Alliance, opposing France in the War of the Spanish Succession.

1704: English forces took Gibraltar.

1707: The Act of Union created a United Kingdom of Great Britain in England and Scotland, with a single Parliament.

1713: By the Treaty of Utrecht, which ended the War of the Spanish Succession, the United Kingdom gained Gibraltar, Hudson Bay, Menorca, Newfoundland and Nova Scotia, as well as a monopoly on carriage of slaves from Africa to America.

1744: France declared War on Britain and Austria, as part of the War of the Austrian Succession.

1746: The Jacobites (supporters of the displaced House of Stuart), who had launched a rebellion in Scotland in the previous year, were finally defeated at Culloden.

1763: By the Treaty of Paris, which ended the Seven Years' War, the United Kingdom secured dominance in India and North America, as well as expanding its territory in West Africa.

1776: Thirteen of the British colonies in North America (the nucleus of the United States of America—USA) declared independence, with the United Kingdom maintaining its war against them.

1788: The first British settlers arrived in Australia.

1789: The first manufacturing machine to be powered by a steam engine was introduced. New technologies enabled an increase in industrial production, and thereby a concentration of the workforce in urban areas, and a decline in the importance of agriculture to the British economy. This process became known as the Industrial Revolution.

1791: The Canada Act gave Canada representative government.

1793: Britain joined the first coalition against revolutionary France, and became its principal opponent for the next 22 years.

1801: The Act of Union brought Ireland into the United Kingdom.

1805: A French invasion of the United Kingdom was prevented by the destruction of the French and Spanish fleets by the Royal Navy at the Battle of Trafalgar.

1806: The French-dominated states of Europe introduced the Continental System, effectively placing a trade embargo on Britain.

1808: British troops, under Arthur Wellesley (later the Duke of Wellington), invaded Portugal, in order to prevent Bonaparte's dominance extending throughout Iberia. The Peninsular Wars continued until 1813, when French troops were expelled from Spain.

1810–25: Increased taxes and prices in the United Kingdom as a result of war and blockades caused popular unrest throughout the country, which remained after the end of the Wars. The decline in prices of agricultural produce, caused by overproduction, led to disturbances in rural areas.

1815: The Congress of Vienna, which determined the peace settlements of the wars with revolutionary France (concluded after the final victory of the Allies at the Battle of Waterloo) confirmed the United Kingdom's imperial pre-eminence. The Corn Laws were introduced, imposing tariffs on imports of foreign grain.

1824: Trade unions were recognized. British colonial expansion in South-East Asia began with the occupation of Singapore and Burma (now Myanmar).

1829: The Catholic Emancipation Act permitted Roman Catholics to become Members of Parliament (MPs). The United Kingdom was one of the powers enforcing the Treaty of Andrinopoulos, and the subsequent London Protocol, by which Greece obtained its independence from Turkey.

1832: The passage of the Reform Bill—which had been rejected by the Lords the previous year, causing popular unrest—modified the electoral system, increasing the representation available in newer towns and cities, and extending the right of franchise.

1833: Slavery was abolished in the British Empire (having been prohibited in the United Kingdom in 1791).

1846: The Corn Laws were repealed, extending the doctrine of free trade to agriculture but destroying the dominant Tory Party (later reconstructed as the Conservative Party).

1854–56: The United Kingdom joined France, Piedmont and Turkey in an alliance against Russia, in the Crimean War.

1858: A mutiny in India was suppressed; all possessions of the East India Company were transferred to the Crown, Queen Victoria becoming Empress of India.

1867: The second Reform Bill extended suffrage to skilled labourers in urban constituencies (similar rights were granted in rural areas by the third Bill in 1884).

1886: The Prime Minister, William Gladstone, introduced the first Home Rule Bill for Ireland; its defeat led to a split in the ruling Liberal party; further attempts to introduce Home Rule were defeated in 1893 and 1913.

1899: Conflict between British and Boer settlements in southern Africa led to the Boer war; after early defeats, British troops forced the surrender of the Boers and the addition of Transvaal and the Orange Free State to the British possessions in the region; the conflicts continued until 1902.

1904: The 'Entente Cordiale' was reached with France, in order to protect the balance of power within Europe; this agreement was joined by France's ally, Russia, three years later.

1911: The Parliament Act reduced the powers of the House of Lords to reject legislation, and introduced salaries for MPs.

1914: Irish Home Rule was introduced; however, its implementation was delayed by the beginning of British involvement in the First World War, when Germany refused to guarantee Belgian neutrality in any conflict.

1914–18: British troops fought in northern France and Belgium, the principal theatre of war. The conflict in the area soon became trench warfare, with relatively small advances made, until the German troops were forced behind the Siegfried line, and, in 1918, Germany was compelled to offer an armistice.

1918: Suffrage was granted to all men over the age of 21, and all women over 30 (the voting age was equalized in 1928).

1919: By the Treaty of Versailles, Britain gained German possessions in east Africa, as well as a mandate over Iraq and Palestine.

1921: Ireland became a dominion within the British Commonwealth (with similar status to Australia and Canada), but six Protestant-dominated counties in the province of Ulster chose to remain in the United Kingdom.

1922: Egypt ceased to be a British protectorate (since 1822).

1926: Increasing discontent at low pay, unemployment and poor working conditions led to a short-lived General Strike. Iraq was granted independence.

1932: Britain agreed a system of preferential tariffs with its former and remaining colonies.

1937: Upon the enactment of its Constitution, Ireland declared itself a republic.

1939: The United Kingdom and France declared war on Nazi Germany after it invaded Poland. During the course of the Second World War, British troops were involved in conflict in Europe, North Africa, Asia and the Pacific.

1940: The 'Blitz', a series of German bombing attacks on major British cities and ports, took place, causing severe damage, most notably in Coventry, London and Plymouth. British troops who had been deployed to defend Belgium and the Netherlands were evacuated from Dunkirk after the capitulation of the two countries. The Battle of Britain was the world's first significant aerial battle, fought between British and German aircraft, chiefly over southern England. The Channel Islands were invaded by German forces and remained occupied until the end of the war.

1941: The USA entered the War.

1942: Having established aerial superiority in the Battle of Britain, British aircraft began intensified bombing raids on German cities.

1944: Allied troops invaded northern France on 'D-day', and were able to advance on Paris and liberate the country. Bombings on Germany increased in intensity.

1945: The Second World War ended. Britain became a founder member of the United Nations (UN). The Labour party came to power, and began the nationalization of sectors of British industry, including coal production (1946) and railways (1947).

1946: The process of granting independence to Britain's colonies and protectorates began. The mandate in Palestine and Jordan was renounced. The following year, Burma was granted independence, and the proposals for the partition and independence of India were enacted.

1949: Ireland was recognized as a republic outside the Commonwealth. The six northern counties remained under British control, however. The United Kingdom was a founder member of the North Atlantic Treaty Organization (NATO).

1956: A joint British–French military expedition to prevent Egypt from nationalizing the Suez Canal was condemned by the USA and the UN; their consequent withdrawal is often considered to be a humiliation for two of the world's largest colonial powers.

1967: A large majority of the population of Gibraltar voted to retain British sovereignty. Two years later the new Gibraltese Constitution included an assurance that the British Government would not negotiate the cession of the territory to another state without formally consulting its population. In the same year the Spanish Government, which in 1963 had initiated a campaign at the UN to reclaim Gibraltar, imposed restrictions against the territory.

1972: After rejections in 1961 and 1967, British membership of the European Communities was approved, and took effect the following year.

1977: The Labour Government of James Callaghan was forced to reduce public spending in order to comply with the terms of a loan from the International Monetary Fund (IMF). The Government became increasingly unpopular as industrial unrest grew.

1979: The Labour Party suffered defeat in the general election, often attributed to the programme of financial stringency imposed as a condition of the IMF's loan. The Conservative Party, led by Margaret Thatcher, was elected to government, and remained in power until 1997.

1982: The Falkland Islands, a small archipelago in the South Atlantic Ocean, and one of the United Kingdom's last remaining overseas possessions, was invaded by Argentina, which claimed sovereignty. A military force was sent to reclaim the islands, and British rule was restored.

1990: Amid increasing popular and party discontent at her leadership, Thatcher resigned from the leadership of the Conservative Party, and consequently the premiership; she was replaced by the Chancellor of the Exchequer, John Major.

1993: The British Parliament ratified the Treaty on European Union, agreed by the European Community member states at Maastricht, the Netherlands, the previous year.

1 May 1997: The Labour Party, led by Anthony (Tony) Blair, won the general election, with a substantial majority, securing 418 of the 659 seats in the House of Commons. The Conservatives saw their representation reduced to 165 seats, compared with 336 at the previous general election in 1993, and the Liberal Democrats obtained 46 seats.

30 June 1997: The United Kingdom transferred the sovereignty of Hong Kong to the People's Republic of China.

September 1997: Referendums were held on the establishment of a Parliament in Scotland and an Assembly in Wales. Both proposals were approved, although the latter was by a narrow margin.

16 October 1998: The former President of Chile, Gen. Augusto Pinochet Ugarte, was arrested in London, following a request for his detention made by Spanish judicial authorities investigating allegations of 'genocide and terrorism' relating to Pinochet's period in office. Following a protracted series of legal hearings, extradition proceedings were halted and Pinochet was allowed to return to Chile on grounds of ill health in March 2000.

March–June 1999: The United Kingdom was one of the principal participants in the military intervention by NATO in the conflict in Yugoslavia.

1 July 1999: Powers were transferred from the British Government to the new legislative bodies in Scotland and Wales, to which elections had been held on 6 May.

November 1999: Legislation was enacted divesting all but 92 hereditary peers of the right to vote in the House of Lords and providing for the establishment of an interim second chamber, pending definitive reform of the House.

April 2000: Extended negotiations between the Spanish and British Governments over the status of Gibraltar were concluded with a compromise agreement.

24 January 2001: The Northern Ireland Secretary, Peter Mandelson, was forced to resign—for the second time in his political career—following allegations that he had assisted two members of the Hinduja family of Indian industrialists in their application for British passports, in return for a £1m. donation to the Government's controversial Millennium Dome project. The resignation resulted in a minor government reorganization. Mandelson was subsequently cleared by an official inquiry of any improper conduct.

16 February 2001: Jointly with the US Air Force, the Royal Air Force (RAF) carried out bombing raids on southern Iraq. The British and US governments stated that the security of their aircraft patrolling the 'no-fly zone' in the region had been threatened, but the strikes nevertheless provoked considerable international condemnation.

The Vatican City

751: The Lombards of northern Italy seized the Exarchate of Ravenna, the lands of the Eastern Roman ('Byzantine') Empire in central Italy, removing the vestigial protection of the original Empire from the powerful Bishop (Pope) of Rome and threatening the effective independence of the Papacy.

756: The ruler of the Franks, Pepin, to whom the Pope, Stephen II, had appealed for help, took the Exarchate of Ravenna from the Lombards and donated it to the Roman patriarch, providing the territorial basis for the Papal States (some Church scholars later claimed this merely reinforced an earlier, fourth century title made by the 'Donation of Constantine').

800: The coronation by the Pope of the Frankish ruler, Charles 'the Great' (Charlemagne), as Emperor in the West, provided the basis for the Holy Roman Empire which came to dominate Germany and northern Italy.

1275: A Concordate between the Holy Roman Emperor and the Pope finally removed any claim of imperial suzerainty over the Papal States (Rome, Romagna, Pentapolis, the March of Ancona and Campagna).

1309: The Papacy was forced to move its headquarters to Avignon, an enclave in southern France, not returning to Rome until 1377, where, one year later, the Great Schism developed, when rival popes were elected.

1417: The Council of Constance ended the Great Schism and the papacy began to reassert its power, although one century later the wealth and corruption of the papal prince of Rome encouraged religious Reformation—in reaction the papal monarchy established its power over the Roman Catholic Church as surely as over its principality.

1797: The invasion of Italy by the revolutionary French leader, Napoleon Bonaparte, led to the abolition of the Papal States, the incarceration of the Pope and the establishment of a Roman Republic. The Papal States were re-established in 1814–15.

1848: Amid Europe-wide unrest, the Pope was driven from Rome and a republic proclaimed, but French troops restored the papacy, maintaining it even when later supporting the creation of a unified Italy.

1866: The Kingdom of Italy was proclaimed, but the Pope, Pius XI, refused formally to cede any territory belonging to the Patrimony of St Peter.

1870: Italian troops occupied Rome (France was at war with Prussia) and Pius IX retreated into the Vatican palace—no Pope was to emerge until 1929.

1871: The Law of Guarantees, defining relations between the Italian state and the Pope, was enacted—the independence and territorial integrity of the Vatican was guaranteed, but the settlement was not accepted.

1929: The Lateran Treaty with the Vatican gave the Roman Catholic Church official status within Italy and recognized the sovereignty of the State of the Vatican City, under the jurisdiction of the Pope.

October 1978: A Pole, Cardinal Karol Wojtyła, took office as Pope John Paul II, becoming the first non-Italian pope to be elected for over 400 years.

March 2000: The Pope made an unprecedented plea to the world's people to forgive 'the past sins of the Church', including racial and ethnic discrimination and the mistreatment of women, minorities and indigenous peoples. No reference was made to specific historical events.

Yugoslavia

168 BC: Illyria (which included modern-day Yugoslavia) was annexed by the Roman Empire and Macedon was finally defeated.

AD 395: Following a division of the administration of the Roman Empire, Illyria was ruled by the Eastern Roman ('Byzantine') Emperor in Constantinople (now Istanbul, Turkey).

5th century: Southern Slav peoples began to move from Pannonia into Illyria and the Balkans.

812: By the Treaty of Aix-la-Chapelle (Aachen), the Byzantine Emperor, Michael I, acknowledged the Frankish (German) ruler, Charles ('the Great'—Charlemagne), as Emperor in the West; German influence over the Slovene-inhabited areas of Carinthia and Carniola was established.

863: The missionary activity of the Byzantine brothers, SS Constantine (Cyril) and Methodius, led to the conversion of the Serbs (including the ancestors of the Bosnians and Montenegrins) and the Bulgars (and Macedonians) to Eastern Orthodox Christianity; a Slavonic liturgy (based on a Macedonian dialect) was introduced with a written language, in the Cyrillic script, which remained common to all the Eastern and Balkan Slavic peoples.

1014: Final defeat of the western Bulgarian, or Macedonian, realm under Samuel by the Byzantine Emperor, Basil II. Later in the century Byzantine influence began to decline.

1102: Croatia's personal union with Hungary effectively, if not finally, linked it to the Hungarian Crown.

1169: Accession of Stefan I Nemanja as Grand Župan (ruler) of Raška; he united the Serb tribes and established a Serbian state.

1187: The Emperor in Constantinople acknowledged Serbian independence, Hungarian conquests in Croatia and Bosnia and the establishment of the second Bulgarian Empire.

1219: St Sava, brother of the Serbian king, Stefan II, was consecrated the first autocephalous archbishop of the Serbian Orthodox Church, at Žiča.

1330: The Serbs defeated the Bulgarians and the Greek Byzantines at the Battle of Velbuzhde (Küstendil).

1346: Establishment of a Serbian patriarchate and the coronation of Stefan Dušan ('the Great') of Raška (1331–55) as Uroš IV, Tsar of the Serbs and Greeks, at Skopje; however, he failed in his ambition to conquer Constantinople (Carigrad).

1377: Stefan (Stjepan) Trvtko I (1353–91) proclaimed himself Tsar of the Bosnians and Serbs, ruling a Bosnia which was now dominated by the heretical 'Church of Bosnia' (*ecclesia Sclavoniae*).

28 June 1389: The Turkish Ottoman Empire, which had already conquered Macedonia, destroyed the Serbian nobility at a battle on the plain of Kosovo Polje (sometimes referred to as 'the Field of Blackbirds').

1459–83: The Ottomans finally incorporated the rest of Serbia into the Empire, following the fall of the Serbian stronghold of Smederovo, and completed the subjugation of Bosnia and Herzegovina; the Montenegrins (Serbs of the principality of Zeta) maintained a semi-independence.

1490: Death of the Hungarian King, Matthias I Corvinus, who had secured modern Croatia and Vojvodina (Slavonia and the Banat) for Hungary and, temporarily, conquered the Habsburg lands.

1526: Louis II and the Hungarian forces were destroyed by the Ottomans at the Battle of Mohács; the Hungarian Crown was claimed as a hereditary possession of the House of Habsburg, but the kingdom itself was subsequently partitioned between the Habsburgs (Croatia) and the Ottomans (Slavonia).

1690: Serbs ('the 30,000 Families', led by Patriarch Arsenije III Crnojević), retreating with Habsburg armies, first settled in Vojvodina.

1697: The Petrović-Njegoš family established the rule of a joint prince and bishop in Montenegro (under the title of Vladika), reigning over the principality until 1918.

1718: The Peace of Passarowitz confirmed the Habsburg liberation of Hungary, including Croatia and Slavonia; the Ottomans ceded the Banat and northern Serbia (but the latter was held only until 1739).

1796: Montenegro, never completely subdued by the Ottomans, was acknowledged as an independent principality.

1804–13: A revolt of the Serbian peasantry against the local Turkish garrison became a popular revolt for autonomy (the First Serbian Uprising), led by Kara Djordje ('Black George') Petrović.

1815: The Congress of Vienna confirmed Austrian rule over Istria and Dalmatia, which were formerly Venetian.

1817: Serbia became an autonomous principality, after the Second Serbian Uprising under Miloš Obrenović, whose house was, from then on, in constant rivalry with the Karadjordjević dynasty.

1848: At a time of revolution in Habsburg and other territories, the Croatian assembly, in Agram (Zagreb), was forced to end consideration of a Southern Slav state.

1851: Danilo II became Vladika of Montenegro, but renounced the title, and the episcopacy, early the next year—he married and reigned as Prince until his assassination in 1860 (a Metropolitan Primate for the Montenegrin Church was appointed in 1855).

1868: Croatia, united with Slavonia, was granted autonomy by Hungary, which, since the *Ausgleich* or Compromise of the previous year, was now a partner in the Habsburg 'Dual Monarchy'.

March 1878: The Treaty of San Stefano concluded the war between Russia, in support of the Orthodox Slavs, and the Ottomans, but the Great Powers rejected the settlement.

July 1878: At the Congress of Berlin, Bulgaria was denied the annexation of Macedonia, Montenegro's independence was confirmed and Serbia's tributary status was ended (it was awarded territory around Niš); Austria-Hungary secured administration rights in Bosnia and Herzegovina and ensured that the Ottomans remained in the Sandžak of Novi Pazar and in Kosovo, as a restraint on Serbian expansion.

1881: Final abolition of the 'Military Frontier' or Krajina (now in Croatia), in which, since the 17th century, the Habsburgs had allowed some autonomy to Serb settlers defending the borders against the Ottomans.

1882: Serbia was proclaimed a kingdom under Milan Obrenović, whose regime was conservative and pro-Habsburg.

1903: Assassination of King Aleksandar I of Serbia; accession of Petar I Karadjordjević, leader of the Radical Party, who was anti-Habsburg and saw the rise of the Southern Slav movement ('Yugoslavism').

1908: The 'Young Turk' uprising in the Ottoman Empire led to disturbances in the Balkans; Austria-Hungary annexed Bosnia and Herzegovina, despite international objections, but its ally, Germany, prevented war against Serbia.

1910: Nikola I, nephew and heir of Danilo II, proclaimed himself King of Montenegro. The secret, Greater Serb society, Union or Death (the 'Black Hand'), was founded by Col Dimitrijević-Apis.

May 1913: The Peace of London concluded the First Balkan War, in which a league of Bulgaria, Greece, Montenegro and Serbia succeeded in removing the Turks from the bulk of their European possessions.

June 1913: Bulgaria attacked Serbia, which was supported by Greece, Montenegro, Romania and the Turks.

August 1913: The Peace of Bucharest concluded the Second Balkan War; Bulgaria lost Macedonia, which was divided between Serbia and Greece; the Sandžak was divided between Serbia and Montenegro; but Austria-Hungary and Italy succeeded in preventing Serbia gaining access to the Adriatic, notably by the recognition of Albanian independence.

28 June 1914: The heir to the Habsburg throne, Archduke Francis Ferdinand, and his wife were assassinated in Sarajevo, the Bosnian capital, by a student, Gavrilo Princip, who was acting for the Serb Black Hand group.

28 July 1914: Austria-Hungary declared war on Serbia, which started the First World War between the Central Powers, of Austria-Hungary and Germany, and the Entente Powers, of France, Russia, Serbia and the United Kingdom.

1915: Serbia, including Macedonia, was conquered by the Central Powers and Bulgaria.

1916: Habsburg troops invaded Montenegro.

July 1917: Serbia and the other Southern Slavs (excluding the Bulgarians) declared their intention to form a unitary state, under the Serbian monarchy.

29 October 1918: Following the defeat and dissolution of the Danubian Monarchy, the Southern Slav (Yugoslav) peoples separated from the Austro-Hungarian system of states (a Southern Slav republic was established on 15 October); Dalmatia, Croatia-Slavonia, Bosnia and Herzegovina, parts of Carinthia, Carniola and the Banat were, subsequently, ceded formally to the new state.

4 December 1918: Proclamation of the Kingdom of Serbs, Croats and Slovenes, which united Serbia and Montenegro with the former Habsburg lands.

August 1921: Prince Aleksandar, Regent of Serbia since 1914 and of the new Kingdom since its formation, became King, upon the ratification of the so-called Vidovdan (St Vitus Day) Constitution. Nikola II, who still maintained a government-in-exile, died in the same year, the last of the Petrović-Njegoš family to have reigned in Montenegro.

3 October 1929: Following the imposition of a royal dictatorship, the country was formally named Yugoslavia.

1931: The dictatorship was suspended by the introduction of a new Constitution, although this did not prevent Croat unrest and the rise of the fascist Ustaša (Rebel) movement.

October 1934: King Aleksandar I of Yugoslavia was assassinated in France by Croatian extremists; his brother, Prince Pavle, became Regent, on behalf of the young King Petar II.

1937: Josip Broz (Tito) became General-Secretary of the Communist Party of Yugoslavia (CPY), which was to become the main partner in the Partisan (National Liberation Army) resistance to the German invasion.

March 1941: A *coup d'état* by air-force officers ousted the Regent and installed King Petar II, who reversed previous policies and aligned himself with the Allied Powers of the Second World War.

10 April 1941: An Independent State of Croatia was established (including much of Bosnia and Herzegovina), with an Ustaše Government under Ante Pavelić.

17 April 1941: German and Italian forces invaded Yugoslavia: Germany annexed Lower Styria and parts of Carinthia; Italy annexed Ljubljana (Laibach) and Dalmatia, and the nominally independent Montenegro became its client; Albania (in personal union with the Italian Crown) annexed Kosovo; part of Vojvodina (eastern Slavonia) was annexed by Hungary; Macedonia was occupied by Bulgaria; the remainder of Serbia was placed under German military administration.

29 November 1943: In the Bosnian town of Jajce, following fierce resistance and civil conflict with the royalist Četniks (Yugoslav Army of the Fatherland) of western Serbia and with the Ustaše regime, Gen. (later Marshal) Tito's Partisans proclaimed their own government for liberated areas (mainly in Bosnia, Croatia and Montenegro); Tito's leadership was subsequently acknowledged by the Allies and the royal Government-in-Exile, although the following year King Petar II was declared deposed.

20 October 1944: Aided by the Soviet Red Army, Belgrade was liberated from German occupying forces.

29 November 1945: Following elections for a Provisional Assembly, the Federative People's Republic of Yugoslavia was proclaimed, with Tito as prime minister.

January 1946: A Soviet-style Constitution, establishing a federation of six republics and two autonomous regions, was adopted.

28 June 1948: Yugoslavia was expelled from the Soviet-dominated Cominform; the break with the USSR ended Yugoslav ambitions for a Balkan federation with Albania and Bulgaria.

November 1952: The Communist Party was renamed the League of Communists of Yugoslavia (LCY) and several liberal reforms were adopted.

January 1953: A new Constitution was adopted, with Tito becoming President of the Republic.

1954: Istria was partitioned between Italy, which gained the city of Trieste, and Yugoslavia. The so-called Novi Sad Agreement proclaimed Serbo-Croat to be one language with two scripts and a number of variants.

1955: Relations with the USSR were normalized.

April 1963: A new Constitution changed the country's name to the Socialist Federal Republic of Yugoslavia (SFRY).

1966: Monetary reform and economic liberalization were introduced; later in the year the reformists secured the fall of Vice-President Aleksandar Ranković, the head of the secret police and an advocate of strong central government.

July 1971: Following the granting of the rights of autonomy to the federal units, Tito introduced a system of collective leadership and the regular rotation of posts; a collective State Presidency for Yugoslavia was established, with Tito as its head.

November 1971: Tito criticized the reformist Croatian leadership, causing them to resign; the suppression of the Croatian 'mass movement', or *Maspok,* and a purge of liberals throughout Yugoslavia followed.

February 1974: A new Constitution was adopted.

May 1979: The principle of rotating leadership was extended to the secretary-ship of the LCY.

4 May 1980: Tito died; his responsibilities were transferred to the collective State Presidency and to the Presidium of the LCY.

March 1981: Protests by students in Priština led to demonstrations by Albanian nationalists throughout Kosovo; the unrest was to continue sporadically throughout the 1980s.

1986: Slobodan Milošević, leader of the Belgrade Communists, became leader of the League of Communists of Serbia.

24–25 April 1987: Thousands of Serbs and Montenegrins, who had gathered at Kosovo Polje to protest at harassment by the Albanian population, clashed with police.

November 1988: Some 100,000 ethnic Albanians demonstrated in Priština, demanding the reinstatement of two Kosovo Party leaders who had been pressured into resigning. An estimated 1m. people demonstrated in Belgrade, against alleged discrimination by the Albanian population of Kosovo. Public demonstrations were banned in Kosovo.

December 1988: Against a background of increasing popular dissatisfaction with economic conditions, Branko Mikulić, the President of the Federal

Executive Council (Yugoslav), and his Government were forced to resign following the Federal Assembly's rejection of the proposed state budget for 1989; three months later a new Government was appointed under Ante Marković.

January 1989: In Montenegro the State Presidency and the Presidium of the local League of Communists resigned as a result of public pressure (a similar situation had occurred in Vojvodina three months previously).

February 1989: Azem Vlasi, a prominent Albanian from Kosovo, was dismissed from the LCY Central Committee, provoking protests in Kosovo, during which federal troops intervened.

May 1989: Slobodan Milošević was elected President of the Serbian State Presidency (and re-elected, in direct elections, in November).

September 1989: The Slovenian Assembly reaffirmed the sovereignty of their Republic and declared its right to secede from the SFRY; thousands demonstrated in Serbia and Montenegro against the perceived threat to the unity of the SFRY.

November 1989: The first direct, secret ballot in Serbia since before the Second World War was held for local, parliamentary and presidential elections, although the Communists continued to dominate the electoral and candidate lists.

December 1989: Serbian enterprises were instructed to sever all links with Slovenia, which retaliated by closing its border with Serbia and implementing reciprocal economic sanctions.

20–23 January 1990: The LCY voted to abolish its leading role in society, but rejected Slovenian proposals to restructure the federal Party; the League of Communists of Slovenia suspended its links with the LCY.

February 1990: The Yugoslav People's Army (YPA—Jugoslovenska Narodna Armija) was deployed in Kosovo for the first time and the federal State Presidency subsequently approved any action by the YPA needed to maintain the *status quo* in Kosovo. The Slovenian Communists changed the name of their party and renounced its links with the LCY.

22 April 1990: In Slovenia Milan Kučan, the leader of the former Communists, was elected as President of the republican Presidency; the opposition DEMOS coalition, which had already won the direct elections to the main Socio-Political Chamber, emerged as the winner in the Chamber of Municipalities.

6–7 May 1990: The Croatian Democratic Union (CDU), the nationalist opposition party, gained 205 of the eventual 351 seats.

15 May 1990: Dr Borisav Jović (Serbia) took over as President of the federal State Presidency.

26 June 1990: The Kosovo Assembly was suspended and its responsibilities assumed by the Serbian Assembly.

2 July 1990: The Slovenian Assembly proclaimed the full sovereignty of the Republic. In a referendum, a majority of Serbians approved the proposed new republican Constitution, which, among other matters, effectively removed the distinct status of the Autonomous Provinces of Kosovo and Vojvodina; 114 deputies of the 180-member Kosovo Assembly declared that Kosovo was, thenceforth, independent of Serbia and a constituent republic of the SFRY; in response, the Serbian Assembly declared the provincial legislation dissolved.

17 July 1990: The League of Communists of Serbia merged with the republican Socialist Alliance of the Working People (a Communist mass organization), to form the Socialist Party of Serbia (SPS); Slobodan Milošević was elected leader.

25 July 1990: The Croatian Assembly approved constitutional changes which reasserted Croatian sovereignty. The leaders of the Serb minority in Croatia, who had formed a 'Serb National Council', proclaimed the right to sovereignty and autonomy for all Croatian Serbs.

13 September 1990: The 111 members of the Kosovo Assembly, who, at a secret session in Kačanik on 7 September, had declared the Assembly to have been re-formed, proclaimed a 'Constitution of the Republic of Kosovo'.

28 September 1990: Serbia's new Constitution formally took effect: the word 'Socialist' was removed from the Republic's title; a multi-party system was established (in accordance with federal provisions of the previous month); the independence of the institutions of the Autonomous Provinces was effectively removed; and Kosovo was renamed Kosovo and Metohija.

19 October 1990: Stipe Mesić was endorsed, by the Federal Assembly, as the new Croatian member of the State Presidency and Vice-President of the collective body.

9 December 1990: Three nationalist parties won most of the seats after the final round of elections to the Assembly of Bosnia and Herzegovina. In similar elections in Macedonia the nationalist opposition, the Internal Macedonian Revolutionary Organization-Democratic Party for Macedonian National Unity (IMRO—DPMNU), won the largest number of seats in the Assembly. In Serbia a presidential election was won by Milošević, with 65% of the votes cast; the first round of the elections to the Assembly was held, despite an opposition boycott. The first-round elections to the presidency and to a new, unicameral Assembly were also held in Montenegro.

16 December 1990: The final round of voting in the Montenegrin Assembly elections took place; the ruling League of Communists of Montenegro won 83 of the 125 seats.

21 December 1990: The Croatian Assembly promulgated a new Constitution, which proclaimed the Republic's full sovereignty and its right to secede from Yugoslavia.

23 December 1990: A referendum, in which an overwhelming majority voted in favour of secession, was held in Slovenia, despite federal warnings of unconstitutionality and economic sanctions. No candidate having won an overall majority in the Montenegrin presidential election, a second round was held and was won by Momir Bulatović, of the League of Communists. The second round of elections to the Serbian Assembly was held; the final results gave 194 of the 250 seats to the ruling SPS.

15 January 1991: The Serbian Assembly elected Dragutin Zelenović, until then the Vojvodina member of the federal State Presidency, as the republican premier.

25 January 1991: The Macedonian Assembly unanimously adopted a declaration of the Republic's sovereignty, including a statement of its right to secede from the federation.

20–21 February 1991: Slovenia initiated its process of 'dissociation' from Yugoslavia, and Croatia asserted the primacy of its Constitution and laws over those of the federation; both Republics, which had declared a mutual defence pact in the previous month, declared their willingness to negotiate a future for Yugoslavia.

9 March 1991: Massive demonstrations, demanding less confrontational policies by the SPS and resignations from the Serbian Government began in Belgrade; many opposition leaders were among those arrested, notably Vuk Drašković of the nationalist Serbian Renewal Movement; President Milošević demanded the deployment of federal troops to suppress the disturbances.

15–21 March 1991: Jović, the President of the federal State Presidency, resigned and, supported by the members for Kosovo and Metohija, Montenegro and Vojvodina, demonstrated the power of the 'Serbian bloc' to render the State Presidency inquorate; however, the YPA rejected political involvement (which was what the Serbian Government was demanding) and the crisis passed when Jović withdrew his resignation.

6 May 1991: The USA suspended all economic aid to Yugoslavia, because of alleged human-rights abuses in Kosovo and Metohija and for the 'destabilization' of the State Presidency.

June 1991: A summit of the republican presidents considered a proposal to make Yugoslavia an alliance of states; by this time an overwhelming majority had voted for independence in Croatia (although the Serb region of Krajina rejected such moves) and Slovenia had enacted legislation enabling its eventual assumption of independent power.

25 June 1991: The Croatian and Slovenian Assemblies declared the independence and sovereignty of their republics, beginning the process of dissociation from the federation.

27 June 1991: The YPA began military operations, mainly in Slovenia, mobilizing to secure the international borders of the SFRY.

30 June 1991: Under pressure from the European Community (EC—known as the European Union from November 1993), Stipe Mesić, a Croat, was confirmed as President of the federal State Presidency (he was due to assume office on 15 May, but was not endorsed by the Serbian bloc, leaving the body in abeyance).

1–5 July 1991: The emergency committee of senior officials of the Conference on Security and Co-operation in Europe (CSCE) and the CSCE Conflict Prevention Centre met for the first time, to discuss the situation in Yugoslavia; the CSCE meetings supported the EC's peace efforts, which continued with agreement on an arms embargo (endorsed by the USA on 8 July), a decision to send in cease-fire observers and the suspension of financial aid to Yugoslavia.

7–8 July 1991: The EC mediating team and representatives of the State Presidency, Croatia and Slovenia agreed that all fighting should cease immediately and that Slovenia and Croatia should have a three-month moratorium on further implementation of their declarations of dissociation. However, fighting continued to escalate in Croatia.

21 August 1991: The federal State Presidency and the republican authorities reached an agreement that provided for the basic economic and political operation of the federation for three months.

26 August 1991: The presidential cease-fire commission collapsed with the resignation of its secretary, who stated that the July agreement had been breached some 200 times and that more than 70 people had been killed. The next day condemnation of Serbia, as the aggressor in the Yugoslav conflict, was general at an EC meeting (a view echoed by the USA on 29 August); the EC proposed new peace measures, but Milošević refused to endorse them.

7 September 1991: An EC-sponsored peace conference on the future of Yugoslavia opened in The Hague (Netherlands), chaired by the former British foreign minister and NATO Secretary-General, Lord Carrington; the federal State Presidency met with all eight members for the last time.

25 September 1991: The UN Security Council unanimously ordered an arms embargo on Yugoslavia.

3 October 1991: The Serbian bloc on the federal State Presidency announced that, because of the imminent threat of war, Serbia was to assume certain powers of the Federal Assembly; the other four Presidency members were not present and repudiated the decision of this 'rump' Presidency and refused to participate in further activities of the body.

8 October 1991: The Croatian Assembly declared all federal laws null and void. Slovenia's independence declaration took effect and recalled all its citizens in federal institutions.

15 October 1991: The Assembly of Bosnia and Herzegovina declared the Republic's sovereignty, emphasizing the inviolability of its borders and its willingness to consider a form of Yugoslav association. As in Croatia, however, the Serb areas rejected such declarations.

19 October 1991: Following a referendum in the province, the Kosovo Assembly-in-Exile declared Kosovo to be an independent and sovereign Republic; the Assembly appointed a provisional coalition government.

26 October 1991: In the Sandžak region (mainly in Serbia, but partly in Montenegro) the Slav Muslims voted for autonomy in a referendum banned by the Serbian authorities.

9–10 November 1991: A referendum of Serbs in Bosnia and Herzegovina indicated overwhelming support for remaining in a common Serb state.

17 November 1991: A new Constitution was enacted in Macedonia, which declared it to be an independent country.

5 December 1991: Stipe Mesić resigned from his post as President of the federal State Presidency, declaring that Yugoslavia had ceased to exist.

20 December 1991: Ante Marković, the federal prime minister, resigned following a vote of 'no confidence'; further resignations followed.

10 January 1992: Sanctions, imposed on Montenegro and Serbia by the EC in the previous year, were lifted from Montenegro.

15 January 1992: The EC recognized the independence of Croatia and Slovenia; numerous countries followed. The Montenegrin Constitution, adopted in November 1991, was amended in order to comply with EC criteria for recognition.

9 March 1992: The first UN peace-keeping forces arrived in the former Yugoslavia, following the endorsement of their deployment by the 'rump' federal State Presidency the previous December. The first in several days of mass protests by opponents of the Serbian Government occurred in Belgrade.

27 April 1992: By adopting a new federal Constitution, Montenegro and Serbia effectively acknowledged the secession of the other four republics, although they claimed to be a continuation of the SFRY, rather than one of a number of successor states and claimed all international functions of the Federation. Under the new Constitution a Federal Republic of Yugoslavia (FRY) was created, with a bicameral legislature and a single head of state replacing the collective State Presidency; the 1990 Serbian abolition of the autonomous status of Kosovo and Vojvodina was confirmed.

11 May 1992: Alleging Serbian involvement in the continued fighting in Croatia and in Bosnia and Herzegovina, the Governments of the EC countries announced their decision to withdraw their ambassadors from the FRY.

24 May 1992: Elections, declared illegal by the Serbian authorities, were held in Kosovo; the Democratic Alliance of Kosovo (DAK) won a majority of seats in this Assembly and its leader, Ibrahim Rugova, was elected President of the self-proclaimed 'Republic of Kosovo'. The 'Kosovo Assembly' was prevented from holding its inaugural session by several hundred Serbian police.

30 May 1992: Economic sanctions were imposed on Serbia and Montenegro by the UN, because of their involvement in the wars in Croatia and Bosnia and Herzegovina.

31 May 1992: The opposition boycotted elections to the new Federal Assembly and the SPS won an overwhelming number of seats in the parliament. The Serbian Democratic Movement (SDM) was formed by a broad alliance of opposition parties; Vuk Drašković was elected leader.

15 June 1992: Dobrica Ćosić was elected President of the FRY.

14 July 1992: Milan Panić, a US businessman of Serbian origin, was elected Prime Minister of the FRY.

26–27 August 1992: At the conference on the former Yugoslavia, held in London (United Kingdom), Panić declared that there was no federal involvement in the conflict in Bosnia and Herzegovina. The state of emergency in Kosovo and Metohija (in force from 1989) was revoked, following a visit to the area by Panić.

10 September 1992: The Federal Minister of Foreign Affairs resigned in protest at the policies of the Prime Minister, Panić; there were further departures from the Federal Executive Council in November.

12 October 1992: A new Montenegrin Constitution was adopted, defining the republic as part of the FRY.

12–13 October 1992: There was rioting in Kosovo and Metohija following the arrest of two ethnic Albanian deputies from the 'Kosovo Assembly' and the banning of an Albanian-language newspaper; Panić attended UN-EC sponsored negotiations in Priština to discuss the reopening of Albanian schools in Kosovo. There were terrorist attacks on Muslims in Pljevlja, in the Sandžak. Supporters of Milošević surrounded the Federal Ministry of Internal Affairs with 48,000 Serbian police and blockaded the building for several weeks.

20 December 1992: Ćosić was re-elected President of Yugoslavia, in a direct election, with some 85% of the votes cast. At a general election the SPS won 47 of the 138 seats in the Federal Assembly. The SPS was also successful in the republican elections, winning 101 of the 250 seats in the Serbian Assembly. The SPS leader, Milošević, was re-elected President of Serbia, with 56% of the votes cast, compared to Panić, who gained 34%. The opposition accused the SPS of electoral malpractice.

29 December 1992: Panić was replaced as federal Prime Minister by a Montenegrin, Rade Kontić.

10 January 1993: Momir Bulatović, of the ruling Democratic Party of Montenegrin Socialists (DPMS), was re-elected President of Montenegro in a second round of voting.

3 February 1993: A new federal Government, comprising the SPS and the DPMS, was formed. The SDM, which had won 49 seats at the December elections, began a boycott of the Serbian Assembly.

10 February 1993: A new Serbian Government, comprised of SPS members and led by Nikola Sainović, officially took office.

5 March 1993: Milo Djukanović formed a new coalition Government in Montenegro.

1 June 1993: Ćosić was removed from office by the Federal Assembly, following accusations that he had conspired with army generals to oust Milošević; there were mass demonstrations in Belgrade in protest at his dismissal. Miloš Radulović was appointed Acting President by the Federal Assembly. On 25 June Zoran Lilić was elected President of the FRY.

26 August 1993: Col-Gen. Momcilo Perisić became Commander-in-Chief of the Yugoslav Army (formerly the YPA); many other army officers were also replaced.

19 December 1993: In further Serbian parliamentary elections the SPS received some 37% of votes cast and 123 seats in the Assembly; the opposition SDM gained 18% of the ballot and 45 seats; the nationalist Serbian Radical Party (SRP) came third with 15.6% of the votes cast and 39 seats. The Democratic Party of Serbia (DSS) won seven seats.

20 December 1993: The Deputy Prime Minister of Montenegro, Mihailo Ljesar, was assassinated in Podgorica (formerly Titograd).

17 March 1994: The Serbian Assembly approved the election of a new republican Government, with Mirko Marjanović as premier.

August 1994: Against a background of increasing tension between President Milošević and the Bosnian Serb leadership, the Serbian Assembly endorsed a peace plan, sponsored by the 'Contact Group' (consisting of France, Germany, Russia, the United Kingdom and the USA), which had earlier been rejected by the Serb Assembly in Bosnia and Herzegovina.

September 1994: A smaller, 14-member Federal Government was appointed, with Kontić retaining the post of Prime Minister. The UN suspended some sanctions against the FRY (mainly relating to travel, sport and culture) after the Serbian leadership imposed a blockade on the Bosnian Serbs.

August 1995: Following a major military offensive by Croatian government troops in the Serb-controlled enclave of the Krajina (in Croatia), over 100,000 Croatian Serbs sought refuge in the FRY, particularly Vojvodina, prompting protests from Hungarians in that region. The Bosnian Serb leadership agreed to allow the FRY to act as its representative during peace negotiations on Bosnia and Herzegovina.

1–21 November 1995: At an air base near Dayton, Ohio (USA), a number of agreements on peace in the former Yugoslavia was reached by the leaderships of Bosnia and Herzegovina, Croatia and the FRY. Later in the month, Milošević dismissed several leading members of the SRP who were opposed to the terms of the Dayton accords. All international sanctions against the FRY were suspended.

14 December 1995: The Dayton accords were signed into treaty in Paris (France).

February 1996: The Yugoslav Government suspended its blockade of Bosnian Serb territories.

28 May 1996: The Serbian Assembly voted to redistribute a number of portfolios in the cabinet; all outgoing ministers were members of the SPS, while the new appointments belonged to the increasingly influential Yugoslav United Left organization, led by Mirjana Marković, the wife of President Milošević.

23 August 1996: The FRY and Croatian Governments finally normalized relations with a treaty of mutual recognition.

3 November 1996: There were federal, Montenegrin and local elections. The SPS-led United List gained 64 of the 138 seats in the federal Chamber of Citizens, followed by the opposition electoral alliance, Zajedno, with 22 seats; ethnic Albanians in Kosovo boycotted the elections. The DPMS won the majority of seats in elections to the Republican Assembly in Montenegro, and also gained control of the majority of municipal assemblies in the republic. The results of the municipal elections in Serbia were unclear.

17 November 1996: Following a second round of voting in local elections in Serbia, provisional results showed that Zajedno had gained control of 14 cities, including Belgrade; however, Zajedno's victory was annulled by the courts, leading to mass demonstrations; a third round of voting was held on 27 November, but was largely boycotted. Further protests against the rulings led to two deaths.

353

5 December 1996: The Serbian interior minister resigned in protest at the temporary ban on two independent radio stations which had reported the demonstrations.

2 January 1997: After an Organization for Security and Co-operation in Europe (OSCE) delegation had declared the Serbian local election results to be valid, the Serbian Orthodox Church, which had hitherto supported Milošević's SPS, issued a statement in support of the opposition's electoral victory.

11 February 1997: After further anti-government demonstrations, the Serbian National Assembly reinstated the municipal election results; opposition leaders announced an end to the protests, although students continued to agitate in support of political reform. The National Assembly also approved a reorganization of the Serbian cabinet.

20 March 1997: Changes in the Federal Government, including additional members from the DPMS, were approved by parliament.

March 1997: The Montenegrin premier, Djukanović, resigned as Deputy Chairman of the DPMS; he had apparently refused to comply with a request from the republican President, Bulatović, to remove any ministers hostile to Milošević from the Montenegrin cabinet.

23 June 1997: The DPMS voted to support the candidacy of Milošević for the federal presidency, but rejected proposals that there should be direct presidential elections in the future, fearing the reduction of Montenegrin influence in Yugoslavian affairs.

15 July 1997: Milošević was elected to be President of the FRY by the Federal Assembly, following the expiry of Lilić's mandate; the conflicts within the DPMS caused the ballot to be held earlier than scheduled. Opposition deputies boycotted the vote and declared its result invalid.

11 July 1997: Bulatović was ousted from the party leadership by a pro-Djukanović faction in the DPMS.

6 August 1997: Bulatović was re-elected leader of the DPMS and nominated as the party's candidate for the Montenegrin presidency. Although the Montenegrin courts invalidated his candidature (as Djukanović was also endorsed as the DPMS nominee), the federal Constitutional Court overturned this decision on 28 August.

21 September 1997: In Serbian legislative elections the United List failed to secure an outright majority, while the nationalist SRP increased its representation to 82 seats and Drašković's Serbian Renewal Movement (SRM) gained 45 seats. In the Serbian presidential contest Lilić, the candidate of the United List attracted the most votes, but not enough to avoid a second round.

1 October 1997: In Priština ethnic Albanian students demonstrated against the Serbian Government's refusal to restore Albanian-language teaching to the curriculum in the province; the protest was dispersed by Serbian security forces.

5 October 1997: Vojislav Šešelj narrowly defeated Lilić in the second round of the Serbian presidential election, but the election was declared constitutionally invalid as less than 50% of the electorate had participated. In the Montenegrin presidential election Bulatović gained 48% of the valid votes cast and Djukanović 47% and, as the two leading candidates, had to contest a second round of voting.

19 October 1997: After a second round of voting Djukanović was elected President of Montenegro, with 50.8% of the votes cast; the OSCE deemed the election generally fair, despite objections from the rival candidate, Bulatović, the incumbent President.

7 December 1997: In a new election to the Serbian presidency none of the candidates gained more than 50% of the votes cast (the United List candidate was now Milan Milutinović, hitherto federal foreign affairs minister, following Lilić's appointment to the federal cabinet in November).

21 December 1997: In the second round of the Serbian presidential election, Milutinović secured 59.2% of the votes cast, compared with Šešelj, who gained 37.5%.

15 January 1998: Djukanović was inaugurated as President of Montenegro, despite violent disturbances following protests by the supporters of Bulatović; the federal premier, Kontić, brokered an agreement between the DPMS factions providing for early legislative elections and a transitional Government (approved in early February).

23 February 1998: The UN further relaxed international sanctions against the FRY, in recognition of its support for the continuing peace process in Bosnia and Herzegovina.

3 March 1998: An international arms embargo was imposed on the FRY, in response to a major offensive by Serbian forces against the separatist insurgents of the Kosovo Liberation Army (KLA)—up to 80 Kosovars died, some of them, allegedly, civilians.

24 March 1998: The Serbian Prime Minister, Marjanović, announced the establishment of a coalition Government comprising 13 SPS members, four from the Yugoslav United Left and 15 representatives of the SRP, including Šešelj, who became a deputy Premier.

7 April 1998: The leadership of the 'Republic of Kosovo', Rugova and the DAK, refused to negotiate with the Serbian President, Milutinović, reiterating that it would only deal with the federal authorities, and with foreign mediation.

355

15 May 1998: Under considerable pressure from the international community (led by the Contact Group prominent in the Bosnian conflict) the federal President, Milošević, met Rugova in Belgrade; the US-brokered meeting was followed by the opening of negotiations between delegations from the two sides in Priština.

19 May 1998: President Milošević appointed Bulatović the new federal premier, having dismissed Kontić the previous day (the Federal Government had lost a confidence vote); Djukanović, the President of Montenegro, immediately declared the new administration to be illegal.

31 May 1998: In elections to an enlarged, 78-seat Republican Assembly in Montenegro, For a Better Life, an alliance led by Djukanović's DPMS, gained an outright majority (42 seats); Bulatović's Socialist People's Party of Montenegro won 29 seats.

13 June 1998: The Contact Group threatened the use of force to bring about an end to the fighting in Kosovo and the withdrawal of Serbian troops, which were allegedly attacking civilians.

17 June 1998: The new Republican Assembly withdrew all 20 Montenegrin members of the upper Chamber of Republics in the Federal Assembly and replaced them with delegates loyal to Djukanović, to ensure that President Milošević could not command the two-thirds majority necessary for constitutional amendments.

16 July 1998: A new Montenegrin Government, headed by Filip Vujanović and comprising representatives of the DPMS, the People's Party of Montenegro and the Social-Democratic Party of Montenegro, was appointed.

23 September 1998: With Resolution 1199 the UN Security Council demanded an immediate cease-fire in Kosovo, the withdrawal of Serbian troops, unrestricted access for humanitarian aid and meaningful negotiations; it threatened further action, assumed by most to include the use of force, if its demands were not met.

28 September 1998: The Serbian Government announced the end of military activity in Kosovo and promised an amnesty to any remaining KLA members; the Serbian legislature agreed to establish a multi-ethnic Interim Executive Council in the province. There were, however, reports of a new Serbian offensive, in which ethnic Albanian civilians, including women and children, had been massacred.

8 October 1998: Following reports of a new Serbian offensive, the international community issued an ultimatum that military force would be employed against the FRY unless UN demands were met by 27 October.

13 October 1998: President Milošević agreed to the presence of a 2,000-strong, OSCE 'verification force' (the Kosovo Diplomatic Observer Mission), to monitor the implementation of the Security Council's demands, and to NATO surveillance flights in FRY airspace; in return, Serbia would retain sovereignty over Kosovo and Metohija, pending negotiations on autonomy for the province. The first members of the Observer Mission arrived in Priština five days later.

20 October 1998: Following a government ban on any foreign radio or television broadcasts and the temporary prohibition of three independent daily newspapers several days previously, the Serbian National Assembly approved controversial legislation further restricting media freedom.

7 December 1998: A proposed peace plan for Kosovo was rejected by the Kosovan Government.

14 December 1998: Serbian security forces attacked KLA troops attempting to transport supplies of armaments from Albania, killing 31; tensions in the region further increased following the discovery, four days later, of the body of the Serbian mayor of Kosovo Polje, Zvonko Bojanić. Heavy fighting subsequently broke out. A 2,300-member NATO 'extraction force' was deployed near the Kosovo border in Macedonia, to effect the evacuation of the OSCE monitors in the event of an attack.

2 January 1999: The cease-fire declared the previous October 1998 was broken; episodes of violence occurred throughout January.

13 January 1999: Serb military and ethnic Albanian prisoners were released following an agreement between the KLA and the Serbian Government.

15 January 1999: The discovery of the bodies of 45 ethnic Albanians in the village of Račak, 30 km south-west of Priština prompted international condemnation of Serbia.

18 January 1999: William Walker, the US head of the OSCE monitoring mission in Kosovo was ordered to leave the country by 21 January after publicly accusing Serbian forces of perpetrating the massacre in Račak. He, however, refused to comply with the order.

6 February 1999: A peace conference, organized by the Contact Group and attended by all groups, convened in Rambouillet, near Paris (France).

23 February 1999: The Serbian and ethnic Albanian delegations, including KLA representatives, agreed, in principle, to accept the peace plan.

18 March 1999: Following a second round of the peace negotiations, the ethnic Albanian delegation formally signed the peace agreement. The Serbian delegation, however, continued to object to certain clauses.

20 March 1999: OSCE monitors left Kosovo; a further 30,000 Serbian forces were subsequently deployed in and around the region.

357

24 March 1999: Following the collapse of negotiations between the US envoy, Richard Holbrooke, and President Milošević, the 19 members of NATO approved a NATO-led aerial bombardment of air defences and military installations in the FRY, notably in Belgrade, Novi Sad, Priština and Podgorica. In response, the Federal Government declared a state of war (which the Montenegrin Government refused to recognize).

30 March 1999: NATO rejected an offer by President Milošević to gradually reduce Serbian security forces in Kosovo if an immediate cease-fire was declared.

April 1999: Serbian security forces in Kosovo intensified the campaign of mass expulsions and large-scale massacres of the Kosovan Albanian civilian population, resulting in an exodus of refugees from the province; by early April over 470,000 ethnic Albanians had fled Kosovo.

6 April 1999: The FRY Government announced that Serbian security forces had unilaterally ceased all operations against the KLA and that negotiations with Rugova had commenced. NATO dismissed the cease-fire announcement as inadequate and continued its operation.

14 April 1999: NATO aircraft mistakenly attacked a convoy of ethnic Albanian refugees in Kosovo, killing about 64.

20 April 1999: The President of Montenegro, Milo Djukanović, refused to comply with an order from President Milošević to place Montenegrin security forces under federal military command.

22 April 1999: The Federal Government and Russia, which had opposed NATO's action, agreed on a proposal for an international presence in Kosovo, under UN auspices and including Russian personnel. NATO, however, reiterated its stance that it should lead any international protection force in the region.

28 April 1999: Vuk Drašković was dismissed from his post of Federal Deputy Prime Minister, following disagreement with President Milošević.

27 May 1999: The UN International Criminal Tribunal for the former Yugoslavia (ICTY) in The Hague (Netherlands) announced the indictment of President Milošević, the Serbian President Milutinović, the Federal Deputy Prime Minister, Nikola Sainović, the Chief of Staff of the federal army, Gen. Dragoljub Ojdanić, and the Serbian Minister of the Interior, Vlajko Stojiljković, on charges of crimes against humanity.

3 June 1999: Following mediation by the President of Finland, Martti Ahtisaari the Serbian National Assembly formally approved a peace plan presented to the FRY Government by EU and Russian envoys. The agreement, based on proposals agreed in May, by the Group of Eight (comprising the seven industrial nations and Russia), provided for the withdrawal of Serbian forces from Kosovo, and the deployment of a joint NATO-Russian peace-keeping force (to be known as KFOR), numbering about 50,000 personnel. Refugees were to be allowed to return to Kosovo, and the province was to achieve some autonomy under an interim administration.

9 June 1999: A Military Technical Agreement, providing for the complete withdrawal of Serbian forces within 11 days, was signed by the FRY and NATO representatives.

10 June 1999: The UN Security Council adopted Resolution 1244 (with the People's Republic of China abstaining) approving the peace plan for Kosovo. NATO formally approved the establishment of the Kosovo Peace Implementation Force (KFOR) and divided Kosovo into five sectors, to be under the control of a member country. The UN Interim Administration Mission in Kosovo (UNMIK) was to assume authority in the region.

14 June 1999: SRP ministers and legislative deputies temporarily suspended participation in the Serbian Government, in protest at President Milošević's acceptance of the Kosovo peace plan.

18 June 1999: Following discussions between the US Defence Secretary, William Cohen, and his Russian counterpart, an agreement was reached whereby 3,600 Russian troops would serve as part of KFOR under NATO command.

20 June 1999: NATO announced the official end to the air campaign, following the withdrawal of Serbian forces from Kosovo; NATO signed an agreement with the KLA whereby the latter was to disarm within 90 days. The Serbian National Assembly formally ended the state of war in the FRY.

16 July 1999: The first meeting was held of the Kosovo Transitional Council (KTC), created as a consultative body to UNMIK; it comprised representatives of the main political parties and ethnic groups in Kosovo.

August 1999: Despite the efforts of KFOR troops to enforce order, increasing violence in Kosovo, particularly in Priština, caused most of the remaining Serbian residents to leave the capital. According to the UN High Commissioner for Refugees, the Serbian population of Priština had decreased from 40,000 to less than 2,000 within a few months.

5 August 1999: The Montenegrin Government drafted a proposal to abolish the federation and replace it with an Association of the States of Serbia and Montenegro and announced that a referendum on independence for the republic would be held if Milošević failed to agree to the demands.

12 August 1999: President Milošević reorganized the Federal Government, introducing new ministers from the SRP.

20 September 1999: NATO agreed to the reconstitution of the KLA as a 5,000-member civil emergency security force, to be known as the Kosovo Protection

Corps; two days later, Serbian representatives to the KTC withdrew participation in protest.

28 September 1999: An escalation in violence between Serbs and Kosovar Albanians culminated in a grenade attack on the market of Kosovo Polje, south of Priština, in which two Serbs were killed and 40 wounded.

15 October 1999: KFOR troops intervened to suppress violent rioting by ethnic Albanians in the northern town of Titova Mitrovice, which was divided into separate Kosovar Albanian and Serbian regions following the conflict.

2 November 1999: Montenegro adopted the Deutsche Mark as its official currency; the decision was subsequently ruled illegal by the Federal Constitutional Court.

9 November 1999: Serbian security forces violently suppressed an anti-government demonstration by students in Belgrade.

15 January 2000: The Serbian paramilitary leader and war-crimes suspect, Zeljko Raznatović (known as Arkan), was shot and killed in Belgrade.

4 February 2000: Five ethnic Albanians were killed in clashes with KFOR troops in Titova Mitrovica.

7 February 2000: The federal defence minister, Pavle Bulatović, was killed in Belgrade. President Milošević subsequently appointed Gen. Dragoljub Ojdanić, a former federal army chief-of-staff who had been indicted by the ICTY, to replace Bulatović.

3 April 2000: Serbian representatives announced that they were to resume participation in the KTC and another multi-ethnic body established by UNMIK, in an effort to encourage Western governments to prevent ethnic violence against the Serb community.

3 May 2000: In what was seen as an attempt by President Milošević to consolidate his position in the event of an opposition victory in federal legislative elections, due to be held later in the year, the Serbian parliament elected a 20-member delegation from the ruling coalition parties to the Federal Chamber of Deputies. The SRM boycotted the legislative session.

13 May 2000: Bosko Perošević, President of the Provincial Government of Vojvodina, was killed in Novi Sad. The Federal Government accused opposition groups of involvement in the killing.

17 May 2000: Following the Serbian Government's decision to close several independent newspapers and television stations, some 30,000 people attended a protest rally in Belgrade; two days earlier an estimated 20,000 had attended a demonstration organized by opposition parties in support of early elections in the republic.

22 May 2000: A Serbian court in Niš sentenced 143 Kosovar Albanians, alleged to be members of the KLA, to prison on charges of terrorism. The individual terms meted out ranged from seven to 13 years.

23–24 May 2000: The FRY Government was not invited to attend the ministerial conference of the implementation of the Dayton agreement; consequently, the People's Republic of China and Russia refused to attend, rendering the conference ineffectual.

11 June 2000: Local elections were held in Podgorica and Herceg Novi; the ruling coalition, 'For a Better Life', won a majority of seats in the Montenegrin capital's municipal assembly. In Herceg Novi the pro-Milošević Coalition for Yugoslavia, led by Bulatović's Socialist People's Party of Montenegro, won 19 out of a possible 35 local council seats, followed by For a Better Life with 14.

12 June 2000: The mandates for the 20 newly-elected deputies from the Serbian Assembly to the Chamber of Republics were verified, causing anger amongst Montenegrin deputies, whose 20-member delegation was ignored by the Federal Assembly in early May.

16 June 2000: The Serbian opposition leader, Drašković, was shot and slightly injured at his holiday home in Budva (Montenegro).

28 June 2000: Leposava Milicević, the hitherto Serbian Minister of Health, was appointed Federal Minister for Religious Affairs.

12 July 2000: Milovan Bojić was appointed Serbian health minister and Kata Lazović became Serbian education minister.

24 July 2000: The Federal Chamber of Republics approved amendments to the Constitution, allowing for the direct election of the federal President and of deputies in the Chamber of Republics; a proposal giving the federal legislature the power to appoint and dismiss members of the federal cabinet, including the Prime Minister, was also approved. The amendments allowed President Milošević, whose term of office had been due to end in 2001, to stand for re-election for two more terms. Opposition parties in both republics condemned the changes.

27 July 2000: President Milošević announced that federal legislative and presidential elections were to be held on 24 September; Djukanović immediately declared that Montenegro would not participate in the elections.

7 August 2000: An alliance of Serbian opposition parties, the Democratic Opposition of Serbia (DOS), nominated Vojislav Kostunica, leader of the Democratic Party of Serbia, as their joint presidential candidate.

24 September 2000: The federal elections took place, amid allegations of electoral malpractice made against Milošević.

26 September 2000: The Federal Election Commission announced that Kostunica had received 48.2% of the votes cast in the presidential election, compared with 40.2% for Milošević, thus necessitating a second round of voting. However, external electoral monitoring organizations estimated that Kostunica had secured over 50% of the ballot and thus Kostunica refused to participate in a second round. In legislative elections to the federal Chamber of Citizens, the DOS won 43.9% of the valid votes cast, equating to 58 of the 108 Serbian seats, the SPS received 33.0% (44 seats), the SRP 8.7% (five seats) and the Socialist People's Party of Montenegro 2.2% of the votes cast, but 28 of the 30 Montenegrin seats. In elections to the 20 Serbian seats in the federal Chamber of Republics, the DOS received 46.2% of the valid votes cast (10 seats) and the SPS won 32.7% (seven seats); and in elections to the 20 Montenegrin seats the Socialist People's Party of Montenegro received 83.3% of votes (19 seats).

28 September 2000: Amid increasing pressure from the international community for Milošević to accept defeat, the Serb Orthodox Church announced that it considered Kostunica to have been elected President. The Chief of General Staff of the Yugoslav Army, Gen. Nebojsa Pavković, declared that his forces would not interfere in the political process.

29 September 2000: Vojislav Šešelj, leader of the SRP, one of the partners in the ruling coalition, officially withdrew his party's support and transferred his allegiance to Kostunica.

1 October 2000: Demonstrations began throughout Yugoslavia in support of Kostunica, urging Milošević to accept that he had lost the presidential election.

4 October 2000: The Constitutional Court declared the presidential election invalid and announced that another election should be held to coincide with the end of Milošević's term of office in mid-2001.

5 October 2000: Amid continued popular demonstrations against Milošević in Belgrade, opposition supporters took control of the parliament buildings and the headquarters of the state broadcasting service. Kostunica declared himself the elected President of the FRY and was referred to as such by the state-run news agency.

6 October 2000: Milošević conceded defeat in the presidential election and recognized the validity of Kostunica's claim to the presidency.

7 October 2000: Kostunica was sworn in as President during a joint session of the new federal Parliament. The Government of Serbia resigned the following day, announcing that legislative elections would be brought forward to December.

9 October 2000: Canada, the USA and the EU agreed to remove sanctions imposed on the FRY during the Kosovo conflict. Numerous countries which had suspended diplomatic relations with the FRY subsequently agreed to their restoration. Momir Bulatović, the federal premier, resigned.

17 October 2000: The SPS and the DOS reached an agreement on the joint governance of Serbia pending legislative elections on 23 December. The Prime Minister was to come from the SPS, making decisions in conjunction with Deputy Prime Ministers from the DOS and the Serbian Renewal Movement.

18 October 2000: The Montenegrin Government announced that it remained committed to independence from the FRY. Kostunica had previously stated that he opposed Montenegrin independence, but was prepared for a referendum to be held on the issue. In the following month the Montenegrin Government announced that a referendum on independence would be held in 2001.

21 October 2000: During a visit to the capital of Bosnia and Herzegovina, Kostunica declared that diplomatic relations between that country and the FRY would be re-established and that the FRY would henceforth co-operate with the ICTY.

24 October 2000: Kostunica admitted that Serbian forces had been responsible for killings in Kosovo; a film detailing atrocities committed by Serbian forces in the province was shown on Yugoslav television in November. The Serbian parliament approved the new transitional Government.

26 October 2000: The FRY was accorded full membership of the EU-initiated Stability Pact for South Eastern Europe.

28 October 2000: In municipal elections held in the province of Kosovo and Metohija the DAK, led by Rugova, secured 58.1% of the votes cast and won control of 21 of the 30 municipalities, including the five major cities. The ethnic Serb population boycotted the elections and the head of the UN administration in Kosovo, Bernard Kouchner, announced he would appoint councillors in Serb-dominated municipalities, pending the arrangement of further elections.

1 November 2000: The FRY, which had previously declined to apply for membership of the UN since the dissolution of the SFRY, was admitted to the organization after an application made by the new regime was accepted.

4 November 2000: The new, multi-party federal Government, led by Zoran Zizić of the Socialist People's Party of Montenegro, was endorsed by the federal parliament.

26 November 2000: The FRY was admitted to membership of the OSCE.

December 2000: Unrest between Serbs and Albanians in southern Serbia caused concern among members of the Government and in the international community.

15 December 2000: The FRY was admitted to the European Bank for Reconstruction and Development.

23 December 2000: In the legislative election in Serbia, the DOS secured 64.1% of the votes cast, equating to 176 of the 250 seats in the National Assembly; the SPS received 13.8% of the ballot (37 seats), the SRP 8.5% (23 seats) and the Serbian Unity Party 5.3% (14 seats).

27 December 2000: Zoran Djindjić, the principal figure in the DOS campaign, was named as Serbian Prime Minister-designate.

25 January 2001: The Serbian National Assembly approved by a large majority the DOS-dominated Government proposed by Djindjić.

24 February 2001: At a meeting of Balkan leaders and EU officials in Skopje (Macedonia), the EU warned that it would withdraw aid from Kosovo if violence between ethnic Albanian guerrillas and Serb forces on the Kosovo–Serbian border continued.

February–March 2001: It was revealed that Milošević, who had been placed under constant police supervision in early February, was under investigation by a special commission established by the Yugoslav Government, in connection with allegations of 'misrule' and corruption, including the illegal export of state funds. In early March Swiss authorities confirmed that more than US$1m. of gold had been shipped from a state-run mine in Serbia to Switzerland at the time of Milošević's election defeat. The ICTY insisted that any domestic charges would have no bearing on the indictment for crimes against humanity, but it remained unclear whether President Kostunica would co-operate with attempts to extradite his predecessor.

7 March 2001: US KFOR troops shot and wounded two Albanian rebel fighters in Kosovo, near the border with Macedonia.

Europa's Regional Surveys of the World

A unique series of regularly revised reference titles aimed at businesses, libraries, universities, government departments, embassies, newspapers and international organizations

'Europa's Regional Surveys of the World are justly renowned for their exceptionally high levels of production, content and accuracy.' *References Reviews*

South America, Central America and the Caribbean

- An incomparable source of factual and statistical information for this vast region
- Reflects the very latest political and economic developments
- Includes contributions from over 30 leading authorities on Latin American and Caribbean affairs
- Provides a systematic survey of each country
- Enlightened commentary on topical issues, such as international trade and the banana war, the environment and the drug crisis

Africa South of the Sahara

- A one-volume library of essential data on all the countries of Sub-Saharan Africa
- Over 1,200 pages of economic and demographic statistics, wide-ranging directory material and authoritative articles
- Contributions from 50 leading experts on African affairs
- Incisive analysis and the latest available information
- Includes details of international organizations active in the region

Central and South Eastern Europe

- This title is one of the two new successor volumes to Europa's award-winning Eastern Europe and the Commonwealth of Independent States
- Includes country-by-country surveys, political, economic and social information
- Detailed articles by acknowledged experts cover issues of regional importance such as integration with the West, social policy and religion, the Macedonian Question
- Coverage of regional organizations, research institutes and periodicals
- A select bibliography and a political profile section

Western Europe

- Over 660 pages of statistics, directory and analytical information
- Introductory essays on the region cover political, economic and social issues ranging from the impact of the European Union to Western Europe's environmental politics and its relations with the wider world
- Acknowledged authorities write on regional and country-specific topics
- Specially prepared for this new edition, chronologies for each country

Eastern Europe, Russia and Central Asia

- First edition of one of two successor volumes to the award-winning Eastern Europe and the Commonwealth of Independent States
- Includes country-by-country surveys, political, economic and social information
- Articles by acknowledged authorities covering regional issues such as the politics of energy and the environment
- Coverage of regional organizations, institutes and periodicals
- A select bibliography and a political profile section

The Middle East and North Africa

- Covers the Middle Eastern world from Algeria to Yemen
- Draws together the events of the past twelve months
- Provides comprehensive information on the United Nations and all major international organizations operating in the area
- A detailed calendar of events, expert articles, up to date statistics and directory information
- An invaluable reference source in business matters relating to the area

The Far East and Australasia

- A systematic survey of all the countries of East Asia, South Asia, South-East Asia, Australasia and the Pacific Islands
- Essential for anyone with a professional interest in this part of the world, the book keeps you up to date with current economic and political developments
- Presents over 1,400 pages of statistics, directory information and expert analysis
- Provides details of all major international organizations active in the region

The USA and Canada

- Invaluable reference guide to the political, economic and social affairs of these two powerful North American nations
- Contributions from over 30 acknowledged authorities
- Specially commissioned articles cover issues such as the USA and the United Nations, Aboriginal Peoples in North America, the Canadian Economy
- Includes wide-ranging statistics and directory information
- Provides geographical and historical introductions to each state/province, data on the economies, and a comprehensive governmental and legislative directory section

For further information on any of the above titles contact our marketing department on:
tel. + 44 (0) 20 2842 2110 fax. + 44(0) 20 7842 2249
e-mail info.europa@tandf.co.uk   www.europapublications.co.uk